P9-DNB-671

WITHDRAWN

WITHDRAWN

JAILS

ANCHOR·PRESS·DOUBLEDAY·

JAILS:
The Ultimate Ghetto

Ronald Goldfarb

ANCHOR PRESS/DOUBLEDAY
GARDEN CITY, NEW YORK
1975

Library of Congress Cataloging in Publication Data

Goldfarb, Ronald L
    Jails, the ultimate ghetto.

    Includes bibliographical references and index.
        1. Prisons—United States.   2. Juvenile detention
homes—United States. I. Title.
HV9471.G64   365′.973
ISBN 0-385-09784-0
Library of Congress Catalog Card Number 74-9450

I dedicate this book to their memories:
Minnie, Rose, David and Joseph, who once said to me:
"Work is work, but a book is forever."

CONTENTS

Acknowledgments

The Twentieth Century Fund aided in financing research for this book. Pearl Schwartz and Glen Bibler, formerly of the Fund, worked with me and were helpful friends. My appreciation also goes to John E. Booth of the Twentieth Century Fund.

Several people helped in the research, writing and editing of this book and I wish to acknowledge formally their contributions.

My former colleague Peter Jaszi did the lion's share of my research and his work on the chapters concerning alcoholics, addicts and sick people were painstaking and major. He also assisted in the research and editing of the juvenile chapter. Without his help, I could not have completed my work in this time. The parts of the book he worked so hard on are truly his as much as mine; although I accept sole responsibility for all the conclusions.

My partner, Linda Singer, helped with parts of Chapter 1 and drafted a substantial part of the legal chapter. She also provided general editorial assistance and good counsel throughout my work. My wife, Joanne Goldfarb, did research on the history and architectural evolution of jails, and conducted numerous interviews for me.

Mary Ann Stein did considerable research and gathered much of the material which was used in the juvenile chapter. Ruth Bell did some research on the historical part of the chapter on the poor laws.

Without all this help, this book could not have been completed in the two and one half years this research project took.

Susan MacDonald, Barbara Johnston and Michelle Wicker helped with the typing. Marianna Moore did, too, along with handling all the details, organization and general administration of this research project. Dorothy Lucht did most of the final preparation of the manuscript and co-ordinated my files. They all have my thanks for their skillful contributions and good will. Jeannette Hopkins' editorial assistance is also appreciated.

Three experts provided particularly important critiques: Allen Breed on the juvenile chapter; Robert DuPont on the narcotics chapter; and Peter Hutt on the chapter on alcoholics. Many other public officials, scholars and experts in the criminal justice field

—too many people to enumerate here—provided me with advice, assistance, materials and encouragement which were very important. They know how obliged I am to them and how grateful I am for their help; but I repeat it here again.

This manuscript has been out of my hands for over a year, thus some of the data referred to and some of the cases in the footnotes may be out of date. However, recent events worth noting have been included in the text.

RONALD L. GOLDFARB

Washington, D.C.
1974

1

〜〜〜〜〜〜〜

JAILS IN AMERICA—
AN INTRODUCTION

> Here I am in the low-down jail,
> Ain't got nobody to go my bail,
> Oh, listen, Cap'n, want you to know,
> You got to reap jes' what you sow.
>
> "Here I Am in This Low Down Jail",
>
> Lawrence Gellert
> *Negro Songs of Protest*
> NY: Am. Music League (1936)

The rural American jail has been sung about through the years in mournful, plaintive country music; the big city jail has become notorious in dramatic news reports of riot and suicide. But beyond the legends and folklore, the scandals and violence, the real, full and sad story of America's jails never has been adequately told.

Jails have been little studied, and widely misunderstood. There is sparse literature on the subject.[1] The more recent pamphlets are textbook treatises on jail management, security and operations; the few available books concentrate on administration: site

[1] One thorough and very useful report on jails is Hans Mattick, "The Contemporary Jails of the United States: An Unknown and Neglected Area of Justice," a chapter in Daniel Glaser's *Handbook in Criminology* (New York: Rand McNally, 1974). Another good survey, entitled "Jails and Criminal Justice," *Prisoners in America* (Englewood Cliffs, N.J.: Prentice-Hall, 1973), was prepared for the Forty-second American Assembly meeting at Arden House in December 1972, by Prof. Edith Elizabeth Flynn, associate director, National Clearinghouse for Criminal Justice Planning and Architecture, University of Illinois.

planning, how to run competent jails, how to control a riot and prevent escapes, how to run a clean kitchen—the nuts-and-bolts problems facing jail personnel. The federal Bureau of Prisons, commonly regarded as leader in progressive penal policies, describes in its recent tome *The Jail: Its Operation and Management,* how to frisk an incoming inmate, how to run a competent count, how to detect contraband. A key goal of the jail, according to this handbook, is the protection and convenience of the jailer. It provides painstaking and petty detail on maintenance of order. Here are samples:

> Women prisoners must be completely separated from male prisoners, with no possibility of communication by sight or sound. [P. 72]

> In large jails where organized games are played, prisoners should be permitted to select their own umpires and referees. However, the recreation supervisor must be constantly on the alert for disagreements among the players. Unless there is an obviously poor call, the supervisor should permit the umpire to make the decisions. [P. 72]

> Prisoners assigned to food service should not be deformed or have skin eruptions or other skin conditions. They should look and be clean. Known homosexuals and sex offenders should not be assigned to food preparation. [P. 143]

The paltry existing literature aims at solving the problems which are created by the institution itself. The editor of the book issued by the Bureau of Prisons says in his preface that the book was written for "the potential users" of jails—"the jail officers and jail administrators." It candidly reports a fact of correctional life, that the real consumers of the system, the clients, are ignored in correctional planning. Institutions are run for the convenience of their administrators, not their real users; this is one obvious reason why they are so unsuccessful.

JAIL: THE NATION'S DUMPING GROUND

A jail is not a prison. A prison houses convicted criminals; no untried people go to prisons. A jail is essentially a pretrial detention center used to hold people until they are tried. But to complicate matters, the jail also has come to be used both as a short-term correctional institution for misdemeanants, and a way station for a random mélange of other defendants. Sometimes people are lost and forgotten in the jails for weeks and months after they could have been legally released. Men convicted but awaiting sentence or appeal, defendants on their way across the country to trial or prison, defendants being moved from one institution to another, immigrants awaiting deportation, military arrestees, people held as material witnesses to a forthcoming trial also crowd the jails, adding to the confusion and the bedlam and complicating the mission of these institutions.

The jail population is composed predominantly either of people who are denied bail because of the seriousness of the offenses with which they were charged or who, because they are poor, cannot afford bail and are forced to waste in jail waiting for a distant trial.

One stark fact of life is that generally people of means never see the inside of a jail. Wealthy people can make bail, get medical treatment, make restitution, pay fines, and generally find alternative techniques to resolve their problems. Noah Pope, a perceptive convict, once told me: "The jail is for the poor, the street is for the rich."

No Lady
Prison didn't improve me none.
There was ten of us girls in the county jail
five white, five black awaitin' trial for sellin shit.
The white girls, they all on probation.
Us black girls, we all go to Dwight. Me, three months gone.
An I ask myself sittin on them concrete benches in the county.
How come? How come me an my sisters going to jail
An the white girls goin back to college?
Their mothers come in here an weep—they get probation.
My mamma come in here—nose spread all over her face—
she weepin too
But I goin to Dwight
An I think about that—But I don't come up with no answers.
Ain't got no money for a lawyer. Hell, I couldn't even make bail.
Met the defender five minutes before my trial
An I done what he said. Didn't seem like no trial to me,
not like T.V.

[*Off Our Backs,* April 1972]

The jail houses a disparate collection of social outcasts and underprivileged people in desperate need of unavailable social services. The jail of any American city is in one author's words, "the traditional dumping ground for the untried, the petty offender, the vagrant, the debtor and beggar, the promiscuous, and the mentally ill." It is the "forgotten, residual institution" for "the public nuisance, the sick and the poor, the morally deviant, and the merely troublesome and rejected."[2] Alcoholics filled half of many jails until recently. A 1967 survey of one city jail and three large county workhouses in one state revealed that more than half of the prisoners sentenced to jail for commission of a crime were there for drunkenness. Huge numbers of narcotics addicts are thrown into jails at random. Others are in jail because they cannot pay a fine; men are there on work release; youngsters and first offenders who could be reached and corrected are thrown together with inveterate criminals who ought to be segregated; mentally ill individuals, and social delinquents like alimony dodgers, all compose parts of this often nightmarish mélange.

. . . sheriffs and jailers are faced with a multitude of problems. The populations of our jails are heterogeneous conglomerations of humanity spewed from the gutters, the alleys, and the city dumps; tumbled about by the tangled complexities of modern life; or losers in calculated and bold ventures in criminal activity. Many are bewildered by the force of circumstance which has brought them to the wrong side of the prison bars.

Unless the jailer and his staff are intelligent, experienced, and trained in workable jail procedures, only contamination and degradation of human personality result, and the jail assuredly becomes a veritable moral cesspool whose stench and sloughings insidiously creep into the far corners of the community.

The inevitable impact of this flow of humanity through American jails affects every community throughout the length and breadth of the United States.

It is an unhappy but well-established fact that far too many jails—hundreds of them—while presumed to be the bulwark of community social protection, actually are little more than the enforced common meeting places for social derelicts who find there the greatest opportunity to infect the casual offender, the weak, the unsophisticated, the morally retarded, and the socially inadequate. Moreover, such jails are often unsuccessful in performing

[2] Flynn, "Jails and Criminal Justice," p. 2.

their basic mission of secure detention. In them, jailers' responsibilities are delegated to the most sophisticated and experienced criminals who proceed to prey upon the majority of other prisoners through tacitly approved kangaroo courts, "sanitary" courts, and other devices and insidious methods concocted by those morally corrupt criminals schooled in the slimy culture of mankind's social backwash.[3]

For about four years, while writing a book about the American correction system, I traveled around the country to view American prisons and correctional programs. One shocking paradox became apparent to me. Our prisons are used to incarcerate men convicted of serious crimes and our jails (while housing some convicted men) primarily hold people who are awaiting trial, who have been convicted of nothing; yet our jails are far worse than our prisons.

I can recall, for example, taking a three-day trip to see a sampling of correctional institutions in Georgia. I had seen eight different prison institutions in a state which was not famous for its progressive correctional institutions. Then I asked to see the Atlanta Jail. I was shocked to discover conditions so horrible I could not believe them. The jail was far worse than the state prisons I had just seen. Inside a relatively modern exterior in a modest, busy part of town was a cramped, dark, dank interior. Large, four-sided cages each held sixteen men, with disheveled beds and an open toilet. Inmates are kept inside these cages twenty-four hours a day throughout their often prolonged stays at the Atlanta Jail. There is no privacy and no activity at all, artificial air and light, and nothing at all to do day and night. A dismal atmosphere, a constant din and a wretched stench pervaded the place.

It has long been known that epidemics can spread from jails to surrounding communities. One such historic disaster occurred about 1750 when an epidemic of typhus fever, then also known as "jail fever," spread from London's Old Bailey Prison to the adjoining courtrooms and was carried home by aldermen, two judges, and several learned counsel. An eminent physician of the day reported the "closeness and stench" of the jail as the cause of the tragedy, and ordered that courts thereafter be provided with

[3] Myrl E. Alexander, *Jail Administration,* Police Science Series (Springfield, Ill.: C. C. Thomas, 1957), pp. 5–6.

bunches of sweet-smelling flowers to overcome the odors of the
jail and ward off disease. There is no record of any attempt to improve conditions in the jail.[4]

The available published surveys of local jails, together with my
own visits to numerous and varied large city and small rural jails,
document conditions of filth, dilapidation, brutality and lack of
hygiene, medical care or any type of constructive programs that
are far worse than those at most prisons for convicted, confirmed
criminals.

> The majority of county and city jails are more or less independ-
> ent units, each having a certain autonomy. The grounds, buildings
> and equipment are owned by the respective counties and cities. In
> a majority of cases the buildings are old, badly designed, poorly
> equipped, and in most instances in need of urgent repairs. They
> are not properly heated, ventilated nor lighted; they do not have
> the necessary facilities for the preparation and service of food;
> proper and adequate provision for bathing and laundering are
> missing; sanitary arrangements are, for the most part, primitive
> and in a bad state of repair; only in rare instances are there proper
> hospital facilities or means for caring for the sick and infirmed;
> religious services are infrequent; educational activities are almost
> completely unknown. . . . Recreation is mostly restricted to card-
> playing, and in general, complete idleness is the order of the day.
> Filth, vermin, homosexuality and degeneracy are rampant, and
> are the rule rather than the exception. Of these there is no more
> pressing nor delicate problem, among the many confronting jail
> administrators today, than the ever-present and increasing prob-
> lem of homosexual behavior among those incarcerated in jails all
> over the nation.[5]

Americans have an edifice complex when it comes to solving
social problems, one commentator has said, and nowhere is this
phenomenon truer than in the world of so-called "correction."
Huge investments are made in concrete shells and steel cells
instead of services; indeed, what is built is often the very antithesis
of a service-oriented environment.

Buildings are crude and inadequate at best and when new;
they commonly are hazardous, venomous, unsafe, unhealthy and

[4] Nick Pappas, ed., *The Jail: Its Operation and Management* (U. S. Bureau
of Prisons), p. 140.
[5] Jones, *American Jails* (Centennial Congress of Corrections, 1970), pp. 5–6.

dangerous, as well as antiquated. According to former Minnesota Commissioner of Corrections Paul Keve, "If I closed all the sub-standard jails in the state there would only be two or three left."

Large, open dormitories are intended for mass storage of people; cells are designed for single occupancy but often are over-crowded with many more. Typical of jail overcrowding is the scene at the St. Louis City Jail. When I toured that medium-sized institution in November 1972, officials advised me that they were overcrowded 77 per cent of the time and that 7 per cent of the inmates had to sleep on the floors of the eight- and two-man cells.

Since there is no national or even regional and sparse statewide central administration of American jails, there is no way to dis-tribute their populations. Most big city jails and some county jails are chronically overcrowded, with as many as four inmates housed in six-by-nine-foot cells, sleeping on the floor and con-fined to their cells or a narrow adjoining corridor for meals and "recreation." Others, generally in rural areas, are often half empty.[6] Since some jails may have only from one to ten sentenced prisoners in custody, rules requiring separation of prisoners by age or sex may mean that they are kept in solitary confinement.

Correctional administrator Myrl Alexander reports that the average jail houses eleven prisoners; but some jails hold thou-sands of inmates. According to the 1970 Law Enforcement Assist-ance Administration census, 5 per cent of the jails surveyed held more inmates than they were designed to hold; of the larger jails (those holding 300 or more) about 30 per cent were overcrowded. In my travels around the country, I never saw a big city jail that was not badly overcrowded, and rarely saw a small country jail that was full (except on the weekends, when they were full of drunks drying out).

Rural jails I have seen are small, ugly, very old warrens that are unsophisticated in their facilities and programs, if what they have could be called that; but they usually provide some modest, if patronizing, civilities. The big bastions in the largest cities are teeming houses of horrors.

One recent survey of Georgia jails, for example, that chronicled the inadequate, hazardous, filthy conditions of that state's 366

---

[6] Hans Mattick and Ronald Sweet, *Illinois Jails—Challenge and Opportunity for the 1970's,* Chap. 4; Preliminary Report of the Governor's Special Com-mittee on Criminal Offenders, State of New York (1968), pp. 205–6.

jails, found 80 in good condition, 151 fair, and 135 deplorable, poor or obsolete. Recent widespread jail riots are symptoms of the increasingly open and violent hostility that is a consequence of the treatment of inmates in our jails.

The absence of programs in jails seems to derive less from a lack of resources (although the absence of any space other than cells and narrow corridors in most jails presents very serious obstacles) than from a lack of imagination. Most jailers prefer to exclude outsiders from jails, citing the troublesome problems of guarding extra people and searching visitors for contraband. The easiest course is to keep inmates locked in their cells, where they can be guarded with the least amount of effort.

Although many of the jails I have visited were dingy and filthy, most inmates are not given even housekeeping chores to keep them busy. The Illinois Jail Survey found that in only 3 per cent of city jails and 14 per cent of county jails were inmates given any sort of work to do. "In general, only the small minority of inmates who are designated as "trusties" are allowed to do more than clean their own cell areas. Even inmates who are remanded to jails in lieu of paying fines are more accurately described as "laying out" rather than "working out" their fines . . ."[7] The inmates simply fester, corrupt one another and, as more than one jailer told me, "figure out ways to break out of here."

Jack Newfield, the author and critic for the *Village Voice,* has called jails "the ultimate ghetto," and he is quite right. Jail inmates, Newfield observed, "are the most powerless people in the society. They have zero power to affect their environment. They have no rights. Their victimization is kept invisible behind thick walls. They inhabit the ultimate ghetto."[8]

THE ORIGIN OF AMERICAN JAILS

The American criminal justice system is closest to the English common law system, from which historically many of our roots grew. In the best study of that system, *English Local Government;*

[7] National Council on Crime and Delinquency, "Correction in the United States," p. 146.
[8] Newfield, *Bread & Roses Too: Reporting About America* (New York: Dutton, 1972), p. 333.

English Prisons Under Local Government, Sidney and Beatrice Webb reported that a few hundred local jails were managed by the sheriffs until the eighteenth century. There were also county jails, city jails, even private jails which were run by ecclesiastical officials and manorial lords. Sheriffs had no correctional role; their only obligation was to prevent escapes, and they carried out this task with cruel and barbaric controls. Not unlike the situation in many jails today, the sheriffs' operations of these early jails rarely were overseen by anyone of any authority and bad conditions were allowed to worsen. The jail and the English workhouse for the poor that developed in later centuries combined to serve as a model for modern American jails.

During the period of time between the American colonial period and the later Jacksonian era, Americans changed their attitudes about how to deal with certain groups of outcasts in their midst: the insane, the poor, children and offenders. Essentially, during the colonial period, these people were treated in a home environment; later on, in the Jacksonian era, institutionalization became "the preferred solution to the problems of poverty, crime, delinquency and insanity." Thus one historian has called the Jacksonian years the Age of the Asylum.

In the first years of the settlement of the New World, the colonists depended on non-institutional techniques, such as settlement laws, to keep strangers and poor people out of a community, and for offenders, on such severe sentencing practices as fines, stocks, pillory, banishment and widespread capital punishment. Jails had another rationale: "Local jails held men caught up in the process of judgment, not those who had completed it: persons awaiting trial, those convicted but not yet punished, debtors who had still to meet their obligations. The idea of serving time in a prison as a method of correction was the invention of a later generation."[9] Colonists did not believe that deviant behavior could be changed in an institution. It was easier to exile an offender from the community or resort to the family for correction.

Jails that did exist in the eighteenth century were run on a household model with the jailer and his family residing on the premises. The inmates were free to dress as they liked, to walk around freely and to provide their own food and other necessities.

[9] D. Rothman, *Discovery of the Asylum* (Boston: Little, Brown, 1972), p. 48.

"So long as they did not cost the town money, inmates could make living arrangements as pleasant and homelike as they wished. A few communities carried this logic to its end and simply dispensed with the jail, allowing those awaiting trial to post security and stay at home. Once assured that the offender would come to court, they saw no difference between the household and the prison."[10]

When in the late eighteenth century, American reformers—predominantly the Quakers in Philadelphia—became outraged by the cruelty of corporal and capital punishment, they devised the penitentiary as an alternative to separate convicted offenders from the rest of society and force them into penitence by imprisoning them. The first penitentiary was nothing more than a remodeled wing of the existing Walnut Street Jail in Philadelphia. Until that time, there was no system of imprisonment and no prisons. Convicted offenders were banished, branded, pilloried, killed or maimed; they were kept in jails only to await trial.

Instead of using such models as the existing English jails and workhouses for the poor, or institutions like hospitals, schools or monasteries, the architects of American jails and their well-intended sponsors chose the huge, ugly, forbidding prison fortress. The jails that proliferated were smaller than their prison counterparts and had fewer facilities; but they were super-secure, fenced, ugly, uncomfortable and unsafe, totally deprived environments.

There was no coherent architectural history or social planning of the jail institution; nor has there been much variation in the function and design of the jail to the present time. The physical form of the place of detention has not evolved from its spontaneous appearance as a secure lockup. The history of the jail is less one of social engineering through architecture than a history of early American attitudes about rectitude and social control and of practical politics and economics in American local government. The trend toward institutionalizing problem people evolved in the name of reform but, as one social historian has concluded, "coercion and not benevolence was at the heart of the movement."[11]

The notorious era of lawlessness in the American "Wild West" which accompanied the homesteading movement, the Gold Rush

[10] D. Rothman, op. cit., p. 56.
[11] Ibid., p. xvi.

and the general westward push of the frontiersmen in the nineteenth century gave rise to the proliferation and transplantation of the local jails started by the East Coast colonists. "The first jail was a building of cottonwood two by fours built in the early 1870s. In its narrow confines of six by eighteen feet as many as forty law breakers were kept at one time, largely cowboys who had shown too much exuberance upon reaching town."[12] Depictions in typical western movies of the town jails of that era are accurate. Small jails like those in western movies—a crude, sparse building with a few cells, a small office in front, an absence of facilities, programs, staff (except for the sheriff's wife, who served the food)—still exist in this country.

In the post-Civil War era some midwestern cities met the challenge of increasing numbers of transient gangs of criminals (the James brothers and their ilk, for example) with anger and harsh measures. Some states instituted "rotary" jails, also called "human squirrel cages,"[13] weird, patented jails that sat within a large brick and barred building. The jail cells were within a permanent steel barred cylinder with one opening on each floor. Inside that was another revolving steel cylinder, also barred, and segmented into ten tiny pie-shaped cells (seven by six feet) with a door opening but no actual door. As the cells revolved past the opening, that opening in effect became the door. Outside this exit was a huge, weighted, barred brace to secure this door. And, as if this was not super-secure enough, the sheriff could keep the whole cylinder revolving all night so that no dexterous and ambitious inmate could saw his way out of this steel jungle.

Some of these specimens still exist.

With the rise of urbanization in the twentieth century came the decay but continuance of the small, old, rural jails and the building of large, new, high-rise, big city jails to handle short-term convicts and the human refuse of the cities for whom no other social agencies existed: the poor, drunks, addicts, mentally ill. As community controls became inadequate to handle the rising numbers of problem people, institutionalization evolved to handle them. The traditional county jail took over for society what per-

[12] Walter A. Lunden, "The Rotary Jail, or Human Squirrel Cage," *Journal of the Society of Architectural Historians* 18, no. 4 (December 1959): 156.
[13] This bizarre Rube Goldbergesque institution is described in Lunden, "The Rotary Jail."

sonal contacts and private associations could not handle. City jails developed to take over local police functions of detention as urbanization increased.

As these institutions grew and proliferated, those notions of reform which initially had prompted their development were discarded in place of simple custody. Overcrowding, lack of classification, rigid rules, all of the typical consequences of institutions, quickly came to characterize life in these early jails.

A paradox developed: as prisons for convicts became more community-oriented, jails servicing mostly pretrial defendants, and some minor offenders, remained essentially punitive, and especially deprived environments. Take one example. In prisons, inmates are provided with work, and indeed sentenced convicts even in the jails have work; but pretrial detainees cannot work while they are in jail (often for prolonged periods) on the ground that it would be unfair and illegal to force a man to work if he is not convicted of a crime and serving a sentence. Prisons added certain therapeutic and non-punitive features like medical and educational facilities; jails for non-serious offenders, innocent people and untried defendants have remained static, and harshly punitive. While some special institutions have been developed to handle some of the prototypical prison population—special institutions for juveniles and the mentally ill, work camps and probation for non-dangerous convicts, for example—"the vast majority of sentenced misdemeanants continued to be sent to local city and county jails."[14]

PROLIFERATION OF JAILS

Our jails touch the lives of more people in the community than all other correctional institutions. One of the nation's leading correctional experts, Hans Mattick, has said that jails are the most important part of the correction system "in terms of numbers and impact." They hold "the highest percentages of innocent and inoffensive persons." Jails are, as the 1967 President's Crime Commission noted, the beginning of the correctional continuum, the distributor and the key filtering point for the criminal justice system.

[14] Mattick, "The Contemporary Jails," p. 23.

There are about 400 prisons in the United States, but a survey conducted in 1967 for the President's Crime Commission estimated that there were about 3,500 jails.[15] There are actually many more since the figure of 3,500 appears to have been derived from the number of counties in the United States; the city jails and workhouses that do not hold prisoners for the counties, are excluded. A recent survey of jails in Illinois found 160 jails in that state (excluding police lockups), of which the Crime Commission survey presumably included only 102 (the number of Illinois counties). If this considerable undercounting of the jails by the Crime Commission was true of other states, one might extrapolate from its figures and arrive at an estimated total of at least 5,250 jails.

Accurate data is hard to come by since almost all jails operate under varied local and not statewide controls (one fifth of all jails are city-run; four fifths are county facilities, according to a 1970 report to the Congress of Corrections) and most keep inadequate records and have no duty to report to a central authority.

A survey of American jails published in late 1970 by the Law Enforcement Assistance Administration of the Department of Justice, provided an advance report of the Bureau of the Census, which had canvassed every municipality having at the time of the 1960 census a population over 1,000. As of one fixed day—March 15, 1970—there were 4,037 locally administered jails (confining inmates for forty-eight hours or more) holding a total of 160,863 people (half this number came from six states alone—New York, California, Texas, Florida, Pennsylvania and Georgia). This total population included 153,063 adults (19 of every 20 were male) and 7,800 juveniles. This survey left out many smaller jails in the states surveyed and did not even survey any jails in several states. According to the LEAA report, 52 per cent of these adult inmates (two thirds of the juveniles) were confined to await trial. An additional 5 per cent had been tried and were awaiting sen-

[15] President's Commission on Law Enforcement and Administration of Justice, *Task Force Report: Corrections* (Washington, D.C.: Government Printing Office, 1967), p. 75; National Council on Crime and Delinquency (hereafter cited as NCCD), "Correction in the United States" (Washington, D.C.: Government Printing Office, 1966), p. 139. The federal Bureau of Prisons cites a figure of 3,100 county jails (including some city jails holding county prisoners). Conversation with Harold Thomas, Jail Inspection Service, October 15, 1970.

tencing or appeal. The rest, more than 69,000 inmates (or 43 per cent of the total) were serving sentences. The annual operating costs ran over $300 million.

In addition to these myriads of conventional jails, almost every police precinct station has a lockup where people may be held after an arrest, usually for a few hours and up to a few days—sometimes more. Although there are no statistics on the number of police precincts in the country, the International Association of Chiefs of Police reports that there are approximately 40,000 police departments, some of which are divided into as many as twenty or thirty precincts. The number of people going through police lockups in a year thus may be in the hundreds of thousands.

The 1967 President's Crime Commission reported more than one million convicted offenders, mostly misdemeanants, served sentences in jails in 1965. The average daily population then serving sentences was 141,303. Although some of these people undoubtedly served more than one jail term in a year and thus were counted more than once, the figure still represents a gross underestimate of the entire jail population, since this survey excluded prisoners serving sentences in facilities where convicted offenders could not serve sentences of at least thirty days. Add to this an unknown annual number of pretrial defendants who comprise more than half of the population of most jails—and persons in jail for violations of motor vehicle laws and other civil offenses, and one could speculate that jails hold from three to four million people annually—perhaps thirty-five times the number handled by all state and federal prisons.

High turnover rates and poor record keeping make accurate data impossible but, according to Professor Mattick, himself a former Cook County Jail official, "the best estimate of the number of jail commitments in the United States each year is at least one and a half million, and may be as many as five and a half million"; the most likely accurate estimate "is probably around 3 million."[16]

It is difficult to determine the financial costs of operating these grim jails, because of incomplete records and because budgets often are merged with those of the larger city or county governments. The jails surveyed for the 1967 Crime Commission (again excluding those that do not hold sentenced prisoners for thirty

[16] Mattick, "The Contemporary Jails," p. 47.

days or more) reported spending an average of $2.87 per day, or $1,046 per year (excluding capital costs) on each sentenced inmate. This figure compares with an average annual operating budget of $1,966 spent by state and federal prisons on each prisoner and $3,613 spent by institutions for juveniles. The LEAA survey reported that the 1969 operating cost of all the nation's jails was $324 million. Dr. Edith Flynn estimated the annual per capita jail cost at $2,000 compared to the $250–$400 per person annual cost of supervision for probation.[17]

Staffing patterns also are revealing. In 1965, more than 19,000 people were employed in the jails surveyed for the Crime Commission, of whom only 500, less than 3 per cent, performed any sort of rehabilitative functions. There was only one social worker for each 850 inmates, one psychologist for each 4,300 and one academic teacher for each 1,300. Some of these professionals worked in jails only part time, and most were concentrated in the large institutions.

The LEAA survey reported that in March 1970, there were 5,676 part-time employees and 28,911 full-time employees in the country's jails. Of the full-timers, more than 30 per cent worked in New York and California; their average earnings were $617 per month. It is not surprising that two thirds of the jails surveyed by LEAA said they had no rehabilitative programs at all. (If institutions receiving no prisoners with sentences greater than thirty days were included, the proportion of jails with no programs doubtless would be considerably higher.)

The LEAA survey reported that 86 per cent of the larger jails (3,319) had no facilities at all for exercise or recreation; nine out of ten had no educational facilities; almost half had no medical facilities; a quarter of them had no visiting facilities; in fact, forty-seven jails in twenty-one states had no toilet facilities.

Philadelphia's superintendent of prisons concedes the problem: "Our problem basically is that we are overwhelmed with detentioners. We are so busy receiving and discharging and sending detentioners to court every day that we have very little time left for our staff to devote to program development."

Jail administration is low on the budget and priorities of most jail administrators. In some rural counties, the jailer is on duty

17 Flynn, "Jails and Criminal Justice," p. 5.

twenty-four hours a day, seven days a week. He sometimes has
other functions, such as cleaning the courthouse. His profit still
may depend on the fee system, under which he keeps any money
he saves from the allotment for the inmates' food and upkeep and
pays any excess out of his own pocket. A 1969 survey pointed out
that full-time jailers were employed in only nine of Utah's thirty-
four jails; in many instances jails were completely unattended and
typically "officials responsible for the operation of the jails were
engaged in other duties, such as driving school buses, escorting
children at school crossings, or working at other employment to
supplement their salaries received as law enforcement officers."[18]

Since most jail employees are law enforcement personnel, often
uninterested in or hostile to their assignments to guard inmates,
people in jail are, according to Mattick, "placed in the hands of
those who are least likely to teach or exhibit [respect for law and
order] . . . the least qualified and poorest paid employees in the
criminal justice system, the jail guards."[19] In almost every jail
which has been the scene of a riot, one of the major aggravating
situations was the bad blood between the inmates and guards.
Often the guards are predominantly white while the inmates are
black or from minority groups. The regime is harshly militaristic;
the atmosphere inevitably is incendiary.

Anthony Russo, thirty-five, was a research analyst at Rand Corporation and was recently indicted in connection with Daniel
Ellsberg for distribution of the Pentagon Papers. Before that he
was imprisoned for forty-seven days for refusal to testify before
a grand jury. His description below is of Los Angeles County Jail.

> Russo: About 6 o'clock I was called to the booking room . . .
> where clerks take the valuables you weren't supposed to have in
> jail . . . The lady behind the window didn't want me to keep my
> reading glasses nor my fountain pen . . . I said, "Please, I'd like
> to keep those because I need them to read. The glasses I have on
> are for long distance . . ." And she replied, "Well, you're not
> gonna need them because you're not gonna be doing much read-
> ing where you're going." Which kind of upset me. I always
> thought that one could read in jail . . . I said, "You're not serious,
> are you?"

[18] "Study of Jails in the State of Utah," p. 3. Research paper of Utah Council
on Criminal Justice Administration, 1969—mimeographed—no other data to
cite.
[19] Mattick, "The Contemporary Jails," p. 80.

A guard walked up, and he said, "You got a problem here?" And I looked at him and I said, "No, I don't have any problem. Do you?" . . . As I was talking with the lady clerk, the guard walked up, grabbed me by the arm and started pushing me out of the room. . . . I walked down the hallway about a hundred feet, when all of a sudden, four guards turned on me and they bodily . . . pushed me through this door, and there I was in a maximum security cell. . . . Concrete, solid, no windows . . . Six other guys . . .

[Russo said he had not made a phone call after he surrendered himself and wanted to call his lawyer. He says he tried unsuccessfully to get a response from two guards sitting outside his door.]

So I began to yell out through there about how those guys were violating my constitutional rights . . . I was getting madder and madder . . . and I began to kick the door . . . as hard as I could and these big metal doors make a lot of noise . . .

I did that for about five minutes and all of a sudden the door flew open and a flying wedge of guards came through, four or five and I was flattened . . . they came through, hit me, pushed me up against the wall, said "Turn around, put your hands against the wall." I did . . . and one hand was jerked away and pushed up behind me really tight.

I felt like my arm was going to be pulled out of its socket. And then the second arm was pulled behind me . . . And then someone kicked my legs out from under me. I felt knees all over me, knees on my head, on my neck. I wasn't struggling . . . It would be ridiculous to struggle . . .

They began to chain up my legs, and they put my wrists in handcuffs . . . really tight . . . so they tied my hands cuffed behind me and my legs shackled together. Then they tied my hands to my ankles, so I was done up in a little neat bow there, lying on my belly . . .

After about half an hour we had the chains loose so I could stand up . . . I was really so mad then that . . . I spun around and chained the door bam!—and did that a couple of times . . .

And all of a sudden the door flew open and . . . the captain was there. He had real authority . . . and he said, "Are you Mr. Russo?" I said, "Yes." He said, "We didn't know who you were." . . . and that made me mad as hell because what that meant was that this was par for the course . . . [Washington *Post*, Feb. 5, 1972, p. A-6, article by B. Bagdikian]

Of the jails surveyed for the Crime Commission, 35 per cent

were more than fifty years old.[20] The LEAA study several years later reported that over 25 per cent of all jail cells in the United States are more than fifty years old (half of these were seventy-five years old; one fourth were more than a century old).[21] Many jails still standing were constructed before the days of plumbing and electricity and I have seen some of these, still in use, which are so crude and despicable that they shock the conscience.

Jails are administered almost exclusively by local governments, although states have taken over administrative responsibility for jails in Rhode Island, Delaware, Connecticut and Alaska. Only six states provide subsidies for local improvement of jails.[22] Only half the states set any standards for local jails, and even fewer states than that (eighteen by last count) inspect their jails to determine whether their standards are being met. Even where inspection uncovers deficiencies, the only way to enforce changes is to close the jails—a politically unlikely solution.

The federal Bureau of Prisons, which runs only two jails (the large and busy Federal Detention Headquarters in New York City and the tiny, remote Federal Detention Center in Florence, Arizona), contracts with local authorities to hold between 3,500 and 4,000 unsentenced federal prisoners each day in 800 local jails.

The bureau has twelve inspectors whose job it is to evaluate these jails. When the inspectors consider a jail unsuitable for federal prisoners, the bureau's only remedy is to revoke its contract and send its prisoners elsewhere. Consequently, the inspectors take into account the needs of the local courts and the available alternatives when rating the 800 jails as acceptable. In some places, federal defendants are kept in a segregated wing of local jails. But many federal detainees are kept in terrible local jails that violate the federal bureau's propounded standards.

Heavy security may be necessary for a few prisoners; but it is unnecessarily expensive and restrictive for the great majority. And, at that, while jails are built like fortresses to secure the small por-

[20] NCCD, "Correction in the United States," p. 146.
[21] Law Enforcement Assistance Administration, *1970 National Jail Census*, National Criminal Justice Information and Statistics Service (U. S. Government Printing Office, 1971), Report SC-1, p. 4 (hereafter cited as *1970 National Jail Census*).
[22] President's Commission on Law Enforcement and Administration of Justice: *Task Force Report: Corrections*, p. 80.

tion of dangerous defendants who must be detained to protect society, in fact, they constantly are broken out of. Jail escapes are a common fact of life; only the ingenuity of each new attempt is newsworthy.

Even this devotion to security is illusory. Security for whom? one might ask. For the prisoners? Reports are common that rapes, attacks and violence between inmates are rampant in jails. For the correctional personnel? Everyone who knows about jails knows that they can only be run at the sufferance or with the acquiescence of the inmates, the society of captives, one scholar called it. And the antagonisms between jail populations and their jailers—between the keepers and the kept—in recent years have been far-flung and incendiary. Attacks on guards, the taking of hostages and the vilifications heaped on jail personnel have prompted correctional unions to demand changes and reforms and raises to compensate for the notorious risks of their now hazardous duties. In fact, even the security from inmates sought for the community is questionable, as escapes become more common.

Thus the perplexing paradox: the dangerous inmates are not kept escape-free; yet the non-dangerous ones are locked in cages like wild animals, deprived of all normal contacts and made to suffer grave and prejudicial deprivations.

Jails are run under the most irrational, annoying rules and de-personalizing, degrading militaristic regulations, all attributed to security requirements—marching to meals, ugly uniforms, counts, routines set to odd times, minimal visitation rights, frisks, shake-downs of personal items. And still, with all that, illicit contraband and deadly weapons are commonplace, assaults and rapes are common, property destruction is rampant.

Racial unrest has become a major problem in jails as the disproportionate number of minority groups who typically compose the bulk of the jailed and imprisoned populations have become more militant, vengeful and politicized. Even the small, silent minority of women in jail are beginning to raise their voices in protest to the prejudices they see visited upon them.

Although conditions and attitudes vary from place to place most local jails discriminate against women. I've been in about a dozen jails, all but one (Cass Co., Neb.) in the eastern U.S. Local jails often exclude women from most or all work, recreational and educational programs, increasing the deadly boredom which is the major reality of life in jail. Male guards are often used to "handle" (and sometimes mis-handle) women inmates. Matrons, as women jail guards are called, often have lower qualifications and lower pay than male guards. [*Off Our Backs,* April 1972]

Riots, property damage, the taking of hostages have become commonplace. People disrespect institutions which do not work for them; this is a fact of life.

CRACKDOWN AT JAIL SEEN AFTER RIOTS

Baltimore, April 6 (AP)—

An immediate crackdown was promised today at City Jail by Warden Hiram Schoonfield in the wake of Wednesday night's prisoner rioting that caused more than $10,000 in damages.

"This is my jail and I've got it back," the warden said.

More than 600 windows were broken, six television sets smashed, steam pipes broken, fire hoses turned on, furniture broken, and tables and bunks splintered in the two-hour rampage that began when a guard ordered a group of inmates away from a window.

Jail officials said the inmates were shouting and gesturing to motorists and pedestrians passing outside the jail.

Jerome Ford, 34, the guard, locked himself on a third-floor catwalk until the inmates were returned to their cells. He was unhurt.

The disturbance lasted until nearly 100 city policemen in riot gear and with tear gas, rifles and shotguns moved in.

Three jail inmates were sexually assaulted by other prisoners during the disturbance, the Baltimore Evening Sun reported.

Schoonfield said, "We have to get respect. We'll just have to go and start locking people up no matter what the courts say. The inmate knows he has support from certain legal agencies."

The warden said that inmates will spend more time in the jail cells and that windows broken will not be replaced by glass but by steel plates.

When three inmates who said they represented the prisoners began making demands to the warden, he said he didn't intend to talk to them, describing the rioters as "vandals—like kids who break out school windows."

"This is absolutely ridiculous," Schoonfield said. "They curse the guards and subject them to all sorts of abuse, they expose themselves to nurses who are hired to help them and they urinate on the walls while en route to the cafeteria. And they have the nerve to say they are mistreated."

One of the saddest aspects about the failures of our jails is their apparent immunity from reform. Criticism of jails comes from all quarters; yet little gets done to change things.

In a few states, I was taken for tours of local prototypical jails by state jail inspectors. All were very pleasant and open men; despite long careers in police and jail work, they seemed critical of the conditions we saw and proud of any modest improvements they could demonstrate. Yet, they seemed part of the fraternity of jailers, at heart, and readily admitted their inability to bring about significant reforms.

Richard W. Velde, associate administrator of the Law Enforcement Assistance Administration of the U. S. Department of Justice, made this statement recently:

> Jails are festering sores in the criminal justice system. There are no model jails anywhere; we know, we tried to find them. Almost nowhere are there rehabilitative programs operated in conjunction with jails. It's harsh to say, but the truth is that jail personnel are the most uneducated, untrained and poorly paid of all personnel in the criminal justice system—and furthermore, there aren't enough of them.
>
> The result is what you would expect, only worse. Jails are, without question, brutal, filthy, cesspools of crime—institutions which serve to brutalize and embitter men to prevent them from returning to a useful role in society.

Sheriff Michael H. Canlis, president of the National Sheriffs' Association, said as recently as October 1970:

> It has been said that most [jails] are only human warehouses. We must ask ourselves, is merely keeping our prisoners secure, enough?
>
> If we are content ourselves with maintaining nothing more than a human warehouse, we are not only perpetrating the so-called failure of an element in the system of criminal justice, but we might, to some degree, be responsible for a contribution for some of the increases in crime. Cited in Richard A. McGee, "Our Sick Jails," *Federal Probation,* March 1971, p. 3.

I shall never forget my first real visit through a jail. As a lawyer, I had had some general contacts with our country's jails. Yet I had never taken a full tour, never had a real view of life inside any jail until I had been a member of the bar for about ten years.

In 1965, my book about bail reform was published and shortly thereafter a local television station did a documentary on the subject, for which I was a consultant. During the filming of the documentary, it was decided that we should shoot some scenes in the District of Columbia Jail, to show what happens to people who cannot afford to make bail. The jail authorities consented to let us go through, and on the appointed day—with TV cameras and cameramen—I showed up at the D. C. Jail and we went through the place to do our filming.

I was so shocked and disgusted by the scene we witnessed that I almost could not pay attention to what it was that we were there to do. I can recall filming a segment in a huge dormitory filled with hundreds of double-decked beds on which perched, lay, slept, a vast army of mostly black, young men dressed in rumpled, soiled denim uniforms.

I had to describe this terrible scene before the camera; but I was so depressed and dismayed I found it very difficult to speak. Most of these people were there simply because they could not afford a bail bond, and were forced to exist, many for prolonged and unrelieved periods of time, in ugly, squalid, teemingly overcrowded conditions.

Standing amidst that clamor, the clutter of that crude dormitory, while hundreds of distant, hostile eyes stared at me and the crowd listened as I described their pathetic state to the public viewers, I cringed. I will never forget that sad scene often replicated in the following years during now countless visits through our country's squalid jails.

Years later, I stayed overnight at this same D. C. Jail as the culmination of a week-long conference designed to expose professionals interested in the correctional world to the realities of the system. Though my stay was brief, while I knew I could get out if I needed to and that I was being protected from the extreme experiences of the place, even this limited experience—being processed in, stripped, mugged, showered, frocked and locked up in a dirty old cell—this night had a most moving impact on me. Being in a jail is a horror.

My first visit to the D. C. Jail had so shocked me that I could barely think of anything else for days. For several days I sat at home, stranded by a snowstorm, with plenty of time to think about what I had seen. I wrote an article based on my vivid recollections of that jail tour, which was published in *The New Republic*. The piece was very strong, written out of the passions I felt at that time.

That article caused a stir in Washington. The day after the magazine article appeared, the local newspapers and other media picked up on the subject. The Washington *Post,* for example, ran a series vividly describing and criticizing conditions at the D. C. Jail. The Bar Association formed a committee to send lawyers into the jail to interview the inmates and make recommendations for reforms. A very powerful local clergyman delivered a strong sermon on this subject at his church that weekend. Senators Robert Kennedy and Joseph Tydings, who were on the D.C. Senate Committee at the time, sent staff to look into the problems of the D. C. Jail.

However, with the passage of not a lot of time the subject went off the front pages and out of the consciousness of the community. Conditions have continued to be very much the same to the present time. I recently came across a worn and yellowed document of the U. S. Senate, Sixtieth Congress, dated January 11, 1909, containing a message from President Theodore Roosevelt asking Congress to respond to a report to him condemning the D. C. Jail for overcrowding, idleness and other "outrageous conditions." The language of critics, muckrakers and observers of jails has had a discouragingly reminiscent ring throughout this century, in the District of Columbia and elsewhere around the country.

In 1972, I joined the city's public defender service in representing all the inmates at the D. C. Jail in a class action litigation in federal court, questioning the constitutionality of these same conditions. In the interim, I have had the frightening experience of participating in an around-the-clock negotiation regarding the grievances of a riotous group of inmates at the jail in October 1972, while they held a dozen guards hostages and threatened the life of the city's humane corrections chief.

And still conditions are critical.

Washington's problems are not unique. A similar example of the sloth of law reform exists in Louisiana. New Orleans is a sophisticated city. It had a mayor who was known for being relatively reform-minded and progressive. It had a sheriff of its jail who, in my conversations with him, impressed me as being most enlightened and open-minded, and willing to try almost anything to improve conditions. Furthermore, a highly regarded, venerable federal district court judge in New Orleans recently ruled that the conditions at the city jail were so terrible as to violate the Constitution.

Spurred by Neighborhood Legal Service lawyers who were critical of the jail and anxious to bring about reforms, and supported by this very strong judicial opinion, and given the climate and political situation in New Orleans, one would have expected that all elements for reform were operating to improve the jail.

Yet when I went there I found the New Orleans Jail to be perhaps the worst one I had seen, anyplace. One enters this large building after walking up a long flight of steps under a portico bearing a standard high-sounding judicial legend, etched in stone. Once inside and past the hallway one enters a high-rise, clanging, cramped, squalid jail.

Interior cells are crowded with groups of pent-up men; blankets and mattresses on the floor hold sleeping bodies. The all-pervading jail reek and din were omnipresent. I saw men chained to the staircase banister lying on mattresses on the hall floors at the foot of the steps amidst the unconcerned traffic of passersby. They were, I was told, mental cases who had caused trouble and needed to be segregated from the other inmates. So they were abandoned, shackled and simply left on the floor all day, ignored, secure, but a sad vision no visitor could forget. The men rarely get out of their cells. Suicides, rapes, assaults are not uncommon. The place was a hopeless nightmare.

Tait, a 21-year-old pre-law student at the University of Maryland, was remanded to the parish prison to await trial on a charge of carrying a concealed weapon. (Like more than one million American offenders, he was unable to post bail—in his case, $500.)

As Tait subsequently told the tale, he was placed in dormitory-style confinement with 30 to 40 other inmates accused of everything from minor offenses to armed robbery and murder. Having been warned by a guard "not to get in any fights," Tait reluctantly obeyed a cellmate's order to take a shower. When he emerged, he discovered that his clothes had been stolen, and when he went to his bunk, he was given a severe beating. That was it—for the first night. For the next nine nights, Tait later reported, he was "forced to act as a sexual outlet to the other inmates." He submitted, he explained, "out of fear for my life and further beatings." At his trial, he was fined $50 and released. [*Newsweek*, September 14, 1970, p. 41]

The 1949 federal Bureau of Prisons' *Handbook of Correctional Institution Design and Construction* now is the general reference work in the field; it is the jail builder's bible. It criticized the use of maximum security facilities for all people in jail as unnecessary overbuilding and wastefully expensive. It also favored separate institutions for the confinement of pretrial detainees and convicts, or at least internal classification within individual institutions. It called for urban facilities large enough to allow for work, recreation and space for professionally staffed programs. And it recommended the use of cells only for intractable inmates and long-term misdemeanants who would not adjust to a dormitory setting: it preferred dormitories (large interior cells which hold from eight to thirty people) for the general (three quarters of the total, according to bureau recommendations) population.

The bureau relied less and less on this handbook through the years; it had come to question some of its own advice and observed that its old formulas were being followed blindly by local officials. It published a series of "How to" pamphlets in the 1960's dealing with prototypical problems of jails: and eventually stopped production of its handbook.

Then, in 1968, LEAA set up and funded the National Clearinghouse for Criminal Justice Planning and Architecture at the University of Illinois. The clearinghouse published a thick looseleaf book on jail guidelines; it also reviews programs and proposals to deal with jail problems; its approval is required when the planning of a new institution is financed under LEAA programs. The guidelines question the fundamental usefulness of incarceration and present a wide array of alternate choices for the resolution of jail problems based on the current and changing state of correctional developments. While the guidelines go into great details about jails, they advocate no model, recommended institution.

The influence of the clearinghouse could be great: its staff of forty-five was consulted regarding 370 projects during its first few years, according to Frederic Moyer, its architect director. It is not committed to propagating institutions, preferring, where it makes sense, the use of community-based alternatives, the renovation of

existing facilities, and smaller and more specific spaces. Moyer
told a White House Conference on Corrections in December 1971,
"With a few exceptions, current correctional architecture is obsolete." He wrote in June 1972 that the clearinghouse's goals run
contrary to "construction of new versions of the old type prison—
or people warehouse—with all its failures."[23] He and his clearinghouse colleague Dr. Edith Flynn are on record as critics of current
jails and supporters of architectural and programmatic reforms
which could initiate an era of wholesome change.[24]

America is still plagued with the progeny of her wedding to
institutionalization. However, in the twentieth century, a movement can be discerned away from complete reliance on institutions
and back to the community for treatment through such techniques
as foster homes, adoption, probation, parole, out-patient medical
care and the like. Even some jails allow work release programs,
volunteer citizens' projects and community programs; but the community's contacts with its jails are minimal.

There is little sign, however, of significant change. The situation
of our jails is a national disgrace.

23 F. Moyer, "In Answer to Questions on Correctional Architecture," American Institute of Architects Journal, June 1972, p. 46.
24 F. Moyer, "Toward a New Era in Correctional Architecture," Proceedings
of the National Conference on Corrections, pp. 150–55. Williamsburg, Va.,
Dec. 1971.

2

JAILS
The Poorhouses of the Twentieth Century

American jails operate primarily as catchall asylums for poor people. Individuals of wealth, property and connections who get into trouble seldom are confined in jail. Public and private social agencies and hospitals, bail bondsmen, attorneys, prosecutors and judges combine to provide an alternative for the middle class and the affluent that is seldom available to the poor. The vast majority of persons in jail are there because they cannot afford to buy their way out of their predicament.

Poor people are in jail because they cannot provide bail or even the bondsmen's premium or because the judge has deliberately set bail so high that in effect preventive detention has been decreed. Or they are in jail because they have no money to pay a fine imposed and have been ordered to work it out in time behind bars, or because they cannot pay alimony or child support or a sum imposed in a civil judgment. They may be in jail because of a contempt citation or simply because they were witness to a crime and are held as material witnesses. But, whatever the legal justification offered, they are jailed primarily because they are poor.

Americans always have assumed that their country has no poor laws or debtors' prisons. The assumption is technically false and seriously misleading. In the past, America has employed the criminal law overtly to punish the poor for their poverty; but today legal institutions serve the same end covertly. Among these institutions, the jail is the most widespread and most pernicious.

THE "POUND OF FLESH" THE LAW DEMANDS

According to ancient practices, the body of a debtor could be physically attached to enforce payment of a debt, and to punish delinquency. Under the early Roman Law of the Twelve Tables, the unsatisfied creditor had an option; he could sell the debtor and his family into slavery, or he could insist on the death penalty. If there were several creditors, each could literally receive his "pound of flesh" when the debtor's carcass was sectioned and divided among them. Later, Roman law introduced the possibility of a reprieve; before disposing of a defaulting judgment debtor, his creditor was required to hold him in chains for sixty days, and then to exhibit him in the marketplace. If no champion appeared to take up the debtor's cause, the options were the same as before: death or slavery.[1]

The pre-Solonic laws of ancient Greece were a degree more humane, merely sanctioning the personal slavery of debtors to unsatisfied creditors. The customs of the Germanic tribes, from which much of the Anglo-Saxon legal tradition derived, did the same.[2] In Anglo-Saxon England itself, "The *wite-theow* [serving-man] may very often have been working out by his labors a debt that was due to his master."[3] In early feudal England (1066–1200) every man's body already belonged to his lord, and not to himself, but as the feudal system declined, economic pressure grew for drastic remedies against debtors. A 1285 statute allowed the jailing of financially embarrassed merchants as a first step toward collecting their debts. By the mid-fourteenth century, the gradual development of the common law had made a special writ (*capias*) available to creditors.

[1] See Note, "Imprisonment for Debt in 1969," 4 *New England Law Review*, p. 227 (1969).
[2] T. Plucknett, *A Concise History of the Common Law*, p. 389 (5th ed. 1956).
[3] F. Pollack and F. Maitland, *The History of English Law*, Vol. II, p. 596 (2d ed. 1968 reprint).

Some dishonest debtors suddenly discovered assets they had overlooked previously; most became prisoners, however, as they were unable to earn their discharge. Confinement, ironically, made repayment of the debt impossible; even worse, the jailed debtor was expected to pay for his own keep or starve.

During the late seventeenth century, a series of remedial statutes eased this harsh practice. Small debtors were empowered to seek their release on proof that they had no sequestered funds. If their creditors insisted, they could be held for up to three months, but at the creditors' expense.[4] During the eighteenth century, the modern law of bankruptcy began taking shape in England; for some debtors, disclosure of assets and assignment of assets to creditors was a permissible way out of confinement. The collection process generally still began with jailing, however. New laws mandated the segregation of debtors from felons; yet debtors' prisons were foul and overcrowded.

In the nineteenth century, in London, there were three major debtors' prisons, including the notorious Fleet. Poor men languished in squalor, sometimes for decades, over tiny debts, while well-connected debtors lived lives of relative comfort, paying their jailers for luxuries while simultaneously avoiding their legal obligations. Attachment against alleged debtors was available easily, and it was often sought in malice. One historian wrote that "Almost every man's liberty is liable to be invaded, be his means what they may; clergymen, gentlemen, merchants, and tradesmen are alike subject to be torn from their families, at almost any moment, and arrested for debts they do not owe."[5]

The critical attention of the Victorian reformers,[6] among them Dickens,[7] spelled the beginning of the end for England's debtors' prisons. The Debtor's Act of 1869 formally abolished imprisonment as a primary remedy against debtors, and as a punitive measure; the practice nevertheless survived as a last resort in debt collection well into the twentieth century.

In America, some of the original colonies, Georgia, for example,

---

[4] See W. Holdsworth, *A History of English Law,* Vol. VIII, p. 235 (1926).
[5] Ibid.
[6] Several parliamentary commissions heard extensive evidence on the abuse of imprisonment for debt during their inquiries into the courts of common law.
[7] Conditions in debtors' prisons were described in a number of the novelist's works, from *David Copperfield* to *Barnaby Rudge.*

were founded primarily as havens for English debtors; they naturally were reluctant to re-enact the rigorous English debtor laws. Imprisonment for debt was constitutionally prohibited in other states, but some colonies followed England's moralistic example. Pennsylvania legislators deliberated intermittently for almost 150 years without rejecting jailing as a permissible sanction, slowly eliminating the worst abuses—by relieving small debtors, limiting the permissible term of imprisonment, and exempting women; but not until 1842 did Pennsylvania formally abolish all imprisonment for debt.[8] And, as recently as 1969, in the state of Maine, debtors were jailed regularly—and legally—for their failures to meet repayment schedules set by court-appointed commissioners.[9]

The English poor laws, and the Houses of Correction for the "able-bodied poor," were introduced gradually throughout the sixteenth century, and codified systematically in 1601.[10] These laws authorized local officers to compel the labor of destitute persons who were deemed able, but unwilling, to work. In practice they were confined indefinitely in "workhouses," where they were paid a nominal sum for their labors, but required to return most of it to pay for their keep.

The poor were put to work, according to Sidney and Beatrice Webb, "partly in order to produce their keep, partly with a view to their reformation of character, and partly with the intention of thereby deterring others from idleness and disorder."[11] Essential to the same statutory scheme were strict anti-vagrancy laws intended to suppress the spread of "idleness and disorder" among the common people.

Like every historical experiment with institutionalization, the workhouse began with what were taken to be benevolent aims and optimistic expectations. Workhouses were intended to be self-supporting communities providing useful work and healthy surroundings, altogether separate from the criminal prisons. The Elizabethan jurist Sir Edward Coke said that "Few or none are

---

[8] See S. Laurence Shaiman, "The History of Imprisonment for Debt and Insolvency Laws in Pennsylvania as They Evolved from the Common Law," 4 *Am. J. Legal Hist.*, p. 205 (1960).

[9] See Note, Chester Darling, "Imprisonment for Debt in 1969," 4 *New England Law Review*, pp. 227, 237–38 (1969).

[10] 43 Elizabeth Ch. 2.

[11] S. and B. Webb, *English Prisons under Local Government*, p. 13 (1906). (Hamden, Conn.: Archon Books, 1963 edition)

committed to the common gaol but they come out worse than they went in. And few are committed to the house of correction but they come out better."[12]

By the end of the seventeenth century, as the Webbs have reported, the distinction between local jails and workhouses blurred. The workhouses' inmates performed little useful work, and the institutions were a continuing drain on the public purse. They were unsafe and unsanitary; rogues and beggars mixed freely with children and the elderly, and the sick contaminated the healthy. Throughout the eighteenth century, attempts at reform—to institute, for example, the segregation of the "deserving" from the "undeserving" poor—failed.[13]

In 1832, the Poor Law Commissioners condemned local workhouse management as inefficient and dishonest, but Parliament retained the system with only minor reforms. The New Poor Law acts continued to degenerate. Debtors joined the workhouse population. Local masters ran their workhouses as the jailers ran their jails. Even useful labor was replaced by cruel make-work schemes such as the crank and the treadmill, or by simple idleness. By 1865, English workhouses and jails were both known simply as "local prisons."

In 1779, a new statute directed that local jails be used to house convicted criminals, until the first of what would become a new system of English national prisons could replace the prevailing practice of transporting offenders to foreign countries. A mix of pretrial and post-conviction prisoners resulted. The innocent and the guilty, the vicious criminals and the harmless poor, the healthy and the sick were crowded together in all-purpose institutions.

That condition still exists in American jails today.

One recent study has noted that colonial families in America generally cared for their own poor relations at home, or had them cared for privately; but the stringent colonial sanctions against vagrancy echoed the English concern with the idle.[14] As the new nation grew, almshouses, austere, regimented establishments with vigorous programs of labor, proliferated as a public welfare solution to the growing problem of the hard-core, urban poor. With

[12] Quoted in Holdsworth, *A History of English Law,* Vol. IV, p. 396 (1924).
[13] See Holdsworth, *A History of English Law,* Vol. X, p. 174 (1938).
[14] D. Rothman, *The Discovery of the Asylum.*

their mixed populations and unprofessional supervision, the American almshouses came to resemble the English workhouses, and eventually, many almshouses simply became jails.

The United States had adopted legal principles fundamentally at odds with the English poor laws, but in practice thousands of people were jailed because they were poor.

The Ransomed Majority in the Jails

Bill, Randy and Emery live in a six-by-eight foot cage in the Wayne County Jail.

They sleep on filthy pads, infested with insects that crawl out and bite them at night. Roaches, mice and an occasional rat roam their cell in the evenings.

The plumbing on the floor above them is defective, causing sewage to seep down into their tiny, stinking cubicle. The moisture has caused much of the paint to peel off the dirty cream-colored walls.

The small seatless toilet bowl sticking out of the far wall is foul beyond description.

One bare lightbulb dangles from exposed wires in a crevice in the wall.

There is no ventilation or central heating.

There are no facilities for exercise.

Bill, 28, has lived in the cage for 2½ months; Randy, 20, for a month and a half, and Emery, 23, for 10 days.

They are not there to be punished. They are cooped up in the closet-size space because they are too poor to post bond and must, therefore, await their trials in the Wayne County Jail.

The average wait is four or five months. During this time the men are "presumed innocent until proven guilty beyond a reasonable doubt," according to the letter of the law. [Excerpt from the Detroit *Free Press*, November 10, 1970, p. 1, Jack Knight, "Legally Innocent Live with Vermin in Filthy Cages"]

It's the day before Christmas, 1970. You get a call from a minister who visits the Monroe County Penitentiary occasionally to counsel the inmates. He just happens to come across a friend of yours, Willie, a sixteen-year-old boy with a record of mental disturbance and petty crime. Willie has been in the pen for two weeks, and you didn't know.

"But why didn't he call me? Why didn't someone tell me?"

"No dime. Didn't know your number. It's pretty hard to call from here. Is there anything you can do? It's only $50 bail, and sixteen is too young to be in there with . . ."

"My God, of course, I'll do everything I can."

So you call the police, and they tell you to call the "Hall of Justice" because they have no record of Willie. No one at the courts can help you either, because they don't keep records in such a way as to tell you what happened to a particular name.

You call back the police. You have to know what day he was arrested, or they can't look up the name for you. Since you don't know when Willie was arrested, you ask that they check every record for about two weeks ago.

In ten minutes an officer tells you he has just checked every record he has. No Willie. "Maybe we didn't arrest him. Try the Sheriff's Office."

After requests to check all their records, the Sheriff's office finds that they arrested Willie sixteen days ago. The charge is "trespassing."

"Bail? We don't keep records of bail here. Try the pen."

You call the penitentiary. You are switched to three sheriffs in various sections of the prison before one finds Willie's name on a list of prisoners. No, they don't know the bail. They don't even know the charge. But you can visit Willie on Tuesdays and Thursdays between the hours of 2 and 4 p.m. . . . [From "Picking Through the Ruins of the County Penitentiary," March 1971, *The Journal,* Rochester, N.Y.]

The largest group now jailed for poverty, however, are those who lack funds for bail. Millions of people who have been arrested but are not yet tried and, therefore, have been convicted of nothing, are in effect punished by imprisonment without trial. Many of them are innocent and many who are not will serve pretrial time of months, even years, that exceeds the time they could receive if eventually convicted. They are in jail because they are victims of the perverse and unfair bail system.

More than half of the people in American jails—52 per cent according to the *1970 National Jail Census* sponsored by the Department of Justice[15]—are pretrial detainees, held for trial because they can't pay for bail. Bail is an economic discrimination: those with the means to afford a bail bond usually go free before trial; those without the required money, property or connections rot in jail. Preventing flight is the supposed reason for pretrial detention, but relatively few defendants awaiting trial actually ever flee. Some have argued that dangerous defendants should be jailed before trial

[15] *1970 National Jail Census,* p. 1.

to protect society from the chance of their repeated offenses. Even granting this constitutionally questionable rationale, the "dangerous" group is a small percentage of all defendants—a good estimate is about 10 per cent.

A 1968 study by the National Bureau of Standards of a sample of District of Columbia arrestees showed that of the defendants who were held in jail, 40 per cent were never convicted.

America got its bail system from England. Between 1000 and 1300, a pretrial system much like our present one evolved under the old common law of England. Judges traveled and conducted trials in various localities intermittently; local sheriffs were responsible for presenting defendants for trial when the judges arrived. The medieval dungeons were places of horror; they were also both expensive and insecure. The sheriff preferred to hand his prisoners over to his friends to await trial. A discriminatory pretrial detention system had begun. Some sheriffs extorted rewards from prisoners in exchange for release; others resorted to vindictive incarcerations. In 1275, the Statute of Westminster I established rules governing bail practices, defining crimes which were bailable and specifying those which were not, shifting control over the process to the judges.

The right to freedom before trial, originally recognized by the Magna Carta, had, theoretically, been assured by the Petition of Right in 1628. After prolonged pretrial detentions for legally bailable offenses continued to occur, the Habeas Corpus Act was passed in 1679, providing defendants with a remedy when improperly incarcerated before conviction. But judges then, as now, set excessively high bail, and thus circumvented the law. The English Bill of Rights, in 1689, then outlawed the imposition of excessive bail.

The U. S. Constitution has provided habeas corpus relief (Article I, section 9), and a prohibition against excessive bail in the Eighth Amendment. It omitted mention of "the underlying right to the remedy of bail itself." In consequence of this oversight, federal and state rules defining bail law have made bail a limitable right, available only for non-capital offenses, for example. However, most statutes require bail, and provide that bail must not be excessive. Former Associate Justice Robert Jackson's oft quoted, now classic statement that bail was intended to be a device to keep people out of jail until their guilt has been adjudicated at trial, and not a gimmick to put them in jail, has turned out to be honored in the breach.

THE ABUSES OF BAIL

The passage of the Bail Reform Act of 1966 aimed to assure release of all defendants charged with non-capital federal offenses irrespective of their financial status. But many thousands of poor defendants remain in jail for lack of bail. No one knows exactly how many such people are in jail but the number is known to be high. The recent *1970 National Jail Census* showed that on a given day recently there were 83,079 pretrial detainees in the 4,037 American jails surveyed. Omitted here were all the smaller cities and towns and the three states whose jail systems are run by the state, Connecticut, Delaware and Rhode Island, and the thousands of jails which confine inmates forty-eight hours or less. One widely quoted estimate stated that in 1963 a million and a half people went to jail for lack of money to secure a bail bond. In Philadelphia alone, nearly 2,000 people were in pretrial detention one day recently because they could not raise the premium for a bail bond, sometimes only forty dollars. During the weeks, months, sometimes years they spend in jail awaiting trial, they lose jobs, their family connections disintegrate.

Former Attorney General Robert F. Kennedy testified about such a typical case before Senator Sam Ervin's Subcommittee on Constitutional Rights on August 4, 1964. "In Glen Cove, New York, Daniel Walker was arrested on suspicion of robbery and spent fifty-five days in jail for want of bail. Meanwhile, he lost his job, his car was repossessed, his credit destroyed, and his wife had to move in with her parents. Later, he was found to be the victim of mistaken identity and was released. But it took him four months simply to find another job."

When someone is arrested or indicted, a hearing is required with minimum delay to determine what disposition should be made pending trial, often months or years later. The judge or substitute judicial officer then either denies bail and the defendant is locked up until his trial, or bail is set. If the defendant can afford to put up or get someone else to put up the bail imposed on condition that he show up for trial, he is freed.[16] One study in 1968 showed that "seven percent of all defendants in Allegheny County [Pennsylvania] could afford to post full bond themselves; everyone else had to pay a bondsman or go to jail."

Few defendants have assistance at this initial, and crucial, bail hearing. The wealthy and connected defendant will have a lawyer and bondsman present in court. But the mass of defendants face this first judicial contact confused and alone.

One survey demonstrated that the presence of counsel doubled a defendant's chances for release: yet only one of four defendants in the average city had counsel.[17] Counsel can argue the grounds for release or bail reduction, assist in the plea bargaining process, when a prosecutor (often assisted by a judge) seeks to persuade the defendant to plead guilty to a lesser charge, thus avoiding trial and prolonged pretrial detention.

If bail is set, a commercial bondsman will write a bond policy insuring the defendant's attendance at trial for a premium, usually 5 to 10 per cent of the amount of the bail set by the judge. The bondsman, in turn, requires indemnity or collateral from the defendant to cover his risk of forfeiture. But a bondsman has no obligation to go bail for a defendant and frequently refuses to do so. Because of this practice, U. S. Court of Appeals Judge Skelly Wright concluded, the unregulated and often questionable bondsmen—not the judges—actually hold the keys to the jails.[18]

This bail system then really amounts to what former Justice Arthur Goldberg called "checkbook justice," a form of capital punishment for the poor. The insurance companies which administer this business through their local bondsmen, who proliferate in the run-down, neon-lit storefronts which inevitably flower around the country's jails and courthouses have a no-risk bonanza, estimated by former Attorney General Robert F. Kennedy, in testimony before the United States Senate, at a quarter of a billion dollars a year. One estimate had ten to twelve million defendants

[16] In some places, the bond only applies until the defendant comes before the trial court. Then another bond may be required, as another also may be when a conviction is secured and appealed. Multiple bonding is a form of compounding the original inequity of money bail; it was used in places where bondsmen had the greatest political clout.

[17] Paul B. Wice, doctoral dissertation filed at the library of the University of Illinois.

[18] *Pannell* v. *United States,* 310 F. 2d 698 (1963).

buying bail bonds each year, covering about 90 per cent of all misdemeanor cases and about 70 per cent of all felony cases. A seventeen-month survey of one Pittsburgh court showed that 40 per cent of those defendants released on bond eventually were cleared of the charges against them; thus "innocent defendants paid out a total of $215,116 to bondsmen who in effect are licensed by the state to make a profit from the plight of the accused threatened with jail."

Bondsmen may bribe police and lawyers or even judges to get referrals; they often cater to racketeers and organized crime. To complete the collusion, a judge who does not wish a certain man released on bond may set bond only to have the bondsman arbitrarily refuse. In return, that judge will be understanding at a later forfeiture hearing involving the same bondsman.

Occasionally, according to reports, bondsmen have exercised dragnet powers to collect absconding defendants far beyond the powers which could be used by the police in similar circumstances. Bondsmen use enforcers, "skip tracers" and informants to locate and capture absconders; arresting them on their own or with the assistance of the local police (the investigators are paid 10 per cent of the bond).

Some judges simply deny bail if they don't like the defendant, his race or background, or the crime with which he is charged. Judges, especially lower court, bail-setting judges, like to proselytize and philosophize about life and law; they frequently will use the bail process to lecture a hapless defendant about his alleged crime, his record, his life. Such idiosyncratic prejudices demean and disgrace the judicial system.

One illustration of judicial manipulation of the bail proceeding was reported by the Bar Association of the City of New York:

> The Court: The only thing I say is this: I'm going to insist that these boys are not to be bailed out. I'm going to set such bail that they will not be bailed out. If the parents will voluntarily agree not to bail them, I'll not set real high bail. But if they don't voluntarily agree, I'll set such high bail they won't be bailed out. Therefore, do you still want the 3rd? I'm giving them the earliest possible date. . . . Let them see what the inside of these jails look like. Maybe that will be a deterrent to them. I don't know.
>
> The Court: All right. February 3rd. I'll give them that date. I won't be in jail and neither will he. Now, these boys, as I see it

have gone beyond children's acts. This is something that shows they don't know when to stop. Maybe a couple of days in jail may solve the problem. I don't know. I'm going to set $5,000 bail on each. Now, I'm leaving word that if a bond is presented, the matter is to be sent back to me, and I'll tell you right now, if they put up $5,000 bail, I'll make it $10,000, and if they put it up to ten, I'll make it $25,000. I want these boys to spend one or two nights in jail. Maybe that is the answer. I don't know what the answer is.

The Court: . . . I think that the only way to teach these boys anything is to give them a taste of the inside of a jail. Maybe that will help. I don't know. I don't know what the answer is. It's a tough situation.[19]

In cities throughout the South, during the civil rights demonstrations of the 1960's, judges arbitrarily denied bail or set it so high that it might as well have been denied. Or they manipulated the bail system. When money bail was available, property was asked for; if property was available, unsecured property was demanded and only one bail (however little) could be insured by one piece of property (however valuable). One civil rights lawyer told me organizations would not go into a city without a "war chest" to solve the inevitable bail problem. The bondsmen often helped the deviousness of the law, turning away a potential financial bonanza by refusing to provide bail in many cases where it was sought. Often egregious things happened to the jailed defendants in the southern jails.

THE COSTS OF PRETRIAL DETENTION

Studies of the Philadelphia Magistrate's Court in the late 1950's showed striking differences in the trial dispositions of jailed as opposed to bailed defendants. The New York City Legal Aid Society, which surveyed about 900 of its cases, also found that a first offender jailed before trial for lack of bail is convicted three times more frequently and goes to prison twice as frequently as defendants free before trial.

Certain prejudices are obvious: a man in jail, unlike his counterpart who is free before trial, cannot consult with his attorney in

---

[19] *People* v. *Ronald Garnett et al.*, docket #184, 185, 186 (January 26, 1960), Magistrate's Court, New York City, Felony Court, Queens County. Transcript pp. 4–5.

the open and continuous way that he could if he was free. Nor can he personally assist in his own defense. He is deprived of his privacy and a normal life. He lives in a gross, dangerous, unhealthy, brutal, nightmarish environment with nothing to do.

When he eventually gets to court he appears not as a free man. Men in jail before trial 1) get indicted by the grand jury more often, 2) plead guilty more often, 3) are convicted at trial more often, 4) are given probation less often, and 5) receive longer prison sentences more often than their counterparts who were free before trial.[20]

There is no need to incarcerate most defendants to protect society, yet the operating costs of jail run into millions of dollars annually in the big cities; and the costs of lost earning capacities and families forced onto welfare roles are high. From standards of public safety and economics—as well as fairness—the money bail system is not socially utilitarian.

One witness at Senate hearings several years ago on the operations of the federal bail system pointed out that with an average cost of only $3.39 per person daily, the annual costs of detaining federal defendants (who are a small fraction of the overall criminal population) ". . . came to about four million dollars a year, and the trend is upward." In Philadelphia, in 1952, pretrial detainees spent a total of 131,683 days in jail at a cost to the city of more than $300,000. The late New York Supreme Court Justice Bernard Botein said that, in 1962, 58,000 people spent almost two million days in New York City detention facilities awaiting trial—at a direct cost to the city of more than $10 million.

One thirty-year-old Puerto Rican, according to a report by New York City's former Correction Board Chairman, William vanden Heuvel, was arrested on November 7, 1970, had his case postponed fifty-five times while he sat in the Tombs for almost two years at a cost to the city of $16,000.

EFFORTS AT BAIL REFORM

In the early 1960's, a number of experimental programs sought to alleviate some of the well-documented and widely considered excesses of the bail system. The National Bail Conference spon-

[20] In Ronald L. Goldfarb, *Ransom: A Critique of the American Bail System* (New York: Harper, 1965), pp. 37–42, these studies are discussed.

sored by the Department of Justice in 1964 focused national attention on these bail reform programs. By mid-1972, an OEO survey of pretrial release programs in the United States had discovered about 100 such programs. Still, the growth and spread of the pretrial release movement in this country was haphazard, disorganized and unpublicized. Many of the early programs are now defunct. Existing projects secure the release of only about 170,000 people annually. Only eight programs screen 15,000 or more defendants each year.[21]

A detailed look at one of these programs, New York City's pioneer Vera Institute of Justice program, the parent of ROR (release on recognizance) programs, demonstrates how they work, when they do work. A retired industrialist-philanthropist, Louis Schweitzer, had learned in 1960 that of almost 115,000 people detained before trial in New York City, only about 31,000 were later convicted and sentenced to incarceration. He decided to do something about this scandalous situation. First he considered establishing a fund to provide bail money for poor people who were worthwhile risks, but abandoned this idea because it would simply ease a system that was intrinsically bad.

The Manhattan Bail Project experiment resulted from his conception. Local law schools, judges, district attorneys, defense lawyers and city officials were consulted. Vera obtained offices in one of Manhattan's criminal court buildings. As prisoners were brought into the detention center each day, law students would interview the defendants before arraignment, asking questions aimed at establishing their community ties as evidence that they would not flee. Detainees were given points for their responses; a certain number of points would qualify them to be recommended by Vera for release on their own recognizance, that is, on trust to return to court for all later proceedings. A recommendation would be made to the court that they be released. Vera undertook to remind the people of their court appearances if they were released.

Those released whom Vera recommended returned for trial a greater percentage of the time than those who were out on bail under the control of bondsmen. As prosecutors and judges became more willing to go along with Vera's recommendations, the num-

---

[21] OEO Office of Planning Research and Evaluation, "Summary of Survey of Pre-Trial Release Programs, OEO Pre-Trial Release Program" (March 21, 1973).

ber qualifying under the program was expanded. At first only persons charged with certain relatively minor offenses were eligible for consideration; as the program proved its effectiveness, these categories were expanded. Vera's successful statistics were widely published and endorsed by influential observers. It cost the city thirteen dollars to put a defendant through the Vera process; it cost the city an average of $120 to confine a defendant pretrial. (In 1962, 58,000 defendants spent 1,700,000 days in New York City jails pretrial, at a cost of over $10,000,000.)

A new Pretrial Services Agency to accelerate and expand the city's release on recognizance program was recently proposed in New York City. Several varieties of the Vera program are in operation elsewhere, including outright release on trust, release on nonfinancial conditions but with outside supervision; release on personal bond (of the defendant without requiring additional personal securities or a third-party surety); and cash bail (defendant provides the court with 10 per cent of the bond, most of which is returned when he comes back for trial).

In most cities with ROR programs, government agencies are the sponsors; about a third are run by private organizations, according to Professor Paul Wice's survey. In St. Louis and Cincinnati, the probation departments administer the program; in Des Moines, a private foundation-funded citizens' group does the job using law students. In some cities, Vista Volunteers assume the Vera role; in the District of Columbia an independent bail agency has been set up under the auspices of the court to conduct the program (in 1970, more than 8,000 suspects were released under its supervision; only about 10 per cent were rearrested); in Tulsa, Oklahoma, a special program of the local bar association provided for local defense lawyers to vouch for the appearance of their clients.

Objective criteria based on set questions and points for proper answers usually are used; in Los Angeles and Chicago, subjective judgments are used, and releases are awarded more often than when objective tests are applied.

In Baltimore, after one year with a Vera-type program, 868 men were approved for ROR; only six failed to appear for trial, and the city was saved more than $500,000, according to a report to the city's courts by the pretrial release program director. In San Antonio, only 2 per cent of more than 1,000 prisoners released on personal bond in 1971 failed to appear for trial, lower than the forfeiture rate for prisoners on commercial bond. More than half went back to their jobs or found new ones, saving welfare costs.[22]

A very large percentage of pretrial detainees in all jails could be safely released if a responsible agency would assume the responsibility for screening and conducting the minimum, interim supervision—usually simply on a phone call or letter—to assure a successful return to court. They are uniformly more successful than bondsmen, according to the few reliable statistics available.

The Milwaukee ROR program found that of 780 released on their own recognizance, seven became involved in further difficulties with the law prior to court disposition, one other died; *all* the remaining 722 prisoners showed up in court. Professor Wice reports that the programs that are the most inclusive appear to have the lowest forfeiture rates. The Wice study of eight cities concluded, nevertheless, that the poorest defendants, who must rely completely on bail reform programs for pretrial release, are released only in one in four cases.

Another reform program used to relieve the overflowing ranks of pretrial detainees also instituted by Vera, and now used in New York City and New Haven, is the expanded use of summonses. In certain categories of relatively minor offenses, a simple summons rather than an arrest is used to order the person to trial or arrested defendants are given a summons to appear in court for a later proceeding and are then released.

In California, citations or summonses may be used in all misdemeanor cases, except when an arrest is necessary to protect the community or the processes of the court. A police officer calls in to a computer-based network system which notifies him within a minute if the defendant is wanted for another crime. If he isn't, he can be given a summons and released.[23]

The procedures employed by the police are simple, quick and much like the ROR interview. Criminal background is checked; questions are asked to determine likelihood of flight with answers given points; a quick corroboration of fundamental facts results in a release.

Public money and police manpower are conserved under this kind of system, and justice is served. A memorandum from Oak-

22 San Antonio *News*, August 13, 1971.
23 Wice, Chap. 10 (hereafter cited as Wice Report).

land Chief of Police Charles Gain to the Oakland Police Department said of the use of citations for adult misdemeanants:

> . . . It is well established that a person who has been arrested but not convicted is, in the eyes of the law, an innocent person; that is the purpose of the trial, and the historical reason for the granting of bail . . . If he lacks the funds for bail, he usually stays in jail, which means that his ability to be released from jail depends on the amount of money he has—a clearly inequitable result. Moreover, in those cases in which the arrested person can make bail, it seems undesirable for the system of justice to depend upon money any more than necessary: if a person can be safely released, the release should be based on that fact rather than upon the payment of a fee . . .[24]

In San Francisco, a misdemeanor citation program has largely replaced the traditional arrest-and-book system. Sgt. Thomas Dempsey, who oversees the program for the patrolmen, spoke of it enthusiastically to the local press: "I'd been a policeman for 18 years, and all this time we'd been locking up people for malicious mischief, shoplifting, those Mickey Mouse deals. As an old-time policeman, the idea of walking up, giving a guy a piece of paper and sending him on his way was hard to accept. It's unbelievable how much time this saves."[25] Wise as this procedure seems to be, its overall use is minimal. In Washington, D.C., where station-house release was authorized by the law setting up the city's bail agency, in 1,037 cases referred to the bail agency in 1969 by the police, 681 were released; but approximately 50,-000 defendants were eligible under the program for such release.

According to the OEO survey, 20 per cent of the known bail projects in the country reported use of field release by police, 39 per cent said station-house ROR was used; 64 per cent reported use of station-house bail.

Millions of summonses are issued each year (the most common form is the traffic ticket). With increasing computerization of police information this technique could be expanded greatly to clear overcrowded jails and to protect poor defendants, many of whom are innocent. Taxpayers' costs for welfare and detention have

[24] Quoted in *California State Bar Journal,* November–December 1972, p. 581.
[25] "San Francisco Police Hail Misdemeanor Citation," *Evening Tribune,* February 25, 1971, p. 1.

been reduced significantly where such programs are used, with no corresponding diminution of public safety.

RELEASE UNDER CONDITIONS

In Washington, D.C., and in the federal system since passage of the Bail Reform Act of 1966, courts may release pretrial defendants on condition that defendants meet certain requirements. They may be asked to give up their passports, stay within the court's jurisdiction, observe a curfew, remain at work or in school, not travel, attend drug counseling courses or vocational training programs, report regularly of their whereabouts. A defendant charged with a non-capital crime must be released on his own recognizance or upon execution of an unsecured appearance bond. The court may condition release into the custody of a supervising person or organization; place restrictions on travel, association or abode, require a 10 per cent cash bail bond, securities, property or cash in lieu of unsecured bail; or "impose any other condition deemed reasonably necessary to assure appearance as required, including a condition requiring that the person return to custody after specified hours."[26] The purpose and goal of the law was to assure release, minimize reliance on and perversion of financially conditioned release, and allow for versatile, imaginative techniques for securing pretrial release and assuring against fugitivism.

Under the cash bail system, pioneered in Chicago and elsewhere in Illinois, a defendant pays 10 per cent of the amount of his bail into court and gets back 9 per cent if he appears (the court keeps 1 per cent to cover its administrative costs), but this system has been challenged on pragmatic grounds (it leads to inflationary bail because judges want to detain) and constitutionally (it discriminates in favor of the defendant who can provide the full bail to the court and then get it all back without paying 1 per cent).

Courts also may release a defendant into the custody of a vouching third party—frequently a member of the clergy, family friend, employer or attorney. In Albuquerque and Tulsa, active third-party custody programs are run by lawyers. Community programs

[26] Pub. L. 89–465, 89th Cong., June 22, 1966, 80 Stat. 214.

in some cities supervise defendants pretrial. In Washington, D.C., a group run mostly by ex-convicts, Bonabond, does this with reported success. In Chicago, the Alliance to End Repression supplements the local court-based release program; in Los Angeles, the HEW-funded Community Justice Center operates a private release program. In Detroit, community organizations participate. Daytime release to go to school or work is rarely used for pretrial defendants, though paradoxically, it is used widely for sentenced convicts. In Orange County, California, under a Legal Aid Warranty Fund, college students can purchase jail insurance providing assistance in obtaining release and counsel.[27] Organizations such as unions long have provided such services; some churches recently have done the same.

Yet money bail remains the major means by which courts deal with defendants. Twice as many defendants, according to Wice's seventy-two-city survey, won release through bondsmen as through their own sources. Poor defendants still are required to languish in jails before their trials, victims of an unnecessary, wasteful, scandalously unjust system.

Legislative efforts in numerous states—California, Missouri and Georgia, for example—proposing statewide reform, have failed; citywide attempts at limited reform have been starved, shrunken and disbanded. The federal reform movement reportedly has been perverted in some places, ignored in others. The rhetoric and some isolated examples of successful reform programs remain; but so do all the problems long noted and deplored; in fact sadly, they have increased in the last decade of reform.

Take the situation in the nation's capital, the only city governed by the Bail Reform Act of 1966 and the testing ground for the first preventive detention law, as well. A survey of bail practices in Washington, D.C., conducted by the Washington *Post*[28] five years after the passage of the Bail Reform Act, found more than 1,100 men in the D. C. Jail, the overwhelming majority—98 per cent—there because they could not come up with relatively small premiums for bail bonds, this despite an active citywide bail

[27] Moore, "Jail Insurance, A New Way to Open Doors," Los Angeles *Times,* October 2, 1970.
[28] Valentine, "Five Years After Reform," Washington *Post,* September 26, 1971, p. 1.

agency which had supervised more than 8,000 released defendants a year at the last count.

Officials of the local police, court and district attorney's offices candidly admit that money bail is used as a cynical subterfuge to incarcerate repeater offenders. One federal judge quoted by *Newsweek* magazine said of the Bail Reform Act, "Under this Act, I'd have to turn a raving maniac loose on the streets." Bondsmen were refusing to provide bail for the increasing number of defendants charged with narcotics offenses because they were bad risks. Police were cracking down on crime in response to political pressures to clean up Washington. Judges interpreted the Bail Reform Act clause to permit setting bail defendants could not afford.

PREVENTIVE DETENTION

There are some persons, though a minority of those arrested, who need close supervision before trial as a matter of public safety. Ironically, many of these persons frequently are able to buy their way out of jail with a bail bond.

Should any persons, regardless of financial resources, be incarcerated during pretrial simply because they are assumed to be dangerous? The idea of preventive detention, in theory, and in practice, has aroused civil libertarians, who point out the inexact, unscientific nature of predicting future offenses and the constitutional problems aroused by jailing somebody without a trial based on suspicion of future acts instead of proof of past offenses.

The dilemma is this: to imprison a man on the mere speculative possibility that he might commit a crime at some future time deprives him of the presumption of innocence both for the crime with which he is charged and prospectively for a crime which it is argued there is a likelihood he will commit. The dilemma is that, on a practical level, if certain people are free before trial, there is a real risk of immediate danger to society. The available evidence indicates that the seriousness of the charge has little to do with the risk of flight if released.

Minor offenders, who are not considered dangerous to society, frequently cannot make money bail and wind up in jail. The more serious offenders, the organized criminals, for example, the big shot racketeers, frequently can afford bail and go free before trial even though they may present a greater and more demonstrable risk of committing future crimes or obstructing justice. San Antonio Judge Archie Brown reported about this paradox to an investigating Citizens' Committee that studied the Bexar County Jail in 1970:

> The saddest thing is that people who are obviously guilty, in cases in which the State has an open and shut case go, "wham, wham" right through. It is the poor devil who is probably innocent, but the police think they have got the right man, and they are working, trying to prove that, then finally they convince the District Attorney to take the complaint and then his investigators try to plug up the loopholes. We find the least likely to be guilty. This is a real sad situation. The guilty get all the service and the one that is half innocent spends too much time in jail.

The practices of the bail system pervert its purposes, in paradoxical ways. Attempts to proscribe formal procedures for preventive detention for the most part have not been successful because critics have been able to demonstrate their inherent pitfalls. While formal preventive detention proposals are attacked and officially forbidden, preventive detention is practiced *sub rosa,* nonetheless. Judges who deem defendants to be dangerous to society simply set bail so high that defendants cannot afford it; in effect, the judge has made a private and largely uncontrolled determination that the prisoner should be preventively detained.

Detractors of officially prescribed preventive detention fear it will lead to detaining many innocent men to catch some guilty ones. Proponents point out that preventive detention now exists unofficially, probably jailing more innocent defendants than official practice would do. When in 1968 the National Bureau of Standards conducted a study for the Justice Department of suspects rearrested on further crimes while free on bail, 11 per cent of the 426 defendants were found to be rearrested.

Few people doubt that in certain classes of cases a compelling argument can be made for society's right to self-protection: in cases involving organized crime and racketeering, flagrant recidivism, criminal insanity and subversion. That something must be done about this category of offenders few could deny. Articulating a scheme which does not do havoc to important constitutional guarantees of the right to trial by jury and the presumption of innocence, however, becomes both difficult and questionable. What quantity of proof of the likelihood of future criminality should be required? How can a judge predict future crime? How can means for preventing abuse of the power be assured?

Critics argue that in parallel situations regarding juveniles, sexual psychopaths and the mentally ill, prophylactic commitments have not worked out well. They make the argument, and this is the fundamental point, that once you get into the business of predicting future crime you end up with erroneous confinements in order to assure appropriate ones. As Harvard law professor Alan Dershowitz has said: "A predictor is likely to be able to spot a large number of persons who would actually commit acts of violence only if he is also willing to imprison a very much larger number of defendants who would not, in fact, engage in violence if released."

To the objection that judges cannot predict future crime, a number of judges have told me that they feel they can make reasonable judgments. One judge said, "You don't have to be a mental giant to know when a man comes before you to be arraigned on Friday for a burglary and his record shows he is an addict and that he was released on bail a week ago, that if you release him again he is going out and do the same thing." Another judge, with a long prosecutorial experience, said to me, "There are widows and orphans in the city who plague my conscience because I try to follow my oath of office and adhere to the Bail Reform Act strictly, even when releasing certain defendants violates my common sense, reason and experience."

In responding to Wice's questionnaires, the majority of judges, prosecutors, public defenders, bail project directors and defense attorneys in seventy-two cities said that increased use of preventive detention would reduce crime (52 per cent) and should be used more often (54 per cent). Forty-eight per cent admitted that preventive detention was practiced in their community.[29]

The few studies that are available show that about 10 per cent of all the people on bail commit further crimes. In 1968 the U. S. Department of Justice funded a survey by the National Bureau of Standards of recidivism rates of 426 charged felons free before

[29] Wice Report, p. 355.

trial in the District of Columbia. Its finding: 11.7 per cent of the defendants surveyed were rearrested for additional felony charges while awaiting trial. In the Indianapolis system, 11 per cent of defendants free before trial were rearrested. Wice's mail survey of seventy-two cities disclosed a 6.8 per cent rearrest rate.

Speedy trials would help the pretrial detainee somewhat, but that remedy does not help the defendant who needs delays to perfect his case. Conditional release begs the question; the category of offender for whom preventive detention might be appropriate is not likely to be controllable short of confinement.

In the District of Columbia, which has experimented with the country's only preventive detention statute to date, only the barest few proceedings to obtain preventive detention have even been sought (eighteen times during the first ten months, according to a recent survey). Because it takes so much time to process a preventive detention proceeding, because of the delay occasioned by all of the legal procedures everyone agrees must surround any constitutional preventive detention practice, DA's hesitate to use it.

It is much easier to get a judge to order high money bond and obtain preventive detention indirectly through this subterfuge. Hundreds of defendants have been detained in the District of Columbia since passage of the Bail Reform Act through their failure to make money bond, though unattainably high money bond should be impermissible under the act. Some lawyers have argued that the only money bond permissible is that which a man can afford and which a judge feels will assure his presence at trial.

The jails are bad enough for convicted people; they are intolerable for people who have not been convicted. Unless the techniques for employing preventive detention are perfected so they can be used with relative ease where appropriate, and until decent facilities can be devised to hold people held under these special circumstances, the profound questions about whether any form of preventive detention could pass constitutional muster and whether it would provide a worse precedent than the problem it is designed to cure may better be deferred. The best balance between the risks of pretrial release and the dangers of pretrial detention has yet to be struck.

Real reform will never come, in my judgment, until we stop game-playing with the money bail system and scrap it. There is something intellectually, philosophically, fundamentally wrong with hinging freedom on money.

Judges should resort to varied, versatile techniques to assure defendants' releases until trial and to insure against the risk of their flight in every case. Only where it is impossible, or where a clear showing of dangerousness of recidivism is proven, should pretrial detention be allowed. And then, it should be allowed only after complete and fair procedures, in decent detention places and for limited periods of time.[30]

DEBTORS IN JAIL

The bail system is the biggest source of jailing for the poor, but it is not the only one. Thousands of persons every year are jailed because they cannot or will not pay fines, judgments, alimony or otherwise conform to orders of a court. With the exception of the defiant person who can obey these orders and does not, these defendants too are economic victims of a judicial system that discriminates against people without money.

Fines. As a form of criminal sentence, fining is older than imprisonment itself. Fines originally were small payments paid by convicted offenders to help feudal overlords defray the expense of trials; the bulk of the monetary reparations for crime went to the victim or his family. As the state took over responsibility for punishing criminals, the king claimed a payment from the offender for the state's participation in bringing the criminal to justice and for the injury done to the public peace. In the twelfth century in England, the victim's share of the reparations began to decrease while the king's share increased. Eventually the king took the entire payment.[31]

Today, fines seem to be imposed routinely to dispose of minor offenses, whether or not the defendants gained financially from their crimes. However, a sentence to pay a fine frequently is stated in the alternative: pay or go to jail. Some pay; many go to jail.

[30] For a thorough description of a proposed pretrial procedure which would deal with release and detention on these criteria, see Goldfarb, *Ransom,* Chap. 7.

[31] Holdsworth, *A History of English Law,* Vol. II, p. 38 (1909); see Ronald L. Goldfarb and Linda R. Singer, *After Conviction* (New York: Simon & Schuster, 1973) (Victim Compensation).

In the federal system and in forty-seven states a person who cannot or will not pay a fine may be imprisoned. In some states there formerly was no limit on the length of time that could be served for non-payment. Non-payment of fines had become a major cause of imprisonment. In 1966, the District of Columbia Crime Commission found, of 1,183 convicted misdemeanants included in a sample, 222 (19 per cent) were fined. Of these, 105 (47 per cent) were imprisoned for non-payment. In the Philadelphia County Jail, according to one recent study, 60 per cent of the inmates had been committed for non-payment of fines.[32] More than 26,000 prisoners were in New York City jails in 1960 for failure to pay fines. In San Joaquin, California, according to a 1968 study, about half the people in jail were there for non-payment of fines in petty, often alcoholic-related cases.[33]

The law in this area is changing, however. In 1907, a United States District Court was faced with a claim that a statute imposing a fine for refusing to submit to a search of one's person or property by a revenue officer contained no authorization of imprisonment if the fine was not paid. Despite the statute's silence, the court ruled that the use of a jail term to enforce payment was too well established a practice to be disregarded.[34]

When the Supreme Court considered the question, in 1907 and again in 1936, it held that a sentencing court had discretion to provide two means of collecting a fine: executing on the debtor's property or putting him in jail. According to the Court, "The choice of pains and penalties, when choice is committed to the discretion of the court, is part of the judicial function."[35]

This reasoning, strained even in the case of recalcitrant defendants who willfully refused to pay a fine they could afford, made no sense when applied to the many poor defendants who lacked the resources to pay. Even where the result of imprisoning an indigent defendant for failure to pay a fine was to keep him in jail beyond the maximum period authorized for an offense

[32] President's Commission on Law Enforcement and Administration of Justice, *Task Force Report: The Courts* (Washington, D.C.: Government Printing Office, 1970), p. 18.
[33] Institute for the Study of Crime and Delinquency, "Model Community Correctional Program," Report II (1970).
[34] *Ex parte Barclay*, 153 Fed. 669, 670 (1907).
[35] *Ex parte Jackson*, 96 U.S. 727 (1877); *Hill* v. *Wampler*, 298 U.S. 460, 463–64 (1936).

by statute, the courts justified the additional hardship imposed by a fiction: the extra jail term was not part of the punishment for the original crime but merely a means of collecting the fine. The New York Court of Appeals articulated this stilted rationale: "A direction in a sentence imposing a fine that defendant stand committed until the fine is paid is no part of the penalty for the offense, but is merely a means of compelling obedience to the judgment of the court."[36]

In a 1950 case, *People* v. *District of Columbia,*[37] the defendant, who had a record of approximately seventy convictions for drunkenness, was found guilty of being drunk in a public park. He was fined and given 150 days in jail if he defaulted (a choice of working off his fine at the rate of fifty cents a day). On appeal, the court repeated the rationale that an alternative sentence to jail "is not imposed as part of the penalty but as a means of compelling payment of the fine."

The appeals court admitted that in this case the alternative sentence of 150 days looked suspiciously as if the trial court decided that because of appellant's record of approximately seventy convictions for drunkenness, he should be confined for more than the thirty days permitted by the statute. The appeals court concluded that the trial court should not evade the legislative penal enactment under the guise of enforcing payment of a fine. But since the defendant could not perform the impossible task of convincing the court that this undoubtedly was the case, he spent his 150 days in jail.

In the 1960's, as the Supreme Court issued related opinions requiring lower courts to furnish poor people with certain basic rights in criminal proceedings, including free lawyers and trial transcripts,[38] it became increasingly anomalous to permit discrimination against the poor for their inability to pay fines.

The first breakthrough came in 1966. A New York trial judge had sentenced a defendant whom he knew to have neither funds nor property (and who also was married and a father) to pay a $500 fine or spend 500 days in jail. The maximum term of imprisonment for the offense, a minor assault, was one year. The

[36] Matter of *McKinney* v. *Hamilton,* 282 N.Y. 393; 26 N.E. 2d 949 (1940).
[37] 75 A. 2d 845.
[38] *Griffin* v. *Illinois,* 351 U.S. 12 (1956); *Douglas* v. *California,* 372 U.S. 353 (1963).

New York Court of Appeals found that the trade-off of one day in jail for every dollar of an unpaid fine was an "absurdly low rate" dating back to 1876, and held that it constituted cruel and unusual punishment where the sentencing court knew that the defendant was indigent and consequently would be imprisoned beyond the maximum term fixed for the crime.[39]

In 1968, a District of Columbia court, reviewing the sentence of an indigent jaywalker (who was a chronic alcoholic) to a $150 fine or to serve sixty days in jail, invalidated the prison sentence because it exceeded the ten-day maximum provided for the offense. The court ruled that "in every case in which the defendant is indigent, a sentence of imprisonment in default of payment of a fine which exceeds the maximum term of imprisonment which could be imposed under the substantive statute as an original sentence is an invalid exercise of the court's discretion for the reason that its only conceivable purpose is to impose a longer term of punishment than is permitted by law."[40] Although the court noted that "a court should not be powerless to compel a contumacious defendant to pay a fine imposed as punishment," it recognized that "no such purpose can possibly be served in the case of an indigent who, although willing to do so, is without funds to pay a fine and avoid the term of imprisonment."

The Supreme Court, in a 1970 decision, agreed.[41] In this case the Court invalidated the imprisonment of an indigent for 101 days beyond the maximum sentence provided by law, to "work off" an unpaid fine and court costs at the rate of five dollars a day. In the opinion of Chief Justice Burger, the Court ruled that "when the aggregate imprisonment exceeds the maximum period fixed by the statute and results directly from an involuntary nonpayment of a fine or court costs we are confronted with an impermissible discrimination which rests on ability to pay"; this discrimination violates the equal protection clause of the Fourteenth Amendment. The Court limited its holding to cases where an indigent defendant is imprisoned for a period beyond the statutory maximum for the offense. However, its reasoning—that a defendant's choice of paying a fine or serving a prison term that is

[39] *People* v. *Saffore,* 18 N.Y. 2d 101; 218 N.E. 2d 686 (1966).
[40] *Sawyer* v. *District of Columbia,* 238 A. 2d 314, 318 (D.C. Mun. App. 1968).
[41] *Williams* v. *Illinois,* 399 U.S. 235 (1970).

greater than the maximum for the offense is illusory if he is indigent—seemed to apply equally to the case where an indigent defendant is given the "choice" of paying a fine or serving a jail term within the statutory ceiling.

A year later, the Supreme Court went the next step. Preston Tate, an indigent, had been convicted in the Corporation Court in Houston, Texas, of nine traffic offenses and fined $425. Unable to pay the fine, he was sentenced to the municipal prison farm for eighty-five days to work off his fine at the rate of five dollars per day. The Texas courts upheld this practice, even though Texas law provided only for fines for this offense and not for imprisonment, though it did require people unable to pay their fines to work them off in jail.

The Supreme Court held that it was an unconstitutional discrimination to subject someone to imprisonment solely because of his indigency. Standards of imprisonment, the Court held, must fall equally on all defendants irrespective of their economic conditions. Quoting one of its earlier decisions, the Supreme Court declared that the equal protection clause of the Fourteenth Amendment "requires that the statutory ceiling placed on imprisonment for any substantive offense be the same for all defendants irrespective of their economic status."[42]

The jailing of indigents for non-payment of fines is self-defeating. The state must undergo the expense of keeping an offender in jail when a judge already has determined imprisonment unnecessary. At the same time the defendant is prevented from earning the money to pay his fine. The state ends up by supporting the defendant and often his family, through welfare payments, as well.

INSTALLMENT PLANS AND WORK SENTENCES

Several approaches have been suggested to broaden the alternatives of a court wishing to impose a fine.

One such plan is the development of more flexible collection methods to give defendants time to pay their fines and authorizing payment of small amounts at periodic intervals.

[42] *Tate* v. *Short,* 401 U.S. 395 (1971).

Since the enactment of the Criminal Justice Administration Act in 1914, British judges have been required to allow a defendant at least seven days to pay any fine. New York changed its procedure in 1962 to permit a forty-eight-hour grace period in response to the adverse publicity given the four-hour jailing (in the court lockup and later in the Tombs) of a public relations executive when he lacked enough cash to pay seven dollars of a twenty-five-dollar fine for a year-old parking ticket and when the clerk refused to accept his check.[43] The adoption of the grace period reduced jailing for non-payment in New York for about 10,000 people annually.

In fourteen states and the federal courts judges may authorize payment of fines at periodic intervals,[44] but there is little evidence that this discretion is used frequently. In Sweden the use of installment payments reduced the number of people imprisoned for failure to pay a fine from over 13,000 in 1932 to 286 in 1940.[45] In addition to authorizing installment payments, the American Law Institute's Model Penal Code would permit courts to allow additional time for payment if necessary or to change the terms of payment.[46] The use of civil attachment and execution to collect unpaid fines might be helpful when defendants are solvent and have property.

The President's Commission on Crime in the District of Columbia recommended that fines be imposed only on those defendants who are likely to be able to pay them, but would provide for possible jailing of others.

> If a fine is to be imposed, it should be set in light of the offender's ability to pay and this information should specifically appear in the presentence report. If the offender cannot pay a fine all at once, periodic installment payments should be established. If it appears that he will not be able to pay a fine under any circumstances, the court should impose a sentence of either imprisonment or probation, whichever is appropriate in the case, and not

---

[43] New York *Herald Tribune*, July 5, 1962, p. 1.
[44] Cal. Penal Code 1205 (1966 Supp.) (misdemeanors); N.Y. Code Crim. Proc. 470-d(1) (b), as amended, N.Y. Sess. Laws 1967, c. 681, 61 (all fines); Mich. Stats. Ann. 28-1075 (1959); Pa. Stats. Ann. tit. 19, 953–56 (1964).
[45] Note, "Fines and Fining—An Evaluation," 101 *U. Pa. L. Rev.* 1013, 1023 (1953).
[46] Model Penal Code 302.1(1), 302.2(2); see also American Bar Association, *Report on* "Minimum Standards for Criminal Justice, Sentencing Alternatives and Procedures" (approved draft, 1968), 2.7(b), pp. 117–23.

offer an offender a false option unrelated to his character or his offense.[47]

A New York law provides that:

> In any case where the defendant is unable to pay a fine imposed by the court, the defendant may at any time apply to the court for resentence. In such case, if the court is satisfied that the defendant is unable to pay the fine, the court must . . . revoke the entire sentence imposed and . . . may impose any sentence it originally could have imposed except that the amount of any fine imposed shall not be in excess of the amount the defendant is able to pay.[48]

A recently enacted Maryland statute contains similar provisions and, in addition, sets maximum periods of imprisonment for non-payment of fines (one third the maximum or ninety days, whichever is less; no more than fifteen days if the offense itself was not subject to punishment by imprisonment; in any case no more than one day for each ten dollars of the unpaid fine).

A new and enlightened Delaware statute has the greatest potential for eliminating imprisonment for non-payment of fines. A person sentenced to a fine who is unable or unwilling to pay may be ordered to report to the commissioner of the Department of Correction for work on public-works projects to discharge the fine. A defendant may be assigned to state, county or municipal agencies or to private employers for standard compensation. Wages not required for his support are withheld until the fine has been discharged. Only if he fails to comply with the work order may the defendant be held in civil contempt of court or imprisoned for less than thirty days for violation of a probation condition. This provision was reported to have reduced the adult prison population in Delaware by 105 inmates in its first five weeks.[49]

Courts generally have some leeway in setting fines for a particular offense. Any fine may impose a greater burden on a poor defendant than a rich one. A judge at least should inquire into the defendant's resources before deciding how much to fine him.

The laws of Switzerland, Finland, Cuba, Sweden and Mexico

[47] President's Commission on Crime in the District of Columbia *Report*, (1967), p. 394.
[48] N.Y. Code Crim. Proc. 470-d(3), as amended, N.Y. Sess. Laws 1967, c. 681, 61.
[49] Md. Ann. Code, art. 38, §4 (1970); 57 Laws of Del., ch. 198 (1970).

explicitly determine the amount of fines according to the means of the offender. Fines are expressed in units approximating the value of one day's work. Values vary depending on the defendant's daily wage, the possibilities for him to earn money and the number of his dependents.[50] A committee of the American Bar Association wisely suggested that this or a similar system is best suited to equalizing the effects of fines on different defendants.[51]

Where terms of payment can be arranged, fines represent a simple, cheap and effective form of punishment. A recent study of chronic drunkenness offenders showed that in five out of six cases there were longer periods of time between arrests when offenders were given fines instead of jail or suspended sentences. More appropriate than fines for the large group of offenders who cannot pay would be a system of work release, with or without partial confinement, that would enable the offenders to earn money or to repair some of the damage caused by their crimes.[52] The few cities that put substantial numbers of minor offenders on work release do allocate some of the participant's earnings to the payment of fines or court costs or court-ordered restitution.[53]

Accurate statistics on how many indigents still are being jailed for non-payment of fines are not available; jail records are incomplete and do not show why a jail sentence is imposed after conviction.

Old sentencing habits die hard, especially in the crucial lower courts of limited or special jurisdiction, courts which impose fines, deal with minor misdemeanor cases and face the practical problem of non-payment of fines.[54]

[50] Derek A. Westen, "Fines, Imprisonment & the Poor: Thirty Dollars or Thirty Days," 57 *Calif. L. Rev.* 778, 813 (1969); Note, "Fines and Fining—An Evaluation," 101 *U. Pa. L. Rev.* 1013, 1024–25 (1953).
[51] American Bar Association, "Report on Minimum Standards for Criminal Justice," pp. 117–23.
[52] Lovald and Stub, "Revolving Door: Reactions of Chronic Drunkenness Offenders to Court Sanctions," 59 *J. Crim. L. C. & P. S.* 525 (1968).
[53] See Goldfarb and Singer, *After Conviction,* Work Release section.
[54] This discussion had to be impressionistic; every authority consulted confirmed the lack of empirical evidence of indigents' non-payment of fines. Along with numerous local court judges who were consulted in 1973 in gathering this information were various experts and authorities. Most helpful were James Frick of the National Center for State Courts, Washington, D.C.; Thomas Russell of the National College of the State Judiciary, Reno, Nevada; and Stephen Goldspeil of the American Bar Association's Traffic Courts Program, Chicago, Illinois.

Shortly after the decision in *Williams* v. *Illinois* struck down the alternative "thirty-dollar-or-thirty-day" sentence, one California magistrate ceased imposing fines, and began committing all sentenced convicted misdemeanants to jail. This illustrates the fallacy of assuming that real reforms in practice automatically follow reformative judicial decisions.

Many judges dislike or distrust the new rule, and refer to it as a form of "negative discrimination." They regard the necessity of providing for deferred fines or fines payable on installment as an unwarranted imposition on the courts, and, therefore, continue to jail indigents for non-payment. Judge Phil Saeida of the Los Angeles Municipal Court, wryly observed in a recent interview: "Law and order is for defendants, not for judges."

Experts on the lower state judiciary report that word of developments in the law filters down from the rhetorical majesty of the Supreme Court in Washington to the dingy rural lower courts in the provinces at a slow pace. Some judges are still unaware of the existence of the *Tate* decision. Furthermore, since many lower trial courts do not appoint counsel for unrepresented indigents with any regularity, there may be no one in court to call a potential violation of *Tate* to the attention of an uninformed judge.

Most courts have no empirical test for determining indigency in petty misdemeanor cases. Each determination is made on the basis of the judge's personal intuition or special knowledge of whether defendants can "come up with the money." Many courts also are reluctant to undertake the bookkeeping effort associated with installment collections. As a result, indigents may be jailed for non-payment not—as before—at the day of sentencing, but weeks or months afterwards, when they fail to settle a deferred fine.

Most judges who employ systems of installment fines report that it is seldom necessary to imprison defendants for non-payment of the installments—an option which the *Tate* decision and its precursors leave available. Judge Saeida could recall this happening to only about ten out of about 300 misdemeanants he had sentenced. A postcard reminder of their obligation usually was sufficient.

Unless the amount of the installments is tied to the defendant's actual financial condition, his eventual fate still may be the jail.

In some Los Angeles courtrooms, commitments for failure to meet installments run as high as 40 per cent of all the defendants sentenced to pay on this basis, a local judge advised.

Several judges consulted on the problem of alternative dispositions for indigent misdemeanants expressed special enthusiasm for the "work sentencing" concept. The indigent who once served thirty wasteful days in jail for non-payment now may spend three afternoons a week cleaning the courthouse to pay off his fine. And although it may be constitutionally dubious (some observers feel enforced labor violates the Thirteenth Amendment's prohibition of slavery), this non-institutional sentencing device is acceptable to many of the lower court judges who actually decide the fate of the poor offender, and it is more constructive than jail.

Civil Debtors. A poor person can end up in jail for other reasons than the lack of money to pay for bail or a fine. Even where statutes and practices exclude imprisonment for debt, individual debtors may be jailed for contempt or violation of criminal statutes where the root of their offense really is their poverty.

Most state constitutions include provisions designed to eliminate or curtail "imprisonment for debt." Although the federal Constitution contains no such language, the federal courts are bound by statute to observe the strictures against imprisonment for debt which apply in the states where they sit.[55]

The prohibitions of the state constitutions are subject to a number of built-in exceptions, of which the most common is a reservation preserving jailing as a technique of collection in cases involving "fraud."[56]

These provisions have put an end to widespread use of old forms of "body execution" as a device to enforce ordinary civil obligations, or to punish debtors who do not satisfy such obligations. In only a few jurisdictions, including New Jersey and Illinois,

[55] 28 U.S.C. §2007. In a purely federal action with the United States as creditor-plaintiff, imprisonment for debt as such would be unavailable, since there exists no federal statute authorizing the remedy or establishing a procedure for it. But a judgment debtor who willfully refused to pay an adjudicated obligation to the United States would be subject to imprisonment for contempt. In similar situations involving private parties, federal courts have the same power as state tribunals to order incarceration. See *Atlas Corp.* v. *DeVilliers,* 455 F. 2d 799 (10th Cir.), *cert. denied,* 405 U.S. 1033 (1971).
[56] A few state constitutions are limited in their coverage to contract debts only, and thus leave local courts with the option to jail for non-payment of other civil obligations, such as money judgments obtained in tort actions.

can a suspected debtor be jailed before his financial obligation has been embodied in a court decree.

In a number of states, of which New Jersey and Illinois again are notable examples, body execution is available by statute as a specialized form of final process against defaulting judgment debtors.[57] While it is not available to aid in the collection of an ordinary judgment debt arising out of a contractual obligation, it may be available against a judgment debtor who is withholding assets fraudulently, whose obligation arises out of a malicious tort such as assault, or who is about to flee.

At worst, body execution is a peculiar legal anachronism. Since in theory no judgment debtor can be imprisoned for non-payment until after a hearing at which he is entitled to raise the defense of his inability to pay, it is unlikely that many indigent defendants are being swept into American jails on this legal pretext.

In Maine, until late in 1971, there was no automatic hearing on the issue of financial capacity before a defaulting debtor was jailed. In practice, petty debtors were commonly being jailed at the whims of the creditors. In testimony before the National Commission on Consumer Finance in 1970, a Maine attorney stated that in the two preceding years, 200 debtors had spent 1,754 days in jails in just two of the state's counties for failure to pay contract debts.[58]

The Maine procedure allowed successful creditors to secure arrest orders for defaulting after-judgment debtors. The creditor also could hold the order, rather than delivering it to the sheriff, and use it to coerce the reluctant debtor, and his frightened family, into making payments. A second abusive procedure allowed an attorney representing a plaintiff-wife in a divorce proceeding routinely to demand his counsel fees from the defendant-husband. If the husband did not pay, whatever the reason, the attorney could force the husband's incarceration without granting the debtor even a hearing to prove his inability to pay. The debtor remained in jail until the attorney-creditor gave permission for his release.

[57] During 1965, twenty-six of the almost 2,800 inmates received at the Union County Jail in New Jersey were listed under the heading "Civil Action." This total apparently represents debtors imprisoned either before or after judgment under the New Jersey body execution statutes. Union County Sheriff's Office, "Annual Report of the Union County Jail—1966" (mimeographed).
[58] Statement of Howard T. Reben, attorney for Pine Tree Legal Assistance, Inc. June 21, 1970.

These procedures were modified drastically in 1971 as a result of a lawsuit brought by legal assistance lawyers. In one case, the husband, whose only assets consisted of less than $100 cash and the clothing he was wearing, remained in jail for eight months until his relatives found money to pay his debt. The court noted that there was no indication that non-payment had resulted from a "deliberate refusal" to pay, or that the debtor had dishonestly handled his assets or in any way concealed them from the attorney. Yet he was not released until the magnanimous lawyer for his former wife wrote to the sheriff, saying: "This will inform you that William Lindsey has satisfied *capias* execution . . . for which he was incarcerated. He may be released from jail if he satisfied your office on the payment of board."[59]

Few of these unfortunate prisoners had the sophistication or the legal assistance to raise the defense of their indigency after they had been jailed. As a result, they often spent months in confinement until a settlement of some kind could be arranged, or until the cash arrears could be shaken loose from the debtor's friends and relations. Maine's jailed debtors suffered the additional indignity and expense of being charged for room and board by their county sheriffs. Some, like twenty-six-year-old Charles Ozois, jailed in York County for failure to make court-ordered alimony and child support payments, had worse luck still. Local press reports described how Ozois' cellmate was charged in an attempted jail break, and Ozois was convicted of conspiracy for not reporting the plan to officials.

When Maine's state and federal courts finally acted, their action was not dramatic. They merely invalidated the practice under which defaulting debtors could be jailed without a prior judicial hearing on their financial capacity.[60] This one modest stroke, however, converted body execution in Maine from a lively evil into a peculiar anachronism.

[59] *Lindsey* v. *County of Cumberland,* 278 A. 2d 391 (Me. 1971).
[60] *Desmond* v. *Hachey,* 315 F. Supp. 328 (D. Me. 1970); *Lindsey* v. *County of Cumberland,* 278 A. 2d 391 (Me. 1971); *Yoder* v. *County of Cumberland,* 278 A. 2d 379 (Me. 1971).

CIVIL CONTEMPT

Body execution, the modern nomenclature for "imprisonment for debt," is now almost non-existent in this country. But the opinion of the Maine Supreme Court in the case of *Yoder* v. *County of Cumberland,* one of the cases which put an end to extensive body execution in that state, concludes with a disquieting dictum:

> Nothing herein decided, or stated, is intended to deprive a court of its powers of *contempt,* in accordance with appropriate procedural guarantees, to ensure compliance with any order or decree, by whatever label designated, issued by the court . . . [C]ontempt is available to a court to enforce its process, decree or order even when the payment of money is involved.[61]

Records are too sparse to tell how many courts impose jail sentences for contempt as a workable substitute for unconstitutional forms of "imprisonment for debt" or how frequently the contempt sanction is applied to debtors whose only real fault is an inability to pay their court-ordered financial obligations.

The states are divided on whether constitutional prohibitions against imprisonment for debt also forbid civil contempt jail sentences for non-payment of money judgments. Other state appellate courts than Maine have held that the contempt sanction is never available to enforce an order to pay specified sums of money, if the underlying obligation is an ordinary contract debt reduced to judgment.[62]

Courts in some jurisdictions have adopted a middle line, holding that while use of the contempt sanction to coerce payment of a money judgment is not inherently repugnant to constitutional prohibitions against imprisonment for debt, it cannot be applied until all the less drastic judicial collection remedies—such as the forced execution sale of the judgment debtor's assets—have been tried and have proved unavailing.[63]

[61] 278 A. 2d at 390.
[62] See, e.g., *Ex parte Preston,* 347 S.W. 2d 938 (Tex. 1961); *Bahre* v. *Bahre,* 230 N.E. 2d 411 (Ind. 1967).
[63] See, e.g., *Maljak* v. *Murphy,* 177 N.W. 2d 228 (Mich. Ct. App. 1970).

Almost every American jail has a small but relatively constant population of contemnors. Because jail records are so inadequate, it is nearly impossible to estimate how many members of those groups have "defied" the committing courts by mere non-payment of civil debts, willful or otherwise.

In Virginia, during 1970, almost 3,900 of the more than 130,-000 prisoners received in local jails were classified in a category labeled "contempt of court and other obstruction of justice."[64] In other jurisdictions the equivalent totals are smaller: during fiscal year 1968–69, only fifty-four of the more than 21,000 prisoners booked into Nebraska jails were contemnors.[65] These aggregates, however, embrace a multitude of evils and offenses: along with some who are confined indefinitely for failing to pay a judgment, they include prisoners sentenced to jail terms for criminal contempt, individuals committed as the result of "direct" contempts such as violent or abusive conduct in the courtroom, witnesses who failed to respond to subpoenas, defendants found to be in defiance of injunctions and other non-monetary court orders, and "prisoners of principle."

Inability to comply with a court order should be a complete defense to any contempt citation; and where a court order directs the payment of money, poverty amounts to inability to comply. As a general rule, the drastic sanction of contempt is reserved for judgment debtors who could pay but refuse to do so. The efficacy of holding them in jail until they comply with a court order, however, is open to question; the legality of the procedure is not.

Uniform tests and standards seldom are applied. The right to a jury trial has not been extended to persons who are in danger of imprisonment for civil contempt. The debtor who cannot convince a judge that he has disclosed all his assets, or that his limited means do not permit him to satisfy a money judgment, may still find himself committed to the equivalent of a twentieth-century debtor's prison. Once a person in these straits has been jailed, his dilemma is remarkably similar to that of imprisoned debtors throughout history. When he is cut off from his community and

---

[64] Commonwealth of Virginia, Department of Welfare and Institutions, "Commitments to County and City Jails and City Jail Farms, Year Ended June 30, 1970" (mimeographed).

[65] Nebraska Department of Economic Development, "For Better or Worse?: Nebraska's Misdemeanant Correctional System" (mimeographed, 1970), p. 11.

his occupation, his financial position can only deteriorate. If he was not obviously indigent when he entered confinement, he soon may become so. Unfortunately, he also may be cut off from the legal aid which he needs to make a new financial showing to the committing court, or to seek review of his original commitment.

In absolute numbers, this population of jailed contemnors from "borderline" financial brackets probably is very small, but their discriminatory imprisonment is unjust and the practice is condemnable, nonetheless.

Alimony and Support. The population of inmates whose only offense is their failure to meet financial obligations to their own families is large. According to most of the appellate courts which have considered the problem, state constitutional prohibitions against imprisonment for non-payment of ordinary debts, even by way of contempt, do not extend to jailing for failure to meet court-ordered property settlement, alimony or child support payments.[66] Nor do such prohibitions bar the jailing of persons who have disobeyed a legislative command to support embodied in a criminal statute.

Family obligations outlive family units, and a husband is more likely to be jailed for failing in his financial obligations to his wife after the two have parted company than before. Derived from English ecclesiastical and common law, the theory of a husband's duties is based on the concept of the wife as a chattel for which the husband was bound to care just as for any other piece of property. Feudal principles of the lord and vassal relationship, by which protection and support of the wife was provided in return for her services as housekeeper and heir-maker; and that the husband was vested with the right to his wife's property, earnings and services at marriage; and that the cost of supporting her was not borne directly by him, but was deducted from the profits he received from the marital relationship.[67]

---

[66] See, e.g., *Hogan* v. *Hogan,* 29 Ohio App. 2d 69; 278 N.E. 2d 367 (1972), which applies Ohio law barring any civil contempt citations for non-payment of contract debts to the situation of an ex-husband who failed to abide by a contractual property settlement which had later been incorporated into a court order of divorce. In essence, the court held that the husband's obligation was no longer a mere contract debt; it was part of an adjudicated financial obligation to his ex-wife, and thus could be enforced by use of the contempt power. See also *Ex parte Preston,* 347 S.W. 2d 938 (Tex. 1961).
[67] M. Paulson, "Support Rights and Duties Between Husband and Wife," 9 *Vanderbilt U. L. Rev.* 709 (1956).

Permanent alimony was an incident of an ecclesiastical decree which did not completely dissolve a marriage.[68] The husband, who gained control of his wife's property at the time of their marriage, retained control; thus it was logical to require him to continue to support his wife.[69] Most state statutes authorize permanent alimony in the discretion of the court.

The related duty of support of minor children also derives from a father's traditional responsibilities. The abandonment and non-support of young people are more than private matters: society has a substantial interest in preventing such neglect. If the father neglects him, the minor child must, of necessity, look to others for financial support—although it is unclear why the obligation to provide that support would, by law, fall upon only one of the child's parents.

A failure to meet financial obligations to one's family may be the first step on either of two alternative paths to jail. The first route is a contempt citation. When the obligation has been the subject of an earlier court decree, non-payment may be treated as civil contempt of court, and the defaulting husband or father may be jailed until he complies with the former order. This use of the contempt power is as old as the civil courts' involvement in intra-family finances. For historical reasons, family obligations generally are regarded as special debts owed not only to the spouse or the child but also indirectly to the community at large. If a breadwinner does not meet his family obligations, the traditional reasoning runs, his dependents are apt to become public charges. Therefore, courts have greater latitude in enforcing such obligations than in assisting the enforcement of ordinary contractual debts owed to strangers.

Contempt is primarily a rich man's road to jail; as such, it is relatively lightly traveled. For the well-to-do and middle class, lawyers and courts become important factors early in family disputes; for them, the "system" consists of separation agreements, divorce decrees, orders for separate maintenance, alimony and

[68] See, e.g., C. Foote, R. Levy, and F. Sander, *Cases and Materials on Family Law* (Boston: Little, 1966), pp. 907–8.
[69] M. Paulson, W. Wadlington, and J. Goebel, Jr., *Cases and Other Materials on Domestic Relations* (Mineola, N.Y.: Foundation Press, 1970), p. 529; J. W. Madden, *Handbook of the Law of Persons and Domestic Relations* (St. Paul, Minn.: West, 1931), 97–89, pp. 319–20.

child support awards, and—in extreme cases—adjudications of civil contempt. Numerous commentators have observed, however, that America harbors a "dual system" of family law. For the poor, the "system" is welfare, paternity proceedings and criminal non-support prosecutions.

The second route to jail for the delinquent family head begins with the non-support prosecution, and it carries heavy traffic. The origins of criminal non-support statutes are linked with those of civil intra-family obligations. Incarceration for failure to support legitimate children was part of a complex seventeenth-century scheme popularly known as the Elizabethan Poor Laws,[70] under which English legislators sought by various devices to deal with the economic problem of children whose parents failed to keep and maintain them. Persons of means, for example, were required to contribute to the maintenance of the poor; in return they received apprentices, who in turn reduced the cost of the burden through their labor.[71]

Because unemployable young people could not offset the costs of their support themselves, their financially able relatives were made legally liable.[72] Local courts determined the amount of liability, buttressed through a system of fines[73] and penal sanctions.[74] Significantly, this new legislation made fathers liable to support all their children, male and female, legitimate and illegitimate. Under the common law only heirs had rights, and other children "remained in [their] father's household[s] at the complete sufferance of the fathers, who could turn [them] out at any moment without regard to the child's need or the father's ability."[75] By injecting a public fiscal interest into the family relationship the English Poor Laws offered some protection to young

---

[70] This discussion relies heavily on J. TenBroek, "California's Dual System of Family Law: Its Origins, Development and Present Status," 16 *Stanford L. Rev.* 257 (1964); W. J. Brockelbank, "The Family Desertion Problem Across State Lines," 383 *The Annals of the American Society of Political and Social Science* 23 (May 1969).

[71] TenBroek, "California's Dual System," pp. 281–83.

[72] Ibid., p. 283; Brockelbank, "The Family Desertion Problem," p. 25.

[73] 43 Eliz. 1, c. 2 SUI (1601), quoted in TenBroek, "California's Dual System," p. 283.

[74] TenBroek, "California's Dual System," p. 285.

[75] Ibid., p. 288; see also, Comment: "Extent of a Parent's Duty to Support," 32 *Yale Law Journal* 825 (1923); Brockelbank, "The Family Desertion Problem," p. 25.

people who previously were completely dependent on their fathers' affection and moral sense.

In America, courts struggled to find a parental obligation to support children: English common law precedents gave them little comfort, and the Poor Laws were not widely imitated. In the 1863 case of *Cromwell* v. *Benjamin,* a New York court found such a duty to be rooted in parentage and the voluntary assumption of obligation "implicit in the act of begetting,"[76] a decision incorporated into the Field Code of 1865. The adoption of the code by other states in effect disseminated the principles of the Cromwell decision.[77] The penal sections of that code made willful omission to furnish such support a misdemeanor.[78]

In the twentieth century, just as the Elizabethan Poor Laws had introduced the state into the once private relationship between parent and child, the "new American poor laws," regulating welfare and public assistance, perpetuated the state's role. Criminal non-support statutes have proliferated, and penalties for a husband's failure to support his wife have been added to sanctions against defaulting fathers. Because the husband's obligation to support his family is deemed to be owed derivatively to the taxpaying general public, as well as the particular child or wife, failure to support can lead to a fine, a jail sentence (with a maximum term of up to two years) or both. It is under these statutes that indigent or near indigent family heads are being jailed today.

New York City's Civil Jail, for example, has long been nicknamed the "Alimony Jail"; it still houses poor or stubborn ex-husbands, although they are only a fraction of its total prisoner population. The incongruity of this special sort of judicial intervention is based on outdated protective attitudes about women.

Contempt proceedings based on court orders relating to intrafamily finances occur less often than non-support prosecutions; but they do occur. In 1961, a less than sympathetic Texan was committed to the Tarrant County Jail for his willful failure to pay a $10,000 court-ordered cash property settlement to his former

[76] 41 Barb. 558, 561 (N.Y. Sup. Ct. 1863), quoted in TenBroek, "California's Dual System," p. 301. See also, Comment, "Extent of a Parent's Duty," p. 827.
[77] See e.g., R. Field and B. Kaplan, *Materials for a Basic Course in Civil Procedure* (Brooklyn: Foundation Press, 1953), p. 311. TenBroek examines New York in detail because the Field Code and its concepts were incorporated into California—his main focus of interest.
[78] TenBroek, "California's Dual System," p. 314.

wife, despite his claim that he was unable to comply because he had flushed the cash in question down the sewer system of the city of Fort Worth.[79]

While inability to pay court-ordered family obligations may provide the impoverished contemnor with a defense, courts take a strict view of what constitutes such inability. In 1955, a railroad conductor in Arkansas was found in contempt for failure to pay alimony and was given a jail sentence of ten days and a fine of fifty dollars. On review, the appellate court reversed on the ground that the man's disobedience of the court order was not willful. The man had stopped making payments after a heart attack and an arthritic condition of the spine put him in the hospital. After several successive visits to the hospital, he was retired from his job. His sick benefits after his severance had amounted to less than the alimony payments he was required to pay; still, the trial court had seen fit to punish him for "contempt" of court. His wife during that time had a job and was not solely dependent on her former husband for her support.[80]

Despite clear rules to the contrary, men continue to be ordered to jail for failures to obey family court orders with which they cannot possibly comply. In one recent Oklahoma case, for example, a man was ordered to surrender to his ex-wife the registration papers for a group of racehorses, as part of their property settlement. Their son, however, was holding the papers in another state, claiming a lien. At three court hearings the man explained his continuing efforts to obtain the papers and his son's refusals. The court, while recognizing his good faith attempts, sentenced him to sixty days in jail.[81] According to one press account, there are always a handful of men in the Civil Jail in New York City serving up to six months for civil contempt for non-payment of alimony and child support. For many, as one inmate stated, "They get one night in this place and they say: I've had it. Let me out. I'll pay." But for some, they simply cannot pay and are forced to sit in jail for half a year.[82]

[79] *Ex parte Preston,* 347 S.W. 2d 938 (Tex. 1961).
[80] *Griffith* v. *Griffith,* 282 S.W. 2d 340 (Ark. 1955).
[81] *Garoutte* v. *Garoutte,* 455 P. 2d 306 (Okla. 1969). Wise enough to announce his intent to appeal the sentence, this contemnor was freed on bond pending an appellate decision, which vacated the contempt citation.
[82] Prial, "Alimony, Child Support or the Civil Jail," New York *Times,* April 8, 1974, p. 1.

A peculiar, and far more significant case is now working its way through the Vermont courts. There a former home builder named George Chicone was held for almost five and a half years in the state prison[83] on a civil contempt citation.

At the core of Chicone's dilemma is a dispute over his financial capability. No one involved in the case disputes that in October of 1967, Chicone had the means to pay the few thousand dollars in arrears which he then owed his divorced wife. Nevertheless, he refused. Shortly after his imprisonment, Chicone's lawyers assert, his property was sold at distress prices under court order; today, they argue, he is completely without means. The judge who originally sentenced Chicone for contempt consistently has taken the position that Chicone is concealing $90,000 in hidden assets.

As a coercive exercise, Vermont's handling of Mr. Chicone was a distinct failure. His hidden assets—if they exist—never came to light, and Chicone himself consistently refused offers of financial aid from friends and relatives. Meanwhile, he suffered a series of debilitating heart attacks in prison, while his wife survived on welfare. In March of 1973, Chicone was released on the strength of a legal technicality, without any final resolution of his dispute with the courts. He now owes his ex-wife more than $20,000 in alimony accrued during his imprisonment, and faces a new contempt citation if he fails to satisfy that debt.[84]

For the moment, George Chicone is free. His unknown counterparts, however, may still be confined in the local jails of states where the open-ended contempt sentence is an approved method for enforcing alimony payments. Moreover, where a case involves minor children and a default on court-ordered child support payments, even courts which refuse to apply the contempt sanction for mere non-payment of alimony may be less reluctant; unlike marriage, they may reason, paternity involves a continuing and

[83] In Vermont, where there are few large local jails, trial judges draw on the prison system, intended to house sentenced criminals from across the state, for substitute facilities. In most states, a prisoner in Chicone's position would be delivered to the jail serving the community where the committing judge sits.

[84] See "Vermont Debtor in Prison 5 Years," New York *Times*, February 18, 1972; Friedman, "Alimony: A Special Kind of Debt," New York *Times*, March 28, 1973.

wholly non-contractual obligation of special biological and social significance.[85]

In most family cases, invocation of the contempt power may prove positively counter-productive. Jailing impairs a husband's ability to work. Rather than encouraging a shattered family to regroup, the jailing of one of its members only hurries its permanent dissolution.

It is impossible to determine the rates of such jailing statistically; in jail reports from states and localities such inmates either are listed under the umbrella heading of "contempt" or relegated to the "other" and "miscellaneous" categories.

Jailing after criminal non-support prosecutions, on the other hand, occurs regularly. Statistics from a number of jurisdictions indicate that such prosecutions contribute substantial numbers of inmates to local jail populations. During fiscal year 1968–69, for example, almost 7 per cent of the prisoners committed to Nebraska jails were sentenced for non-support—1,440 prisoners in total. The non-support offense was third only to public drunkenness and drunk driving as a cause of jailing.[86] In Virginia, during fiscal 1969–70, more than 2 per cent of all jail commitments—a total of 3,247—were for non-support and "other offenses against family and children."[87] Almost 4 per cent of the roughly 4,500 prisoners received at the Milwaukee, Wisconsin, county jail during 1966 were non-support cases.[88]

Other jails, especially those in predominantly rural areas, report no equivalent concentration of non-support prisoners. Out of about 1,000 bookings at the Corvallis and Benton County, Oregon, jail in 1965, only one was made on a non-support

[85] For one recent case upholding the constitutionality of jailing for contempt in non-support cases, see Matter of *Chase* v. *Brooke, Layton* 27 N.Y. 2d 700, 314 N.Y.S. 2d 15 (1972).
[86] Nebraska Department of Economic Development, "For Better or Worse?: Nebraska's Misdemeanant Correctional System" (mimeographed, 1970), p. 11.
[87] Commonwealth of Virginia, Department of Welfare and Institutions, "Commitments to County and City Jails and City Jail Farms, Year Ended June 30, 1970," table 11. This total apparently includes persons sentenced for offenses such as child abuse, as well as those whose only crime is non-support or desertion. The widespread use of a general "family offense" category in jail statistics makes wholly authoritative estimates of the extent of jailing for non-support impossible.
[88] Milwaukee County Sheriff's Department, "Milwaukee County House of Correction, Annual Report—1966" (mimeographed).

charge.[89] And in March 1969, in Alaskan jails and prisons, only one individual was incarcerated for non-support.[90]

In typical urban jurisdictions, on the other hand, non-support is not an uncommon cause of jailing. Unlike a civil contempt sentence, a sentence for criminal non-support is a fixed term: the maximum may be as long as two years in jail. Probation may be available for men convicted of non-support on the condition that they reassume their family obligations,[91] but many family court judges operate on the theory that exposing an unwilling or impecunious parent to at least a "taste of jail" is a healthy corrective measure.

Although indigency clearly is a good defense to contempt, it is not recognized as a defense to criminal non-support in all jurisdictions. The Iowa Supreme Court recently considered a case in which an unemployed defendant from Cedar Rapids appealed his thirty-day sentence to the Linn County Jail, arguing that he was being punished unconstitutionally for his inability to support his minor child. His case was a typical one; his troubles began with a proceeding to establish his paternity of a child. This was followed by a court order directing the payment of support. Non-payment, in turn, led directly to criminal prosecution. If one reads between the lines of cases like this another pattern appears to emerge: the female head of a fatherless household applies for welfare, and is pressured, subtly, or not so subtly, into bringing a paternity suit; she gets her welfare checks, while the absent and often penniless father becomes a target for prosecution.

[89] Oregon State Board of Control, Corrections Division, "Report on the Corvallis and Benton County Jail" (mimeographed, 1967).

[90] Alaska Comprehensive Statewide Planning Project for Vocational Rehabilitation Services, *A Survey of Public Offenders* (May 1970).

[91] The option of probation is a theoretically important one: the theory is that the hanging threat of a jail sentence to be served if probation is revoked will convert defaulting husbands and fathers into responsible providers. Family courts generally do not operate probation services for non-support offenders. The sentence of probation is pronounced, usually after the entry of a guilty plea, without any judicial inquiry into the offender's financial situation; the probationer receives no effective guidance or supervision to help him comply with the conditions of his sentence. Under such circumstances, the likelihood of compliance is low; when the probationer next is accused of failure to support, the court has the option to forgive his delinquency again or to revoke his probation and jail him summarily. For too many non-support defendants this sort of "assembly-line probation" does not substitute for jailing but merely defers it.

In the Iowa case, the court dealt with the defense of indigency:

> [T]he statute under which he was tried and convicted does not punish for inability to support; it punishes only the willful refusal to do so.

> . . . [T]he statute under which the defendant was sentenced makes no invidious distinction between rich and poor. All who willfully fail to support their children are equally subject to its punitive provisions.

> Defendant complains, too, because the trial court postponed commencement of his sentence for ten days to give him the opportunity to find employment. Only when he was unable to do so was he directed to submit to his punishment. He says this shows he was actually sentenced to jail because of inability, rather than willful refusal to support his child. There is no record to show what course the trial court intended to follow if defendant had found a job; but, whatever it was, it could not vitiate the jury verdict that his failure to support was willful.[92]

This Iowa decision does not hold that inability to pay might not, under some circumstances, save a non-support defendant from jail. It does suggest that courts take a generally dim view of defaulting parents' protestations of indigency, and that mere inability to pay, however extreme, may not always be enough to forestall jailing. But to say that all defaulting husbands are treated equally is to echo Anatole France's comment that the rich and poor alike are forbidden to sleep under bridges on cold nights.

Inability to pay may be a bar to a non-support prosecution. However, the decisions generally hold that the prosecution has no affirmative duty to prove a defendant's ability to support his children. The burden of proof on this issue lies with the defendant. In a recent Missouri case, a St. Louis hospital worker with a weekly take-home of about eighty dollars had been divorced from his wife, with a court order to pay fifty dollars monthly to support his four young children. Subsequently, his ex-wife went on welfare and he was charged with criminal non-support, tried and sentenced to a six-month term in the St. Louis workhouse. At his trial, the defendant tried to show that he had paid as much as he could

[92] *State* v. *Hopp,* 190 N.W. 2d 836, 837 (Iowa 1971).

afford and that his wife had disclaimed any desire for further support payments from him.

The Missouri Supreme Court upheld his conviction and sentence, reasoning that while its reading of the state constitutional provisions prohibiting imprisonment for debt would have barred any attempt to jail him for contempt, this did not bar a criminal non-support prosecution. The court found evidence of finances "sufficient to show his ability to contribute support to his children."[93]

Where vigorous enforcement of criminal non-support statutes is local policy, only that minority of absent fathers and husbands who can be traced easily are prosecuted.[94] Obviously, there is no correlation between the ease with which an absent father or husband can be traced and his ability to meet his family obligations.

A study of the Lake County, Illinois, Family Court conducted in the mid-fifties, demonstrated that the threat of jailing did little to promote the actual collection of financial obligations. In almost 90 per cent of the cases studied, there were arrearages or complete failures to support. Yet in almost half these cases, the defaulting husband was under a court order to pay support, and theoretically subject to summary imprisonment if he failed to meet his decreed obligation.[95] Apparently, most defaulting husbands were either beyond the practical reach of the court, or were able to forestall their imprisonment indefinitely by presenting reasonable excuses for their non-compliance.

The existence of criminal non-support statutes works a particular injustice on the poor. Theoretically, rich and poor may be equally subject to the jailing sanction; in practice, only the poor are affected. This inequity is reinforced by the peculiar methods by which criminal non-support prosecutions often are set in motion. Too often, the wife's co-operation in instituting a prosecution is exacted as *quid pro quo* for admission to the aid for dependent children welfare rolls. Too often, the criminal non-support prosecution is used as a means of checking a so-called "welfare fraud" or symbolically placating a public dissatisfaction over wel-

[93] *State* v. *Davis,* 469 S.W. 2d 1 (Mo. 1971).
[94] Thomas Willging and John Ellsmore, "The 'Dual System' in Action: Jail for Non-Support," 1969 *Toledo L. Rev.* 348, 353, 368–74 n. 6.
[95] Henry H. Foster and Doris Jonas Freed, "Unequal Protection: Poverty and Family Law," 42 *Indiana L. Jrnl.* 192, 207 n. 5 (1966).

fare costs—rather than as a means of compelling parents who could, but do not, support their children to do so.

Generally, the legal support obligation arose from a meeting between the district attorney and the parent, when the parent was interrogated and threatened with prosecution until he signed a "voluntary agreement" to pay a stipulated monthly sum for child support. In one county, the judge called all non-support cases together and told the fathers to plead guilty and receive probation. This was done without a presentence report and without knowledge of any of the defendants' backgrounds or circumstances. Some had prior convictions, or had violated support agreements painstakingly tailored for them by welfare workers. Others were simply not guilty. One man, for example, earned fifty-six dollars per week, was supporting eight children already, was physically handicapped and qualified for welfare himself. Nevertheless, he was convicted and placed on probation. For many defendants, this sort of probationary sentence is merely another step on the road to jail.

One California county used this tactic to get poor people off the welfare rolls by exploiting the courts' power to jail for failure to support. The district attorney typically charged both the mother and the father of children receiving aid for dependent children with non-support. If the mother pleaded not guilty, she often would be convicted and jailed. If she pleaded guilty, as the judge advised, she would be placed on probation on condition that she remove her children from the welfare rolls and go to work. This was done, according to one commentator, ". . . without regard to health or ability to work, the children's need for a mother in the home, provisions for the children's care, availability of employment, or eligibility of the family for public aid. Thus did they seek to solve at a penal stroke the human and social problems of welfare."[96] Further study of non-support enforcement practices is required. Sanford H. Kadish said in 1967:

[96] TenBroek, "California's Dual System of Family Law: Its Origins, Development and Present Status," 17 *Stanford L. Rev.* 614, 663–63 (1964). These anecdotes reflect the situation in California as of the late fifties and early sixties. Since that time, the nationwide "welfare rights" movement has experienced some success in checking legal abuses affecting welfare mothers, but there is no indication that the movement has concerned itself with the criminal jeopardy faced by the absent fathers of welfare families.

In a number of instances which, taken together, consume a significant portion of law-enforcement resources, the criminal law is used neither to protect against serious misbehavior through the medium of crime and punishment nor to conform standards of private morality, but rather to provide social services to needy segments of the community . . . [T]he deserted mother, and the creditor have been the chief beneficiary. In each instance, the gains have been dubious in view of the toll exacted on effective law enforcement . . . [T]he criminal process is being used to provide a service which indisputably, the State has an obligation to provide [but] it makes little sense to provide it through the already over-burdened criminal processes.[97]

Over-crowded conditions, not considerations of justice, may be forcing judges to make readjustments. Too many more serious offenders await sentencing. In the District of Columbia, adjudications of civil contempt for non-support usually include a stay of execution. The defaulting husband is given additional time in which to pay the arrears he owes; if he fails to do so, the court marshals can execute the contempt order and take him into custody without further judicial action. The hope is that the threat of execution and jailing may be sufficient coercive incentive to pay; in fact, the marshals give low priority to executions based on contempt adjudications in non-support cases.[98]

In some courts, many men sentenced to jail for non-support make an appeal, are released on a low appeal bond, and use the extra time to find money to pay their accumulated obligations. One available option is individualized marital counseling. One study report on correctional systems said that the successes of optional counseling in San Joaquin County, California, were notable enough to prompt the re-allocation of county resources now devoted to collection efforts to provide mandatory counseling.[99]

[97] Kadish, "The Crisis of Over-Criminalization," 374 *The Annals of the American Society of Political and Social Science* (November 1967): 157, 165–67.

[98] Interview, Mr. John M. Bischoff, chief deputy clerk, Family Division, Superior Court of the District of Columbia courts.

[99] Institute for the Study of Crime and Delinquency, "Model Community Correctional Program," Report III (mimeographed, 1970), pp. 94–100. Another finding of this study is that conventional enforcement of support techniques results in no net savings for local governments; in San Joaquin County, the real cost of collecting from defaulting husbands exceeded the county's share of the welfare payments their wives were receiving because of their defaults.

Jailing sanctions were reserved for cases where counseling had failed. A provision for work furlough was built into every jail sentence for non-support.

Another more radical proposal would provide public insurance for support. Mandatory payroll deductions would be applied, like those existing under the Social Security and unemployment insurance systems, to create a general fund for support in case of marital breakdowns. Collections from the fund would be automatic, and subject to none of the bitterness and uncertainty which now characterizes the enforcement of support orders.[100]

The Practicing Law Institute has recommended the use of a mandatory payroll deduction plan, similar to the wage garnishment system employed in the collection of ordinary civil judgments.[101] Wisconsin's wage assignment law provides public rebates to employers to cover extra bookkeeping costs, while simplifying the lives of persons under court support orders.[102]

Other proposals for more efficient collection of support obligations include the requirement of a bond posted in court at the time when a support obligation first is decreed, and the use of jail sentences with provisions for work furlough or part-time custody.[103]

Material Witnesses. Almost every local prosecutor has statutory authority to take into custody witnesses to crimes who may flee the jurisdiction or otherwise become unavailable. The "material witness" is treated much like a pretrial detainee; at a court hearing, bail is set to secure his appearance, and if he cannot make bail, he is remanded to jail.

In a few states, such as Illinois, statutes theoretically forbid the holding of material witnesses in the same facilities used to detain accused criminals without segregation. However, alternative hold-

[100] Foster and Freed, "Unequal Protection," pp. 192, 210.
[101] Practice Law Institute, *Tactics and Strategy Under the New Divorce Law* (Course Handbook Series, No. 33, 1970), p. 168.
[102] Wis. Stat. §52.055 (1973).
[103] The bonding procedure was once in force in Pennsylvania, but has been abolished. See Foote, et al., *Cases and Materials on Family Law,* p. 939. Variants on the "part-time" jailing proposal for defaulting parents are now being tested in various California jurisdictions; this alternative also is specifically permitted under New York State statutes.

ing areas are often unavailable, and statutes like the one in Illinois are simply ignored.[104]

Generally, material witnesses merely join the general local jail population. Because their total numbers are few, and their power and influence negligible, they are among the lost men and women of the jailing system. No statistics are maintained to reveal how often material witnesses are detained or how long their detention lasts.

In some respects, the dilemma of the jailed material witness is more acute than that of the accused pretrial detainee. The size of the bonds set for their release may be as high or higher.[105] In theory, the accused detainee has the constitutional right to a speedy trial; he may be able to secure release by convincing the authorities that they have no case against him. The material witness, however, has no clear constitutional right to an early disposition of the case in which he has become entangled. Since he is charged with no offense, he cannot clear himself; he must await trial at the whims of courts, prosecutors and defendants. It is unclear whether indigent material witnesses, like indigent defendants, must be afforded the right to appointed counsel at their bond hearings.

The detention of many material witnesses often is nothing more than a prosecutorial excuse to investigate their involvement in a crime, with a view toward eventually charging them with a crime,[106] and an evasion of the witness' constitutional guarantees.[107]

When Ed Goodman, manager of New York City's radio station WBAI-FM, was sentenced in 1973 to Manhattan's Civil Jail for

---

[104] See Mattick and Sweet, *Illinois Jails: Challenge and Opportunity for the 1970's*, p. 121.

[105] In one New York case, a material witness in a bookmaking prosecution was held in lieu of $250,000 bond. See Note, "Confining Material Witnesses in Criminal Cases," 20 *William and Mary L. Rev.* 164 (1963).

[106] The facts in *Ex parte Grzyeskowick*, 255 N.W. 359 (Mich. 1934) provide an example. The imprisoned material witness seeking release was a bartender who had been present during a murder at his tavern. Although not suspected in the crime itself, he had fled immediately afterwards, registering in a local hotel under a false name. Police suspected—although finally they could not establish—that he had taken a hand in attempts to conceal the body.

[107] *Mallory* v. *United States*, 354 U.S. 449 (1957); *Henry* v. *United States*, 361 U.S. 98 (1959), holding that an arrestee must get a judicial hearing within a reasonable time and that mere suspicion is not adequate probable cause to justify an arrest.

contempt of court,[108] he met one such unfortunate inmate. Goodman remarked in his diary:

> The Civil Jail is a curious institution, filled not only with no criminals but with people who are not even charged with crimes. Of the twelve male inmates here at present, I'm the only one who has been convicted of breaking a law. Though the jail has a reputation for housing those unable to pay alimony, in fact it houses primarily "material witnesses" . . . who lack the money to meet bail, which is set very high—from $30,000 to $50,000. The racial mix here reflects that of most jails. There are three whites, including myself. The rest are black and there's one Puerto Rican.

> I spend most of my first night talking with Louis. Louis is black, born and raised in Montgomery. He got into drugs at a tender age and in 1967, at 22, he sold a joint to a narc and was sentenced to fifty years in jail . . . After 10 months in the Alabama State Penitentiary he escaped and had been hiding and staying "clean" ever since. One day as he was about to buy a hamburger, several men burst from a diner on the lower East Side after robbing it. Shortly afterwards, Louis was picked up as a material witness, though he claims he cannot identify the thieves. Of course, his record was discovered and after this case he faces extradition to Alabama.

> . . . Louis showed me a letter by a recently departed Henry Fellows . . . and signed by the seven inmates here at the time.

> My name is Henry Fellows. I am being held prisoner in the Civil Jail as a material witness against my will. I cannot believe that my civil rights are not being violated according to the constitution. Because I have committed no crime nor aided or abetted no crime, I have cooperated with the D.A. fully in his investigation and willingly taken a lie detector test. My life is neither in danger, nor will I flee, yet I am held in communicado. All my mail and phone calls must be approved by the D.A. yet the perpetrator of the offense is free to call or write who he pleases because he happens to be rich and can make a big deal and pursues his desires as he sees fit, even commit another crime if he deems it necessary to his survival . . .[109]

---

[108] Appropriately enough, his contempt consisted of a refusal to surrender tape recordings made during a rebellion at another city jail, the Tombs.
[109] Goodman, "On 44 Hours in Civil Jail," in *More: A Journalism Review*, April 1972.

In 1953, eleven of the twenty-six male prisoners in the Essex County, New Jersey, House of Detention were held as material witnesses.[110] In 1965, only four of the more than 1,000 prisoners received at Oregon's Corvallis and Benton County jails were material witnesses.[111] In the same year, about 1 per cent of the 2,700 inmates received at New Jersey's Union County Jail fell into this classification.[112] During 1970, jails throughout the state of Virginia held 187 material witnesses, out of a total of more than 130,000 prisoners received.[113]

Case law on the subject indicates that a conventional term of detention is the life of the grand jury investigating the crime in connection with which a material witness is being held. In the late 1950's, two migrant farm workers—one a resident of Baltimore, Maryland, the other of New Orleans, Louisiana—had the bad fortune to witness a murder in Rhode Island. They were held two days before receiving any hearing, and then shipped to a state correctional facility for holding in lieu of $5,000 bail each. There they spent 156 days in the general convict population before they were freed on writs of habeas corpus by a court which found that neither the materiality of their testimony nor their personal dependability had ever been the subject of judicial inquiry.[114] Eventually, the state legislature passed a special bill authorizing these two men to sue for damages, and the state Supreme Court awarded them $3,750 to compensate for their lost time and the indignity of their experience.[115] At that, they did better than most.

[110] Sol Rubin, Jr., and Sherwood Norman, *Procedures, Practices and Laws Affecting Essex County Institutions* (National Probation and Parole Association, 1953). The House of Detention, the smaller of the county's two holding facilities, was used to house the bulk of the material witnesses detained in the jurisdiction.

[111] Oregon State Board of Control, Corrections Division, "Report on the Corvallis and Benton County Jail."

[112] Union County Sheriff's Office, "Annual Report of the Union County Jail—1966."

[113] Commonwealth of Virginia, Department of Welfare and Institutions, "Commitments to County and City Jails and City Jail Farms, Year Ended June 30, 1970."

[114] *Quince v. Langlois*, 149 A. 2d 549 (R.I. 1959).

[115] *Quince v. State*, 179 A. 2d 485 (R.I. 1967).

JUSTICE ACCORDING TO ABILITY TO PAY

The late Associate Justice of the United States Supreme Court Hugo Black once said that the ideal of the judicial system should be that the kind of justice a man gets must never depend on the amount of money he has. Yet the subjects described in this chapter show, sadly but clearly, that our system of justice operates discriminately against the poor. At great social cost and risk, our jails are filled with people who are there solely because they are too poor to avoid it. All evidence shows that society gains nothing from their detention and loses much—public money, public safety and social self-respect.

Jail, like the prison system it farms for, is no more than a public welfare part of our correctional process. People of means may seek correction of their delinquency in alternate, private practices and institutions. Poor people do not know about these alternatives, and if they knew, could not afford them. When society assumes responsibility for delinquents, it does not use those techniques which are customarily used by people with money. It punishes the poor. In doing so, the justice system is subject to the charge that it is prejudicially and intolerably classist.

Someone once asked me when I made similar comments in a speech recently, where in this country I had ever seen such an outlandish system actually operate, as if my notion of private, community-based replacements for correctional institutions was utopian. "Here," I suggested; and one could say the same about the situation in any city in this country. The informal, private system which people of means and status use to correct and treat their own wards is essentially private, usually community-based, and much more effective and in the long run more economic than are our public jails.

What businessman arrested for being drunk in public ends up in jail? Typically, he is taken home, sobered up, called a sport and the episode is laughed over. If he is an addict or mentally ill, he may end up in a private, therapeutic hospital; in any event, he will be treated and pitied for the sick man he is. What white collar criminal or organized crime magnate waits for trial in jail? However anti-social his capacities, this man is released until the last possible minute, usually after trial and conviction. What affluent person goes to jail because he did not pay bail, a fine, alimony, a civil judgment? Only the perversely adamant one, and at that only by choice. He has alternatives if he chooses to use them. What juvenile delinquent goes to jail or to a juvenile detention center for playing hooky, giving his parents a tough time, getting pregnant, having family problems or even committing mischief or crimes? Affluent children are tutored, treated; they make restitution; they are taken to professionals to solve their problems. Rarely do they end up in jail.

Alternatives to replace jails for defendants who are incarcerated for strictly economic reasons, then, are not radical innovations. They are the usual ways that society deals with these problems—for those whom it regards as respectable and decent. Jails are the other way; the way reserved for the poor.

3

CONFINEMENT
OF THE SICK

Anyone who visits any local jail will observe immediately that many prisoners are obviously seriously ill. Most authorities generally agree that certain chronic disease conditions—including heart ailments, tuberculosis, venereal disease, dental problems, diabetes and psychological or emotional disturbances—are widespread among jail prisoners. Many inmates have physical injuries. But, because routine medical examinations at intake are not even given in most jails, and tend to be cursory or superficial where they are performed, inmates frequently are neither referred to other more appropriate public institutions nor adequately cared for during their confinement.

Because most people who are sent to jail are poor and unsophisticated, and because minority group members and slum dwellers are represented out of proportion to their numbers in the general population, inmates suffer not only from the diseases which afflict Americans of all classes, but from diseases which thrive among the disadvantaged. The apparently high incidence of tuberculosis among jail inmates is a case in point. Upper- and middle-class Americans tend to view TB as a thing of the past, but for many of the poor who have never had a complete medical checkup, and have lived all their lives in urban squalor, this debilitating disease is a problem. Not knowing or even suspecting that they are tubercular, they may live for years with the disease's lingering symptoms. If they are jailed, their condition generally will continue to go unrecognized and their TB may be communicated to other, previously uninfected inmates.

In jail, an individual has no control over his own physical well-being. That power belongs to his jailers, who too often are unsympathetic or ill informed and do not discharge their responsibility to provide medical care. When a prisoner is denied maintenance medication, forced to consume an inappropriate diet, or thrust into a closed and stressful environment, the person becomes even more vulnerable to disease than he has been outside the jail, even in a deprived environment.

For example, while there is no data to show that jail populations include an inordinately high percentage of epileptics, epileptic seizures are not uncommon in jails. There is reason to suspect that the deprivations of detention have triggered severe overt symptoms in individuals whose condition ordinarily is mild or dormant. The typical jail scene is bedlam; even to the untrained observer the atmosphere is stressful and the population contains individuals who show signs of mental illness. Some of these sick people contribute to the inhuman conditions in jails; others are victims of it; all ought to be somewhere else.

Jailers tend to give equivocal and evasive answers when asked about the medical care they provide. The arrangements for health services in their jails are, at best, informal and haphazard. According to the recent *1970 National Jail Census,* by jail administrators' own reports, 49 per cent of the more than 3,300 jails surveyed have no medical facilities whatsoever.[1] A 1966 study of Illinois jails asked jailers whether they maintained "medical facilities." Five said they had adequate medical infirmaries; a large number reported that the health "facility" was nothing more than a meagerly supplied first-aid cabinet. One sheriff said he had a supply of "aspirin, Tums, and band-aids around someplace."[2]

If physical facilities for medical services in jails are shocking, professional staffing is even more grossly inadequate. A survey of 266 county and city jails in Oklahoma reported:

> No jails were found to have a staff physician or nurse. The closest arrangement to medical professionals on staff is the contract agreement which 39 jails have with either local private physicians or publicly employed county doctors.

[1] *1970 National Jail Census,* p. 19. As a general matter, even the most thorough state jail surveys provide no information on the number and type of infirmaries, first-aid rooms or other jail "medical facilities." See, e.g., "Oklahoma Jails, A Report to the Oklahoma Crime Commission" (mimeographed, April 1972).

[2] Mattick and Sweet, *Illinois Jails,* p. 183.

Jails most frequently avail themselves of local hospital emergency room facilities for sick or injured prisoners. One-hundred-eight are served by a private physician that is available on call.[3]

Standing arrangements for professional services in Oklahoma—and throughout the country—usually are geared to meet only emergency situations. Full or part-time jail physicians are almost unknown outside the largest urban jurisdictions; trained jail nurses are almost as rare.

The "on-call" physician, theoretically available in emergencies on a contract or fee-for-service basis, is the jail's most common professional medical resource. Of ninety Nebraska county jails surveyed in 1969, 69 per cent had a "private physician on call"; 7 per cent had physicians who also made regular "sick call" visits; 4 per cent had no physician assigned on any basis. The authors of the Nebraska survey concluded that "the major responsibility for administering medication rests with the jailor."[4]

This conclusion is applicable to the vast majority of American jails. Untrained custodial personnel of necessity must assume responsibilities for which they have no qualifications and often little interest.

In Illinois, the 1966 jail survey found that at about 63 per cent of the state's city jails and about half its county jails, the "jail physician" visited less than once a month: no doctor ever visited at about 24 per cent of the city jails and 10 per cent of the county institutions. Only 1.7 per cent of the county jails, and 3 per cent of the city jails reported a daily physician's visit. As the authors of the survey observed:

> A jail administrator can be trained to give first aid, to differentiate drunkenness from sickness or injuries producing stupor or coma, and to identify clear symptoms of common diseases so that he can make a preliminary check to detect any conditions requiring immediate medical care. But such a preliminary examination by an administrator should be regarded only as a "stopgap measure" until the prisoner can be examined by a physician. An untrained jailer simply is not qualified to determine whether an inmate needs medical care or should be separated from other inmates. Nor is he qualified to prescribe medical treatment programs.[5]

[3] "Oklahoma Jails."
[4] Nebraska Department of Economic Development, "For Better or Worse?: Nebraska's Misdemeanant Correctional System," p. 36.
[5] Mattick and Sweet, *Illinois Jails,* pp. 168–69.

In practice, jail administrators routinely diagnose, prescribe to, and treat inmates. It is not surprising that even seriously ill jail prisoners frequently go without care. The jailer is first and last a custodian; his natural first reaction to any prisoner's medical complaints is one of mistrust. Malingering by prisoners may be common, but jailers' suspicions of malingering are exaggerated. One Illinois sheriff reportedly followed the diagnostic routine of asking a complaining inmate to "sit for a while to see if he will shut up"; any inmate who did not persist with his complaint was dismissed as a fraud.[6]

American jails generally do not give entering inmates medical examinations. In Illinois in 1966, almost half the jails surveyed reported that no inmate ever received an intake checkup. Only four jails reported medical examinations, and those only for prisoners who complained or showed obvious symptoms of illness.[7]

By failing to provide routine medical checkups to all entering inmates, jailers turn their backs on a unique opportunity to intervene constructively in the troubled lives of prisoners with medical disabilities.

Jails fail to perform the routine, inexpensive laboratory tests which can discover previously undiagnosed disease which could be cured or controlled by available medical technology. They fail to provide simple, corrective medical services such as minor surgery or new drug regimens which could improve a prisoner's well-being and outlook.

Dental care is another illustration. Many jail inmates have never received regular dental care; their conditions may have caused pain and embarrassment; they can become barriers to social adaptation and employment. In almost any American jail, dental care is provided only in "emergencies," and under conditions which effectively limit the available treatment to extractions.

Institutions which house women (a small minority of the total jail population) have one special, although occasional, problem. Some women prisoners are pregnant; some give birth in jail. The present jail institution does little but exacerbate their especially difficult experience. The detention of pregnant women clearly should be avoided where possible. It seems even more obvious

6 Ibid., p. 171.
7 Ibid., pp. 170–71.

that women should not be forced to give birth in jails or to keep or remain with their infants in such institutions.

The Riker's Island Women's Detention Center has opened a prenatal clinic for its inmates.[8] The new clinic provides counseling on abortion and planned parenthood, gives special VD care (required by an "alarming number of inmates"), prescribes special diets and vitamins, and assists with the placement of babies. At this institution, forty out of 600 inmates are pregnant at any one time and more than 200 women use the clinic facilities each month.

In 1972, the American Medical Association, in conjunction with the American Bar Association, conducted a questionnaire survey of 2,930 jails regarding the state of their mental care personnel and facilities. They did not reach any juvenile detention facilities, overnight lockups, drunk tanks or jails in seven states. They received 1,159 responses, which, however incomplete, nonetheless compose the most current and fulsome panorama of the field of medical care and jails at this time. Their findings are worth quoting:

Facilities in Jails

According to respondents, there are limited facilities within jails for the provision of medical care to inmate populations: 65.5 percent of the responding jails had *only* first aid facilities, while 16.7 percent had no internal medical facilities. Only 17.4 percent of responding jails had facilities for alcoholics, 13.1 percent for the mentally ill and 9.1 percent for drug addicts.

Jails for the most part rely on community medical facilities to provide care for their inmate populations. The most frequently used institutional sources of care are government hospitals, indicated by 47.5 percent of responding jails, and private hospitals, indicated by 41.8 percent of respondents. Physicians' offices reportedly serve as sources of medical care for 62.6 percent of responding jails.

Medical Personnel Available to Jails

Respondents indicated that medical personnel in jails were available on an extremely limited basis: in only 440 (38.0 percent) of the responding jails were physicians available on a regularly scheduled basis, and only in 586 (50.6 percent) responding jails were physicians available on an on call basis. In 360 jails (31.1

8 "Inmates Praise Prenatal Clinic," New York *Times,* April 15, 1973.

percent), *no* physicians were available to provide medical care to inmates.

Most jails have no formal arrangements with physicians to provide medical care; physicians are just called as needed, as indicated by 902 jails (77.8 percent). Physicians are primarily reimbursed on a fee-for-services basis, indicated by 844 jails (72.8 percent) of respondents, while in only 222 jails (23.5 percent) are they reimbursed on a salary basis.

Of the responding jails, only 438 (37.8 percent) claimed availability of a dentist, 215 (18.6 percent) availability of nurses, 244 (21.1 percent) availability of social workers, and 176 (15.2 percent) availability of psychologists.

Although prescription drugs are dispensed to inmates in 97.8 percent of responding jails, in 81.6 percent of responding jails medications are dispensed by *non-medical* personnel, although often on physicians' orders.

Sanitary inspections are made in jails on a regular basis in 87.3 percent of responding jails. However in only 49.0 percent are inspections provided on a monthly basis or more frequently.[9]

The prescription for improving the quality of health care in American jails as they presently exist is a simple if expensive one. Construction of adequate infirmaries, dispensaries, examining rooms and dental offices within the jails, creation of routine medical intake procedures, employment of more full- and part-time health care professionals, increased use of medical paraprofessionals and significantly upgraded first-aid and diagnostic training for custodial staff are required.

No dramatic change in the delivery of medical care to jail inmates can be accomplished without the creation of formal hospital-jail affiliations. Institutional relationships between local hospitals and jails generally are informal; prisoners receive emergency room treatment on an occasional basis. By sharing responsibility for the physical welfare of inmates with competent medical agencies, jail administrations can take a step toward improving the health care opportunities of the impoverished men or women in confinement.

[9] American Medical Association Center for Health Services, *Medical Care in U.S. Jails—a 1972 AMA Survey* (1973).

MENTALLY SICK INMATES

Neither Jimmie Jones nor a D. C. Superior Court paper ordering a mental examination for him ever reached St. Elizabeth's Hospital.

The paper, ordering a mental examination for the 37-year-old drifter prior to his second-degree murder trial, is lodged somewhere between the court, the jail and the hospital.

Jones, of no fixed address, was found Tuesday morning hanging from a crossbar in his cell at D.C. jail on the 28th day of his wait for space at St. Elizabeth's.

Superior Court Chief Judge Harold Greene has launched an investigation into the lengthy delay after the order was issued.

Noting that there is usually a backlog of cases for mental examinations there for the court, Greene commented, "As far as I'm concerned, it's just inexcusable to put mentally ill people in jail.

"This is something we'll have to address ourselves to and . . . stop sending the suspect to jail where he can harm others and others can harm him," he said.[10]

Improving the delivery of mental health care to jail inmates involves special, serious problems. Mentally ill inmates—and indeed all inmates with character disorders or markedly abnormal behavior patterns—create security problems as well as medical dilemmas for jail administrators. Not only should they be diagnosed and, so far as possible, treated; they also must be protected from themselves and other inmates, and prevented from endangering others or disrupting the tense, delicate balance of the jail environment. Note the following, rather typical incidents:

On the seventh floor of the Wayne County Jail a naked man with light brown hair and pale white skin sits on the edge of his cot and stares fixedly at a wall in his cell with vacant blue eyes.

A few cells away a thin young man weeps bitterly and moans and talks to himself for hours at a time. When a guard passes his cell, the prisoner is likely to leap up and yell obscenities and threaten to kill him.

Nearby, a wizened, old man with a small gray beard stands

[10] Taylor, "Inmate Killed Self While Waiting Mental Test," Washington *Post*, November 30, 1972, p. 63.

scrutinizing everything that goes on in the hallway with wide, darting eyes. He doesn't speak, but he wears a permanent, barely perceptible smile.

These men are inmates in what is called the "mental ward" in the Wayne County Jail, located in downtown Detroit. Many of them obviously need immediate psychiatric care. They may spend six or eight months in the Wayne County Jail before they get it.

"A bunch of them belong in a psychiatric hospital," said a deputy on duty in the ward, "but we can't send them out of here unless the court orders them."

Wayne County sheriff William Lucas said that the jail has a psychiatrist who "diagnoses and gives medication."

The psychiatrist does not have time for psychiatric treatment of individual inmates, Lucas explained, but "he does give them medication. They're chemically restrained now."

A guard, who did not want his name used, said: "Some of them go nuts because they can't stand it in those little dirty cells day after day.

"At first they start screaming to get out. Then they get this funny look in their eyes. We put them in the ward for their own protection because the other inmates get scared when somebody goes crazy, and they'll beat him up. They think it'll spread to them, I guess."

"Do you think it's fun listening to those guys in there crying and yelling and howling all day long?" a guard asked. "There's nothing we can do for them. We just have to listen."

Iron mesh is welded to the inside of the bars enclosing the cell. It was put there, a deputy said, because inmates kept running head-first into the bars, trying to injure or kill themselves.[11]

City Sgt. Andrew J. Winston said today there is nothing his staff at the City Jail can do to prevent someone from killing himself unless jail personnel have been warned that the individual has suicidal tendencies.

Winston's comment came in the wake of the death of Richard Farris Kennett, 16, of the 300 block W. 26th St., who was found

[11] Knight, "Jail Mental Cases Get Minimum Care," Detroit *Free Press*, November 21, 1970, p. 1.

hanging by a sheet attached to the bars above the door of his cell at the jail.

According to a police report about Kennett's death, the youth had told another inmate that he intended to kill himself. However, Winston said today the suicide threat had not been reported to jail personnel.

According to Winston, Kennett had been placed in an isolation cell at his mother's request after the youth had complained that other juvenile inmates had attempted to force him to commit unnatural sex acts.[12]

Psychological and behavioral aberrations which attract little attention in a heterogeneous free society may become sources of danger and unrest in the closed society of the jail. Homosexuality is a case in point.

However they happen to arrive in jails, homosexuals pose special problems. The fact of life is that homosexuals (men and women) seem to be in abundance in all correctional institutions, whether by choice or fortuity. They present special problems in these institutions for obvious reasons. For the jailer, inmate homosexuality is primarily a problem of security. In its training materials on jail administration, for example, the U. S. Bureau of Prisons notes that:

> The homosexual prisoner is a threat to the safety and good order of the jail and a moral and physical danger to other inmates. Whenever homosexuals are found among the jail's population, they should be segregated immediately and kept under close and constant supervision. There is nothing the jail can do to correct the cause of the homosexual's abnormality; the jailer's responsibility is to control the homosexual, keep him segregated, and prevent him from introducing other inmates to abnormal sexual behavior.[13]

The jailer who follows this advice literally, however, will tend to concentrate his attention on the obvious cases: the blatant transvestites and demonstratively effeminate or lesbian prisoners. But although these inmates undoubtedly create a temptation for their sexually deprived fellow prisoners, they do not participate in the

[12] "Nothing We Can Do, Jail Official Says," November 18, 1970.
[13] Bureau of Prisons, U. S. Department of Justice, "Unusual Prisoners in the Jail" (Correspondence Course for Jailers, No. 8, n.d.), pp. 10–11.

most violent, corrupting and dangerous episodes of jail homosexuality, except as victims.

Any inquiry into sexual practices in detention reveals that the most troubling incidents—gang rapes, victimizations of youthful prisoners, sexually related beatings—are initiated by men who may not even be practicing homosexuals in the free world, and certainly are not easily identifiable as homosexuals in jail. No simple visual inspection will enable a jailer to isolate the prisoners with the greatest capacity for homosexual aggression.

There have been recent reports of gang rapes in jail with clearly racial overtones. Aside from the violent acts of jail inmates who rape other inmates as a reaction to the unique frustrations and bizarre environments of correctional institutions, there is some indication that at least in isolated cases, gang rapes of inmates are conducted as a special manifestation of deep racial antagonisms that exist in society at large and which are exacerbated in jails. These kinds of incidents are ugly in every situation, are never to be condoned and can constitute only a particularly vicious and condemnable form of criminal conduct which should not be excused. These acts should be prosecuted however one might sympathize with the broader social provocations of which they are a manifestation.

A much more difficult problem, and one which could be ameliorated by reform measures, involves the weak person who is preyed upon by homosexuals or others who while not homosexual are driven to or tempted into homosexual acts when they are in jail. This person, along with the non-violent homosexual of choice, should be carefully protected when involuntarily incarcerated in public institutions. To the extent that these people can be diverted from the jail by assignment to alternative institutions, such measures should be encouraged. To the extent that alternative institutions are not available, emphatic and special procedures for their protection must be enforced.

The precarious emotional condition of some prisoners is apparent to jail administrators, either because they are being held for medico-legal action, or because they display symptoms, such as suicidal behavior, which are too obvious to be overlooked or ignored. Some of these are: non-criminal prisoners confined in connection with a state civil commitment proceeding; others are criminal defendants for whom an assertion of incompetency to stand trial has been made or an insanity defense has been initiated.

But many other inmates have serious mental and emotional problems with dangerous and self-destructive potential which are not recognized at intake or during detention. They generally do not receive even the minimal attention afforded identified inmates.

Occasional press reports of a suicide in jail, a disturbance by violent inmates, an act of mutilation or some other exotic but regular jail occurrence bring these tragic cases to public attention.

The jails get these sick people by default. In its widely circulated correspondence course for local jailers, the United States Bureau of Prisons noted:

> Enlightened treatment of the mentally ill hinges upon the availability of local hospital facilities . . . [and] effective legal procedures which . . . will permit expeditious placement of the mentally ill in hospitals for temporary care as well as their commitment for treatment after determination of mental competency has been made.
>
> Until the community can provide adequately for the mentally ill, the jail will continue to face the problem of housing them. Some will be prisoners awaiting trial; others will be charged with no offense but held awaiting sanity hearings or pending removal to a state hospital. In the prisoner group there will be those suspected of mental illness and held for psychiatric examination and legal determination and those who at the time of arrest or commitment gave no evidence of a psychosis but during confinement began to exhibit signs of mental illness.[14]

Beyond this blanket description of the problem, however, the bureau has little practical advice to give: mentally ill prisoners should be carefully supervised (provided they are recognized); they should be examined by the jail physician (provided there is a jail physician); and they should quickly be transferred to other, more appropriate custodial settings (provided other institutions are available and willing to accept them).

On one point, however, the bureau's pamphlet is emphatic: "Padded cells should never be used for the confinement of the mentally ill or any other person." Incidents of death from burns and smoke inhalation in accidentally or intentionally fired padded jail cells are a familiar part of the dismal history of American

14 Bureau of Prisons, op. cit., pp. 7–8.

jails. In 1970, a fifty-one-year-old Massachusetts woman serving a short sentence for drunkenness in Boston's Charles Street Jail died as a result of a blaze in a padded isolation cell. According to the sheriff, the prisoner had made herself "a constant source of trouble to us by disturbing the other prisoners and setting three fires in her own cell and trying once to take her own life with bed sheets." A local mental hospital had rejected her as a security risk, and her fellow prisoners had petitioned the jailers to remove her from their cell block. So she had been transferred to the padded cell, where she died.[15]

Yet, despite the bureau's admonition, the padded cell remains perhaps the most common provision for dealing with the mentally ill jail inmate—common, that is, in jails which make any special provision whatsoever. The city jail in Defiance, Ohio, was built in 1956 with the problem of the psychotic inmate in mind. In late 1971, an inspection report from the state sheriffs' association included the terse comment: "Padding in padded cell was half destroyed by mentally disturbed prisoner."[16]

Although early nineteenth-century reforms resulted in the near banishment of chains, fetters and other gross mechanical restraints from hospitals and sanitaria built to house the insane, such devices still are employed in local lockups.

Mental disease is no respecter of economic and social class. Its incidence is general throughout the population at large. But few middle-class or well-to-do sufferers need fear being held in a padded cell or subjected to other equally anachronistic penal restraints. This treatment is reserved for the poor, whose access to private medical help is minimal, and whose first contacts with the public system of mental health care delivery often are made in local jails. For Americans with means and sophistication, doctors' offices and private sanitariums are the typical way stations on the path to longer-term psychiatric treatment. For an indigent American—whether he has been charged with a crime or merely observed behaving "strangely"—the "doctor's office" is often a jail cell.

The problem of managing the mentally ill inmates of city and

15 Kurkjian, "Probe Asked in Fire Death in Hub Jail," Boston *Globe,* March 9, 1970, p. 1.
16 Buckeye State Sheriffs' Association, "County Jail Survey" (mimeographed).

county jails is complicated by the difficulties of identification. The prisoner population group is composed of some disturbed inmates who are in jail because of some real or suspected mental illness: non-criminals awaiting the examination which may lead to their civil commitment to state hospitals; defendants awaiting a psychiatric evaluation or a determination of their competency to stand trial; and individuals who have been adjudicated "incompetent" or "insane," but whose placement in a medical-custodial facility remains pending.

A second group of mentally ill jail inmates is even more difficult to manage effectively. It consists of detainees and sentenced prisoners with psychological problems—ranging from mild neuroses to flagrant psychoses. Into this group falls the bulk of the jails' serious suicide risks, the preponderance of their aggressive-assaultive prisoners, and no doubt many of the inmates who create serious disciplinary problems. Their symptoms—and their diseases —go unnoticed during routine and perfunctory intake processing, and reveal themselves only later, when it is too late to prevent a death, a wounding, an incident of self-mutilation or an irreversible episode of psychological deterioration.

Any solution to the problem of the mentally ill inmate in American jails must identify the inmates whose mental and psychological problems now go unnoted and unattended; and it must provide appropriate alternative placements or in-jail services for those disturbed prisoners who are identifiable because of their legal status or their obvious symptoms.

Although the manifest, documented inadequacies of public mental health establishments are outside the scope of this discussion, it should be noted that state hospitals and asylums reportedly are not much ahead of local jails as examples of institutional efficiency; for a shocking number of indigent or low-income sufferers from mental disease, the states provide nothing more than warehousing, even in the specialized institutions they have designated to receive them. To divert a man or woman from the restraining cells of a local jail to the "back ward" of a state hospital has only one, dubious advantage—it removes the burden of responsibility for a generalized failure to treat the individual from an agency which can excuse itself by citing the inappropriateness of the task, and settles that responsibility squarely with an agency which cannot beg off so readily.

Ultimately, nothing short of a major reorganization of American health care delivery systems, emphasizing the provision of psychological care and preventive mental hygiene services in the community, will have a far-reaching impact on the mentally ill jail inmate. Meanwhile, however, new diagnostic and treatment services must be introduced in jails and lockups; new alternatives to jail custody must be provided.

Because of the scanty available jail statistics, no one knows how many inmates suffer mental illness and need special health care as a result. Even as to the discrete group of self-identified disturbed inmates, no evidence is available to show the type and severity of their psychological problems or the lengths of time they spend incarcerated in local jails because of them.

The practice of confining individuals in non-medical institutions because of some mental or behavioral peculiarity has historic roots in America. The early almshouses, which performed many functions now exercised by jails, held lunatics along with vagrants, unemployables and assorted nuisances. Their inmates usually were men and women unknown to local householders, confined only until they would be moved on. In this population of strangers there undoubtedly were a significant number whose only offense was a streak of non-conforming behavior pronounced enough to appear unnatural to the close-knit community into which they had strayed.

With the trend toward medical institutionalization of the insane, the numbers of indigent sufferers in non-medical custodial facilities also swelled. One historian reported that "not all the members of the mentally ill found a place in a hospital, and a good number among the aged and chronic poor remained in almshouses and jails . . ."[17] From its inception, professional mental health care too often was a prerogative of the well-to-do. And as the acceptance of the therapeutic idea rose, there was a parallel increase in community intolerance for peculiar behavior. Whatever the economic and cultural factors, more and more disturbed people found their way to jail. By the twentieth century, as statutes providing for compulsory commitment of the mentally ill proliferated, the number of men and women jailed for insanity throughout the United States became truly significant.

[17] David Rothman, *The Discovery of the Asylum,* p. 130 (Little, Brown, Boston, Mass.), (1971).

In 1902, one pioneering attempt to describe a local jail population in statistical terms revealed an extremely low rate of commitments for reason of insanity: out of 1,035 prisoners entering the Rockford, Illinois, city jail in that year, only one was jailed as "crazy," and one other was committed as "sick."[18]

Today, the situation is different. Most available "offense category" breakdowns reveal sizable groups of persons held in jail as "mental" cases. In Virginia, during fiscal year 1969–70, over 1,500 prisoners, more than 1 per cent of all those annually committed to jails, were "held for mental commission or hospital."[19] In Oklahoma, during 1970, prisoners being held for a "sanity hearing" made up almost the same total, and the same proportion of the overall jail population.[20] In Nebraska, during fiscal year 1968–69, the proportion of all jail prisoners held for mental health hearings was higher—almost 2 per cent.[21] Although the absolute number of prisoners involved was smaller than in more populous states, it was greater than the total number of prisoners booked that year in Nebraska for forgery and grand larceny charges combined.

The jailing of "mental cases" is not limited to cities and towns, although it is concentrated there. During 1969, only 2 of the more than 500 prisoners booked into the Hood River County, Oregon, jail were classified as "mental"; in a neighboring rural (Wasco) County, 20 of about 650 bookings fell into this classification;[22] in another group of mixed urban-rural counties (Marion, Polk and Yamhill), 38 of the approximately 6,300 individual jail bookings were categorized under the heading "mental disease."[23] Thus the jails would appear to hold a significant number of people

18 F. Lewis, ed., *The City Jail: A Symposium* (1903). In other respects, the population statistics outlined in this study seem remarkably contemporary. For example, 362 prisoners—almost 35 per cent of the total—were committed on drunkenness charges.
19 Commonwealth of Virginia, Department of Welfare and Institutions, "Commitments to County and City Jails and City Jail Farms, Year Ended June 30, 1970," table II, p. 4.
20 "Oklahoma Jails," table 7.
21 Nebraska Department of Economic Development, "For Better or Worse? Nebraska's Misdemeanant Correctional System," p. 11.
22 State of Oregon, Corrections Division, "Region 9 Correctional Feasibility Study: Supplemental Report, Jail Data Analysis" (mimeographed, n.d.), pp. 8–11.
23 State of Oregon, Corrections Division, "Research Findings, District 3 Correctional Feasibility Study" (mimeographed, September 1971), p. 30.

—a reasonable speculation would be 1 per cent of the national daily inmate population of over 160,000 inmates—who are charged with or suspected of no crime, and whose only offense against their communities is some appearance of mental abnormality. Jail prisoners who first are booked on a criminal charge, and later detained for some action involving their mental condition (for example, after they have entered an insanity plea or a question has been raised as to their competency to stand trial), are not included in this total; generally, they continue to be reported under the offense category described in their initial booking.

Non-criminal mentally ill jail inmates are medical detainees in the custody of the law. The fact that significant proportions of the individuals who are processed through the official medical-judicial system designed to deal with suspected insanity spend time in jail is confirmed by court records as well as new jail bookings data. In the mid-1960's, a survey of Oklahoma county judges revealed that in each of forty local jurisdictions, as many as 25 per cent of the individuals who appeared in court for sanity hearings previously had been detained in jail; four jurisdictions reported a pre-hearing jailing rate of over 75 per cent.[24] The time these prisoners spend in jail before some disposition can be significant: in the Oklahoma survey, for example, periods of detention ranging from three to five days—before any judicial action was taken—were found to be common. Even after an adjudication of mental illness or incompetency, jail detention can continue, often for long periods, before a medical placement is made and a transfer of the patient-prisoner actually is completed.

The presence of medical detainees in jail is to some extent a reflection of the operation of the prevailing and varying "civil commitment" statutes. In a few jurisdictions, only a judicial finding of "dangerousness"—the likelihood that a mentally ill person will harm himself or others if allowed to remain at large—will justify involuntary long-term institutionalization.[25] In the others, commitment also can take place after a finding that an individual is "incompetent" to manage his own affairs or that he requires

[24] Oklahoma State Department of Health, "County Judges' Views on Mental Health" (Planning Comm. Report No. 3, mimeographed, 1964), p. 7.
[25] The states where statutes take this narrow approach to the grounds for commitment include Arizona, Arkansas, the District of Columbia, Florida, Massachusetts, Missouri and Nevada.

treatment but cannot or will not seek it himself. In almost every jurisdiction, the commitment process can be initiated by presenting the court with certificates by physicians who have examined an individual and concluded that he is mentally ill. Many civil commitment statutes also allow relatives, friends and public officials —including police—to initiate civil commitment proceedings by petitions filed without supporting medical documentation.

Some mental health laws also vest the police with specific authority to arrest individuals who appear to exhibit serious symptoms of a "dangerous" mental illness, and to detain them until they can be given a psychiatric examination or preliminary judicial hearing—which in turn often will trigger the formal commitment machinery.[26] Some of these statutes specify that detention following a police pickup shall be in a medical setting whenever practical. Others contain no such protective provisions.[27]

In practice, however, and sometimes contrary to the letter of statutes, local jails are employed widely as an initial place of detention for individuals picked up "on suspicion" of mental illness. In communities where there are no specialized residential mental health facilities, or no specialized facilities which are willing to assume responsibility for the secure custody of indigents, the jails are the only resource available to the police. Police officials in one rural, western state said that they have no place other than their jails to detain mentally ill people.

It is on the street that the eventual fate of many mentally dis-

---

[26] See, e.g., Colorado Rev. Stats. Chap. 71-1-3 (1963), authorizing any peace officer to take a person suspected of dangerous mental illness into "protective custody" and hold him in a "suitable place for custody" pending court action.
[27] The new Florida mental health law appears to contemplate that no person shall be detained except in a medical setting; it provides police with authority to deliver mental health pickups to the "nearest receiving facility for examination and treatment" (Florida Rev. Stats. 394.463 [1972 Pocket part]).

The Oregon law, which mandates that pickups shall be transported to a hospital "forthwith," also requires that no allegedly mentally ill person be maintained in a jail or prison provided another place "suitable for the comfortable, safe and humane confinement of such person" is available (Oregon Rev. Stats. 426.10 & 462.215 [1971 Replacement part]). As state jail surveys show, however, the jailing of the mentally ill is far from uncommon in Oregon.

In other states, the laws governing emergency police action in mental health cases apparently describe procedures under which pickups will be jailed first and hospitalized only after a threshold medical examination. See, e.g., Massachusetts Ann. Laws, ch. 123, §12(a); and North Dakota Century Code Ann., ch. 25-03.

turbed individuals often will be determined. If their behavior is threatening, distracting or even "peculiar," and the police get a citizen's complaint, they may choose to act on their own initiative. If a disturbed individual appears to have an established place in his community, he may be handled informally—escorted to his home, to the office of his physician or psychiatrist or even to a private, voluntary mental health institution. If the individual appears poor, homeless and friendless, he will be escorted to a public hospital or a jail.

Police pickups do not account for all the non-criminals committed to American jails as "mental" cases. Although most state civil commitment statutes allow a person suspected of mental illness to remain free in the interim between the filing of a petition and the issuing of a judicial commitment order hearing,[28] this policy is subject to significant exceptions. The most common exception authorizes courts to order apprehension and detention of individuals who appear likely—on the facts alleged in a commitment petition or after a preliminary examination and hearing—to injure themselves or others if not restrained. Although such detention should be in a medical setting, the jail often is the only available facility.

Various rationales are advanced for failing to transfer civil detainees from jails to hospitals to await mental health hearings. In a survey of Oklahoma county judges,[29] the following explanations were tendered: the complete unavailability of local hospitals; the refusal of available local hospitals to accept pre-hearing detainees as patients; the reluctance of local doctors to perform the paperwork required for a medical referral; the lack of county funds to subsidize bed space for indigent pre-hearing prisoners in fee-paying institutions; the absence of transportation services to move such prisoners between jail, hospital and courthouse; and the general reliance of judges and jailers on speedy hearings and

---

[28] Not every state's commitment procedure incorporates this policy; in Mississippi, for example, the process begins when any citizen files an affidavit alleging that another is mentally ill; without any hearing, and without any consideration of dangerousness, the clerk of court then issues an order directing that the allegedly ill person be taken into custody and held—apparently in jail—until examined by two physicians. Mississippi Code Ann., Title 41.21.5 (1972).

[29] Under Oklahoma law, a judge may order up to thirty days of detention before any commitment hearing is held, if medical evidence suggests dangerousness. Oklahoma Rev. Stats., Title 43A, 55 (1973 Pocket Supplement).

early transfer of adjudicated prisoner-patients to long-term state custodial facilities.[30] These justifications are typical of those which support the general reliance on jails to hold persons accused or suspected of mental illness, a reliance which is especially widespread outside metropolitan and urban areas.[31]

The treatment a disturbed man or woman receives in jail far too typically is inadequate, sometimes shocking. In an Illinois jail survey recently, jail officials were asked how they handled their "non-violent" mentally ill inmates. More than 15 per cent of city jails, and more than 18 per cent of county jails reported that they do *"nothing"* out of the ordinary for these prisoners; a few others limited special services to attempts to contact the prisoners' families and efforts to segregate the mentally ill from the general inmate population. Roughly 7 per cent of both city and county jails reported using special close surveillance and seeking medical evaluations. About half apparently begin to arrange a transfer to the custody of a hospital—or another jail.

The same study revealed that where violent mentally ill inmates are involved, roughly half the jails surveyed take immediate action to arrange or accelerate a transfer to medical custody—in most cases by physically delivering the inmate to a nearby general or mental hospital. The other half do not attempt to transfer violent, mentally ill inmates. Instead, they deal with them according to their own improvised methods, of which the most common are "isolation" (the use of solitary confinement, often in a cell, and occasionally in a security cell specially designed to prevent accidental or intentional self-injury) and "restraint" (the use of chains, handcuffs, straitjackets and other appliances of control). According to the Illinois survey, "[O]ne jail 'calms them down' with cold water, using a fire hose from the Fire Department next door."[32]

One other technique for the handling of mentally ill jail inmates—the use of tranquilizing or depressant drugs—is noteworthy, although there is little hard information to indicate how

[30] Oklahoma State Department of Health, "County Judges' Views on Mental Health," pp. 12–15.
[31] The reluctance of hospitals to receive pre-adjudication mental patients is due to more than conservatism or financial self-interest. Those prisoners are unknown quantities, and many have at least been accused of dangerousness. Where a hospital lacks a special security ward, its administrator naturally may avoid accepting such referrals as a matter of policy.
[32] Mattick and Sweet, *Illinois Jails*, pp. 174–78.

widely it is employed. In its 1967 inspection survey of the Wayne County Jail in Detroit, Michigan, the National Council on Crime and Delinquency found that almost 8 per cent of the more than 1,000 inmates were receiving some form of "control medication."[33]

The dangers inherent in any attempt to substitute pharmacological stopgaps for individual psychiatric care are clear. Not all mentally ill individuals respond similarly to control medication, and in some individual cases an ordinarily beneficial drug may be antagonistic. Few nurses, nurses' aides or overworked general-duty physicians have the skills or time required to prescribe psychoactive drugs properly in a jail infirmary. In most urban jails, the work of dispensing medication generally is delegated by default to paraprofessional or non-professional custodial employees. If the substitution of chemical restraints for physical restraints is a step in the direction of humanizing the treatment of jail inmates, it is a step which should be taken with professionalism and extreme caution.

The jails house two other groups of "self-identifying" mentally ill inmates: criminal defendants awaiting a determination of mental competency to stand trial, and defendants who have been adjudicated incompetent or insane and are awaiting a medical transfer. In general, they are subjected to the same policies of neglect and abuse to which their non-criminal counterparts are exposed, but they often are held for longer periods. Because the essence of non-criminal civil commitment procedures is an implied challenge to the allegedly insane or incompetent individual's rights to live free from legal or medical interference, their cases have priority and usually are heard early. Moreover, the non-criminal, civilly committed individual generally is easier to place in a public mental facility after his hearing than the prisoner-patient who first entered jail under a criminal charge.

[33] National Council on Crime and Delinquency, "Adult Detention Needs in Wayne County, Michigan: A Survey of the Wayne County Jail" (mimeographed, 1968), p. 30. The same study found that the jail was almost wholly without other adequate means of dealing with disturbed prisoners. It had no specialized facilities or specially trained staff for this segment of the population, and could not rely on any secure custody hospital to accept transfers. The NCCD did not indicate how many of the inmates taking medication had been identified as mentally ill, and how many were receiving drugs either at their own request or merely because they had been identified as disciplinary problems.

When a jailed criminal defendant or his attorney raises the issue of mental incompetency to stand trial, the prisoner's chances of obtaining pretrial release become virtually non-existent. During his wait for transfer to the secure ward of a mental hospital for examination, the defendant who has raised the issue of incompetency receives the same treatment for his illness as any other disturbed inmate—little or none.

A medical examination is a necessary preliminary to a competency hearing, and as one commentator noted:

> Mental observations are almost always conducted on an in-patient basis because the court may feel that one who is of questionable competence may not be able to understand and comply with the conditions of release. If the hospital is full, the patient is held in jail until there is a vacancy.

Recently, in the District of Columbia, the jail stay for persons awaiting competency examinations was two to three months—a backlog so acute that the local chief judge took the extraordinary step of ordering that psychiatric examinations be conducted in the unfavorable atmosphere of the jail cellblocks themselves.[34]

After a defendant has been found incompetent to stand trial, his experience with the jailing system may not be over. Generally, he will be returned to jail to await a medical placement; his wait may stretch into months. In 1967, the NCCD team surveying Detroit's Wayne County Jail found that some of the prisoners in the two cellblocks reserved for mental cases had been in jail for as long as 250 and 300 days. They described the handling of one female inmate who was adjudicated incompetent in early August and remained in the jail until early December. Much of the time, the overtly psychotic woman, whose symptoms were clear and who had been declared to have a mental illness by the court, received no treatment: "She lay in her own bodily excretion and the trash that accumulated daily from food service. Jail staff did not attempt to bathe her, but did spray her with disinfectant."[35]

Throughout the network of American jails, a substantial number of mentally ill prisoners are being held by default because they are found to be in need of hospitalization, but have not yet

[34] Paul Aaron Chernoff and William Gray Schaffer, "Defending the Mentally Ill: Ethical Quicksand," 10 *Am. Crim. L. Rev.* 505, 515 (1972).
[35] NCCD, "Adult Detention Needs in Wayne County, Michigan."

Confinement of the Sick 103

been placed; or as punishment for defending themselves against criminal charges by asserting the insanity defense. It would be unrealistic to pretend that speeding the processes of transfer and referral necessarily would imply long-term medical benefits for the mentally ill inmates who now are held in jail; at the least, however, it would serve to remove them from the awful environment of the jail, where, to borrow a hackneyed phrase, they are "likely to injure themselves or others."

While the prospect of the identified disturbed inmate is bleak, the predicament of the inmate whose illness has not been recognized or diagnosed is worse still. When an inmate's mental condition has been called to their attention, jailers often will act out of personal and institutional self-interest to segregate that inmate from the general population and to intensify the level of his custodial supervision. The undiagnosed or unrecognized sufferer from mental illness, however, will not even receive these minimal benefits. Instead, he will be left prey to the exploitation of other inmates and—more significantly—to the vagaries of his own disease.

Since few jails have regular arrangements to obtain psychiatric medical services, and since intensive psychological testing and evaluation is rarely a feature of the jail intake process, there is no accurate count of the incidence of various mental disorders among inmates.[36]

One state—Alaska—recently has conducted a survey of physical and mental afflictions "handicapping" citizens who are incarcerated in local jails, state institutions and federal prisons. The survey found that almost 5 per cent of all prisoners suffer from severe psychotic or psychoneurotic disorders.[37] One cannot generalize from the results of this study, which surveyed a peculiar local population with research techniques which the study report itself characterized as "quick and dirty." However, the real incidence of mental disorders in typical American prisoner populations probably is higher than the Alaska figures suggest.[38]

[36] Statistics cannot even be estimated from analogy to long-term state or federal prison populations, since the literature on mental illness in prison is almost as inadequate as the literature on mental illness in jail.
[37] Alaska Comprehensive Statewide Planning Project for Vocational Rehabilitation Services, *A Survey of Public Offenders*, p. 15.
[38] The Alaskan survey, for example, found no prisoners suffering from mental retardation. But a recent nationwide sampling of state penal facilities (ex-

Without hard statistical evidence, there are two means to estimate the dimensions of the problem of untreated, undetected
mental illness among jail inmates. The first is to review existing
criminological and psychiatric literature discussing the high rates
of correlation between mental and emotional disturbances and
certain forms of criminal behavior. In all probability, any psychiatric evaluation of jail populations would reveal rates of mental
illness higher than those which characterize the free population,
and higher still than those which characterize populations of prisoners sentenced to long terms for serious criminal offenses. In
the jails, the process of selection which returns large numbers of
stable one-time offenders to the free world, diverts large numbers
of seriously disturbed offenders to medical custody, and funnels
large numbers of non-disturbed "professional" felons into long-
term correctional institutions, has not yet begun. The jails are
catchalls for "problem people."

Many of their most seriously disturbed inmates are those who
are involved in chronic cycles of petty criminal conduct—the
drunks, the vagrants, the chronic disturbers of the public peace.
These individuals may never be institutionalized elsewhere than
in jails; but they will be jailed repeatedly.

The second and perhaps the best proof of the reality and proportion of mental illness in the jails is the impression one invariably
receives walking through the exercise yard, dayroom or tier of
cells in any jail. Even a layman can observe the blank gazes, the
paralyzing disassociation and the irrational outbursts which in the
free world would be considered signals of some underlying mental
or emotional disturbance. Listening to these inmates, one can hear
real grievances blend into irrational obsessions, realistic details
evolve into grotesque fantasies. Some of these inmates had serious
psychological disabilities when they were jailed; others developed
symptoms in reaction to the conditions of jail life. Whatever their
personal histories, it takes no medical degree to know that many
of these people are mentally disturbed.

In the hurly-burly of jail life, however, their condition often
passes unnoticed and untreated. The rare part-time jail psychiatrist

cluding local jails) revealed that almost 10 per cent of all incarcerated persons
were retarded individuals with I.Q. scores lower than 69. See Bertram S.
Brown and Thomas F. Courtless, "The Mentally Retarded in Penal and Correctional Institutions," *Amer. J. Psych.* 124 #9 (1968): pp. 1164–65.

or psychologist generally is too pressed by the routine work of classification, testing and court liaison to consider devoting any substantial amount of his time to treatment. One psychiatrist experienced in correctional work told me that his work was frustrated because he spent all his time dealing with institution-induced anxieties and thus never got to the inmates' basic problems which led to their incarceration in the first instance.

The typical mentally disturbed inmate simply deteriorates quietly; any attempt he makes to call attention to himself is likely to be dismissed by the jail staff as a calculated play to attract special attention or consideration. When a disturbed prisoner erupts into violence, he generally will be handled as a disciplinary problem, and not as a sick man. The results, whether they take the form of a reprimand, a deprivation of privileges, or a spell in solitary confinement, merely serve to exacerbate the prisoner's mental condition.

Suicide. Attempts at suicide, one of the prisoner's common methods of "crying for help," commonly pass unnoticed in the bedlam of jail life.

During NCCD's 1967 survey of the Wayne County Jail, four successful suicides in the Detroit institution were reported. All four had past histories of suicidal behavior known to public agencies and reflected in records to which the jail staff had access. Yet only two of the four prisoners had received special handling —confinement to the "mental ward"—during the jail stays preceding their deaths.[39] One inmate interviewed by the surveyors was obviously suicidal, having stabbed himself in the chest that very night. This fact was unknown to the attending guard on his cell-block.

Not all jail suicides and suicide risks derive from the mentally ill. Some are results of the effect of the oppressive conditions of jails upon the less than hardy inmates they house. After cautioning that "[i]t is not always possible to identify the suicidal person in advance," the U. S. Bureau of Prisons goes on to advise local jailers to keep a close eye on:

Narcotic addicts and alcoholics during the withdrawal and sobering-up processes;
Psychotics;

[39] NCCD, "Adult Detention Needs in Wayne County, Michigan."

Persons held for murder or other offenses involving a possible death penalty;

Respected members of the community arrested for the first time, particularly on sex or morals charges . . . ;

Prisoners who have received bad news—the death of a family member, desertion by a wife or sweetheart, denial of an appeal, etc.;

The aging individual, abandoned by his family, who may feel he has nothing left to live for.[40]

Suicide risks often can be identified; it is because the jailing system is so poorly adapted to the task of identification that so many attempts occur.

In urban areas, recently withdrawn narcotics addicts (not necessarily those actually in the throes of the physical withdrawal) account for about half the successful jail suicides. The other half almost invariably have some past record of mental illness or emotional disturbance, often including previous suicide attempts. In the area of suicide prevention, improved record keeping, along with increased exchange of information between jails and other institutions, would be likely to save lives.

Consider, for example, the case of William Wing, a thirty-year-old Chinese immigrant arrested in New York City in mid-1972, after stabbing his father fatally and himself in the chest. About two weeks later, Wing was dead—a jail suicide by hanging. The story of Wing's two weeks in Manhattan's Tombs is a tale of crossed signals, missing files and lost opportunities.[41]

Wing was first noted as a suicide risk by the police officers who arrested him. Hospitalized after his arrest, he was observed by a psychiatrist who recorded his diagnosis as "totally psychotic, suicidal and extremely depressed." This information, however, never reached the jail, and when Wing entered detention, the staff did not know that his obvious stab wounds had resulted from a prior suicide attempt. Once in jail, Wing was examined by two staff psychologists. The first found him suicidal and recommended his transfer to a mental observation floor. His report was lost or misfiled. The second—who interviewed Wing two days later in the

[40] Bureau of Prisons, U. S. Department of Justice, "Unusual Prisoners in the Jails," pp. 9–10.
[41] McFadden, "Anatomy of Jail Suicide: Man Lost in the System" New York *Times,* October 15, 1972, p. 1.

cellblock, without quiet, privacy or a chance to familiarize himself with the prisoner's background—found him "apparently not suicidal." He was wrong. The next day Wing constructed a makeshift noose out of his bedsheets and took his own life.

Reflecting on the case, the head psychiatrist for the New York City prison system concluded that by the time of the second interview, Wing "had made a definite decision to commit suicide, was no longer crying out for help and was hiding his intentions so he could follow through on them." Adequate social and medical information on jail inmates, he noted, was "the exception rather than the rule." A Corrections Department spokesman, enlightening the situation, noted that the "paper work that should have followed him was trailing behind him."

William Wing died in New York City, where the jails already provide more psychological services to inmates than are provided in any other major urban jurisdiction.[42] Most city jails do not even gather the essential information which New York too often loses in the shuffle of files and bodies. Yet the signals of suicidal behavior usually are apparent, if anyone is willing to look. Psychiatrist Bruce L. Danto, who studied the ten successful suicides at Detroit's Wayne County Jail during 1969–70, noted that "7 out of 10 had some suspected history of mental illness, and 5 out of 10 had a definite history of suicide attempts or statements." Even in a jail where "psychiatric treatment or diagnostic evaluation was unheard of," prisoner records reflected this much vital information about the suicidal inmates.[43]

In another study, Dr. Danto reported that the successful suicidal jail inmate presents a typical and recognizable profile, different from that of other successful suicides. In the free world, most successful suicides are white males, over fifty years; living alone and suffering from some recent personal loss; usually, the suicide has a past history of attempts and has been drinking just before

[42] Gordon Chase, New York City's health services administrator, recently reported that the city prison system is served by 137 mental health personnel, and that the mental observation floor of the Tombs is staffed with "three psychiatrists, one part-time social worker, two psychiatric nurses, a full-time mental health supervisor, and six mental health workers, two of whom speak Spanish" (Sibley, "Health Care Rise is Cited in Jails," New York *Times,* February 17, 1972, p. 41).

[43] Danto, "Suicide at the Wayne County Jail: 1967–70." *Police Science Quarterly* 34 (1971).

his successful attempt. The means of self-destruction employed by successful free world suicides are varied but almost always violent. By contrast, the successful inmate suicide

> is one who is male, white or black with almost equal incidence, under 30 and who chooses hanging as his chief means . . . He may or may not have communicated his suicide plan to another inmate or guard . . . A preamble to the act is isolation from other persons, as well as a goading statement by the guard: "Listen, Mac, if you're gonna bump yourself off, don't do it on my shift."[44]

This suicide "profile" could be a useful starting point for a suicide prevention effort. Combined with available information about the mental condition and background of individual prisoners, it should be possible to identify many of those inmates whose mental illness would tend to lead them to harm themselves.

Better information systems and upgraded staff training are not enough to solve the jail suicide problem. The most crucial factor is the sensitivity shown by staff members (physicians and guards) in their dealings with disturbed inmates. No amount of sophistication will suffice if human, sympathetic treatment is not the rule in jail.

Far too often, however, institutional arrangements and staff attitudes within local jails tend to reinforce, rather than to offset the suicidal tendencies of disturbed prisoners. In one recent instance, for example, the staff of the Suffolk County, New York, Jail were confronted with a classic "slow suicide"—a thirty-year-old burglary suspect. During his two years in custody, he had been shuffled around between the jail and a series of state hospitals, where he had been diagnosed as mentally ill. During much of his time in jail, he suffered from periodic catatonia; during the two weeks preceding his death from malnutrition, he had refused all food and his weight had fallen to eighty-five pounds. Yet he was not force-fed, fed intravenously or transferred out of the jail's mental ward into a medical facility. According to reports, a jail doctor had observed that "when he gets hungry, he'll eat."[45]

Dr. Danto has pointed out that withdrawal from social contacts

[44] Danto, "The Suicidal Inmate," *The Police Chief*, August 1971, p. 56.
[45] Andelman, "Mentally Ill Burglary Suspect Dies in the Suffolk County Jail," New York *Times*, May 12, 1972, p. 82, col. 1.

is a common early sign of an impending jail suicide. In suggesting a suicide prevention guide for jail staffers, he points out that "[d]epressed and suicidal threateners or attempters must not be kept in isolation," and recommends dormitory housing for this group of jail inmates. Most jails isolate mentally or emotionally disturbed inmates as a matter of policy, without regard to the impact of this policy on their self-destructive tendencies. Rather than encouraging potentially suicidal prisoners to associate with less disturbed inmates, who might be able to act as supporters and even "rescuers," the jails either separate identified suicide risks from all regular inmate contacts, or confine them in company only with other depressed, withdrawn individuals.

Jail administrators continue to regard suicide as a conventional security problem, which can be solved by the construction of new facilities, rather than as an exceptional human problem which can be resolved only by new attitudes and administrative patterns. In 1970, for example, Superintendent Winston Moore of Chicago's Cook County Jail, had this comment on a recent rash of inmate suicides:

> We don't have any facilities for those with extreme suicidal tendencies. . . . What we need is to build a dormitory where there are no bars or pipes where a man can hang himself and where they can be watched continually.[46]

The bricks-and-mortar approach to the problem of the mentally ill inmate is doomed to failure; suicidal prisoners will continue to slip through the cracks in the prevailing architectural design; and even if they temporarily are prevented from destroying themselves physically, they will continue to deteriorate psychologically.

Dr. Danto proposes another rule for jail suicide prevention, which is violated in practice every day in every American jail: "The rescuer guard or deputy must take all threats of suicide seriously."[47] To ignore a potentially suicidal inmate's cries for help is, in effect, to dare him to take his own life. In fact, jail staff members are notoriously case-hardened. Merely because most inmates who threaten suicide do not attempt it, and most of those

---

[46] Petraque, "State Unit to Probe Jail Hangings Here," Chicago *Sun-Times*, March 25, 1970; Brennon and Dolan, "Jail Death Autopsy: No Sign of Anything but Suicide," Chicago *Sun-Times*, March 14, 1970.
[47] Danto, "The Suicidal Inmate," pp. 56, 58.

who attempt it do not succeed, overworked and disinterested jail personnel tend to assume that every threat or signal is a sham.

During one recent six-week period, two inmates of the Alexandria, Virginia, city jail hanged themselves in their cells. Both had shown signs of mental disturbance in interviews conducted by a part-time jail physician the day before their deaths; neither had been referred to a nearby maximum-security psychiatric care facility, although space was available. According to the pragmatic jail doctor:

> A couple of cases like this make you jittery . . . but I don't think you can send everyone who indicates a mental illness. Some of them are great bluffers and just want out of jail. You have to make some judgments.[48]

So long as jail administrators continue to make their "judgments" on the basis of cynicism and institutional self-interest, jail inmates will continue to die at their own hands in significant numbers. Since inmates are in jail involuntarily, and since jails are public institutions, the public cannot shrug off this phenomenon as inevitable, voluntary acts of personal self-destruction.

Improvements in record keeping, upgrading of psychological testing and revisions in staff attitudes could do much to control jail suicide, the most obvious and horrifying consequence of the inappropriate jailing of the mentally ill. But such reforms will have only a superficial impact as long as disturbed persons continue to be consigned to local jails in the first place.

Liaison between jails and public mental hospitals and the elimination of practices which bar or delay the transfer of disturbed inmates would be a limited help. State hospitals already are overcrowded and understaffed and cannot be expected to welcome patients transferred from the jails. Finally, there remains a serious question, for the individual prisoner, as to how much improvement the environment of a state mental hospital (an institution which also has been criticized) would represent over the jail.

A better, if more difficult plan to improve the lot of mentally ill jail inmates would be to increase the availability of a wide range of mental health care resources. The indigent inmate cannot readily be treated like the offender who can afford to pay for private

---

[48] Edwards, "Two Inmates Hanged Selves With Aid Only 6 Blocks Away," Washington *Post*, P.B.–1 March 19, 1973.

psychiatric services; even if the funds were available, the doctors are not. But the jail inmate who has the dual misfortune of being poor and mentally disturbed at least can be afforded the same types of care which are available in the free world through public community health centers.

For some inmates, this would mean bringing psychotherapists into the jails to conduct group therapy sessions. Through group work, inmates could be assisted in dealing with the immediate pressures of jail life, and even in beginning a longer-term course of recovery. Group therapy has proven its effectiveness—and its economy—with free patients.[49] In some cities, it is available even to the poor, through community mental health centers. Its use inside the jails of those same cities has not been reported.

For other jail inmates, participation in community mental health programs would mean a transfer, not to a distant custodial hospital, but to a short-term residential facility located in the community itself. Such facilities exist in growing numbers; their establishment represents part of a public health approach to mental illness which recognizes that temporary intervention often succeeds where warehousing fails.[50] Such facilities would be appropriate to receive seriously troubled prisoners who now languish in jail awaiting a trial or a competency hearing. Many of these prisoners pose no serious threat, except to themselves. There is no justification for a blanket policy under which these prisoners must be held only in secure facilities. Even for those disturbed inmates who do require custodial supervision, community treatment centers may still be a solution, since many of these centers maintain small "secure" wards. Other prisoners who are now being detained on account of their mental condition may need no residential care whatsoever and could be released pending a disposition of their cases, and assisted in making use of community mental health sources during the interim.

Overall there is a need for more judicial sensitivity to the problem of the mentally ill. Whenever a prisoner is detained in jail primarily because he is alleged to be mentally ill (pending civil

---

[49] See Harold I. Kaplan and Benjamin Sadock, *Comprehensive Group Psychotherapy* (Baltimore: Williams & Wilkins, 1971).
[50] See Glasscote, "The Community Mental Health Center: An Interim Appraisal" (American Psychiatric Association, 1969); and "Task Force Report No. 4: Community Mental Health Centers" (American Psychiatric Association, December 1972).

commitment proceedings) or denied pretrial release because of a suspected mental condition (pending a hearing on competency to stand trial), the committing authority should consider two questions.

First, it should ask what interest, if any, detention would serve. Too often, the detention of the mentally ill is a mere reflex, unrelated to any real social need or medical consideration. In other instances (competency examinations, for example), detention may serve only the convenience of the courts and their diagnostic arms—interests which should not be permitted to outweigh the potential harm to the person detained.

Second, if the committing authority finds that detention would serve some necessary, legitimate interest, it should consider whether some less restrictive alternative institution than the jail would serve as well, imposing fewer burdens on the prisoner and his prospective jailers.

The inappropriate detention of the mentally ill is not a problem which can be solved by jail administrators alone. It should not even be a problem of the criminal justice system. As long as the jails continue to be used as a dumping ground for the people society prefers to ignore, the jail will continue to be little more than a makeshift madhouse, a pointed reminder that the general liberalization of our public attitudes towards the mentally ill has yet to benefit the poorest, most unsophisticated and least powerful Americans.

4

NARCOTICS ADDICTS
IN JAIL

Chronic, compulsive self-administration of narcotic drugs today is generally regarded as a disease.[1] Yet most addicts are not under treatment in hospitals, community mental health clinics or physicians' offices. They are on the streets or behind bars. Dr. John Kramer, a psychiatric authority on the treatment of addicts, has observed cynically: "The only treatment modality available everywhere is prison or jail."[2]

THE HEROIN EPIDEMIC AND CRIMINAL RISK

Certain addicts are protected by status from prosecution. "Professional addicts"—physicians and nurses, who favor the synthetic narcotics such as Demerol—are seldom arrested or jailed. Rarely are the patients of private physicians who prescribe narcotics for non-medical purposes exposed and punished. "Medical addicts"— who receive authorized maintenance dosages of various opiumlike

[1] See, e.g., Joint Committee of the American Bar Association and the American Medical Association, *Drug Addiction: Crime or Disease* (Bloomington: Indiana Univ. Press, 1961); President's Advisory Commission on Narcotic and Drug Abuse Report (Washington, D.C.: Government Printing Office, 1963).
[2] Statement of Dr. John C. Kramer in "Narcotics Research, Rehabilitation and Treatment," Hearings before the Select Committee on Crime of the House of Representatives, 92d Cong., 1st sess., 665 (1971).

drugs for pain relief—are beyond the reach of the law. It is the
"street addicts," primarily the poor and unprotected, who are convicted as criminals because of their habit or activities related to
securing a supply of drugs to satisfy that habit. Hence, punitive
treatment of drug users is selective as to race and class and economic circumstances.

Estimates of the extent of narcotic addiction, and the rate of its
increase, have differed. The heroin "epidemic," however, was an
undeniable fact of American life in the late 1960's and early
1970's. Before its recent assimilation into the Drug Enforcement
Administration (DEA), the federal Bureau of Narcotics and Dangerous Drugs (BNDD) kept an estimated tally of narcotics
abusers: in 1968, 100,000 "addict-users"; in 1969, 315,000; in
1970, 524,000; in 1971, 559,000. In 1971, the director of the
National Institute of Mental Health (NIMH) gave Congress a
more conservative figure, noting that an accurate estimate was impossible: "Our best guess is a quarter of a million."[3] This was an
increase of 100 per cent over the NIMH estimate for 1970.
About a year later, it was reported that the new federal Special
Action Office for Drug Abuse Prevention (SAODAP) "leans toward . . . a national estimate of 300,000."[4] During the same
years, guesses as to the national growth rate of new addiction also
varied, but estimates as high as—or higher than—10 per cent annually were not uncommon.

Documentation of the heroin epidemic was reinforced by data
from major cities where the disease was prevalent. The Narcotics
Register maintained by the Health Services Administration listed an
increase in new "users" of 19,836 for New York in 1968;
31,770 in 1969; and 48,137 in 1970. The Mayor's Narcotics
Control Council estimated that between 1964 and 1970, 316,918
New Yorkers were "habitual and compulsive users" of narcotics
(heroin, morphine, Demerol and methadone).[5]

[3] Statement of Dr. Bertram Brown, "Narcotics Research, Rehabilitation and
Treatment," Hearings before the Select Committee on Crime of the House
of Representatives, 92d Cong., 2d sess., pt. 2, 440 (1971). In 1970, NIMH
had estimated only 125,000. As with all such increases, we cannot know
how much of this one was attributable to improved estimating techniques.
[4] Markham, "Heroin Addict Numbers Game," New York *Times,* June 6,
1972, p. 18.
[5] Burnham, "City's Drug Users Place at 300,000 in 7-Year Period," New York
Times, May 1, 1972, p. 1. Unlike the federal addict "Register" initiated by
BNDD and now maintained by DEA, the New York City Register is com-

A careful analysis of rates of death from narcotic overdose and self-reported narcotics use in selected sample populations in Washington, D.C., concluded that the local epidemic began between 1964 and 1966 and became "increasingly widespread at least through 1968."[6] In 1971, the Narcotics Treatment Administration (NTA) estimated that there were approximately 22,000 addicts in the District of Columbia.

Recent trends in the growth of addiction are more difficult to gauge. The federal government has retired from the business of estimating addiction nationwide, in part because it recognized that its efforts were compromised by insurmountable problems of definition and statistical method.

As is true of other social indices upon which public attention has focused, estimates of addiction tend to become unreliable as screening and reporting become more sensitive and more thorough; apparent incidence may increase more rapidly than real incidence. The BNDD's former estimates, for example, were based on the assumption that the ratio between an annual count of drug-law arrests involving "known addicts" (those whose names were reported to the bureau's Register by local law enforcement and public health authorities) and the total of known addicts equaled the ratio between an annual count of all drug law arrests and a total of all addicts, "known" and unknown. Either improved local record keeping or differential law enforcement was likely to be incorrectly reflected as apparent growth in the estimated addict census. The Register itself was criticized as almost wholly unreliable,[7] and private physicians probably concealed the identities of many addicts, as some apparently do also in the case of venereal disease, to protect persons regarded by the community as respectable and hence deserving of protection. Moreover, the steps BNDD took to correct for statistical bias in its estimates may have incor-

piled for research use only; in theory, its contents are not open to law enforcement agencies. Among the sources contributing names to this local compilation are hospitals and physicians, drug treatment programs and police. Some part of the 1968–70 increase is due to improved reporting. And of the 316,918 addicts, not all were still active in 1970. Even taking these qualifications into consideration, the data lends credibility to estimates that this city's addicts numbered at least 150,000 in the early seventies.

[6] Robert L. DuPont, "Profile of a Heroin Addiction Epidemic and an Initial Treatment Response," *N.E.J.M.* 285 (1971): 320.

[7] See William Butler Eldridge, *Narcotics and the Law* (New York: Amer. Bar Fndatn., 1962), pp. 66–78.

porated its policy biases; high figures were consistent with BNDD's position that conventional anti-drug law enforcement required intensification.

The task of estimating the current extent of addiction is further complicated by new evidence, which strongly suggests that some cities have "turned the corner" in efforts to combat its spread. In Washington, D.C., a close analysis of measures including drug arrests, opiate overdose deaths and treatment program records led researchers to conclude that that city's heroin epidemic hit peaks as early as 1969, and "appears to be waning" in 1973.[8] As of February 1973, NTA estimated that there were only 2,000 to 3,000 untreated heroin addicts in the District—a dramatic contrast with its estimates for earlier periods. In New York City, recent analyses of the Narcotics Register have led officials to conclude that heroin addiction is now "declining markedly."[9] It should be noted, however, that these data reflect the situation in two cities where the local heroin epidemic began early, and where efforts to combat it through combined law enforcement-treatment strategies have been particularly aggressive. Encouraging findings for Washington and New York are not inconsistent with the continued growth of heroin addiction in other urban—and non-urban—areas.

Despite the advice of reputable medical authorities, the typical "street" addict is treated not as a sick person but as a criminal.[10] Although the United States Supreme Court ruled in *Robinson* v.

---

[8] Robert L. DuPont and Mark H. Greene, "The Dynamics of a Heroin Addiction Epidemic," *Science* 181 (1973): 716.

[9] Farber, "Heroin Addiction is Reported Down," New York *Times,* September 9, 1973, p. 34.

[10] Throughout the following discussion, the term "addict" will be used to describe those inmates who come to local short-term prisons or detention facilities from the subculture of narcotics use. The term necessarily conceals the diversity of this population. Recognizing that some men and women involved in heroin use are either light or erratic consumers, some authorities favor general use of the broader label "addict-user." But the mere "user" is less likely than the compulsive consumer to be jailed, and does not require the same special treatment services. Alternative labels for the jailed heroin user's disease—ranging from the World Health Organization's preferred "drug dependence of the morphine type" to the fashionable euphemism "drug abuse" —are in some respects less serviceable than "addiction." Although the term "addict" does carry pejorative overtones, it is regularly employed by those who deal with narcotics users on a day-to-day basis; its use here should not be taken to imply a lack of compassion for the "addict," or a failure to recognize the complexity of the disease with which he is afflicted.

California[11] that the status of addiction, in itself, cannot be punished as a crime, every other aspect of an addict's life-style—including sale, possession or use of narcotic drugs, and possession of narcotics "paraphernalia" (syringes, glassine envelopes, improvised "cookers," etc.)—is penalized under federal, state and local criminal laws. In a number of jurisdictions, mere association with narcotics addicts has been made punishable.[12] But the middle-class or affluent users generally escape detection. Police seldom invade their homes and they need not resort to the streets for supply.

Poverty makes criminals of many addicts. The suburban teen-ager's habit may be financed by his parents directly or indirectly. But the ghetto youth, like the adult, often is unemployed or without resources, and thus moves into an endless round of acquisitive criminality to finance his habit. Heroin, the favored drug of "street addicts," is available only in the illicit market. Data on the cost of street heroin are derived almost exclusively from the reports of addicts themselves; even though the quest for prestige or the desire to obtain preferential medical treatment may lead addicts to overstate the price of their drug use, the average cost of a heroin habit ranges between twenty-five and fifty dollars per day.[13]

Data compiled by economist John Holahan suggest that only a tiny minority of the heroin customers, probably fewer than 5 per cent, support their habits legally.[14] Between 15 and 30 per cent traffic in drugs (taking the profits in cash or in kind), or perform services for dealers or traffickers to finance their personal needs.

[11] 370 U.S. 660 (1962).
[12] See Eldridge, *Narcotics and the Law,* pp. 149–93, for state laws forbidding "resort" to places where narcotics are used.
[13] In most cities, narcotics are the only habit-forming illicit drugs so expensive that large numbers of users must commit non-drug crimes. Where heroin use is suppressed, however, secondary crackdowns on once inexpensive drugs substituted by former heroin addicts—such as amphetamines—may produce new drug-related crime by driving up street prices. The tendency of former heroin addicts to substitute non-opiate drugs has been documented; there is no clear indication as to the effect this tendency ultimately may have on the price structure of the illicit market, or on the criminal conduct of its customers.
[14] John F. Holahan, "The Economics of Heroin," *Dealing with Drug Abuse* (Drug Abuse Survey Project, 1972), pp. 255, 289–93, citing Mark Moore, *Policy Concerning Drug Abuse in New York State,* Vol. III: *Economics of Heroin Distribution,* Croton-on-Hudson, N.Y.: (1970), p. 66.

Thus from 65 to 80 per cent or more must support their habits primarily through other criminal activities. For female addicts, prostitution is a typical choice; many male addicts specialize in burglaries. Minor property crimes which yield hard cash or readily salable merchandise—shoplifting, pickpocketing and other larcenies —also are common among addicts.

Because criminality is a symptom of the disease of addiction, the jails today are housing many of its victims. According to a 1969 study of the District of Columbia Jail, 45 per cent of all its inmates were addicted to heroin, probably a significant increase over previous years.[15] About forty "known addicts"—persons already familiar to law enforcement officials as heroin users—were booked into the D. C. Jail in 1958. By 1968, the number of annual "known addict" bookings was over 420, still only an undetermined fraction of the total number of addicts booked. Of this increase of 1,000 per cent in a decade, only a part can be attributed to improvements in police and custodial information gathering.

New York City's commissioner of correction stated in mid-1970 that of a one-day population of 14,324 jailed prisoners, 42 per cent of the men and 70 per cent of the women were "hard-core" narcotics addicts. Addiction rates among sentenced prisoners were roughly the same.[16] In late 1971 the city's Department of Correction estimated that half of its prisoners were addicts.

Denver's director of corrections reports that about 10 per cent of the city's jail inmates are charged with narcotics offenses, but that it is his "clinical impression" that about 40 per cent actually are addicts.[17] An official of the Georgia Narcotics Treatment Program (GNTP), in a recent interview, stated that 40 per cent of Atlanta area jail bookings after felony arrests involve heroin users.[18]

[15] Nicholas J. Kozel, Barry S. Brown and Robert L. DuPont, "A Study of Narcotics Addicted Offenders at the D. C. Jail," *Int'l J. Addictions* 7 (1972): 443. Adams, Meadows, and Reynolds, "Narcotic-involved Inmates in the Department of Corrections" (D. C. Department of Corrections Research Report No. 12, 1969).

[16] "Crime in America—Heroin Importation, Distribution, Packaging and Paraphernalia," Hearings before the Select Committee on Crime of the House of Representatives, 91st Cong., 2d sess., 215 (1970).

[17] Correspondence from William R. Nelson, director of corrections, Denver, Colorado, June 27, 1972, on file at Goldfarb and Singer, Washington, D.C.

[18] Wilson Parker, jail coordinator of GNTP, spoke on several occasions to my associate, Peter Jaszi. Interviews referred to in this chapter, and not

A special American Bar Association committee reported that according to recent "informal estimates," 33 per cent to 50 per cent of the holdups, burglaries, muggings and thefts in the nation's thirty-four major urban centers could be attributed to heroin addicts.[19] This situation can be used to generate a minimum estimate of the number of heroin addicts apprehended by police annually. Adding one third of more than 400,000 arrests for offenses correlated with heroin use (the categories of "robbery," "burglary," "housebreaking," "larceny-theft" and "prostitution and commercialized vice") reported to the FBI by police in cities with populations of over 250,000, to one half of the roughly 300,000 drug law arrests reported by all urban police departments, yields an annual total of almost 200,000 charges against addicts "cleared by arrest."[20] And almost every arrested addict represented in this total was held, for periods ranging from hours to months, in police lockups, courthouse bullpens, detention facilities and local jails.

It is a fact of street life that, at some point in his career, almost every street addict—that is, the urban poor, especially the minority group poor—will be jailed. Of 750 New York City addiction treatment patients ranging from twenty to fifty years of age, each of whom had used heroin for at least four years, 91 per cent had been jailed in the past.[21]

The user-victims of the drug trade are punished, but the commercial wholesalers of the trade, the major dealers and victimizers, remain almost immune from arrest and jailing. Their reliance on

described in the first person, were conducted on my behalf by Mr. Peter Jaszi in the summer and fall of 1972.

[19] American Bar Association, Special Committee on Crime Prevention and Control, "New Perspectives on Urban Crime" (1972), p. 25.

[20] This total, based on data contained in the FBI's *Uniform Crime Reports for the United States,* Washington, D.C.: Government Printing Office (1972) is conservative. The calculation errs in this direction in assuming that only one third of the offenses considered were committed by addicts, and in excluding altogether categories of offenses to which addicts are not especially prone; likewise, the assumption that only one half of all drug law violations are committed by addicts is almost certainly overgenerous. The failure of the FBI statistics to discount for multiple charges against single offenders probably is offset by the compulsive and repetitive nature of addicts' criminality, which makes them more liable to arrest than non-addicts committing similar offenses.

[21] Vincent P. Dole, Marie E. Nyswander, and Alan Warner, "Successful Treatment of 750 Criminal Addicts," *J.A.M.A.* 206 (1968): 2708, 2710.

subordinates and their private arrangements with corrupt law enforcement personnel often insulate major dealers. They will remain immune until new intensified efforts to reduce the heroin supply through vigorous investigation and prosecution of suppliers and wholesalers, like those of the new federal Drug Enforcement Agency (DEA), produce substantial results. Thus, the jails are used to punish those who are sick and in need of treatment. Those who have nurtured and spread the disease too often go free.

"TREATMENT" IN JAIL

The arrested addict usually is confined first in a station house lockup.[22] In these undersupervised and chronically overcrowded facilities, where medical attention is non-existent or is limited to first aid, the addict can expect to be overlooked—even if he is in severe withdrawal.

So far, he has been convicted of nothing. Technically, he's innocent until proved guilty. Yet he is, in effect, already punished. After hours or days in the lockup, the addict is taken to court for arraignment, often passing through a central holding jail, a courthouse tank or both. Those who are fortunate—relatively prosperous drug traffickers, prostitutes whose pimps will post cash bail, some first offenders—may post station house bail and leave the jailing system, returning to the street and to heroin. In most jurisdictions, they do so without having even been identified as addicts.

The least fortunate addict is without cash or contacts, and must await a bail hearing. He has begun to feel the effects of narcotic deprivation, and when he faces the judge who could order his release on personal recognizance or surety, he may be soaked in sweat, shaken by spasms and tormented by anxiety. His appearance does not inspire confidence; he is refused affordable bail and is packed off to the central jail to await trial.

In his cell, if he has avoided identification as an addict, he will have escaped the attention which could bring additional charges or an assignment to segregation within the jail. As described in

[22] Throughout the following discussion, attention will be concentrated on urban jailing.

Chapter 3, in most American jails medical screening at intake is non-existent, haphazard or perfunctory. There are few on-duty physicians. Available personnel lack either the experience to diagnose addiction, or the medical means to forestall withdrawal distress or to treat it symptomatically. Early signs of withdrawal may be overlooked in the confusion of processing, or noted and ignored.

The addict is now at least twelve or fifteen hours from his last injection of heroin. The intensity of his suffering will grow after the cell door closes. If he cries out loud enough, he may receive aspirin or tranquilizers in his cell. If he is seen in extreme withdrawal, he may be transferred to a medical cell or a local hospital. Too often, nothing is done:

> . . . [T]he other girl I had known on the street. I knew she was a confirmed addict. And when they had her in the house of detention, you see, they had one whole block which they called the tank, that is where they put all the drug addicts. If you are really sick they deadlock you, you don't come out of the cell for anything. The only way you can see—there is a little hole . . . and you can look through. . . . And I personally saw this girl lying on the floor—I don't want to make anyone sick but I am going to tell this—she was throwing up and it was actually black. I myself have thrown up kicking a habit, but I have never seen anything like that before—that was the worst I have ever seen.

> And we called the matron, and the matron said "let her alone, she will be all right, all those junkies are the same."

> The doctor in charge there said she didn't like drug addicts anyway; she used to say they were the lowest type of humanity—which I don't think is fair—however, one of the girls was working in the hospital when they took her to the hospital. They put her in a wheel chair and took her to the hospital, and when she got there she was dying, and they waited all this time to give her a shot of morphine. It was too late.

> Later on we learned from the girl who worked upstairs in the hospital that it was on her papers that she died from drug addiction.[23]

[23] Testimony of Beverly Lee Roman, "Illicit Narcotics Traffic Subcommission on the Improvement of the Federal Criminal Code," Hearings before the Committee on the Judiciary, U. S. Senate, pt. 2, 84th Cong., 1st sess., 554–55 (1955).

However extreme this case, "cold turkey" withdrawal and unsystematic or unscientific withdrawal treatment are typical of American jails. Many addicts entering jail after arrest for a high-risk street crime are already in early withdrawal; those who have "fixed" shortly before arrest must wait for the feared symptoms to begin.

The problem of withdrawal in the experience of the jailed addict, can, of course, be exaggerated. Some observers believe that because the purity of the heroin available on the street has decreased, some regular heroin users are now able to endure sudden deprivation without manifesting the classic withdrawal symptoms. Nevertheless, these are the symptoms which all jailed addicts fear, and which many jailed addicts do in fact suffer.

In 1700, an English physician observed that the sudden cessation of heavy opium eating led to

> Great, and even intolerable Distresses, Anxieties and Depressions of Spirits, which in a few days commonly end in almost miserable *Death,* attended by strange *Agonies.*[24]

Withdrawal from heroin and other narcotics can be fatal to the old, the weak and the sick; but unlike withdrawal from alcohol or barbiturates, it is not a threat to life in itself. However, the clinical prognosis makes little difference to the addict in withdrawal. Although some physicians regard withdrawal distress as psychosomatic, to the addict the experience is immediate and often terrifying. Here is one expert's description of the experience:

> About twelve hours after the last dose of morphine or heroin, the addict begins to grow uneasy. A sense of weakness overcomes him, he yawns, shivers, and sweats all at the same time while a watery discharge pours from the eyes and inside the nose. . . . For a few hours, he falls into an abnormal tossing, restless sleep . . . On awakening, eighteen to twenty-four hours after his last dose of the drug . . . [t]he yawning may become so violent as to dislocate the jaw, watery mucus pours from the nose and copious tears from the eyes. The pupils are widely dilated, the hair on the skin stands up and the skin itself is cold and shows the typical goose flesh which in the parlance of the addict is called "cold turkey." . . .
> . . . [h]is bowels begin to act with fantastic violence; great

[24] J. Jones, *The Mysteries of Opium Revealed,* quoted in Alethea Hayter, *Opium and the Romantic Imagination,* London: Faber and Faber (1968) p. 24.

waves of contraction pass over the walls of the stomach, causing explosive vomiting, the vomit being frequently stained with blood. So extreme are the contractions of the intestines that the surface of the abdomen appears corrugated and knotted . . . The abdominal pain is severe and rapidly increases. Constant purging takes place and as many as sixty large watery stools may be passed in a day. . . .

. . . [I]n a desperate effort to gain comfort from the chills that rack his body he covers himself with every blanket he can find. His whole body is shaken by twitchings and his feet kick involuntarily, the origin of the addict's term, "kicking the habit."

Throughout the period of withdrawal the unfortunate addict obtains neither sleep nor rest. . . . As he neither eats nor drinks he rapidly becomes emaciated and may lose as much as ten pounds in twenty-four hours. . . . The symptoms begin to subside of themselves by the sixth or seventh day, but the patient is left desperately weak, nervous, restless and often suffers from stubborn colitis.[25]

When the potency of street heroin is low, even those with expensive habits suffer less intensely, and for shorter periods. Addicts' experiences differ according to their age, overall physical health, duration and pattern of heroin use, use of other drugs in combination with heroin; and the environment of withdrawal. Dr. Andrew Weil says that in a supportive setting with strong positive suggestion, a heroin addict can undergo comfortable withdrawal with no medication other than aspirin.[26]

There can be no worse place to withdraw than a noisy, cramped, unsanitary cell surrounded by bitter, frightened prisoners, watched by apathetic or hostile keepers, with little to anticipate except conviction and sentence.

Withdrawal distress may even be reinforced by law enforcement officials as a device to help them trap pushers, and informers may be recruited in jail by the police. Conventional drug law enforcement depends heavily on the services of addict-informers, and the station house lockup is a rich potential source of "stool pigeons." In 1965, Alfred Lindesmith described some of the tactics used:

The police sometimes offer an addict leniency if he agrees to turn

25 Robert S. DeRopp, *Drugs and the Mind,* New York: St. Martin's Press (1957), pp. 152–54.
26 Andrew Weil, "Altered Status of Consciousness," in *Dealing with Drug Abuse* (Drug Abuse Survey Project, A Report to the Ford Foundation), New York: Praeger (1972), pp. 324, 333.

in one or more peddlars. The most effective reward of all is that the informer may be allowed to continue his habit, at least temporarily.

The most effective punishment used to induce addicts to talk and to cooperate is, of course, the withdrawal distress. This is frequently supplemented, depending upon the inclinations of the police officer, by all the usual third-degree tactics. The low social status of the addict and his characteristic lack of means make the use of rough tactics relatively attractive and safe.

In view of the addict's unusual vulnerability to police pressure it is small wonder that the narcotics police in some cases have estimated that fifty percent or more of those arrested break down under pressure and agree to cooperate.[27]

While the use of withdrawal as a lever probably has been curtailed by recent court decisions circumscribing "custodial interrogation," and while the abuses described by Lindesmith can occur only in the early phase of pretrial jailing, it is nevertheless noteworthy that some jailers may have a positive interest in aggravating the addict's suffering.

The private suffering of jailed addicts seldom evokes much concern, but the public consequences of withdrawal compel attention. Suicide is the most forceful cry of help an addict can make. Urban jails are plagued by high rates of attempted and completed inmate suicide; and suicides are often addicts. Death has been their only available relief from horror and anxiety. As of 1971, in New York City jails, "twenty-two of our thirty five suicides over the past four years were drug addicts."[28] The city's commissioner of correction described his system's experience:

> We get a higher percentage of drug addicts who are successful in ending their lives than non-addicts and we find that the addicts commonly do end their lives within a very short period after their confinement, within 1, 2 or 3 days. Again, it is part of the depression associated with withdrawal.[29]

[27] A. Lindesmith, *The Addict and the Law* (New York: Vintage, 1965), pp. 47–48.
[28] "Proposal for Department of Correction—Methadone Detoxification in Detention" (mimeographed, n.d.), p. 3.
[29] Testimony of George McGrath, "Crime in America—Heroin Importation, Distribution, Packaging and Paraphernalia," Hearings before the Select Committee on Crime of the House of Representatives, 91st Cong., 2d sess., 217–18 (1970).

The suicidal impulse of an addict-inmate can outlast his overt withdrawal symptoms. One psychiatric expert says, "Coming off drugs is like plunging into a cold stream. Realization of past behavior becomes very real, too real. It becomes distorted, and a tremendous feeling of guilt sets in."[30]

The anguish of jail withdrawal can also lead to random violence. The uprisings in New York City's Manhattan Men's House of Detention (the "Tombs") in October 1970 were attributed to a variety of causes. Chief among them was the inadequate medical management of addict-prisoners in an overcrowded jail where about half the population were addicts:

> If an addict is forced to experience [withdrawal] symptoms without medical treatment while locked in a cell, he becomes resentful and violent, or despondent. Crowding together resentful and violent individuals can lead to a riot.[31]

CONTRABAND TRAFFIC

Some inmates never withdraw completely from drugs; they maintain their habits in jail. In fact, one client told me his brother was "hooked" on drugs while in jail; before that he had not used drugs. The underground economy of urban jails facilitates drug traffic. "Time-men"—short-term sentenced prisoners who are free on bond before sentencing—often bring narcotics into jail. One ex-addict recalled preparing for court by concealing a condom stuffed with heroin in his rectum:

> So when I finally landed in the hypo tank for a ninety-day jolt, I was ready to do something for the guys there . . . And of course, the Trustee. We had to take care of him. We gave a mail-runner a buck or two to bring us a hypodermic and I had had no trouble squeezing the stuff out, and we all fixed.[32]

Even a small syringe can be smuggled by the same technique.

Bizarre isolated incidents underline the difficulty of testing secu-

[30] Dr. Ephraim Ramirez, quoted in "No One Cares," *Newsweek*, March 2, 1970, p. 52.
[31] "Proposal for Department of Correction—Methadone Detoxification in Detention," p. 2.
[32] Guy Endore, *Synanon* (Garden City, N.Y.: Doubleday, 1968), p. 27.

rity measures against inmates' ingenuity. Recently, for example, a Detroit inmate was discovered to be receiving heroin in the hollow buttons of a jacket he had repeatedly been permitted to send out for dry cleaning.[33] Narcotics and narcotics paraphernalia reach inmates through visitors and in mail. In the mid-fifties, Philadelphia had to struggle to stem the flow of heroin-laden birthday cards.[34]

More generally, it is difficult or impossible to catch narcotic contraband hidden in visitors' clothes or taped to their bodies without turning a local jail into a maximum security prison. And in any event, poorly paid and corrupt jail employees directed by inmate-dealers, or operating as independent entrepreneurs, are the inmates' most important source. Jail employees usually can deal with near impunity, and the temptation is great. An analysis of the Law Enforcement Assistance Administration's *1970 National Jail Census* shows that the salaries of line officers and non-professional civilian employees average no more than $500 per month. And, in Atlanta, to take one example, a bag of heroin which brings eight dollars on the street reportedly goes for fifty dollars in the City Jail.

A 1970 crackdown on inmate drug use at the Jefferson Parish Jail near New Orleans, Louisiana, required the firing of seven guards.[35] In 1972, investigations of institutions as diverse as the Nassau County Jail in Mineola, New York, and the City Jail in Baltimore, Maryland, revealed extensive narcotics traffic and widespread staff complicity. Indictments are pending against several former guards at the Long Island facility[36] and in Baltimore, a special grand jury heard reports that inmates could

approach one of the guards engaged in trafficking and request him to go to a certain location, where he would be given money. The

---

[33] Knight, "Heroin Follows Victims Behind County Jail Bars," Detroit *Free Press,* November 22, 1970.

[34] See testimony of Randolph E. Wise, commissioner of correction, "Illicit Narcotics Traffic," Hearings before the Subcommittee on Improvements in the Federal Criminal Code of the Committee on the Judiciary, U. S. Senate, 84th Cong., 1st sess., pt. 2, 530 (1955).

[35] Filiatreau, "Shooting Up," New Orleans *Courier-Journal,* August 31, 1970 at 1, col.

[36] "Jail Investigations by Prisoners," *NCCD News,* May–June 1972, p. 4; Andelman, "Sheriff of Nassau Suspends 16 Guards," New York *Times,* June 13, 1972.

guard would then bring in as much as a bundle (twenty-five bags) of heroin into the jail . . .

[A] youthful inmate stated, in the presence of the guards, that if he were given $10.00 it would take him approximately fifteen minutes to get a bag of heroin.

Shakedown searches had uncovered hypodermic syringes in the Baltimore cellblocks. An inmate who arrived at the city court-house, having been brought under guard from the jail, turned over five bags of heroin to police. One prisoner in "medical isola-tion"—separated by three secure steel doors from all other sections of the jail—had succeeded in obtaining and injecting an overdose of heroin. Attempts to apprehend trafficking officers had failed; when a "strip-search" of employees had been ordered to expose a suspected smuggler, "the guard ran out of the jail and has yet to return."[37]

Once inside the jail, heroin moves as easily as—or even more easily than—other contraband. A Detroit reporter learned in 1970 that heroin reached prisoners through the antiquated ventilation system:

As the grates are in the same place in every cell, and because there is a small space between the floor and the wall on the other side of the grate, it is possible for an inmate on the sixth floor to lower heroin to a friend on the second floor, with neither man having to move from his inevitably dark, bug-infested cell.[38]

The addicted inmate is a willing captive of the smugglers sup-plying the jail. He takes what he can get and with it high risks from variation in quality and adulteration of the drug. He injects drugs in a filthy setting with a communal hypodermic and with high risk of infections. Narcotics-related deaths in urban jails are grim testi-mony to the inmates' persistence.[39] When narcotics are unavail-able, they will attempt to steal or deal to obtain some reputedly euphorogenic substance from the jail infirmary. Deprived of all drugs, they may even risk injecting themselves with such "bizarre

[37] "Report of the January 1972 Term—Extended, Grand Jury of Baltimore City, In re: The Baltimore City Jail" (mimeographed, July 1972).
[38] Knight, "Heroin Follows Victims."
[39] See, e.g., Petaeque, "Inmates on Dope: Autopsies," Chicago *Sun-Times*, September 13, 1970.

drug substitutes as plain water from the tap, Kool-Aid, and lukewarm coffee . . ."[40]

RELEASE, RELAPSE AND READDICTION

The addict who is held in jail for any length of time, without a contact in the contraband narcotics traffic, will be forced to withdraw—sometimes with medical assistance, but usually without. The addict who eventually makes bond, whose charges are dropped, who receives a sentence of probation or who serves out time on a short jail sentence, returns almost inevitably to heroin use, often within hours of leaving jail. Relapse and readdiction are the result.

The relapse rates which characterize addicts released from jail have not been measured directly. They can, however, be judged by the performance of analogous groups of detoxified users. Of a sample of voluntary patients who returned to New York City from the U. S. Public Health Service Hospital at Lexington, Kentucky, after an average of six weeks of detoxification treatment and enforced abstinence, 91 per cent relapsed within six months of discharge; after their initial relapses, some of these addicts reattained abstinence, but the majority did not.[41] On returning to the community, they experienced needs and pressures similar to those which first led them to drug use; the handicaps generated by a history of addiction were not easily exorcised.

Traditionally, the detoxified addict has been regarded as "cured" when his physical dependence on narcotics, of which withdrawal distress is symptomatic, appears to be at an end. Today, it is generally recognized that addiction outlasts detoxification. A "cured" addict's tendency to relapse has been attributed by some investigators to environmental pressures and by others to personality de-

---

[40] Filiatreau, "Shooting Up."

[41] Many of these patients were "voluntary" only in contrast to the Lexington patients actually serving sentences for federal offenses. The "voluntary" group included many addicts who had been offered self-referral to Lexington as an informal alternative to prosecution in jurisdictions without local addiction treatment resources. For a description of the "revisionist approach" to the Lexington experience, which suggests that statistics bearing on initial relapse, read alone, only supply an overly discouraging perspective on the detoxified addict's fate, see James V. DeLong, "Treatment and Rehabilitation," in *Dealing with Drug Abuse*, p. 185.

fects. "Metabolic" theorists of addiction argue that addiction causes permanent physiological changes. Other medical commentators maintain that "secondary" withdrawal symptoms, such as minor abnormalities in blood pressure, heart rate and respiratory functioning, persist for months after the classical "primary" withdrawal symptoms disappear and may prompt the detoxified addict to seek relief in heroin.[42] Psychological conditioning is also cited as a cause of relapse; it is notable that even ex-addicts who have served long drug-free prison sentences sometimes experience the early symptoms of withdrawal, and hence a stimulus to renewed drug use, when they return to the neighborhoods where their addiction was spawned.[43]

Treatment of jailed addicts is not, on the whole, humane. Even if it were it would not prevent relapse and readdiction on release. Released addict-inmates require help in finding effective medical treatment if they are to escape the subculture of criminal addiction. And, beyond treatment, addicts require the means of achieving adequate lives without illegal drugs. But the primary question remains—how can society justify treatment of the sick by confining them in jail; especially addict-inmates, so many of whom generally do desire help. Among short-term sentenced addicts interviewed in 1968 at New York City's Riker's Island Penitentiary, a majority were said to desire treatment for their addiction.[44] Addicts studied in the District of Columbia Jail also appeared to wish to stop their drug use, and to be receptive to participation in community treatment programs.[45]

A HISTORY OF ADDICTION AND DETOXIFICATION

Early in the twentieth century, a large number of Americans—estimates vary from 100,000 to 1,000,000—were addicted to nar-

[42] W. R. Martin et al., "Tolerance to and Physical Dependence on Morphine in Rats," *Psychopharmacologia* 4 (1963): 247.
[43] See Jerome Jaffee, "Narcotic Analgesics," in Louis S. Goodman and Alfred Gilman, eds., *The Pharmalogical Basis of Therapeutics* (New York: Macmillan, 1970).
[44] New York City, Department of Correction, "Methadone Detoxification Detention—Background and Theory" (mimeographed, n.d.), p. 1.
[45] Kozel, Brown, and DuPont, "A Study of Narcotics Addicted Offenders at the D. C. Jail."

cotic drugs. Addicts came from every class and calling; their condition generally was ignored or tolerated. Morphine, an opium derivative, first used widely in this country as a pain killer on Civil War field hospitals, had become "God's Own Medicine" to physicians and drugstore customers. In 1880, one medical text listed fifty-four diseases (including nymphomania and alcoholism) which could be treated by morphine injections. Many patients did, however, become addicts in the course of medical treatment. Others "doctored" themselves. Many white, middle-class women, for example, took inexpensive narcotics orally—no prescription needed —purchasing them either by name or compounded in innocuously labeled patent medicines like Mrs. Winslow's Soothing Syrup.

The nature of the American addict population was to change quickly and dramatically. By the 1920's, most of the nation's narcotics users were to be found among the urban poor, and jails had begun to receive a new type of inmate, the "criminal addict." Local detention facilities and short-term correctional institutions were wholly unprepared to receive these prisoners. Yet as early as 1914, an estimated 1 per cent of the 16,000 annual admissions to Manhattan's City Prison were "narcotic habitues,"[46] many of whom were youths sixteen or eighteen with several years of drug use already behind them, and almost none of whom had begun as "medical addicts."

The federal Harrison Act of 1914, criminalizing possession or use of non-prescription narcotics, and the tide of restrictive state and local legislation which preceded and accompanied it, drove the use of morphine, heroin and codein underground, and provided a business bonanza for the underworld. The fear that widespread narcotics addiction would somehow produce a wave of crime and depravity spurred the enactment of these statutes.[47] The statutes were to become self-fulfilling prophecies.

Enforcement of these new laws made addicts into outlaws, dependent on an illicit market for their supply. It prompted many to abandon drug use, but thousands of others formed the core of

[46] Perry M. Lichtenstein, "Narcotic Addiction," *N.Y. Med. J.* 100 (November 14, 1914): 962.
[47] For a description of the semi-hysterical public reaction to the disclosure of the prevalence of drug use in early twentieth-century America, and the perverse medico-legal response, see David F. Musto, *The American Disease* (New Haven: Yale Univ. Press, 1973).

a new "criminal-addict subculture."[48] In a matter of years, the addiction in America lost its heterogeneous and middle-class character; it was transformed into a disease of the poor and, by definition and necessity, into a disease with criminal overtones.

In 1937, Dr. Ben Reitman, who had been a physician at two major midwestern jails and a "prisoner in about fifty jails throughout America," observed:

> . . . I am certain that the majority of all drug addicts have their genesis in the Underworld. . . . For the past ten years it has been difficult for a drug addict to legitimately, legally obtain drugs. The largest source of narcotics is in the Underworld. And most drug addicts have to have an Underworld connection to obtain them.[49]

This "underworld" was not the organized crime we know today, but the society of "prostitutes, pimps, and criminals," the natural, inevitable local milieu of the typical addict, then and now.

As the new subculture of addiction emerged, heroin rapidly became its staple. Discovered in 1898, heroin was first hailed as a "non-addictive" opium derivative, and employed as a cure for morphine addiction. By 1924, its addictive properties were apparent, and its importation and manufacture were banned by federal law. Many European physicians still prefer heroin over other analgesics, but it has been excluded from America's legitimate pharmacopoeia. Illicit traffickers came to favor it over morphine because its powder is easier to conceal and market than vials of the liquid morphine, and three to four times more potent. As heroin became more widely and inexpensively available than morphine, consumers too came to prefer it.

This new preference was reflected in the histories of the growing numbers of narcotics users who found their way to jail. In 1930, almost 84 per cent of a sample of addicted defendants from

---

[48] For an account of the differing impacts of anti-drug law enforcement on members of one local population of addicts, see J. Ball, *Narcotic Addiction in Kentucky* (1971). For a sociological analysis of the process by which the "dominant culture" created the new subculture, see David W. Maurer, "The Subculture of the Criminal Narcotic Addict," in *Drug Abuse; Data and Debate,* Paul Blachly, ed., Springfield, Ill.: Charles C. Thomas (1969), p. 14.
[49] Bingham Dai, *Opium Addiction in Chicago* (Montclair, N.J.: Patterson Smith Reprint Series, 1970), p. 42. Bingham Dai's 1937 study is a valuable collection of case histories and sociological observations documenting the emergence of the criminal addict subculture in the "Second City," a process somewhat more gradual than that reported in retrospective studies focusing on New York.

the New York City criminal courts were heroin users;[50] only sixteen years before, it had been reported, "the drug used for hypodermic injection is almost always morphine."[51]

The shift to heroin coincided with the virtual abandonment of the addict population by the medical profession. Many responsible physicians had found the treatment of addicts frustrating and unrewarding, even before narcotics users became the focus of public fear and legal sanctions. After this transformation, most of the small number of physicians who risked disgrace—and possible prosecution—as "dope doctors" were decidedly unprofessional in their dealings with addict "patients." The Harrison Narcotics Act of 1914—on its face a revenue and information-gathering measure —had placed no limits on a doctor's discretion to dispense narcotics to addicts. It restricted narcotics transfers by individuals, drug companies and pharmacies, but exempted prescriptions for "legitimate medical purposes," made in the course of professional practice "by registered and licensed physicians."

Federal law enforcement agencies, however, immediately began to usurp the medical profession's power of self-regulation, arguing that prescriptions to addicts could not be "legitimate."[52] Under the Treasury Department's interpretation, unregistered persons found in possession of narcotics were subject to the criminal penalties of the act; so, also, were private doctors prescribing narcotics to maintain addicts' habits or even to relieve the suffering of addicts cut off from their supplies.

Rulings of the Supreme Court were cited to support the interpretation. By 1922, it appeared that the Harrison Act allowed for no medical dispensation of narcotics to addicts except as part of an institutional detoxification "cure."[53] One historian of ad-

---

[50] Half were charged with possession of drugs and half with non-drug offenses. "Report of the Mayor's Committee on Drug Addiction to the Honorable Richard C. Patterson, Jr., Commissioner of Corrections, New York City," *Am. J. Psych.* 87 (1930): pp. 433, 437.

[51] Lichtenstein, "Narcotic Addiction."

[52] In the Treasury, enforcement duties initially were assigned to the Internal Revenue Service; it was succeeded by the Prohibition Bureau, and in 1930 by the Bureau of Narcotics. In 1968, it became the Bureau of Narcotics and Dangerous Drugs, and was transferred to the Department of Justice. Today, federal anti-drug policing is conducted by Justice's Drug Enforcement Administration (DEA).

[53] The leading cases in this series are *Webb* v. *United States,* 249 U.S. 96 (1919); *Jin Fuey Moy* v. *United States,* 254 U.S. 189 (1920); and *United States* v. *Behrman,* 258 U.S. 280 (1922).

diction noted that, since "addicts were not accepted at hospitals," this exception was "mainly theoretical."[54]

In 1925, in *Linder* v. *United States* the Supreme Court ruled that the prescription of narcotics to alleviate withdrawal was proper, and that "good faith" in treatment of addiction was a medical, and not a legal, issue.[55] This decision failed to change the patterns of Harrison Act enforcement. Soon after *Linder,* Treasury officials sought congressional confirmation of the broad role they had assumed.[56] When this drive failed, they continued to enforce the Harrison Act as they had before 1925. As one commentator, Rufus King, has noted: "Doctors were bullied and threatened, and those who were adamant went to prison. . . . The addict-patient vanished, and the addict-criminal emerged in his place."[57] King has estimated that 5,000 doctors were imprisoned for Harrison Act violations between 1914 and 1938.

Even today, official publications interpreting federal narcotic laws ignore the *Linder* opinion, or circumvent it.[58] Law enforcement policy on the discretion of the private physician was frozen by administrative fiat in the restrictive posture of the early 1920's.

In general, physicians have no guidelines to indicate how and when they may prescribe narcotics to addicts without risking prosecution. Prescriptions for heroin are, of course, absolutely forbidden, and recent regulations promulgated by the Food and Drug Administration (FDA) effectively bar private physicians from prescribing the synthetic narcotic methadone to private addict-patients. No such directives exist, however, where the vast majority of other narcotics, including morphine, are concerned.

[54] Lindesmith, *The Addict and the Law,* p. 7.
[55] *Linder* v. *United States,* 268 U.S. 5 (1925).
[56] See Musto, *The American Disease,* pp. 187–89.
[57] King, "Law Enforcement Policies," 22 *Law and Contemporary Problems* 113 (1957). See James V. DeLong, "Treatment and Rehabilitation," in Ford Foundation Report *Dealing with Drug Abuse,* pp. 173, 176. For an account of the federal harassment which ended one well-intentioned Philadelphia physician's attempts to treat addicts as patients in the mid-fifties, see "Illicit Narcotics Traffic," Hearings before the Subcommittee on the Improvements in the Federal Criminal Code of the Committee on the Judiciary, U. S. Senate, 84th Cong., 1st sess., pt. 2, 444 (1955).
[58] The preceding discussion draws on several sources. Among the most useful are Lindesmith's *The Addict and the Law,* especially Chap. 1; Rufus King's "The Harrison Narcotics Act: Jailing the Healers and the Sick," 62 *Yale L. J.* 736 (1953); and a recent note, "Methadone Maintenance and the Heroin Addict," 69 *Yale L. J.* 1175 (1969).

Any proscribed prescription to a known addict may lead to suspension from practice, crushing legal fees and possible conviction. The general abdication of responsibility for the treatment of addiction by private physicians was, therefore, understandable.[59]

As physicians ceased to prescribe drugs to addicts in the 1920's and early thirties, morphine gave way in popularity to heroin, the favorite of drug peddlers. Addicts discovered the evils of dilution, uncertain supply and price manipulation. They learned firsthand the peculiar dangers of chronic, unsupervised self-administration of narcotics uncertain in quality and potency: unexpected overdoses, poisoning from toxic adulterants, and "needle infections" like viral hepatitis, malaria and endocarditis.

The penal system took over from the medical system. Prison administrators and jailers replaced physicians as the administrators of the addicts' fate. Reporting in 1930 on the New York statutes which presaged the Harrison Act, a panel observed that

> . . . the endeavor to control the spread of drugs by these restrictive and punitive measures did not control the situation. They forced the courts to take cognizance of the crime of possession of narcotics, and to place the responsibility for the rehabilitation of these addicts on the penal institutions during the period of custodial care.[60]

This development was hardly desirable. Although no effective treatment for addiction was known to medicine in the early twentieth century, anti-drug law enforcement had the effect of relieving any pressure on the medical community to discover such a treatment. In the meantime, the practical, short-term medical needs of jailed addicts too often were unmet. Jails—institutions designed for "custodial care" of prisoners awaiting disposition and serving short sentences—were totally unequipped to care for addicts.

Ironically, the quality and humanity of the short-term care available to jailed addicts diminished as the addict-prisoner became a more familiar type of inmate. In 1923,

---

[59] The Harrison Act has been superseded by the Comprehensive Drug Abuse Prevention and Treatment Act of 1970, P.L. 91–616, which relies on the federal power to regulate interstate commerce, rather than on the federal taxing power, for its sanction. Like the old act, however, the new one leaves physicians in legal limbo.

[60] "Report of the Mayor's Committee on Drug Addiction to the Honorable Richard C. Patterson, Jr.," pp. 433, 447.

. . . the workhouse alone in New York City handled 1,292 cases
that were either sentenced for violating the sanitary code (possession or selling) or were self-committed for cure, and there was a
total of 2,663 cases committed to institutions with drug addiction.
Those not sent to the workhouse were committed to the penitentiary, the New York City Reformatory, or the city prisons.[61]

These figures, referring only to sentenced prisoners self-identified
as addicts or convicted of drug offenses, grossly understated the
size of the addicted inmate population in New York City's jails at
the time. When it is considered that the quality of the narcotics
then available through illicit channels was high, the dimensions
of the narcotic withdrawal problem in the city's cellblocks can be
imagined. Since 1914, addicts in some New York City institutions
had been receiving narcotic detoxification treatment as a matter
of course; morphine injections of diminishing potency were administered to addicts serving short sentences, many of whom had
been hustled briskly from the streets into the City Prison.[62] This
treatment had the effect of minimizing, although not eliminating,
the stress and discomfort associated with withdrawal.

Morphine detoxification continued to be provided for some
sentenced prisoners in New York City into the 1930's. In a recent
interview, former Commissioner of Correction (1934–40) Austin
MacCormick recalled the routine early in his administration: for
seven to ten days, addict-inmates at the Correctional Hospital on
Welfare Island would insert their arms into a slot like "the window
in a cashier's gate" to receive injections. The regimen was hardly
individualized, but the treatment worked. Unfortunately, it was
difficult to administer; to be effective, morphine must be given
intravenously three or four times a day. Also, the diversion of
morphine supplies to prisoners not in treatment was a constant
danger. The availability of detoxification services could not grow
in pace with the growth of the addict population in the jails; and
this medical service was gradually curtailed.

In 1930, a New York City blue-ribbon medical panel concluded
that while non-narcotic drugs were nearly useless in relieving
withdrawal, every addict should be withdrawn as rapidly as was
consistent with his long-term physical health, and that younger

[61] Lawrence Kolb, "Drug Addiction in Its Relation to Crime," *Mental Hygiene* IX (1925): pp. 74, 85.
[62] Lichtenstein, "Narcotic Addiction."

addicts should be withdrawn without any decreasing-dose morphine treatment. Members of the panel believed that abrupt withdrawal has a "very impressive mental effect . . . with a striking
feeling of relief when . . . over," while morphine detoxification
"subconsciously impresses on [addicts'] minds that they need
the narcotic to control their symptoms."[63] These comments presaged an argument that local correctional administrators would
later use to justify their failure to provide treatment to addict-
inmates—that the rigors of withdrawal are a first step in moral
and psychological regeneration. Such a rationale appears in-
distinguishable from the assertion that the addict deserves to suffer
for his disease. It was this type of super-moralism that spurred
the criminal narcotics epidemic, impeded innovative response
to the epidemic, and compounded the problem it provoked.

By the 1940's, New York City's early experiments with morphine detoxification in jail had been forgotten; other, less effective regimens, employing a variety of mild non-narcotic
tranquilizing drugs such as chlorpromazine, were in use with
addict-inmates. Tranquilizer treatment, which is still the best medical care for addicts in withdrawal which most jails have to offer,
does simplify the jailer's work. Tranquilizers can subdue some
overt symptoms of acute withdrawal, including muscle spasms and
insomnia, and make for a quieter jail. But they do not address
the causes of withdrawal distress, or alleviate its subjective symptoms. Nor do they help the addict who has passed out of the acute
phase of withdrawal, and is suffering the subtler symptoms of
the chronic phase. For certain addicts, tranquilizers may make
withdrawal worse.[64]

Ironically, in-jail tranquilizer treatment was superior to the care
offered by New York City's public hospitals, which maintained a
closed-door policy toward street addicts in withdrawal into the
1950's; precisely because some of those who were ill sought to
be jailed, the quality of in-jail treatment was reduced yet again.
One prison psychiatrist reported:

> Addicts . . . would provoke their own arrest—on vagrancy or
> other minor charges—in order to receive a short sentence during

[63] "Report of the Mayor's Committee on Drug Addiction, to the Honorable
Richard C. Patterson, Jr.," pp. 433, 446, 518.
[64] Jaffee, "Narcotic Analgesics."

which the prison would provide medical attention for withdrawal symptoms.

But, he went on,

Toward the end of the decade . . . The city prisons refused to treat addicts, discouraged their imprisonment for medical help, and in effect rejected them from the jails they were substituting for adequate hospitals . . .[65]

Addicts were pariahs everywhere. Eventually services for poor voluntary addict-patients did develop at certain institutions, like Manhattan's Riverside Hospital. But addicts committed to jail still received no effective withdrawal treatment of any kind.

The history of addiction and in-jail detoxification in New York City is not typical of every American jurisdiction. Since at least 1914, New York has led the nation consistently in its local addict census; on occasion, it has led as well in innovative responses to the problem of addiction. The early experiments with morphine detoxification in the city's jails were one example. In most jurisdictions, historical short-term care for jailed addicts has been consistently as inadequate and inhumane as was the care offered in New York during the 1950's and sixties. Significantly, it was in the jails of New York City that the value of one promising if controversial approach to institutional detoxification was tested in the early 1970's.

SCIENTIFIC METHADONE DETOXIFICATION

A simple and inexpensive system of narcotic detoxification, employing methadone, has been available for more than twenty-five years. Methadone is a wholly synthetic narcotic with properties which make it unique among opioid drugs: when administered orally, it suppresses withdrawal symptoms for twenty-four to thirty-six hours, far longer than either morphine or heroin. De-

[65] Yves Joseph Kron and Edward M. Brown, *Mainline to Nowhere: The Making of a Heroin Addict* (New York: Pantheon, 1965), p. 74. As an addict's heroin use continues, his so-called "tolerance" increases rapidly. After a brief period of addiction, he may require fifty dollars' worth of drugs to produce the euphoric effect he once obtained from ten dollars' worth. Withdrawal or detoxification diminishes tolerance, and allows the addict to begin again with an inexpensive habit.

veloped to meet Germany's shortage of opium-based pain-killers
in the late years of the Second World War, it was originally chris-
tened Dolophine after Adolph Hitler, an interesting bit of history
since some critics now charge that its use is a fascistic genocidal
conspiracy by the establishment against blacks.[66]

Shortly after the war, physicians at the U. S. Public Health
Service Hospital at Lexington, Kentucky, a prison-like institution
housing addicted federal prisoners and voluntary patients, found
that methadone could be used for detoxification as effectively as
morphine, and more efficiently.[67] A single daily oral dose of
methadone did the work of three or four intravenous morphine
detoxification doses. Dr. Nathan Eddy, a distinguished medical
authority, recently wrote that "[T]he employment of oral methadone substitutes [is] an almost routine means of minimizing the
withdrawal sickness whatever the opiate upon which the patient
is dependent."[68]

Methadone detoxification was unknown in jails until 1969, and
remains a rarity today. The first American short-term facility to
employ the procedure was the District of Columbia Jail, where
an administrative order outlining a detoxification routine was promulgated in late 1969; unfortunately, the terms of that order
have never been fully implemented. The procedure was introduced at the Milwaukee County Jail and the San Diego County
Jail in 1970,[69] and is used now at city or county jails serving New
York City, Denver, Buffalo, Washington, D.C., and Cincinnati; in
1973, it was being planned for Miami and Atlanta, among other

[66] These critics refer, of course, to its use in methadone *maintenance,* a long-
term therapeutic technique which along with methadone *detoxification* relies
on a common chemical agent.

[67] Isbell et al., "Tolerance and Addiction Liability of 6-dimethylamino-4-4-
diphenyl-Heptanone-3 (methadon)," *J.A.M.A.* 135 (1947): 888.

[68] Nathan Eddy, "Methadone Maintenance for the Management of Persons
with Drug Dependence of Morphine Type" (Washington, D.C.: Government
Printing Office, Bureau of Narcotics and Dangerous Drugs, mimeographed,
n.d.) p. 3. The phenomenon of "cross-tolerance," permits the free substitution of one narcotic for another in an addict's regimen, including the substitution of synthetic narcotics for opium-based preparations.

[69] San Diego authorities operate under a provision of the California Code
which mandates "medical aid as necessary to ease any symptoms of withdrawal" for the addict in custody, and a general discussion of detoxification
alternatives; for an account of the legal challenge which prompted the voluntary adoption of a plan in San Diego, see Goldin, "Methadone Detoxification:
A Non-Controversial Solution to In-Custody Narcotics Withdrawal," 47
Cal. S. Bar J. 14 (1972).

cities.[70] The comprehensive New York City detoxification system is a model.

In March 1971, New York City's Commissioner of Correction Benjamin Malcolm invited Dr. Vincent Dole, an expert on addiction therapy, to review treatment of addicts in city jails. Since mid-1970, a limited number of detainees had been receiving methadone detoxification at small clinics in the Tombs and in the dismal and ancient Women's House of Detention on lower Manhattan; acute cases could be transferred to the Riker's Island Reformatory Infirmary for detoxification. This humane reform had been an innovation of Malcolm's predecessor, George McGrath, who also had moved to house some addict-inmates in dormitories rather than the traditional high security cellblocks. At the Brooklyn Men's House of Detention, this new custodial policy improved the addicts' lot; but at the Tombs, addicts remained on the riot-prone ninth floor, in a double tier of cramped two-man cells set aside for troublemakers and security risks. And at the Tombs in 1971, fewer than eighty of the more than 1,000 addicts committed every month were being scientifically detoxified.

This was the situation when Dr. Dole first visited the Tombs. As a physician, Dole said that he saw a repository for sick men. As a pioneer of methadone maintenance therapy, he saw a manageable problem in the delivery of specialized health services. After surveying the problem, Dr. Dole announced: "Monday, we start."

Within days, Dole had recruited teams of volunteers: physicians, nurses and former heroin addicts. In consultation with jail administrators and personnel, he outlined new methadone detoxification procedures for the Department of Correction. Between late March and early May the teams detoxified 1,336 inmates in the Tombs, and the program won acceptance from both inmates and the initially skeptical guards.[71]

The city health department provides medical staff; former heroin addicts, most on methadone maintenance, supply their hard-bought expertise as "medical aides" and "addiction special-

[70] This list includes systems responding to requests for information directed to major urban population centers in June 1972, as well as those identified by my associates or noted in published articles.
[71] For a description of the medical routine, see Dole, "Detoxification of Sick Addicts in Prison," *J.A.M.A.* 220 (1972): 366. Care was taken to make methadone detoxification compatible with the ordinary jail routine.

ists" salaried by the Department of Correction.[72] The mass detoxification procedure described below was observed in the Tombs. It has been successfully imitated in other New York City jails.

Every new inmate committed to the Tombs negotiates a series of checkpoints before assignment to a cell. Under a prominent hand-lettered sign declaring, "There is no pain medication in this clinic," doctors complete medical history forms. Seriously ill prisoners are routed to an infirmary or hospital. Prisoners addicted to heroin are diagnosed and offered methadone detoxification. Diagnosis is based on indicia of prolonged heroin use and the early symptoms of withdrawal: "general appearance, tracks, other skin lesions, dilated pupils, sweating, gastro-intestinal disturbances."[73] Even for qualified physicians, misdiagnosis is always a risk; a prisoner with tracks or needle scars, for example, may have been injecting cocaine or amphetamines. Another may identify himself as an addict and request detoxification, but show none of the classic signs or symptoms of addiction. The former heroin addicts who assist at intake often recognize atypical patterns of heroin use and pick out prisoners shamming addiction.[74]

To discourage non-addicts simulating addiction, staff outlines the risk of methadone overdosage for individuals who are not currently tolerant to opiates. Those who prefer "cold turkey" withdrawal may choose that course; occasionally, addicts who refused assistance at first enter the methadone program a day or two later. A standard dosage schedule is rubber-stamped on the inmate's medical record card and signed by the examining physician. This is the inmate's prescription. Ordinarily, it calls for six and one half days of diminishing methadone doses.[75]

[72] Most are active methadone maintenance patients. For a discussion of methadone maintenance, see p. 154, below.
[73] Department of Corrections and Health Services Administration, New York City, "Detoxification of Narcotics Addicts in Detention" (mimeographed, December 15, 1971), p. 1.
[74] If the team is in doubt, the inmate is assigned to the detoxification area for "special observation" without medication. If withdrawal symptoms develop, treatment is begun; otherwise, he is transferred to the general population. In an interview, Dr. Dole estimated about 5 per cent of the inmates under the programs' supervision at any time are on special observation.
[75] There is an alternative standard schedule for those arrested while active in high-dose methadone maintenance treatment. Withdrawal from methadone is similar to heroin withdrawal, but more protracted and characterized by

The first dose, available immediately after diagnosis, is of special importance. Detoxification patients are routinely assigned to cells on the Tombs' ninth floor. But when the jail census is far above capacity, new inmates are crowded indiscriminately into the first-floor bullpens, large screened cells with wooden benches fixed to the walls, to await cell assignments. For the addict there, early diagnosis and treatment may be the only safeguards against suffering.

The ninth-floor cellblock itself is bleak and forbidding. It houses a maximum of 120 men. On the morning of a recent visit, several cells were uninhabitable and the backwash from defective plumbing overflowed onto the floor of the walkways. Even the occupied cells were hardly fit for occupation. No windows light the cells on one side of each tier; on the other side, weak diffused sunlight filtered through glass-brick panels screened by heavy bars. Each cell scarcely accommodates narrow tiered bunks with dirty, inch-thick vinyl-covered mattresses, a toilet, a washbowl—and two men. Some cell doors were solid steel, and the men behind them communicated with the walkway only through narrow slots cut at chest level.

The ninth-floor dayroom was no more inviting. It was separated from a corridor leading to elevators by a pair of massive bar-screens, set about four feet apart; a high railed catwalk guarded the opaque windows opposite. Long steel tables with rigidly attached benches nearly filled the room. The only other furniture was an ancient barber's chair. There was no recreational equipment.

The detoxification program adapted to this unpromising en-

---

more generalized muscle pains. When a new inmate's status as a high-dose methadone patient has been authoritatively verified by Rockefeller University staff who maintain communications with jails and community clinics, he is detoxified from a higher initial dosage level, gradually reduced over a ten-day period. The November 1971 death of an eighteen-year-old inmate of the New York City Adolescent Remand Shelter from an apparent methadone overdose, after he evidently had misrepresented himself as an active methadone maintenance patient, dramatized the importance of tight, uniform verification procedures (Markham, "Youth's Methadone Death in Jail Being Studied," New York *Times,* December 1, 1971).

Detoxification of adolescent addicts holds special risks of accidental overdose; an alternative, standard low-dose detoxification schedule is prescribed for all young inmates who are not specifically diagnosed by a specially qualified physician as requiring more intensive treatment.

vironment. Physicians and paramedical staff make rounds in the cellblock, where the bitter clamor of the prisoners blends with undertones of medical consultation. In the dayroom, inmates in outfits ranging from work clothes to cut-off satin trousers—the Tombs issues no uniforms—await medication and pass some of their time off lockup discussing their drug histories with counselors. Many are long-standing addicts, their arms and torsos pitted by needle scars. All are sick men.

The medication is dispensed rapidly and efficiently, morning and evening, when a uniformed nurse wheels the methadone cart between the bar-screens. Each inmate's name is called as his blue medical card is pulled from a file box and reviewed. The current dose indicated on his stamped prescription schedule is prepared by dissolving all or part of a methadone disk in water. Before an inmate can begin his second day of medication, a physician or medical aide must verify the initial diagnosis and check for unexpected reactions to methadone. An inmate can refuse any dose of methadone he feels he does not need, or discontinue treatment completely by refusing two consecutive doses.

There are strict precautions to prevent inmates from receiving unscheduled doses, hoarding medication, or diverting it for sale. Each dose is passed through a small gate into the dayroom; when it has actually been consumed, the corresponding entry on the prescription schedule is canceled. Cigarettes, laxatives—and in the evenings, a light sleeping medication—also are distributed on request, and skin lesions and infections are treated by a medical aide. Many of the patients are chronic petty offenders, who knew the inside of the Tombs long before the introduction of methadone detoxification, and speak with the authority of experience. They confirm official reports that things are better now.

Methadone detoxification was made available, in mid-1971, to addicted prisoners in all New York City detention facilities, from the stacked cellblocks of the forbidding Adolescent Remand Shelter on Riker's Island to the cells and dormitories of the facilities known as Old and New Queens. Wherever the program was installed, it changed the jails by adapting to them.

By the spring of 1972, more than 22,000 heroin addicts had been detoxified in New York City jails, and since the methadone detoxification program was expanded city-wide, there had been no jail suicides or attempts by heroin addicts in withdrawal.[76]

Dr. Dole, in a recent interview, observed that the dispensation of methadone for detoxification is mere "first aid," a procedure which could become impersonal and mechanical. In most jails, whatever their medical facilities, the addict-detainee meets only alienating inattention. Much of the success of the New York program has been ascribed not to the medication, but to the work of the former street addicts who circulate among the prisoners to discuss their individual drug problems and prospects for finding long-term treatment after release. In New York City, Dr. Dole has said, the jailed addict is a "patient," who "knows he is being treated by people who understand his problem and have some sympathy for it."[77]

The New York City detoxification program has limitations. Heavy heroin users do not always escape discomfort; cost factors make individualized prescriptions infeasible; the danger of over-treatment dictates low standard methadone dosages; and the press of new admissions requires rapid turnover and short detoxification schedules. The ideal of optimum care for every patient is compromised by the need to provide safe, adequate care for many. And there have been reports recently of more deaths due to methadone overdose than heroin overdose, though not in the jails.

Another serious shortcoming of the program is due to the very nature of pretrial detention. Addict-detainees are transferred to the general jail population after detoxification, and there, like other inmates, they wait weeks or months for disposition. The therapeutic contact is broken; gradually the detoxified addict loses any interest he may have developed in continuing addiction treatment, and on release he often returns immediately to heroin.[78]

The day-to-day operational problems of the New York City detoxification program have been relatively specialized. In its early months, many addicts did not participate, fearing that by accepting detoxification, they risked attracting the attention of the New York

[76] Dole, "Detoxification of Sick Addicts in Prison," p. 366.
[77] Testimony of Dr. Vincent Dole, "Treatment and Rehabilitation of Narcotics Addicts," Hearings before Subcommittee No. 4 of the Committee on the Judiciary, House of Representatives, 92d Cong., 1st sess., 388 (1971).
[78] In Manhattan and Brooklyn, vigorous efforts have begun to link in-jail detoxification with therapeutic aftercare.

State Narcotic Addiction Control Commission (NACC), and becoming subject to involuntary commitment. As a former inmate of the Women's House of Detention put it:

> The problem with [detoxification] is that you get the Rockefeller papers on your head. That's Rockefeller's program to cure all junkies. You get sent for nine months, I think, to some place upstate which is worse than a jail. Most women say they would rather stay in the Women's House than go there.
>
> If you don't admit you're a junkie, then you go through cold turkey.

The reluctant addicts had read the law correctly, and as Dr. Dole recalled, NACC was then "pulling people off the Detox floor, interfering with their medication and sending them back—having found them to be 'not addicted.'" However, no addict was ever actually committed because he chose detoxification, and the addicts' fears abated even before NACC suspended its expeditions into the jails.[79] Today, program administrators are trying to ensure that addicts confined elsewhere than in detoxification areas —in psychiatric observation or other specialized sections of the New York jails—receive detoxification treatment regularly.

In other cities, in-jail methadone detoxification has been attended by more fundamental difficulties. At institutions like the District of Columbia Jail, methadone is employed only as a stopgap for addicts in active withdrawal. On any given day, 600 addicts may be scattered throughout the D. C. Jail, and as many as 100 men may need detoxification. Unlike the New York City program, however, the Washington program does not supply methadone to all identified addicts; each prescription for detoxification is treated as an isolated case by the overworked medical staff, and dispensing methadone is only the part-time job of a single nurse. Inmates complain that dispensation is haphazard, and assert that their requests for methadone frequently are ignored by guards and doctors. Even so, they are more fortunate than inmates of the D.C. Women's Detention Center, where there is no detoxification service at all.

[79] Ironically, some addicts accused of non-drug offenses now seek commitment to NACC, because the program has reduced length of custodial incarceration in treatment centers to three to six months. An addict committed into NACC often will return to the street on aftercare sooner than he would be paroled from prison after conviction.

In other cities, some individual jail physicians have experimented with methadone detoxification without mastering the principles of the treatment; the programs that resulted usually have been short-lived. The result has been to give detoxification treatment itself an undeservedly bad local reputation.

In most local programs, however, initial dosage levels are adequate, and detoxification periods are equivalent to those observed in the New York City jails: Milwaukee uses a flexible four-to-seven-day schedule; Denver, a standard nine-day regimen; and Cincinnati a five-to-twenty-one-day detoxification routine. But even these medically sound programs do not reach all the new inmates who might benefit.

Experienced nurses, jail officers and paraprofessionals can be invaluable diagnostic assistants; they also can manage an addict's detoxification once a diagnosis has been made and a prescription written. But maximum effectiveness requires that a qualified doctor see every new inmate at—or very soon after—the time he is committed to jail. Most jails do not provide for routine medical examinations at intake.

In Denver, non-expert jail personnel are relied upon to identify candidates for treatment; in Washington, D.C., and Cincinnati that responsibility is diffused; in Milwaukee, it is shifted to the jailed addicts themselves.

At the Denver County Jail inmates are not systematically examined for signs of addiction, but "all inmates are given a cursory medical check by the nurses where symptoms of narcotic withdrawal frequently are identified."[80] Local jail administrators recognize the limitations of this procedure and plan to use federal funds to improve medical screening.

At the District of Columbia Jail medical intake screening is less than uniform. The jail employs no urinalysis procedures of its own, and candidates for detoxification either are self-identified, identified by the trained nurses assigned to the jail's detoxification services, or identified during the routine physical examination which jail physicians generally administer sometime after the booking of a new prisoner is completed. Occasionally, addicts in need of detoxification are identified only by hearsay. At the end of a day's interviews with newly arraigned defendants, the court-

[80] Correspondence from William R. Nelson, director of corrections, Denver, Colorado, June 27, 1972, on file at Goldfarb and Singer, Washington, D.C.

house staff of Narcotics Treatment Administration (NTA) phones the jail a list of persons committed to detention and believed to be experiencing severe withdrawal distress; some then receive decreasing-dose methadone in the cellblocks.

At the Hamilton County Jail in Cincinnati, detoxification is provided by the city's independent Methadone Treatment Center. If a jailed addict

> is observed by qualified staff of the correctional institution to be undergoing withdrawal symptoms—a call is made to the Center and an interviewer goes to the jail to determine his addiction, length and degree. This data is brought back to the Center and evaluated by [the] consulting physician and a . . . detox schedule is established for that particular individual.[81]

Only "in the instance where the Center cannot be contacted (overnight)" can jail personnel administer a single, small dose of methadone without prior authorization.

At the Milwaukee County Jail, an addict must talk his way into the program by "admitting addiction" in circumstantial detail to non-medical intake interviewers. According to jail administrators:

> Most prisoners will not implicate themselves to further criminal charges by admitting they are addicts . . . If an inmate is charged with possession of a narcotic, he usually will admit to his addiction. However, if he is charged with theft, he may deny his addiction . . .[82]

Addicts fear that they may incriminate themselves by requesting detoxification. Admissions of addiction may damage a defendant at trial on a drug-related charge. Moreover, detailed admissions may lead indirectly to new narcotics arrests. Unfortunately, detoxification programs do not give participants formal guarantees

---

[81] Correspondence from John L. Smith, director, Methadone Treatment Center, Cincinnati, Ohio, July 13, 1972, on file at Goldfarb and Singer. The center is a methadone maintenance treatment clinic, which conducts in-jail detoxification as an ancillary service to the addict population.

[82] Correspondence from Michael S. Walker, sheriff, County of Milwaukee, and Lt. Alvin H. Petersen, county jail commanding officer, August 21, 1972, on file at Goldfarb and Singer, Washington, D.C. On an average, eleven addicts are detoxified monthly in Milwaukee, but no estimates of the number of addicts refusing to admit addiction are available. The program is deemed an "unqualified success" in relieving tension, reducing demands on staff, forestalling suicidal behavior, eliminating the need to refer addict-inmates to local hospitals and preventing acute illness.

of confidentiality. If they did, more addict-inmates might seek help.

These makeshift procedures are in sharp contrast to the New York City routine, which is designed to identify all addicts quickly and systematically and then to take the initiative in offering treatment. Without such a routine, some sick addicts inevitably will be overlooked or excluded, while others—ruled by their almost reflexive secretiveness—will conceal their addiction and suffer needlessly, and still others will receive no care until their suffering has become acute. There are few cogent arguments against providing voluntary, systematic detoxification to jailed addicts: the medication, for example, costs as little as sixty-five cents per patient. The medical personnel needed to make a program work are expensive, but innovative deployment policies can drive down this cost as well. In Atlanta, where the Georgia Narcotics Treatment Program (GNTP) has responsibility for jail detoxification, full coverage is provided at minimum cost: at the Atlanta City Jail, which receives most new prisoners, a full-time medical team is on duty. Other holding jails in the metropolitan area are visited daily by a "mobile intake unit."[83] Even this streamlined procedure involves real costs, however, and not every urban jailing system can depend on an independent agency to pay the bills. For jails with small addict populations, the per-patient cost of systematic detoxification will be especially high. In many jurisdictions, adequate medical provision for jailed addicts will come only as the delivery of all health services to men and women in jail is upgraded.

Too often, however, detoxification is omitted from jail programs for non-fiscal reasons. Some jail officials confuse short-term detoxification through decreasing doses of methadone with long-term maintenance treatment using the drug in constant "stabilization" doses. In a recent survey, the physician in charge at the

[83] All prisoners receiving detoxification in Atlanta will be officially enrolled in the GNTP, with identification cards like those held by patients who enter the program's community clinics for long-term addiction therapy. GNTP's central offices will keep current records on the progress of each prisoner's detoxification, to assure that the *course* of detoxification will not be interrupted as prisoners are transferred among facilities in the Atlanta jail complex, and to minimize the paperwork and delay facing releasees who seek long-term treatment in the community after detoxification in jail.

Memphis, Tennessee, jail "indicated a reluctance to use methadone since that would be 'continuing a habit.' "[84]

Other officials distrust methadone detoxification because they believe the program will be abused by prisoners who do not need treatment. A district attorney testified before Congress:

> One of the things you constantly have to watch out for is the kid who comes in there and the first thing he is saying when the jail door closes is, get me the methadone, because the word is out among that breed that you can get this stuff if you qualify and you may have a guy coming in there that isn't really an addict at all, and he wants methadone because he is going to get high.
>
> Two days in jail high beats 2 days any other way. So he wants it.[85]

Detoxification doses of methadone can produce euphoria, as well as overdose, in non-tolerant individuals. A real addict's need for detoxification, however, cannot be measured by the presence or the duration of overt withdrawal symptoms; subtler forms of discomfort persist when the sweating and shaking are at an end. Systematic intake screening is as effective in guaranteeing that non-addicts cannot receive methadone as in assuring that addicts can.

Few jail administrators openly advocate "cold turkey" withdrawal as the addict's just desert; but many contend that treatment short of methadone detoxification is consistent with "hard-nosed" law enforcement and sound medical practice. Captain David Carter, jail commander in Phoenix, Arizona, believes that the jailed addict should be treated as "a violator of the law, not as a sick or handicapped person." Thus, in his jail,

> The medication prescribed usually consists of Thorazine 100 mgs. and Valium 10 mgs. twice a day for 3 or 4 days. This is supplemented by 2 or 3 ounces of sweet syrup administered two or three times daily for 4 or 5 days. This treatment has proved very effective. We have had very little trouble in bringing these people

[84] Goldin, "Methadone Detoxification," pp. 14, 18, n. 7.
[85] Testimony of Fairfax County Commonwealth Attorney Robert Horan, "Narcotics Research, Rehabilitation and Treatment," Hearings before the Select Committee on Crime of the House of Representatives, 92d Cong., 2d sess., pt. 1, 269 (1971). The Fairfax County Jail provided forty-eight hours of methadone detoxification, a regimen inadequate to relieve severe withdrawal.

down and the primary reason is that we do not pamper them in
any way.[86]

Tranquilized addicts may be more tractable than those who go
"cold turkey"—but outside the jails, methadone detoxification is
the medically preferred treatment for withdrawal sickness. Once
an addict has been identified, the routine of methadone detoxification actually is less time-consuming than the administration of
more expensive tranquilizers. Where methadone detoxification has
been introduced, jailed addicts have simply been granted the medical options available to free patients who are under treatment for
withdrawal by hospitals or private physicians.

TREATMENT ALTERNATIVES

Instant medical "cures" for narcotics addiction have been widely
discredited; few experts, for example, would endorse once popular
techniques of shock therapy, although similarly bizarre treatments still are sometimes employed with disastrous results. The
use of "carbon dioxide therapy" at Philadelphia's Hahnemann
Hospital, for example, is under investigation following the death of
a patient who was repeatedly placed into comas by this technique.[87]

Nevertheless, because of the near inevitability of relapse and
readdiction among once detoxified addicts who receive no effective
therapeutic support, the search for new and better modes of
addiction treatment continues. And in long-term therapy, as in
short-term detoxification treatment, jailed addicts receive care of
the poorest quality. As a rule, the most promising therapeutic
programs are open mainly to free, self-referred patients. The addict who has been fortunate enough to avoid arrest has opportunities for treatment which generally are unavailable to the addict
awaiting trial in detention or serving a short jail sentence.

Broadly speaking, every existing mode of addiction treatment
is informed by one of two dominant therapeutic theories.

The "detoxification-abstinence" theory maintains that the only

[86] Correspondence from Captain David E. Carter, Maricopa County Sheriff's
Department, on file at Goldfarb and Singer, Washington, D.C.
[87] Abraham, "Doctors Probe Hahnemann Drug Therapy," Philadelphia *Bulletin,* 23, 1972.

successful treatments are geared toward living without drugs, and that any program must attempt to stabilize and to support its patients in a drug-free state.

For those who advocate the "eclectic" school, on the other hand, total abstinence is regarded as ultimately desirable, but a patient's success is measured by more pragmatic standards, such as improved health, satisfactory job performance, stable relationships with family and friends, participation in community organizations, decreased criminal activities and normal social functioning.[88]

"Detoxification-abstinence" programs include involuntary hospitalization emphasizing public responsibility and care, and residential "therapeutic communities" emphasizing individual initiative and collective self-help. Despite their obvious differences in approach, both sorts of programs assume that the process of achieving abstinence must begin in a specialized, closed environment.

It is striking, and more than a little discouraging, that the detoxification-abstinence approach to the treatment of poor or indigent addicts was introduced at a time when similar approaches had been widely tested and uniformly discredited with fee-paying patients. For two decades after 1914, hundreds of private sanatoria specializing in detoxification "cures" had flourished. The most popular were a chain of "hospitals" managed by Charles B. Towns, a super salesman with no formal medical training; the "Towns treatment" promised results in five days, and its practitioners avoided hard questions as to its long-term value by avoiding follow-up studies of their discharged patients. American medicine's romance with Towns and his ilk was short-lived. As psychiatrist-historian Dr. David Musto has written:

> The year 1930 may be taken as the close of the era of therapeutic optimism with regard to opiate addiction . . . Everything had been tried and everything failed; the relapse rate was appalling. When Congress established narcotic institutions in 1929 the primary reason for federal aid to addiction was not to provide treatment; the Lexington and Fort Worth narcotic "farms" were unmistakably built for the large numbers of jailed addicts who had crowded federal penitentiaries. But in the debate over au-

88 Freedman, "Drug Addiction: An Eclectic View." *J.A.M.A.* 197 (1966): 878.

thorization, the main hope was expressed that through these hospitals effective treatment or a new discovery would begin to wipe out the addiction menace.[89]

Unmistakably, the new federal therapeutic plan for criminal addicts was an anachronism from the beginning. The only hope of the new institutions was that longer institutionalization under conditions more rigorous than those of the private sanatoria, might accomplish detoxification cures where the private sanatoria had failed.

The early history of modern detoxification-abstinence treatment began in an atmosphere of optimism, with the U. S. Public Health Service hospitals at Lexington, Kentucky, and Fort Worth, Texas. Opened in the 1930's to provide scientific detoxification for all comers, including convicted prisoners and defendants who had avoided minor charges by volunteering for the "cure," they closed their doors to voluntary patients in 1972 on a note of failure.[90] (Lexington is now primarily a research hospital concentrating on problems of addiction. The Fort Worth facility has become a co-educational federal prison for addicts, alcoholics and other drug abusers.) Rehabilitative services took second place to elaborate security precautions and few patients remained drug-free after leaving. Most patients came from distant cities, and it proved impossible to provide continuing help; such follow-up care as was provided proved ineffective.[91] One former staff physician termed the experience counter-productive: "It is highly likely that a patient's withdrawal treatment in one of these institutions will increase his underworld connections by scores."[92]

In the 1950's, a number of urban public hospitals opened their own specialized detoxification wards, staffed with social workers

[89] David Musto, *The American Disease*, p. 85.

[90] Recent "revisionist" studies of the records of the federal narcotics hospitals have tended to mitigate somewhat the extent of their failure. It has been noted that while well over 90 per cent of their patients did relapse to narcotics use, some of the same patients ultimately abandoned narcotics use completely; whether this tendency toward abstinence on the part of some addicts is attributable to the institutional experience, or could be observed in any cross section of criminal addicts, remains an open question.

[91] S. Maddux, A. Berliner, and W. Bates, *Engaging Opioid Addicts in a Continuum of Services* (1971). Texas Christian Univ. Press, Fort Worth, Texas.

[92] Marie Elizabeth Nyswander, *The Drug Addict as a Patient* (New York: Grune and Stratton, 1956), p. 116.

and psychologists; most of their patients also relapsed almost immediately on discharge.[93]

Private "ambulatory withdrawal" treatment had a brief vogue in the mid-1950's. Physicians used non-narcotic drugs and supportive psychotherapy to detoxify patients successfully without hospitalization, but the promise of individualized psychiatric aftercare proved illusory. Only a small minority of the addict population ever could have afforded such care. Dr. Marie Nyswander, who pioneered these techniques in New York City, concluded that drug addicts, "like other patients with medical illnesses . . . may neither need nor want psychiatric help."[94]

Proponents of detoxification-abstinence treatment argued for the necessity of newer and stricter procedures to withdraw addicts and reform their personalities before returning them to the community. The governmental response was involuntary hospitalization; the private response was the therapeutic community. The lesson of these experiments, taken together, seems clear: a detoxified addict cannot be expected to abstain from heroin without effective continuing treatment when he returns to the streets.

Since around 1960, a variety of treatment techniques has been developed and experimented with in this country. The major ones are Methadone Maintenance, Therapeutic Community, Outpatient Abstinence Treatment, Narcotic Antagonists, and Civil Commitment.*

---

[93] See, e.g., R. Trussel, "A Follow-up Study of Treated Adolescent Narcotics Users" (Columbia School of Public Health and Social Work, mimeographed, 1959).

[94] Nyswander, *The Drug Addict*, p. 141.

* The following are a selection of the best and most useful sources dealing with these treatment approaches:

METHADONE MAINTENANCE

Dole and Nyswander, "A Medical Treatment for Discetylmorphine (Heroin) Addiction," 193 *J.A.M.A.* 646, 649 (1965).

Dole, Nyswander and Warner, "Successful Treatment of 750 Criminal Addicts," 206 *J.A.M.A.* 2708, 2711, 2709, 2710 (1968).

Jaffee, "Methadone Maintenance: Variation in Outcome Criteria as a Function of Dose" in *Proceedings, Third National Conference on Methadone Maintenance* 37, 38 (GPO, 1971).

Gearing, "Methadone—A Valid Treatment Technique," reprinted in "Narcotics Research, Rehabilitation, and Treatment," Hearings before the Select Committee on Crime, U. S. House of Representatives, 92d Cong., 1st sess., pt. 1, 138, 140 (1971).

Newman, "Methadone Maintenance Treatment; Special Problems of

All of these programs evolved in the context of community programs, although some of them have been used in correctional institutions and although overwhelmingly the clientele has come from past, present and what are likely to be future correctional institution inhabitants. The users, or, if you will, clients of these programs had been people who either came voluntarily or were referred by other social welfare agencies. But by this time the criminal justice system, faced with rising addiction and addict-related crimes, was beginning to face up to the need to incorporate or associate with drug treatment programs.

While telling the story of these interesting developments is not the purpose of this chapter or book, and space does not permit

Government-Controlled Programs," in *Proceedings, Third National Conference on Methadone Maintenance* 121 (GPO, 1971).

HEROIN MAINTENANCE

E. Schur, *Narcotic Addiction in Britain and America: The Impact of Public Policy* (1962).
May, "Addiction and Control in Great Britain," *Dealing With Drug Abuse* 345 (Drug Abuse Services Project 1972).

THERAPEUTIC COMMUNITY

G. Endore, *Synanon* (1968), L. Yablonsky, *Synanon: The Tunnel Back* (1965), and D. Casriel, *So Fair a House* (1963).
Volker and Cressy, "Differential Association and the Rehabilitation of Drug Addicts," 69 *Am. J. Soc.* 129 (1968).
L. Brill and L. Lieberman, *Authority and Addiction* (1969).
"The New York City Program," *Addicts and Drug Abusers* 73 (N. Strauss ed. 1971).

NARCOTIC ANTAGONISTS

Grupp, "The Nalline Test I—Development and Implementation," *J. Criminal Law, Criminology and Police Science* 296 (1970).
Fink, "A Rational Therapy of Opium Dependence: Narcotic Antagonists," in *Drug Abuse: Proceedings of the International Conference* 173, 175 (C. Zerafonetis ed. 1972).
Testimony of Dr. Philip Kurlan, in "Narcotics Research, Rehabilitation and Treatment," Hearings before the Select Committee on Crime, U. S. House of Representatives, 92d Cong., 1st sess., pt. 2, 506–7 (1971).

CIVIL COMMITMENT

Kramer and Bass, "Institutionalization Patterns Among Civilly Committed Addicts," 208 *J.A.M.A.* 2297 (1968).
Murtagh, "Criminal Justice," in *Addicts and Drug Abusers: Current Approaches to the Problem* 62, 69–70 (N. Strauss ed. 1971).
McGlothlin, Tabbush, Chambers, and Jamison, "Alternative Approaches to Opiate Addiction Control: Cost, Benefits and Potential" (Bureau of Narcotics and Dangerous Drugs, mimeographed, June 1972).

elaboration, the briefest mention of these programs here is necessary to understand the recommendations which follow.

METHADONE MAINTENANCE

Methadone, in addition to satisfying the addict's craving for narcotics, blocks the effects of heroin. It represents the fastest growing, if not already the most prevalent form of addict therapy. The essence of the treatment consists of the substitution of a legal and apparently benign, although addictive, narcotic for heroin in the drug use patterns of heroin users.

Most medical authorities and experienced program administrators have accepted methadone maintenance as the best available, pragmatic treatment solution to the heroin-addiction problem.

However, the program is not without critics who are concerned with possible medical side effects and with the diversion of public attention from underlying social problems that cause addiction. The advocates' chief claim is that the people maintained on methadone are in every functional sense like non-addicts. Since their "habit" is cheaply, easily, and legally supported, they are free to devote their energies to normal life-styles and constructive activity.

HEROIN MAINTENANCE

A related, but little used, approach is heroin maintenance, the essence of which is to supply established addicts with an inexpensive legal, medical source of their drug of choice. There is no such program in this country now.

Heroin maintenance is a treatment that has been discussed widely but is not now being practiced and has not been practiced in this country except in ambiguous and isolated experiments in the 1920's. While current considerations of this treatment are very critical and emotion-laden, the available historic experience was, if inconclusive, relatively successful, as has been the experience in other countries, chiefly Great Britain, where heroin maintenance is a primary treatment technique.

Critics note the radically different nature of the problems and conditions then and there.

THERAPEUTIC COMMUNITY

The essence of therapeutic community treatment consists of a period of residence in a structured communal setting where the one invariable rule is abstinence from drug use and where abstinence and stability is rewarded by increased responsibility in the day-to-day management of the affairs of the group.

Success figures are ambiguous and subject to dispute. However, it is not disputed that the cost of providing therapeutic community treatment for even a substantial minority of narcotics addicted people in the United States would be great.

The therapeutic community is one of the most widely praised in theory and least usable in practice of existing treatment approaches. Skeptics argue that few professionals have the ability to administer such a program and few addicts the abilities to graduate from a therapeutic community and remain drug-free in the community at large. Proponents argue, moralistically perhaps, that the only way to quit drugs is to quit and that, for this reason, this is the only true answer to addiction. Zealously they claim that conquering addiction is essentially a matter of self-control with a lot of social help. They point to successful use of this form of treatment in other fields.

Outpatient abstinence is an offshoot of the therapeutic community; it is a catch-all category for a variety of approaches emphasizing drug-free living in a non-institutional setting. Under the outpatient abstinence approach, a person is not a full-time patient in an ongoing program but has access to supportive counseling or necessary services on an emergency basis to assist him in living without drugs.

NARCOTIC ANTAGONISTS

Pharmacological literature establishes that there exists a class of non-narcotic drugs, which, although they cannot satisfy an addict's craving for narcotics, can, like methadone, block the euphoric effects of narcotics. Prime examples are Naloxone, Cyclazocine, and Nalline.

There are experimental programs but no full-fledged treatment programs using narcotic antagonists as a primary mode of therapy. Medical researchers have reported success with small experimental group programs. Unlike methadone treatment, narcotic-antagonists treatment contains no built-in pharmacological incentive (it itself is not addictive) to induce the addict in treatment to continue to receive doses of the antagonist drug rather than returning to heroin. Thus, program dropouts can be expected, even though the treatment is pharmacologically effective so long as persons remain in programs.

CIVIL COMMITMENT

Civil commitment is not a true treatment approach. Key experiments have been attempted in California and New York. While they opened with great hope, their results and practices generally have been condemned.

The essence of this concept is quarantine. The committed addict is removed from the community and placed in an institution which, depending on the program, may be much like a prison, a hospital, or a sanitarium. The period of enforced abstinence which this commitment entails is expected, along with available special treatment services, particularly counseling, to assist the addict in remaining drug-free when his term of commitment is completed. Advocates claim that the community is spared the necessity of dealing directly with the addict during the period of his "quarantine."

MULTI-MODALITY

Multi-modality programs claim the versatility of drawing from any of the above techniques within one administrative structure. The Illinois Drug Program, the Narcotics Treatment Administration of Washington, D.C., are prime examples of this approach.

Advocates urge that this eclectic approach tailors the best working program to the needs of the individual client and avoids doctrinaire allegiances and claims of panaceas. Cynics charge that multi-modality treatment has more to do with political tact than with medical wisdom.

NEW ROLES FOR JAILS:
IDENTIFICATION AND TREATMENT INTERVENTION

In most American cities, the jailing system and the addiction treatment establishment exist in isolation from each other. Addicts in detention are destined either for imprisonment or for return to the sad cycle of release, readdiction and rearrest. Addicts in treatment are unlikely to be arrested and jailed; when they are, their treatment terminates abruptly. If an addict volunteers for treatment, he is regarded as a patient; if he is arrested, he is regarded as a prisoner.

Conventional jailing of addicts is an exercise in futility. Scientific in-jail detoxification services make the jailing experience more humane; but alone it is not a cure. An addict may show real interest in treatment during his first days in jail, but his motivation will be dissipated in detention or overlooked in the courts unless supported by continued counseling and follow-up treatment services. Yet voluntary treatment services, including those which enjoy the confidence of a local addict population, enroll only a fraction of its members, and a smaller fraction still of criminally active addicts. In an interview, Dr. Vincent Dole said that as few as 25 per cent of New York City's heroin users may be responsible for the bulk of the city's drug-related crime, a "hard-core" which includes those addicts least likely to volunteer for treatment.

One practical strategy would encourage treatment programs to seek new clients not only in the streets, but in the jails, which are the natural way stations for criminal addicts. The jails have unique potential to become links between the criminal justice and public health systems. The jailing of addicts can become a first step toward individualized treatment, rather than a substitute for it. With such a beginning step, the now visionary objective of providing treatment to all heroin addicts could become a practical goal.

Innovations in jailing practices may further the goal of equality of therapeutic opportunity for all compulsive drug users. When a businessman's family learns that he is dependent on barbiturates, or a physician's associates discover him to be addicted to prescription narcotics, the individual is offered a range of private treatment services, and forcefully urged to select one. When a criminal addict is arrested for a drug-related offense, he is jailed and effectively cut off from the treatment alternatives. Such differential response is as counterproductive as it is unjust. If the functions of the jail are to be rethought, a new jailing system can aim to provide addict-inmates with practical access to care equivalent to that enjoyed by ordinary consumers of health services.

The jail can then become a center for diagnosis, education and referral—a process which must begin with the identification of addicts in jail populations. Today, jail time is dead time. Few cities keep records of how many addicts are taken into custody; systematic screening of arrestees for drug dependence is rare. The addict usually leaves detention much as he entered: a cipher to his keepers and a burden to himself. In a revamped jailing system, the time in detention can become an opportunity to compile a medical and social history, to introduce him to various local addiction treatment programs and even to arrange for placement in a community program after release.

Using local holding facilities for an effective diagnostic role would require extensive jail reform: different staff, new attitudes and some new facilities. An additional proposed new function for the jail—the direct delivery of addiction treatment services—is more speculative. Many addicts now spend months in local cells, either as detainees or as sentenced prisoners. Certain methods of addiction therapy which have proved their worth in the community may be adaptable for use within the closed environment of the jail itself, and community programs may be able to enroll inmates even before their release.

STRATEGIES OF TREATMENT INTERVENTION

Gradually, the criminal justice system is coming to realize that addiction is a treatable disease, and that criminality is simply its most obvious symptom. Reforms of the criminal justice system can affect the addiction problem materially. The jail, in particular, could be converted to a useful function: it is a logical point at which to identify large numbers of once anonymous addicts and refer them to appropriate treatment.

To the extent that treatment is effective, such a use of the jail will benefit individual addicts. It will also advance an interest which conventional anti-drug law enforcement has alone failed to serve—the community's interest in addiction prevention and control.

The proposition that bringing large numbers of persons currently addicted to heroin into treatment can effect the recruitment of new addicts—and thus, lower the rate of new drug-related crime —runs counter to two popular myths of addiction. One is the belief that the leering "pusher," haunting the schoolyards and alleyways with his baited "free samples," is the chief cause of the spread of addiction. Field surveys of adolescent narcotics use indicate that street traffickers actually do little to develop their markets. Instead, they are sought out by young men and women who were first introduced to narcotics by their contemporaries growing up in settings where "experimental" drug use in response to boredom, frustration or simple curiosity is a regular and widespread part of growing up.[95]

Treatment intervention cannot reach the social determinants of adolescent narcotic use, which one researcher found to be "associated with a triad of neighborhood characteristics . . . widespread poverty, low level of education, and high proportions of broken families and other deviant family arrangements.[96] It can achieve something which the prosecution of traffickers alone cannot: a reduction in the availability of the narcotics which are a necessary condition of drug experimentation, accomplished by limiting the number of active addicts.

The other myth of addiction is that most potential addicts are psychologically weak—so predisposed to the use of narcotics or so susceptible to their effects that they would continue to succumb even if the availability of the drugs were substantially reduced. In 1925, psychiatrist Dr. Lawrence Kolb expressed the view that addicts "are recruited almost exclusively from among persons who

[95] The relative infrequency with which young addicts are introduced to drug use by adult "pushers" is one of the findings of Isidor Chein et al. in *The Road to H: Narcotics, Delinquency and Social Policy* (New York: Basic Books, 1964), the report of one major survey which directly addressed the questions of how, when and where addiction begins.

[96] Isidor Chein, "Narcotics Use Among Juveniles," in John A. O'Donnell and John C. Ball, eds., *Narcotic Addiction* (New York: Harper & Row, 1966), pp. 123, 138.

are neurotic or who have some form of twisted personality."[97] More recently, proponents of this "psychogenic theory" of addiction have sought the typical "addictive personality," without notable success. One scholar of addiction, Alfred Lindesmith, has dismissed the notion as a myth, which

> . . . stems in part from the fact that the consequence of addiction in this country, and the processing of addicts through the legal apparatus make them all seem somewhat alike. The post-addiction similarities are then assumed to have been in existence prior to the addiction.[98]

Most experts agree that some addicts are the victims of their psychological susceptibilities. But current medical research on the genesis of addiction indicates psychologically "normal" persons can be caught in addictive traps after experimental or casual exposure to narcotics.

Theorists have suggested that some individuals have inborn sensitivities to addiction which are triggered by the first dose of an opiate.[99] Others suggest that narcotics use can cause long-lasting changes in the metabolism of any user, or reduce his neurological capacity to withstand stress without the aid of narcotics.[100]

Still other authorities theorize that compulsive narcotics use is a "response" to which anyone can be "conditioned."[101] Finally,

[97] Kolb, "Types and Characteristics of Drug Addicts," 9 *Mental Hygiene* (1925): 300, 313.
[98] Lindesmith, "Basic Problems in the Social Psychology of Addiction and a Theory," in O'Donnell and Ball, eds., *Narcotic Addiction,* pp. 91, 100, 107.
[99] The selective "genetic" hypothesis is explored in Avram Goldstein, Lewis Aronow, and Sumner Kalman, *Principles of Drug Action,* New York: Hoeber (1968), pp. 474–75; and in Vincent P. Dole and Marie E. Nyswander, "Methadone Maintenance and Its Implications for Theories of Narcotic Addiction," in A. Wikler, ed., *The Addictive States,* Baltimore: Williams & Williams (1967), p. 359.
[100] The metabolic hypothesis, proposed by Vincent P. Dole and Marie E. Nyswander, "Heroin Addiction—A Metabolic Disease," 120 *Arch. Int. Med.* (1967) 19, is discussed in clinical detail in Schuster, "Tolerance and Physical Dependence," *Narcotic Drugs: Biochemical Pharmacology,* New York: Plenum Press (Doris Clouet, ed., 1971). A neurological sensitivity hypothesis is detailed in Martin, "Pathophysiology of Narcotic Addiction: Possible Roles of Protracted Abstinence in Relapse," *Drug Abuse: Proceedings of the International Conference,* Philadelphia: Lea & Febiger, p. 153 (C. Zarafonetis ed. 1971).
[101] For the argument that addicts are negatively conditioned by the experience of relief from physical withdrawal symptoms, see Alfred Lindesmith, *Narcotic Addiction* (rev. ed., 1967). For the contrary argument that

at least one iconoclastic expert recently has argued that narcotics are not addictive at all, and that heroin use is only one expression of a universal human fascination with psychoactive drugs of all varieties.[102]

None of these theories have been proved or disproved. Work with laboratory animals does support the general proposition that addiction is readily contracted by psychologically normal individuals. Pharmacologist Dr. Julian Villerreal has summarized the experiments:

> The fact that "simple-minded" animals show very much the same behavioral response to drugs which are self-administered indicates that we do not need to invoke attributes peculiar to the psychology of man to account for drug seeking behavior. With rats and monkeys there are no generation gaps, no identity crises, and no desperation because of the evils of society . . . All monkeys that are given full access to morphine . . . will develop the predictable patterns of strong self-administration behavior . . . [t]he differences between human drug users and non-users may turn out to be primarily differences in the access to drugs for self-administration, differences in the tendency to do the initial experimentation which will allow the drug to exert its predictable behavioral effects, or differences in the strength of competing behaviors which are incompatible with drug use.[103]

Historically, law enforcement strategies have not curtailed the availability of illicit drugs; they may have stimulated drug experimentation by lending narcotics the romantic appeal of "forbidden fruit" for despairing inner-city youths and disenchanted suburban teen-agers.

Alone, treatment strategies also may fail to check the narcotics epidemic effectively, since voluntary therapeutic programs often do not enroll the most active—and in an epidemiological sense, the most potentially "infectious"—addicts. Co-ordinated strategies for law enforcement and treatment, however, may succeed in insuring

---

they have experienced positive reinforcement, see Wikler, "Conditioning Factors in Opiate Addiction and Relapse," in *Narcotics*, N.Y.: McGraw-Hill (Blakiston Div.), pp. 85, 87 (D. Wilner & G. Kasenbaum, eds., 1965).

[102] See Andrew T. Weil, *The Natural Mind* (Boston: Houghton Mifflin, 1972).

[103] Statement of Julian E. Villerreal, "Narcotics Research, Rehabilitation and Treatment," Hearings before the Select Committee on Crime of the House of Representatives, 92d Cong., 1st sess., pt. 2, p. 503 (1971).

that the elusive goal of treating all the addicts in the community—and thus assuring against a continued heroin epidemic—is accomplished.

TREATMENT AND THE JAILING SYSTEM

Through "treatment intervention," the jailing of criminal addicts can be minimized or avoided altogether. Police lockups, detention facilities or local short-term prisons are potential points of intervention. Police officers can refer addicts to treatment without completing formal arrests or without taking suspects into protracted custody. Judges can release addicts on bond, with a condition of treatment, immediately after their first preliminary court appearances. "Addict diversion" plans can intervene later in a pretrial period, and probation to treatment programs can go into effect after disposition of criminal charges. In-jail treatment programs can operate while a sentence is served, while the process of postrelease referral can come into effect near the end of a convicted addict's jail sentence.

Informal arrangements to substitute treatment for criminal processing are as old as the problem of addiction. However, formal treatment intervention is a new development, and some modes of intervention have received little practical testing. Even those which have been tested in practice have not accumulated large amounts of research data. Intervention programs place the needs of their clients before the curiosity of evaluators.[104] Herman Joseph, director of New York City's Probation Methadone Program, has stated emphatically that double-blind studies and other research techniques, "have no place in probation, parole, or court affiliated services" for addicts. In assessing the promise of any proposed intervention project, one must test the design against the question: Will the program be capable of bringing large numbers of addicts into treatment without undermining their chances for success as patients? Experience alone can confirm expectations.

In evaluating the prospects of any treatment intervention scheme, it is desirable to consider how much scope it allows for

---

[104] Joseph, "Court Services," *Proceedings: Third National Conference on Methadone Maintenance* (Washington, D.C.: Government Printing Office, 1971), pp. 106, 197.

voluntarism on the part of individual addicts in seeking care and selecting particular modes of therapy. The balance which a program strikes between voluntarism and coercion may be the most important single indicator of its likely success. Most authorities on addiction therapy agree that personal motivation is basic to successful treatment. Voluntarism is a therapeutic ideal, and outright compulsion subverts the treatment process. Dr. Vincent Dole has observed: "The first thing that must be established is a relationship of trust. You are not going to trust me as a doctor when you have a cop behind you pushing you at me."[105] When patients are referred to treatment from the criminal process, some tension between personal motivation and outside pressure is inevitable.

To recruit large numbers of addicts, treatment intervention plans must rely on the coercive potential of the criminal justice system. This reliance is not necessarily anti-therapeutic in itself, since outside pressure can reinforce or precede inner motivation. The new self-referred "volunteer" patient, with a ruinously expensive habit or a distraught family, like the jailed addict facing prosecution or incarceration, is not completely free. Once in treatment, each may discover that life without heroin is more attractive than the vagaries of addiction.

Nevertheless, a treatment intervention plan that ignores voluntarism may doom itself to failure. California's civil commitment program abandoned voluntarism altogether and, although thousands of addicts have been drafted from the courts into the program, few appear to have reaped benefit from the imposed treatment. In dramatic contrast is the early intervention program of the Vera Institute of Justice and the New York City Police Department, which stresses voluntarism.

EARLY INTERVENTION:
ALTERNATIVES TO ARREST AND JAIL

In the Vera-NYPD program an outreach team of two officers and an ex-addict patrols the high-addiction neighborhoods of

[105] Testimony of Dr. Vincent Dole, "Treatment and Rehabilitation of Narcotics Addicts," Hearings before Subcommittee No. 4 of the Committee on the Judiciary, House of Representatives, 92d Cong., 1st sess., pt. 1, p. 397 (1971).

Bedford-Stuyvesant; they can offer a street addict immediate enrollment in one of the long-term treatment programs at Vera's local Addiction Research and Treatment Center (ARTC). If the same addict had been approached by an ordinary police patrol, he might have been subject to search and arrest for possession of narcotics; under the ground rules of this experiment, the addict who rejects help is free to go his own way. The members of the team are selective; during about seven weeks in late 1972, they approached only 150 addicts, of whom about two thirds refused to participate. Eventually fifteen of the 150 were actually enrolled. Of these volunteers one died and one was arrested; the thirteen remaining continued to be active in ARTC's methadone maintenance program.[106]

Other early treatment intervention devices are geared to enroll more addicts than Vera's outreach plan, while still avoiding extremes of compulsion. Several jurisdictions are now considering adopting plans modeled on Vera's, but with coercive pressure—police would have the option of issuing summonses to addicts charged with minor narcotics offenses instead of booking them into jail, and if the addicts then entered treatment, these summonses eventually could be quashed.

Treatment intervention devices which channel addicts into treatment before they have been jailed, or even before they have been formally arrested, must rely on the expertise of experienced policemen and "street-wise" ex-addicts to identify potential patients. They can be expected to involve only a limited number of individuals.

ADDICT IDENTIFICATION

Most treatment intervention schemes would depend in vain on the jails for addict identification. In jails without an effective medical intake screening, addicts are noticed only if they identify themselves or are already "known," or if they are in obvious withdrawal.

[106] In a recent interview, Vera's W. Richard Rykken also cited the experiment's success in recruiting addicts who would not otherwise have entered a program. On the average, the participants had used heroin for eight years; only one, however, had ever been in treatment, and only one was on a waiting list when approached.

In New York City, however, several treatment intervention services recruit among the addicts identified by the Department of Correction's methadone detoxification program for detainees. In other jurisdictions, addicted prisoners are identified by urine testing. Unlike New York's addict identification procedure, this simple and economic expedient requires no special medical facilities or staff; a prisoner's sample is labeled by a nurse or jailer, and shipped off for analysis at a central laboratory. Lab costs are low, and the results can be available within hours.[107] Although urinalysis cannot identify an addict, it can disclose use of heroin within twenty-four to forty-eight hours before booking. To maximize the number of addicts identified where urinalysis is employed, "urine screens" should test as many new prisoners as possible soon after arrest. In many cities, all urine testing can be conducted at the single strategic site where all new prisoners are first held.

In metropolitan Atlanta, where an arrestee may be taken to any of five local jails, and held for several days before arraignment, the Georgia Narcotics Treatment Program (GNTP) has established urine screening programs in each facility, conducted by the regular jail staff. More than 90 per cent of the inmates approached have co-operated voluntarily.

The GNTP urine screening project originated as a research study limited to prisoners booked on felony charges. Preliminary results indicate that about half the prisoners booked on felony charges in Fulton County, and about 35 per cent of those booked in De Kalb County, have used heroin shortly before their arrest. In Cobb and De Kalb counties, prisoners requested to give a urine sample have been routinely informed that the results will be used for research purposes only; in Fulton County, they have received no similar assurances.

Planned uses for GNTP's jail urine sample results include identifying prisoners in need of methadone detoxification and locating potential patients for long-term addiction therapy.[108]

[107] The most widely employed technique of laboratory analysis, thin-layer chromatography, involves a typical turn-around time of twenty-four hours, and a per sample cost of two to three dollars. New techniques, such as gas chromatography, produce results more quickly; they are also less expensive and more discriminating.

[108] For a description of the referral mechanism which GNTP contemplates, see p. 170 below.

No inmate can be compelled—legally or practically—to give up a urine sample, or to submit to an interview concerning his drug use. Resistance and distrust can be serious obstacles; in Wilmington, Delaware, during the first week of urine screening in the central police lockup, half the prisoners approached refused to participate.[109] Clear explanations of the test's purposes, of restrictions on the use of test results, and of the benefits to be derived from co-operation must be explained if the program is to succeed.

PRETRIAL RELEASE TO TREATMENT

In 1970, more than 40 per cent of the defendants in Superior Court in Washington, D.C., tested positive for heroin use. A comprehensive addict identification system using urine screening and interviewing was established: identification may lead directly to pretrial release on bond with a condition of treatment. A unit of NTA conducts screening in the city's courthouse bullpens, the crowded, noisy tanks into which recent arrestees are emptied each morning for holding until arraignment. The pre-arraignment interviews identify some addicts who test "clean" on the urine test.

Centralized testing like the Washington plan misses the addicts who have already been released on station-house bond. Even where station-house bond is allowed on minor charges, such as public drunkenness, addicts also may be overlooked; some feign drunkenness to avoid more serious charges. In Washington, a significant number of candidates for treatment intervention may slip into the routine of criminal processing—although not directly into the jails—through this gap in the identification screen.

On a typical morning, Washington's NTA screening staff sees thirty to forty prisoners; on a busy day, as many as eighty. A counselor tells each prisoner that he is seeking a urine sample and a brief interview concerning the prisoner's history of drug use and treatment. He explains that if the prisoner consents, an evaluation report will be available to the judge at the upcoming arraignment

109 The Wilmington urine screen program is a part of the federally funded TASC (Treatment Alternatives to Street Crime) project, described below at p. 171. Urine samples are collected not by jail personnel, but by project interviewers, who provide twenty-four-hour coverage at the lockup.

hearing, to the prosecutor and defense attorney, and to the agency which oversees pretrial release. Finally, the counselor outlines the closely observed informal agreement under which interview and test results are used only to determine conditions of release, and not as evidence at trial. The counselor makes no promises to secure a prisoner's co-operation. He does explain that some identified addicts are released pending trial to participate in NTA treatment, and that unfavorable inferences—justified or not—are often drawn from a refusal to undergo screening. Although the constitutionality of this subtly coercive procedure may be open to questions, its efficacy is not. An estimated 98 per cent of all defendants—addicts and non-addicts—agree to participate.

Urine samples are analyzed in a modern courthouse laboratory; within hours, detailed results of a gas chromatography analysis are coded on each prisoner's interview form and reviewed by the NTA staff. When there is a substantial discrepancy between a prisoner's test results and his self-reported drug use, a new interview or a new test may be arranged before arraignment.

In most jurisdictions, including some with addict identification systems, addiction is not taken into formal account at arraignment. Where there are no special provisions for the pretrial release of addicts, "known" addicts find conventional release on bond difficult to obtain.

In Washington, D.C., an arraignment judge can recognize an addict's tendency toward compulsive criminality without consigning him to detention. With the NTA report on an addict-prisoner before him, the judge can require participation in "narcotics treatment and surveillance" as a special condition when he sets bail.

An addict who accepts pretrial treatment must meet other conventional conditions to qualify for release, whether on money bond, on personal surety, on personal recognizance, or in third-party custody. If he qualifies, he is escorted to the NTA offices in the courthouse, where he usually is directed to report to NTA's Central Medical Intake Unit. The addict is free pending trial, and the responsibility for following through is his. When he reports for intake, he is treated as a voluntary patient. He receives a physical examination, selects a program of treatment, and is referred to a community clinic providing methadone detoxification, supervised abstinence or methadone maintenance. When a releasee who has tested positive for heroin use denies his addiction, NTA may require only that he report for periodic urine surveillance. If he tests "clean" for two and one half to three weeks, he is considered to have satisfied the narcotics-related condition of release; if he tests "dirty" on more than one occasion, he then is directed to report for treatment.

The District of Columbia introduced addict identification and "treatment-conditioned bond" to eliminate unnecessary pretrial detention, but a few of the judges who sit in arraignment court reacted by setting particularly stiff release conditions for identified addicts. Overall, however, the findings of a recent study by the staff of the ABA Special Committee on Urban Crime Prevention and Control are that the chances that an addict would be jailed to await trial appear to have diminished.[110] About 4,500 individual addicts were identified in Washington lockups during 1971, and 1,700 of them were released to treatment by Superior Court at least once; a smaller number were released by United States District Court, where no tabulation was maintained.

Many of these contacts with NTA did not develop into continuing therapeutic relationships. More than 60 per cent of the addicts released by Superior Court during 1971 abandoned treatment sometime before their court cases were concluded. Half of these simply had never reported to NTA. Of the addicts who did comply with special conditions of pretrial release pending a legal disposition of their cases, fewer than half remained afterwards as NTA voluntary patients to pass the six months' mark in treatment,[111] which is regarded as a turning point because most therapeutic programs report that a majority of the patients who remain this long will persist indefinitely.

The District of Columbia experiment with treatment-conditioned bond cannot be discounted. Because it excludes no addict on the

[110] According to a recent study of the Washington experience, judicial use of the treatment-conditioned bond was on the increase during 1971; pretrial referrals to treatment in the last half of the year exceeded those in the first half by 42.7 per cent. American Bar Association, Special Committee on Crime Prevention and Control, "The Case for Pre-Trial Diversion of Heroin Addicts from the Criminal Justice System" (mimeographed staff report, 1972), p. 61 (hereafter cited as ABA Staff Report).

[111] ABA Staff Report, p. 79. In contrast to NTA's "criminal justice referrals," more than half of all the self-referred patients who volunteer for intake do achieve the "six months' plateau." See Comptroller General of the United States, "Narcotics Research, Rehabilitation and Treatment in the District of Columbia" (Washington, D.C.: Government Printing Office, 1971).

basis of predetermined eligibility criteria, the treatment-bond program has resulted in a large number of initial therapeutic referrals. Those patients who remain in treatment are clear successes, and many of them are long-time criminal addicts who might never have volunteered for treatment. The ABA study suggests some reasons why the Washington release-to-treatment program was not even more successful during the survey period. Addicts who entered treatment under it often risked likely failure by choosing detoxification or abstinence therapy over methadone maintenance. Also, addicts who were out of compliance seldom had their bonds revoked.[112] During 1971, according to the ABA survey, "[O]nly 21.7 percent of these violations were ever reported to the court. In almost all of these cases no action was ever taken." The program did not provide intensive supervision and counseling to criminal justice patients.

Better medical assignments, stricter enforcement of treatment conditions, and more individualized supervision could contribute to the success of a pretrial treatment intervention system. In Washington itself, the experience of the Narcotics Addict Legal Services Project (NALSP) showed that close supervision can make a difference. Of one group of addicts on treatment bond to whom were assigned individual volunteer attorneys, almost half stayed in treatment after legal dispositions, to reach the "six-months' plateau."

The lawyers did well for their NALSP clients in court: fewer than 9 per cent eventually were imprisoned, as compared to 33 per cent of a control group; almost 65 per cent received probation (usually with a condition of continuing treatment), compared to only 44 per cent of the controls. The NALSP clients' treatment successes owed most to their lawyers' practical, non-legal assistance. When an addict was released on bond, his NALSP lawyer often went with him to NTA, assuring that the formal court referral became a real medical contact. While a client's case was pending, the NALSP lawyer was his contact and his counselor; a client who seemed likely to drop out of treatment often was persuaded to remain.[113]

---

[112] ABA Staff Report, p. 61.
[113] Washington Lawyers' Committee for Civil Rights Under Law, "Final Report and Evaluation of the Narcotic Addict Legal Services Program" (mimeographed, May 31, 1972), pp. 2, 28–30.

The rushed and routinized atmosphere of an arraignment court, which permits no detailed inquiry into an addict-defendant's background or motivation, is hardly ideal for initiating medical treatment intervention. Personalized attention during the treatment period—whether provided by lawyers, program staff or community volunteers—can compensate for the impersonality with which release on treatment bond begins.

Pretrial release to treatment can be a dead end. Until late 1973, when a successful program participant's case was advancing toward disposition in Washington, his pretrial treatment record was no ground for deferring or dismissing the prosecution. Today, a small number of addicts with minimal prior records, charged with minor offenses—no more than several hundred annually—are being permitted to earn outright dismissals by completing ten months of successful treatment. The overwhelming majority of the participants in the treatment bond program, however, still return to the criminal process for conventional processing. If they are convicted, their sentences may make further treatment impossible. Probation conditioned on continuing treatment sometimes is granted, but since the sentencing judge usually has little pretrial treatment data before him, such dispositions are merely fortuitous. Little substantive treatment information—favorable or unfavorable—is included in the pre-sentence reports of addict-defendants who have been free on bond in Washington. Critics of the Probation Department ascribe this failure to apathy and overwork; its defenders cite pretrial difficulties in obtaining medical records from NTA. Robert Bailey of NTA's Criminal Justice Surveillance Unit estimates that 80 per cent of the releasees who go to trial with favorable treatment records receive probation. Addicts on bond, however, have no way of knowing this. The ABA study found that only 360 of 1,716 releasees eventually were sentenced to probation, and many of these probationers apparently were not required to continue treatment. Overall, pretrial treatment experience did not appear influential at sentencing.

The Georgia Narcotics Treatment Program (GNTP) is building on Washington's experience. Participation in Atlanta's treatment bond program will be limited to addict-defendants who have expressed an interest in treatment during a pre-arraignment interview. To provide additional incentive, GNTP is encouraging local courts to adopt a liberal probation policy for addicts who comply with special conditions. When participants do not comply, conditions of release will be strictly enforced, and bench warrants will be issued routinely against treatment dropouts.[114]

Atlanta's program is intended to be both more selective and more coercive than Washington's. Success would be had at the cost of involving a smaller overall proportion of the addicts identified in jails.

In Wilmington, Delaware, the pretrial release program initiated in August 1972, provides for even more preliminary selection. Prisoners charged with felonies are automatically excluded from participation; others must agree to enter an in-patient detoxification center for a minimum of ten days after being admitted to bond. In the program's first week of operation, over twenty-five addicts were identified; only one eventually was released on a treatment-conditioned bond.[115]

This venture was part of the first of a series of Treatment Alternatives to Street Crime (TASC) projects jointly sponsored by the Special Action Office for Drug Abuse Prevention (SAODAP), the Law Enforcement Assistance Administration (LEAA) and the National Institute of Mental Health (NIMH). Through these projects—operating in Wilmington, Philadelphia, the federal courts of the Southern District of New York and planned in twenty-three other cities—federal funds and technical assistance are channeled to localities implementing all or part of the following plan:

> Drug dependent arrestees will be identified through urinalysis screening and interviews after police processing. The arraignment judge will be given the results of this identification in order to determine whether the arrestee will be offered treatment as a con-

---

[114] The ABA report on the Washington program notes that strict, uniform enforcement is not necessarily anti-therapeutic, when revocation proceedings are initiated by an independent enforcement unit, and not by the treatment staff themselves:

> Encounters between addicts and staff should be neither adversarial nor overly authoritarian. The coercive influence of the court system should be used in a positive rather than a negative way, with less emphasis on the punitive aspects of failure to comply with treatment conditions and greater emphasis on the personal rewards which would accompany retention in treatment. [ABA Staff Report, p. 87]

[115] The Wilmington program has another limitation. According to its director, John Lemle, the outpatient services available to addicts released to treatment are traditionally abstinence-oriented. There is no present plan to assist these addicts in entering methadone maintenance treatment.

dition of bail. Detoxification will begin where necessary. Continuous evaluation and follow-up will take place during treatment until an individual's case comes up for trial. The judiciary may then take into account the cooperation of the addict and the success of his treatment program to that point, and may determine that the addict should remain in treatment as an alternative to prosecution or to possible incarceration.[116]

The "addict diversion" aspect of TASC is a distinct and promising treatment intervention device.

ADDICT DIVERSION

Pretrial addict diversion is intended to remove selected offenders from the criminal process temporarily to participate in community-based rehabilitation. The prospect of dismissal of charges provides an incentive to persevere. At the same time, local courts and jails derive substantial cost savings.[117]

Informal addict diversion is as old as addiction. The middle-class and professional addict traditionally has had what amounts to an option to choose between a sanatorium and a cell. Into the 1960's, the open-door federal narcotics hospitals were populated largely with poor criminal addicts who had exchanged a promise to take the "cure" for a break from a local judge or prosecutor.

In several states and in the federal system, new statutory provisions for addict diversion have proved overrestrictive and inflexible. In Connecticut and Illinois, diversion is handled on a case-by-case basis; specific prosecutorial concurrence is required in each decision to route an addict out of the criminal justice system, and few addicts actually benefit from the statutes. In Massachusetts, the law provides mandatory diversion on request, but only to first offenders charged with certain drug law violations. In New York the statutory alternative to prosecution has been a minimum of thirty-six months' civil commitment; to avoid this, addict-misdemeanants facing short sentences have sought opportunities to plead guilty with a stipulation of non-addiction.

[116] News release dated April 14, 1972, from Executive Office of the President, Special Action Office for Drug Abuse Prevention.
[117] The following discussion depends on the survey of issues and programs in John Bellassai and Phyllis Segal, "Addict Diversion: An Alternative Approach for the Criminal Justice System," 60 *Geo. L. J.* 667 (1972).

The Federal Controlled Substances Act of 1970 authorized addict diversion, but only for addicts charged with simple possession of narcotics, and only after there has been a conditional guilty plea which can become final automatically on failure in treatment. Title I of the Narcotics Addict Rehabilitation Act of 1966 (NARA), intended to divert substantial numbers of federal offenders, has proved useful to only a handful. NARA I's medical and legal eligibility requirements are strict, but its most severe limitation is complete reliance on local U. S. Attorneys, who may have little time or taste for "social work," to initiate and supervise diversion.[118]

After direct federal addiction treatment was limited to NARA patients, Title III's "voluntary commitment" provisions sometimes were employed as a makeshift diversion device in states with no treatment intervention programs of their own. If an addict agrees to apply under Title III, or is actually accepted under it, his local charges are quashed. Such procedures have obvious limitations. They cannot accommodate large numbers of criminal addicts, at least as long as NARA continues to reject many applicants as medically unsuitable. A local court loses its powers of supervision and control when it dismisses a NARA patient's charges; although Title III treatment theoretically is mandatory after acceptance, the federal program itself has no practical sanctions to apply against dropouts.[119]

Advocates of large-scale addict diversion reject statutory or discretionary models, and argue for flexible and minimally restrictive eligibility standards. They propose systems fitted to local needs, codified in rules of court or adopted as practical working arrangements between criminal justice and treatment personnel. They challenge the logic of diverting addicts arrested for simple possession while jailing those arrested for burglary, when almost all street addicts steal regularly to finance their habits. They question programs which cannot give addicts with long drug-related

---

[118] On the underutilization of NARA I, see above, and Comptroller General of the United States, "Limited Use of Federal Programs to Commit Narcotics Addicts for Treatment and Rehabilitation" (General Accounting Office, September 20, 1971).

[119] For a description of local improvisation with Title III, see Jack G. Collins and D. Richard Hammersley, "The NARA Act of 1966 in Oregon: An Interim Report," 7 *Willamette L. J.* 385 (1971).

criminal records their first practical chance to escape the subculture of addiction.

Proponents of diversion also question whether each addict's fate should depend on prosecutorial discretion. If he has met basic exclusionary criteria and is well motivated, they argue, he should have a right to enter treatment; if he succeeds over a specified period, he should be rewarded with an automatic *nolle prosequi*. Only such a "pure" design for diversion, advocates say, can offer a complete alternative to criminal processing.

Pragmatic supporters of diversion are more interested in the realities than the purity of design. A local district attorney may never concede his authority over criminal prosecutions to a medical program; if veto power is the price of his participation, the real issue is how constructively he will exercise it. If a guilty plea is the price of diversion, the typical addict will not be damaged; one more conviction will not add much to the stigma of his existing record. The advocates contend that the success of diversion depends on acceptance. The diversion of burglary defendants into community treatment may frighten the public unduly. Restrictive eligibility requirements may, therefore, be necessary if there is to be any program at all.

Victim compensation offers a possible compromise. Most drug-related crime is property crime. An addict in diversion could seek to compensate victims of drug addicts' crimes. Unlike active criminal addicts, addicts in treatment can and do hold jobs and earn adequate wages. Public dissatisfaction with a plan which "coddles" addicts might be allayed by victim compensation, and an addict's willingness to make restoration is a prime test of motivation for treatment.

The offer of diversion to addicts is justified by the knowledge that addicts are sick, and that society's self-interest is involved. An addict who is not diverted will generate social costs until he gets treatment. The earlier he can be diverted, the less his personal and social deterioration will prejudice prospects for success of treatment.

At its best, diversion could improve on the therapeutic promise of voluntary addiction treatment by adding close supervision and constructive coercion. Unlike treatment on bond, treatment during diversion cannot be imposed without consulting the addict-defendant, but when diverted, the addict must submit to control. He acquires an immediate practical stake in success.

In some cities, local judges, prosecutors and treatment administrators are able to agree on an adequate working design for diversion; in others, they cannot. In Philadelphia, before TASC, the district attorney's office deferred prosecution in many drug-related cases, as part of the Accelerated Rehabilitative Disposition (ARD) program for minor offenders. Diverted addicts were not required to participate in treatment; to obtain a dismissal, they simply needed to remain arrest-free for two years. Philadelphia's program records do not show how many of the 2,500 defendants diverted annually under ARD were drug addicts. Estimates are from 50 to 80 per cent. Michael English, an authority on addict diversion who has observed the Philadelphia program, believes that about 20 per cent of all addicts appearing in the Court of Common Pleas received deferred prosecution. The introduction of a federally funded TASC program has made existing provisions for addict diversion in that city more systematic and explicit; it has also linked the courts and the treatment programs directly for the first time.

In Wilmington, the local TASC program may embrace the concept of deferred prosecution for addicts; if it is decided to do so, diversion will proceed on a case-by-case basis. In proportion to the number of addicts passing through the city's lockup, the number diverted will be small.

In Washington, D.C., a full-scale addict diversion plan proposed by the ABA Special Committee staff and the Lawyers' Committee for Civil Rights (LCCR) was blocked when the United States Attorney's office insisted on limiting eligibility to petty misdemeanants and retaining veto power even over them. One participant in the negotiations, Roderick Boggs of the LCRR, attributed the deadlock to the Nixon administration's reluctance to release narcotics addicts onto the streets of the nation's crime-control demonstration city. After the ABA Staff Report, the U. S. Attorney's office agreed to a diversion program limited to addicts charged with simple possession or possession of narcotics paraphernalia. This plan, the Superior Court Narcotics Pretrial Intervention Project, envisioned a limited practical test of "pure" addict diversion.

Candidates for diversion are selected from among those addicts released on a treatment-conditioned bond at arraignment who have demonstrated motivation by complying with their treatment conditions at least for three weeks. The U. S. Attorney's office has agreed to delegate the work of selecting candidates for participation, all of whom must meet minimum eligibility criteria, to an independent, court-affiliated project staff. NTA's multi-modality treatment program supplies medical services to program participants. The project staff provides special counseling and vocational services.

The program's design exhibits one peculiarity. In order to qualify, an addict must enter a conditional plea of guilty. After six months of successful participation in treatment, he is permitted to withdraw the plea; but if he is terminated by the project during the first six months of treatment, a judgment of conviction based on his plea will be entered, and conventional sentencing will follow. After a total of ten months of successful treatment, the addict earns an automatic, unconditional dismissal.

In New York City, restrictive pretrial release policies make it practical to concentrate recruiting efforts on addicts in post-arraignment detention. In a jurisdiction with more liberal bond policies, a diversion program recruiting clients only from detention would miss many eligible addicts. In most cities, intake for a comprehensive addict diversion program must reach addicts free on bond—with or without a treatment condition—and jailed addicts as well. Eligible addict-defendants should find routes to treatment leading from "threshold jails"—police lockups and courthouse holding pens—as well as central detention facilities.

New York City's two pilot projects have accumulated the most practical experience with addict diversion. The Tombs "Release Program" is sponsored by the Department of Correction's methadone detoxification system, the "Court Referral Project" by the city's Addiction Services Agency (ASA). Each plan routes addicts into treatment at pretrial and post-plea stages. Neither is affiliated with a multi-modality treatment program, since New York City has none; each makes its own diagnoses and completes its own referrals. Both have reached significant accommodations with the city's jails. By diverting treatable addicts from jail, they aim to end needless long-term pretrial detention, and to avoid needless prosecution of sick men and women.

Early in his experience at the Tombs, Dr. Vincent Dole discovered that many of the addicts on the detoxification floor wanted to continue treatment after release. In October 1971, he secured a commitment from the Beth Israel Hospital to provide methadone maintenance treatment for Tombs releasees at a special outpatient clinic in Harlem. The Manhattan DA would not grant to all releasees adjournments in contemplation of dismissal; Dr. Dole would not accept a counter-proposal that all releasees be required to plead their way into treatment. Basic eligibility criteria also were in dispute. Eventually, they agreed to disagree: they circumvented the impasse, deciding that the Release Program would proceed case by case. No addict would be excluded automatically by past record or present charge; the DA's office could, nevertheless, reject any candidate or require him to plead before release.

Between October 1971 and May 1972, 1,000 inmates were interviewed by the former street addict medical aides. Forty were rejected as ineligible, most of whom desired only drug-free treatment, which the program clinic could not offer. Before the Harlem clinic reached capacity and referrals ceased temporarily, 266 inmates were released to treatment. The participants have not equaled the records of the city's free, self-referred methadone maintenance patients because they display "greater social deterioration" and a "lesser degree of motivation," characteristics which Dr. Dole attributes to their representing "a fair sample of the most criminally active, anti-social group of heroin users."[120] By May 1972, 61 per cent of the original 266 were still active in treatment and arrest-free. Of the 12 per cent rearrested, half were considered "salvageable" by the clinical staff—good candidates for readmission after a resolution of their court cases.

As the DA's office relaxed its views on eligibility, inmates charged with possession and sale of heroin in small quantities began to be considered for the Release Program. The majority of releasees were still petty misdemeanants, but some charged with crimes as serious as armed robbery were accepted.

Dr. Dole believes that release programs can reach "hard-core" addicts with methadone maintenance treatment, although they seldom will seek it voluntarily. He also cites the Release Program's initial successes to confirm his belief in the value of short-

[120] Dole, "Release Program, Manhattan House of Detention" (mimeographed, July 24, 1972).

term "diagnostic detention."[121] He would take the next step of replacing detoxification areas of antiquated city jails with separate, specialized diagnostic detention centers, complete with medical facilities, offices for community treatment programs, and even on-site courtrooms. Addicts could be directed quickly into treatment, by diversion or non-custodial sentencing. In Dr. Dole's view, the diagnostic detention centers would be the embodiment of a new partnership between law and medicine in the treatment of criminal addiction, where doctors and judges could co-operate in dispensing substantial services to the addict population.

In January 1972, ASA's Court Referral Project began in the Brooklyn Criminal Court and the jails which feed it. Its staff of lawyers, ex-addicts, and paraprofessionals, performs an essentially medical referral service: matching its addict-clients with treatment programs of all descriptions.

The referral project succeeded an informal program through which detainees and other defendants met with representatives of community treatment programs. Many addicts were accepted for treatment and were released after an adjournment of trial or a guilty plea. The program to which each addict went after release was the luck of the draw—it was the program which had been holding office hours in rotation when he was first called for his interview. The result, not surprisingly, was a high failure rate for court-referred patients.

The Court Referral Project was designed to improve on this haphazard pattern of assignments, and to build on the Tombs' experiences with diagnostic work-ups during detoxification. The

---

121 This concept need not be restricted to heroin addicts:

A period of two weeks in detention could serve a useful purpose for many individuals, charged with a crime, if it is used for needed treatment and evaluation. Medical examination could show whether or not a desire has contributed to the alleged anti-social behavior. Narcotics addiction is the outstanding example of crime produced by disease. Treatment of addiction is needed to deal with the underlying cause of addicts' theft and robbery. Psychosis and brain damage likewise calls for appropriate medical management . . .

What is needed in detention is a systematic analysis of the detainee's problems, and mobilization of legal, social and medical resources to deal with them. [Statement of Dr. Vincent Dole, "Treatment and Rehabilitation of Narcotics Addicts," Hearings before Subcommittee No. 4 of the Committee on the Judiciary, House of Representatives, 92d Cong., 1st sess. (1971).]

project took the referral process beyond the courthouse into the jail libraries, dayrooms and cellblocks, where interviewers now meet addict-detainees.[122]

Of the 200 prisoners who pass through detoxification weekly in Brooklyn, about 70 per cent are clearly ineligible under the working understanding between the project and the DA. Among those excluded are all addicts charged with serious felonies, including burglary; crimes of violence, except simple assault; narcotics sales in any amount; and firearms violations. The background of detainees interviewed is thoroughly investigated, the options in addiction therapy are fully explained and program preferences—if any—are determined.

About one in four is washed out for lack of motivation. The others are matched with programs—highly motivated addicts with programs of minimal supervision, less motivated addicts with programs of greater holding power. Occasionally, a match conflicts with a client's own treatment preferences; if the project staff believes that he will benefit only from methadone maintenance, and he opposes all chemotherapy, the referral process may be at an end. It is a first principle of the Court Referral Project that "no defendant will be placed in a treatment which he does not wish to enter."[123]

When a match has been made, the treatment program selected must accept the referral; with drug-free programs, this usually takes only hours or days, but for methadone maintenance the interval can be from ten days to two weeks, a delay that hampers the project's efforts to effect placements: "As a result of the time lapse, many defendants refuse to apply [for methadone maintenance] even though this modality is their choice for treatment."[124] The project staff takes each case to a daily conference with the DA's staff. Through July 1972, about half of the defendants they proposed were rejected. Of the rest, about one third

[122] A prisoner who is not in detoxification may also request an interview with the referral project staff. Other requests come from addicts free on pretrial bond, and from addicts on probation or parole who have been cited for violations. Occasionally, the project is asked to conduct an interview by a judge seeking alternatives to penal sentencing, or by a probation officer preparing a presentence report.

[123] Addiction Services Agency, the City of New York, "Description of the Court Referral Project" (mimeographed) (n.d.).

[124] ASA Court Referral Project, "Quarterly Report, April 1, 1972–July 1, 1972" (mimeographed, 1972).

were approved for referral on an adjourned trial basis; most of the rest were required to plead.[125] The project opposes the mandatory plea on principle; but it finds that clients with prior criminal records are little affected in practice. The DA's office, for its part, has never required a plea from an eligible first offender.

The administrators of the Court Referral Project believe that without the restrictive eligibility standards, the number of successful referrals could be doubled. They anticipate gradual relaxation of these standards. The staff has been able to convince the prosecutors to waive their exclusionary policies in certain cases. As a rule, for example, no addict charged with a residential burglary will be considered for pretrial diversion or post-plea referral to treatment by the DA's office. But where special facts appear, such as a close relationship between the burglar and the proprietor of the burgled premises, exceptions sometimes are made.

In its first seven months of operation, the project conducted almost 1,400 interviews. It placed 350 clients, of whom almost 69.4 per cent remained active in treatment and arrest-free as of July 1972. Discounting commitments to the prison hospitals of the Narcotic Addiction Control Commission (NACC), the success rate was about 65 per cent. NACC commitment—which is regarded as overrestrictive and minimally therapeutic—is the one form of treatment which the referral project staff have attempted to dissuade clients from accepting; the project completes such referrals only when a client insists, or when he is a NACC absconder with warrants against him which NACC cannot be persuaded to withdraw. Only about 40 per cent of all placements were to methadone maintenance programs; most of the balance were to therapeutic communities and other drug-free programs with generally poor holding records. A few went to an experimental outpatient antagonist clinic at the Kings County Hospital.

The clients of the Court Referral Project who showed this remarkable progress were young, hard-core heroin addicts, averaging twenty-four years of age, seven prior arrests, three convictions and more than two years of prison time. Before treatment intervention, they were being held in lieu of bail averaging $1,500.[126]

[125] About 10 per cent of the project's referrals were convicted addicts awaiting sentence or probation with treatment.
[126] ASA Court Referral Project, "Quarterly Report: April 1, 1972–July 1, 1972," p. 5.

The success of the Court Referral Project is due to the care it takes to match addicts and programs, the energy with which it resists attempts from the bench to second-guess its placements,[127] and to the personalized attention it devotes to its clients. Project staff members accompany clients from the courtroom to the treatment program to forestall slippage and relapse during the crucial hours after release. If a client shows signs of failure in his assigned program, the project attempts to arrange a new court referral.

Up to the moment of the judicial referral hearing, clients can and do reject the project's services; even in court, some have reversed themselves to choose thirty or ninety days of confinement over a longer period of supervised community care. Clients' active and voluntary participation in the referral process has been an additional factor in their treatment success.

Early release from jail is the obvious and key spur to clients' participation. It serves the interest of the Department of Correction, as well. Project administrators estimate that the total cost of each completed referral is $300. Addicts assisted by the project average only twelve days in the Brooklyn Men's House of Detention; other inmates, thirty-five days of pretrial detention. With the daily cost of holding a prisoner in Brooklyn thirteen dollars, the public saves $299 for every addict-inmate the project refers. The project is now funded by federal grants, but has demonstrated that locally financed addict diversion could pay its own way.

The Court Referral Project has the potential to provide service in volume. In September 1972, the Court Referral Project expanded its operations into Manhattan, where it now co-operates

---

[127] Every Court Referral Project placement must, of course, receive the judicial sanction after it is granted the prosecutorial blessing. And in court, difficulties can arise:

> There are . . . certain numbers of the judiciary who still believe that jail will "cure" an addict . . . [T]his type of judge will still send an addict to prison, even though the sentence is a short one (e.g., 60 to 90 days).

> The other problem is the bias certain judges have against one type of treatment or another . . . [I]t is usually impossible to convince that judge that his "clinical" evaluation of a defendant's needs might be incorrect. If the Court insists on sending an addict to treatment, completely opposite to our recommendation, it is our policy to withdraw from the case. [ASA Court Referral Project, "Quarterly Report April 1, 1972–July 1, 1972," p. 3.]

with the Tombs Release Program. Project administrators believe that citywide expansion would bring 10,000 addicts into treatment annually if prosecutorial ground rules were relaxed to include motivated addicts charged with drug-related offenses such as sale of narcotics and burglary. Of that total, 6,500 or 7,000 could be predicted to succeed on their first referral. A jail-based diversion program on this scale could have a major impact on the city's heroin epidemic.

Many communities will adopt addict diversion on their own. Others will follow the lure of federal money; still others may soon be operating such programs in response to new judicial interpretations of narcotics law.

In *Watson* v. *United States*,[128] a case involving an addict-trafficker, the U. S. Court of Appeals in Washington, D.C., suggested that addiction would be a good defense for a user charged with simple possession of narcotics. Some D.C. trial courts recognized addiction as a defense.[129] Then, in a major test case, *United States* v. *Moore,* after hearing arguments that possession of heroin is the inevitable result of a disease condition over which an addict had no control, and that to punish such possession would violate both the common-law rule that there can be no offense without intent and the Eighth Amendment guarantee against excessive punishment, the D.C. federal appeals court repudiated its earlier suggestion.[130] In a five-to-four decision, a majority of the court concluded that the penal-rehabilitative approach to the treatment of narcotics offenders was not so thoroughly discredited that it could be discarded through judicial action. In opinions which filled more than 200 pages, both the majority and the dissenters noted that little is known with certainty about either the etiology or the treatment of addiction. Although the decision in

128 439 F. 2d 442 (D.C. Cir. 1970) (*en banc*). See Note, "Emerging Recognition of Pharmacological Duress as a Defense to Possession of Narcotics," 59 *Geo. L. J.* 761 (1971).
129 *United States* v. *Ashton,* 317 F. Supp. 860 (D.D.C. 1970) (indictment dismissed on uncontroverted proof of addiction); *United States* v. *Lindsey,* 324 F. Supp. 55 (D.D.C. 1971) (defense of criminal incapacity recognized but evidence of addiction found insufficient); *United States* v. *Allen* (D.C. Super. Ct. Nos. 41333-70 & 21031-70, February 10, 1971) (information dismissed on uncontroverted proof of addiction); *United States* v. *Bowser* (D.C. Super. Ct. No. 45504-70, February 24, 1971) (jury instruction recognizing defense granted; verdict of not guilty).
130 *United States* v. *Moore,* 158 U.S. App. D.C. 375, 486 F. 2d 1139 (1973).

Moore represents a temporary setback in the campaign to rationalize narcotics law enforcement, the court clearly left the door open
for reconsideration of the issues posed, based upon new medical
evidence.

The recognition that it was certainly unjust, and possibly unconstitutional, to punish chronic alcoholics for drunkenness stirred
the development of new alcoholic detoxification centers. Extension
of the defense of "pharmacological duress" to addicts, if and when
such extension comes, would be likely to stimulate interest in
the development of new non-criminal dispositions for comparable
defendants. Of the available alternatives to punishment, the most
practical and promising is limited-term commitment to outpatient
addiction treatment. Addict diversion now begins with a plea of
guilty or an adjournment of trial. In the future, it may begin with
a verdict of "not guilty by reason of addiction."

PROBATION FOR ADDICTS

Although addicts routinely are sentenced to conventional[131]
probation after convictions for minor offenses, most jurisdictions
make no special provisions for their treatment on probation. Addicts who participate in addiction therapy on probation can, however, fulfill the typical goals and conditions of probation more
successfully. In the mid-1960's, experienced New York City probation supervisors noted dramatic changes when their addicted
clients enrolled in voluntary methadone programs:

> Probationers who were previously anxious, unproductive, and
> anti-social when addicted to heroin, became normal human beings
> and were quickly reabsorbed into the community through employ-
> ment and healthier social lives. Also, those with additional emo-
> tional or social problems could be reached and referred for
> help.[132]

[131] "Conventional" probation—in which release following a guilty plea or a
conviction at trial is granted on conditions set at the discretion of the court,
with the advice of pre-sentence reports prepared by probation officers—
differs from the sort of probation which is a practical substitute for addict
diversion, and follows a clear understanding that a guilty plea will result
in release to treatment.
[132] Herman Joseph and Vincent P. Dole, "Methadone Patients on Probation
and Parole," *Federal Probation,* June 1970, pp. 42, 47.

The burdens of the probationers were eased, and the work of their supervisors was simplified.

By 1970, officials of the city's probation department had concluded that treatment programs were not capable of returning a substantial number of addicts to normal functioning within the community.[133] An estimated 40 per cent of their clients were heroin users, and only those enrolled in methadone maintenance were making consistent progress. Many had been discouraged from enrolling in public methadone programs by long waiting lists. Others had been frustrated by the difficulties of reporting regularly to both a treatment clinic and a probation officer.

With the help of Beth Israel Hospital, the city Probation Department opened a special methadone clinic in its own Manhattan offices. Probationers could begin treatment without long delay. The new Probation Methadone Clinic served 125 patients, with a casework staff of three specially trained supervisors. Two years later, there are five such clinics (two in Manhattan, one each in Brooklyn, the Bronx and Queens), serving more than 600 probationers. In late 1972, 85 per cent of the patients who had begun treatment under the program had remained active in treatment and arrest-free during their probation; the majority had continued in treatment afterwards.[134] By all indices of success in treatment —with the significant exception of improved job status—program participants did about as well as New York City's free, self-referred methadone patients.

Medically, the Probation Methadone Program offers few services beyond methadone and the group therapy sessions in which a few probationers take part. Herman Joseph, the program's director, attributes much of its success to the commitment and expertise of its probation supervisors, who are especially trained to provide counseling services and supervision, and carry heavy caseloads

[133] Joseph and Dale, op. cit., p. 42.
[134] When a probationer and his supervisor agree that he has made satisfactory progress, the department recommends that his initial one-to-three-year term of probation be terminated. After formal court action, the former probationer can transfer to one of New York City's non-specialized methadone maintenance programs, again bypassing waiting lists. Most program participants transfer between six months and a year after beginning treatment. As of September 1972, the Probation Methadone Program had admitted 822 patient-clients; 98 had been terminated unfavorably and 91 transferred on completing probation; 50 were awaiting transfer and the balance remained in treatment at a probation clinic.

—usually around sixty-five clients each. A program participant reporting daily for medication finds daily counseling available as well, either from his supervisor or from one of the successful methadone patients who work in the program as research assistants.

Joseph believes that the most critical factor in the program's success is the voluntary nature of the decision to begin and remain in treatment. Every addict who joins the program is free on probation; he earns no legal concessions by volunteering. Methadone maintenance is never mandated by a sentence of conventional probation in the New York City criminal courts, and program participants "are free to withdraw . . . treatment without fear of violating conditions of their probation."[135] Since no probationer enters the program against his will, treatment efforts need not be geared to the demands of a hostile or reluctant faction of patients. Because participants have chosen methadone maintenance for themselves, they regard it as a valuable medical service rather than a burdensome imposition. Supervisors can work flexibly with those who lapse temporarily, attempting to bring them back into methadone treatment or to place them in other, more appropriate programs.[136]

Without compromising its special philosophy of treatment, the New York City Probation Methadone Program is moving to recruit additional voluntary patients from among the addicts being held for trial in the city's jails.

At its inception, the program dealt only with volunteers who already had passed through the jails and the courts. Once an addict's term of probation began, he could request methadone treatment at any time, on his own initiative or at the suggestion of his case supervisor. Like all New York City methadone maintenance patients, participants were required to be at least eighteen years old, and to have been addicted for at least two years.

[135] Joseph, "Court Services and Methadone Treatment: The New York City Probation Programs," Proceedings, Third National Conference on Methadone Treatment (Washington, D.C.: Government Printing Office, 1971), pp. 104, 107.

[136] Some of the participants in the Probation Methadone Program have been released with a general condition requiring them to "seek treatment, if addicted." Whether a particular probationer *is* addicted is a question for his supervisor; the choice of treatments is for the probationer himself. Since unsupervised abstinence qualifies as "treatment," a probationer may elect to treat himself.

Probationers with addicted husbands or wives were required to persuade their spouses to enter treatment also before they would be accepted themselves. If he passed a required physical examination, and met basic eligibility criteria, a probationer could be admitted to the program about ten days later.

For addicts released on probation directly from detention, these ten days are a time of special danger, when they are most liable to relapse, readdiction and possible rearrest.

Probation officers working in the Tombs have begun to experiment with interviewing candidates during detention, and completing paperwork before the disposition of their cases. If they are sentenced to probation, they will be able to go directly from the courtroom to the clinic.[137]

The administrators of the program do not expect to increase enrollment dramatically during their experiment. They admit that the program benefits only those addicts who need a special mix of medical care and close supervision.

As an alternative to jailing, addiction treatment on probation is of greatest importance for sentenced prisoners. In many jurisdictions, the addict-misdemeanants who are treated successfully on probation in New York City would serve thirty days to a year in a jail or local prison, returning eventually to heroin and crime. Treatment on probation can reduce the jail population and interrupt the cycle of arrest, punishment, relapse and rearrest.

The design of the New York City Probation Methadone Program has not been imitated directly in other jurisdictions,[138] but special probation for addicts is gradually gaining currency. Some cities are without formal programs, but employ treatment on probation regularly. In Cincinnati, for example, judges, probation

[137] In working up addicts' cases, probation officers will rely on interview forms prepared by the staff of the Department of Correction's detoxification program. Use of this resource will speed the preparation of pre-sentence reports on addict-defendants. If their wait in detention between detoxification and release on probation can be reduced, addict-probationers will begin treatment while their motivation is still strong.

[138] Such imitation has been confined to the New York City area. The office of the U. S. Attorney for the Southern District of New York has promoted a specialized methadone clinic for federal addict-offenders—both probationers and defendants on adjourned trial status—with TASC financing from the federal government. The New York State Division of Parole plans a Manhattan parole methadone clinic for former addicts released from upstate prisons.

officials and treatment administrators have agreed that treatment at a local methadone maintenance clinic can be imposed as a condition of probation.[139]

In other jurisdictions, treatment on probation has been reduced to a system. Recent legislation authorizes Georgia courts to require treatment during probation,[140] that state's addict-probationers can be sentenced to the care of the multi-modality Georgia Narcotics Treatment Program (GNTP), which prescribes treatment, usually methadone maintenance, for referred probationers. Failure to observe "[s]trict adherence to the treatment program requirements . . . is likely to result in a revocation of their probation."[141] While the GNTP treatment staff does not police compliance, it reports the lack of it to the probation supervisor. The supervisor determines "how many days missed attendance or how many dirty urines will be considered a violation," and when probation should be revoked.

GNTP treatment personnel note that many pre-sentence reports on addict-defendants still contain no recommendations for treatment; late in 1972, only about fifty probationers were enrolled with GNTP at court direction. In Georgia—and elsewhere—the suspicion and skepticism of probation officers must be overcome before large numbers of convicted addicts can be treated in the community.

Many probation officers distrust methadone maintenance as a "substitute addiction," but a unified program for treatment on probation need not rely on methadone as its only resource. In New York City, several case supervisors now work exclusively with clients who are in residential therapeutic drug-free communities. Specialized clinics dispensing narcotic antagonist drugs could supply another medical alternative for addict-probationers.

Exclusive reliance on methadone will reinforce professional and community resistance against treatment-conditioned probation;

[139] Correspondence from John L. Smith, director, Methadone Treatment Center, Cincinnati, Ohio, July 13, 1972, on file at Goldfarb and Singer, Washington, D.C.
[140] "Narcotics Research, Rehabilitation and Treatment," Hearings before the Select Committee on Crime of the House of Representatives, 92d Cong., 1st sess., 624 (1971).
[141] Georgia Narcotics Treatment Program, "Some Suggested Procedures for Referral of Individuals on Probation to the Georgia Narcotics Treatment Program" (mimeographed, January 1972), p. 2.

such reliance also may result in the jailing of some addicts with short or sporadic histories of heroin use, who do not qualify for maintenance programs, while others with "substantial histories of opiate use" are placed directly on methadone and probation.[142] The range of treatment services available must reflect the diversity of the addict population, if youthful addicts and addicts who oppose methadone are to be kept from jail.

THERAPY IN JAIL

For the addict-defendant who has not been diverted or sentenced to probation, criminal processing may end where it began —in a local jail. While many convicted heroin users are in state and federal prisons, jails which serve as city and county prisons are crowded with addicts serving short sentences. A few jails conduct token group therapy sessions or arrange occasional visits from volunteer counselors. Fewer still make an attempt to provide real treatment during incarceration.

Many forms of treatment used in the community cannot be adapted to penal institutions. Treatment authorities agree that there is little sense in providing methadone maintenance in jail. If contraband traffic is controlled, the jailed addict does not need the protection which methadone maintenance offers; his craving for narcotics tends to be activated not in jail, but in the community where he is exposed to other drug users.

Therapeutic community treatment is not necessarily inappropriate to a penal institution. Its use has been pioneered at the federal prison in Danbury, Connecticut, where convicted criminal addicts live and work together in designated sections of the institution. Prisoners pass through a twelve-month residential "cycle," then return to the general prison population to await release. In an ordinary therapeutic community, residence is open-ended, and residents are not expected to graduate by a fixed date. In other respects, the Danbury program imitates its free world models closely. To a surprising degree, participants make their own rules and manage their treatment. When they first enter one of the Dan-

---

[142] See John Kramer, "Parole, Probation, Police and Methadone Maintenance," in S. Einstein, ed., *Methadone Maintenance* (1971) 104, at 107 New York: Marcel Dekker, Inc., 1971.

bury communities, they are assigned menial tasks, but as the residential "cycle" progresses, they assume increasing responsibility. A federal judge who visited Danbury came away shocked by the brutal intensity of its inmate-managed encounter sessions. By contrast, a recent Danbury graduate—now living drug-free and working as a juvenile detention counselor—spoke of the program with enthusiasm.

A few local jails have established therapeutic communities for sentenced addicts, drawing heavily on the Danbury model. At the Dade County Stockade, the Miami Drug Treatment Program conducts a community for sentenced male addicts; a similar community for female inmates will be available soon.

Jail-based therapeutic communities encounter problems which facilities for long-term sentenced prisoners avoid. Continuity of residence in a jail is difficult to maintain. Sentenced addicts in local jails can expect early release whether or not they participate in a therapeutic community program, and thus have no special incentive to join.

Addiction is, at least in part, an environmental disease; no amount of preparation in an artificial atmosphere of a therapeutic community will arm most former addicts to resist the pressures of the street. The double artificiality of a therapeutic community operating within a penal institution makes it questionable whether graduates will be fully prepared to avoid relapse upon release.

POST-RELEASE TREATMENT

No in-jail program can forestall relapse and readdiction on release. Addicts serving short jail sentences are best helped through programs which assist them in getting treatment after release with a minimum of inconvenience and delay.

Jail inmates could volunteer for admission to community methadone programs, or be stabilized on maintenance doses before their release, as shown in a New Orleans pilot project initiated by Judge Andrew Buccaro. According to a 1971 report: "10 of the most chronic offenders—'revolving door shoplifters'—were started on programs while still incarcerated. Seven of these ten patients are currently doing well."[143]

[143] Wm. A. Bloom and E. Ward Sudderth, "Methadone in New Orleans Patients, Problems and Police," in Einstein, *Methadone Maintenance,* at 127.

The experiment in pre-release methadone induction at the New Orleans Parish Prison was a therapeutic success; apparently it was a bureaucratic failure. Sheriff Louis Hyde said, in a recent interview, that it had been discontinued for "administrative" reasons. In Connecticut, however, where all jails operate under state authority, pre-release induction is still being practiced. Hartford State Jail inmates can enroll in local methadone programs before discharge, to continue as voluntary outpatients at community clinics afterwards.

In other jurisdictions, there is active informal co-operation between jails and addiction treatment programs. A psychiatrist affiliated with the Jackson County Jail in Kansas City, Missouri, described that city's past-release program:

> Many prisoners find their times of greatest stress are when they are ready to leave the jail. These prisoners are afraid they will again become addicted to Heroin when they leave the Jackson County Jail. These prisoners are advised to go immediately to the Methadone Program at the Western Missouri Mental Health Center or the University of Kansas Medical Center when they leave the jail so they again can start on Methadone rather than getting Heroin on the street.[144]

If antagonist treatment becomes more widespread, in-jail stabilization for prisoners who elect it would be a logical development. Free world therapeutic communities, which cannot begin to assist addicts during incarceration, could send representatives to visit local jails and interview interested prisoners, so that space could be reserved for qualifying addict-inmates to enter immediately after release.

JAILING AND CASE-FINDING: POTENTIAL FOR ABUSE

The jail has considerable potential as a case-finding facility for community-based addiction treatment. One New York City treatment administrator recently said it: "We haven't really begun to tap the Tombs."

But the specter of civil commitment has cast a shadow over all

[144] Correspondence from Carleton L. Lindgren, M.D., undated (received July 24, 1972), on file at Goldfarb and Singer, Washington, D.C.

New York City's recent innovations with in-jail addict detoxification and referral. New York State addict commitment legislation has authorized the Narcotic Addiction Control Commission to proceed against addicts identified in detention. NACC has deferred to New York City's community-based treatment programs and addict diversion programs, but there can be no assurance this policy will persist, especially in the face of the harsh new statutory minimum penalties which now apply to persons convicted of drug law violations in the state. If "addict quarantine" should have a new vogue, New York jails may become the first stop along the route to NACC's prison-hospitals.

In California, the jails have been regularly employed in the intake phase of civil commitment. The California legislation authorized the diagnostic detention of suspected addicts in a "suitable medical institution," even when they are not currently charged with any offense. Since February 1966, the designated institution in Los Angeles County has been the Central Jail Infirmary. When the jail assumed this new function, the Los Angeles police estimated that as many as 1,500 "civil addicts" a year might pass into commitment through the infirmary.

The case-finding potential of the jails can be misused. Most heroin addicts are amenable to one or another of the treatments available in the community. If the jails funnel them against their will into medically dubious institutional programs, the repressive policies which first created the problem of criminal addiction will be perpetuated and reinforced.

The addict inmate in jail is not a new problem, but he is a major one. At best, inadequate jails have been an indifferent way station for addicts in trouble; at worst, they have been incubators for addicts, places to get hooked, halls of horrors for desperate addicts in need of help.

But with some ingenuity and change, jails, or their metropolitan detention center counterparts of the future, could serve positive, useful roles in the handling of narcotics addicts.

Most obviously and most simply, they could be centers for detoxification. While this humane process is no cure to addiction, it is the first step in that direction. The pretrial period is a prime time to identify a major portion of the addict population, to diagnose and classify addicts.

The jail could serve a long-term role in diverting addicts into appropriate treatment programs in the community, or in referring them to treatment programs in jail if they cannot be released.

To take these steps would transform a negative institution into a positive one, and channel people away from troubled, punitive conditions into treatment-oriented, corrective programs.

5

ALCOHOLICS IN JAIL

As I walked through the modest Greenville, Mississippi, City Jail one Tuesday morning in May 1971, with Sheriff W. C. Burney, taking what for me had become the typical tour and asking my by now stock questions, we came to the subject of alcoholics. Greenville has a substantial number of them in its jail; they compose a regular part of its clientele, just as is the case in every other city. As we talked, we passed a cell housing several men. One very worn old man ambled over toward us. Sheriff Burney said to me, nodding in his direction: "Now, that guy must have been in here fifty times since I've been around; let's ask him." The man came toward us, a frightened, inquisitive look on his seedy face. "How many times you been in here with me _____," Sheriff Burney asked him. "About a hundred and fifty times," he replied.

Later, having seen the rest of this jail, as we sat sipping coffee in the sheriff's office, we came back to the subject of alcoholics. "People call us about them; it's a big public issue around here. Some people are frightened when they see a menacing-looking drunk coming toward them and call us to get him off the streets. Others see a man laid out on the street and think he's dead of a heart attack or somethin' and call us or the hospital. They just want them off the streets, and I don't blame them," he said.

"But," he admitted, "it's a waste sending most of them to jail. We get 'em for a few days, clean 'em up; they get some decent food and some rest. Then they go to court, get a fine—maybe a short sentence, a few days or weeks, then they're back on the street again and drunk that night. What good have we done?" Alcoholics Anonymous is a help, he said, "they pull one out from time to time." But they are not enough. And, he added, "Some of the alcoholics are so disgusting, I hate to let them in my jail."

When I asked the sheriff what he would prefer to see done instead, he said he would send alcoholics to some treatment-oriented facility more like a hospital than a jail. "It wouldn't help all of them, of course," he admitted, "but it would do some good for some of them, without doubt." That would be more than the costly, ceremonious, revolving door system presently used in America's jails to deal with the common drunk.

Sheriff L. B. Williams, long-time chief of the Bolivar County Jail in Cleveland, Mississippi, felt differently. When I asked him if he found fault with the routine jailing of alcoholics, he said: "We put 'em upstairs and let 'em sweat it out. Sometimes I send up a cup full of whiskey to help 'em out. But this does as good as and costs less than taking them to hospital. I do call in a doctor if they get the DT's."

Walking to my office at the Justice Department just about every day for about four years in the early 1960's, as I passed the corner of Ninth Street and Constitution Avenue, invariably I had to sidestep a cluster of drunks who would be panhandling, loitering or in the winter lying on the ground across a wide grate through which emanated enough hot air to keep them from freezing in their stuporous, street sleep.

When I asked the superintendent of the D. C. Jail in those days about his drunk population, he said:

"Drunks are brought into our jail by the droves, especially on Mondays. The largest number of cases have to do with the progeny of minor intoxication-related charges—disorderly conduct, etc."

"My brother worked a day and a half processing in alcoholics and quit," one prison official said. "If you can get past the stench, the sight of these alcoholics could make you sick," said another. "I asked one how he could live on the streets in the winter with just a suit coat on, and he opened his shirt and I saw that his body was wrapped in old, decayed newspapers. When we took the papers off the man, some of the skin came off with it. I lost my breakfast.

"One alcoholic wore eight pairs of rubbers to keep warm when he slept on the streets. As we took them off and got down to the last pair, part of his foot came off. We sent him to the hospital and they laid him down with his feet out the window in blankets—the smell was so bad."

At the D. C. Jail, these alcoholics were thrown in at random with all the other inmates awaiting court action in minor cases. When I asked one of the officials how he felt about this, he said that the police are probably saving a lot of lives by arresting these people, but that the jail is not the place to deal with them after they are picked up from the streets. Proper hospitalization might help alcoholics; it surely would relieve the jails' overpopulation problem.

CLASSLESS DRUG: CLASS-ORIENTED LAWS

Beverage alcohol is America's drug of choice. How many people use it is impossible to determine. How many misuse it is also difficult to ascertain. In 1962, Mark Keller of the Rutgers Center for Alcohol Studies estimated that 4.5 million Americans could be classified "alcoholics."[1] Don Callahan, an authority on drinking problems, states that 9 per cent of the population (approximately 6,500,000 persons) are seriously afflicted heavy drinkers.[2] A special federal task force recently found that "about 9 million men and women are alcohol abusers and alcoholic individuals."[3] Alcoholism is the third most serious American public health problem (after cancer and heart disease).

Legal and social responses to deviant drinking are heavily biased against certain social classes, yet drinking and alcoholism are classless. "Heavy drinkers" exist in comparable percentages in all economic, educational and professional classes. (In the most comprehensive recent survey of alcohol use in America, only

[1] Keller, "The Definition of Alcoholism and the Estimation of its Prevalence" in D. Pittman and C. Snyder, eds., *Society, Culture and Drinking Patterns* (New York: J. Wylie, 1962), pp. 310, 312. This estimate is based on mortality rates for cirrhosis of the liver and corresponds to a relatively restrictive definition of "alcoholism" which excludes many other drinkers, whose day-to-day functioning is impaired by alcohol use.

[2] D. Callahan, *The Problem Drinker*. The class of "problem drinkers"—men and women who experience some medical or social difficulty because of alcohol use—may number as many as thirty million.

[3] U. S. Department of Health, Education, and Welfare, *First Special Report to the U. S. Congress on Alcohol and Health* (Washington, D.C.: Government Printing Office, 1971), p. viii.

upper-middle-class persons over sixty years of age showed a markedly lower rate of "heavy drinking" than members of other groups.)[4]

Yet, the laws against drunkenness have come to be applied discriminately to lower-status persons, primarily.

The costs generated by problem drinking throughout American society are high, totaling $15 billion by one recent estimate.[5] About $10 million of this is in lost work time. According to the General Accounting Office, the U. S. Army alone loses the equivalent of $120 million annually through the absenteeism and impaired productivity of alcoholic personnel. $3 billion takes the form of property damage, private medical expenses and other direct losses. According to the National Safety Council, alcohol-related traffic accidents in themselves generate costs of $1.8 billion annually, along with half of all traffic fatalities. The remaining $2 billion is expended in cash or kind through public service programs for alcoholics and their families. The indirect costs of alcohol abuse—the personal suffering and social disruption—cannot be assigned a dollar value.

Buried somewhere in the national bill for alcohol abuse is a relatively small but shockingly anomalous item: the costs of enforcing the public drunkenness laws. The most comprehensive study of this expense item was made in Atlanta, Georgia, during 1961. For roughly 50,000 arrests, the cost of apprehending, detaining, trying and jailing drunkenness offenders totaled about $870,000.[6] If Atlanta's examples were typical of the costs of drunkenness law enforcement, the nation's bill for expenses stemming from two million arrests for intoxication and equivalent offenses would be about $35 million. But Atlanta is not typical: a drunk arrest is estimated to take fifteen minutes in Atlanta, but in some cities it may consume up to three hours of police time. Because Atlanta prosecutes so many drunkenness offenders, court processing is cost-efficient. And while the average cost of maintain-

[4] D. Callahan, J. Cisin, and H. Cressley, *American Drinking Practices* (1969), pp. 26–27.
[5] U. S. Department of Health, Education, and Welfare, *First Special Report to the U. S. Congress on Alcohol and Health,* p. viii.
[6] See President's Commission on Law Enforcement and Administration of Justice, *Task Force Report: Drunkenness* (Washington, D.C.: Government Printing Office, 1967), pp. 98–99.

ing a sentenced inmate in Atlanta's jails was estimated in 1961 at $1.69, other jails today report a cost as high as eight or nine dollars. Estimating a conservative four dollars per inmate-day, the direct cost of jailing convicted drunkenness offenders alone may approach $50 million annually in the 1970's.[7] If Atlanta is viewed as a city where drunkenness law enforcement is exceptionally efficient and if a decade of cost inflation is taken into account, the national cost of such enforcement overall appears to be in the hundreds of millions of dollars. This expense is incurred in an ineffective attempt to control the behavior of an unfortunate minority of Americans who make up no more than 10 to 15 per cent of the total population of serious problem drinkers.[8] It is one by-product of a pattern of legal discrimination against lower-class alcohol abusers which is as old as the nation itself.

The United States historically has been ambivalent about the use of alcohol. In striking contrast to the general acceptance of a norm of abstinence in Moslem cultures, or the prevailing permissive attitude toward drinking in some European nations and Japan,[9] America has been torn between the "Wets" and the "Drys" —between permissiveness and punitive measures toward use.

As early as 1619, the Virginia Colony adopted a rigid anti-drunkenness statute, which in effect made the first offender an offender against God's law, subject to a private reproof from his minister. The second offender was dealt with as an offender against public morals, with a public dressing down as his due. But the third offender, the colonial prototype of today's "chronic drunkenness offender," was punished as a criminal, with a twelve-hour spell in the stocks and a fine.

The Virginia Colony's ordinance—the first example of American drunkenness law—derives from an English statute of James I, adopted in 1606, for "repressing the odious and loathsome sin of drunkenness." Drunkenness was described in the preamble as

[7] This figure is based on an estimate of 12,200,000 man-days of time served, which is explained in detail below at pp. 226–27.

[8] This is the estimate of the Joint Information Service of the American Psychiatric Association and the National Association for Mental Health, in S. Cahn, *The Treatment of Alcoholics* (New York: Oxford Univ. Press, 1967).

[9] For a description of a nation with general tolerance for alcohol use—and an insignificant rate of problem drinking—see G. Lolli et al., *Alcoholism in Italian Culture* (Rutgers Center for Alcohol Studies, 1964).

the root and foundation of many other enormous sins, as blood-shed, stabbing, murder, swearing, fornication, adultery and such like, the great dishonor of God, and of our nation, the overthrow of many good arts and manual trades, the disabling of divers workmen, and the general impoverishing of many good subjects, abusively wasting the good creatures of God.

Mere public drunkenness previously had not been an offense at English common law. The act of 1606, however, prescribed stiff penalties: a fine of five shillings for each offense, to be paid over to the local churchwardens, and six hours in the stocks for any violator unable to produce this substantial sum.

The English statute's concern with the social fallouts of drunkenness, particularly among the laboring classes, anticipated a pattern in legislation and law enforcement that grew to dominance in post-Revolutionary America. In colonial times, alcohol use as such had not been regarded as a social or legal problem, and informal social control over drinking behavior prevailed in the relatively close-knit colonial communities. Beer and wine were served at meals. The tavern was an important social center. As towns grew, drunkenness increased, but it still was readily contained.[10]

In post-Revolutionary America, an ambivalence toward drinking grew more pronounced and internalized social and religious controls waned. As the laboring and artisan classes asserted new social and economic independence, drunkenness among these common classes came to be viewed by the power structure as a growing moral danger.

The aristocratic legislators and magistrates of the young republic assumed the leadership of the organized temperance movement; they also reacted forcefully to the presence of the public inebriate. They enforced existing statutes prohibiting drunkenness with new vigor. Drunkards were punished under the harsher provisions of acts against vagrancy and vagabondage. And new statutory drunkenness law, much of it still in force today, had its origins in these last decades of the eighteenth century, as the "responsible" classes took steps against intemperance of their charges. The modern criminal justice system in the United States is their direct heir.

[10] See Gosfield, "Status Conflicts and the Changing Ideologies of the American Temperance Movement," in Pittman and Snyder, eds., *Society, Culture and Drinking Patterns.*

To the public man of 1800, the apparent spread of inebriety was more than an aesthetic blight and an offense against morality; it was a portent of anarchy, and a manifest threat to the social order. Post-colonial officials, like the prison supervisors who filled their journals with "case histories" detailing how young criminals had come to grief through drink, took the causal relationship between intemperance and serious crime as a central premise. Drunkenness law began to be enforced with a pronounced class bias. Drunk or sober, the substantial townsman was seen as neither a threat to the established order nor a potential recruit to a life of crime. The drunken laborer or migrant was both.

The promise of a sober, tractable and industrious lower-class population depended on individual reformation, and reformation came to be dependent upon correctional confinement. In the early nineteenth century offenders were less often fined, flogged and publicly humiliated than they had been earlier; incarceration in local jails or workhouses was substituted instead. A sentence of penal confinement would, it was reasoned, deter the drunkard from future misconduct, wean him from drink and evil society, and reintroduce him to the virtues of regular work and personal discipline. There has been little change in official policy to this day.

A survey of local jails, poorhouses and other public holding facilities throughout the Northeast, conducted in 1833–34 by the temperance pamphleteer and propagandist Samuel Chipman, disclosed what its author had hoped to find: an overwhelming majority of "intemperates" in every jail polled. The descriptive notes accompanying the statistics, however, show that most of these inmates were simple drunkenness offenders.

By the 1830's, jailing for drunkenness was common practice, Chipman's comments show. The futile "revolving door" cycle, the practice of repeatedly jailing a relatively small number of chronic offenders, had begun. Of the jail in Erie County, New York, for example, he noted:

> The number of *commitments*, in this jail, in proportion to the number of *persons* committed, is larger than I have found in any other; but in every jail I find that many of the intemperate have been committed repeatedly, and *always* occasioned by ardent spirit. In some instances the intemperate spend more than half the time in prison *solely* on account of their intemperance.

Judge Benjamin Whitman of the Boston Police Court told Chipman that during his eleven years on the bench in the early nineteenth century, 1,661 of all the 9,661 cases examined by him were "tried on the direct charge of being common drunkards!" Of the rest,

> such as vagabonds, assaults and batteries, lewd and lascivious conduct, and every species of crime . . . I am satisfied that more than one-half of the same were directly or indirectly caused by intemperance.

The FBI's *Uniform Crime Reports* estimate that in 1972 police made 1,676,800 arrests for "drunkenness," out of a total of about 8,712,400 arrests for all non-traffic offenses. This total is more than double that for the next largest offense category in the FBI's breakdown, "larceny-theft" (829,900). The same statistics also show 696,800 arrests for disorderly conduct and 66,000 arrests for vagrancy—both designations frequently employed to cover mere drunkenness, because of police lack of statutory authority to arrest for drunkenness, or because of inexplicable enforcement traditions. Until 1966, for example, the overwhelming majority of non-belligerent inebriates arrested in New York City were routinely booked, charged and convicted of "disorderly conduct."[11] In other jurisdictions, charges of public drunkenness, vagrancy or disorderly conduct are used interchangeably, at the whim or discretion of the arresting officer. A well-established practice of taking public intoxicants into overnight custody without any formal charge thrives in a number of jurisdictions. Such "arrests" are likely not to appear at all in statistical reports.

Two million arrests for simple drunkenness in 1972 would be a conservative estimate; the total may well run as high as 2.5 million, and these estimates do not include alcohol-related arrests on such misdemeanor charges as panhandling, obstructing a sidewalk, using loud and boisterous language. Nor do they include the 796,800 or so arrests for driving under the influence (DWI).[12]

Striking ironies in the treatment of offenders reflect the class bias characteristic of society's response to drunkenness begun a century and a half ago. Furthermore, enforcement policies also

11 John M. Murtagh, "Arrests for Public Intoxication," 35 *Fordham L. Rev.* (1966), p. 1.
12 The estimate is that of the FBI's *Uniform Crime Reports for the United States* (Washington, D.C.: Government Printing Office, 1972).

ignore the public safety element of law enforcement. The laws against the genuinely menacing offense of driving under the influence are grossly underenforced as the statutes prohibiting public drunkenness are overenforced. If drinking drivers actually cause 180 million auto accidents annually, or about 500,000 a day (as the National Safety Council has estimated), an annual total approaching only 800,000 DWI arrests appears as nothing more than a modest gesture toward controlling this dangerous behavior.

The DWI arrestee can expect to receive a reasonably fair trial, and ordinarily will not be jailed after a conviction. He generally will have been out on bail awaiting trial. He is likely to receive a revocation of his driver's permit, a suspended sentence, or a fine in an amount which he is able to pay.

A simple drunkenness offender will be held in jail, will be sentenced usually on a guilty plea without a trial and will serve a jail sentence sufficient to disrupt whatever tenuous order exists in his personal life. He usually is committed to jail or fined an amount he cannot pay or both.

The sanctions most commonly applied to the DWI offender have little or no impact on his future misconduct. According to a California survey, as many as 85 per cent of those penalized for driving under the influence by license revocation simply continue to drive.

The aberrant drinking behavior of motorists is a genuine threat to public safety; simple drunkenness usually is not. It is a paradox then that offenders who are more dangerous to society are thus punished less severely and less summarily than those who are generally of no danger at all.

DRUNKENNESS LAWS AND THEIR ENFORCEMENT

The offenders who bear the brunt of the laws prohibiting intoxication—the public "drunks"[13] who are arrested and jailed

---

[13] In the technical literature, the jail inmates with whom this chapter is concerned are antiseptically characterized as "chronic drunkenness offenders," a label which is sometimes abbreviated as "C.D.O."; occasionally, they are even termed "chronic police case inebriates." No simpler designation would be accurately descriptive. Many of these men are not "alcoholics," as that status is defined medically. Nor can they be called "drunkards," for while many are hard drinkers, some do not become seriously intoxicated frequently

repeatedly—are a relatively small and homogeneous, and decidedly disadvantaged subclass of the American population. Their histories and fates are tied up in the day-to-day workings of the criminal justice system, but their problems begin with the drunkenness laws—and related statutes—as they are written.

Drunkenness laws are peculiarly archaic as well as discriminatory. Some are genuine relics, like the Pennsylvania act of 1794, declared unconstitutional in 1969 by a judge of Philadelphia's municipal court, which forbade all "drunkenness," presumably private as well as public, and prescribed the curious penalty of a sixty-seven-cent fine. But as recently as 1967, New York State adopted a "new" statute re-creating the crime of simple public intoxication. Statutes in a few states—Connecticut, Florida, Nebraska, Ohio and Pennsylvania—make drunkenness itself or the condition of being "found intoxicated" in public or private, a criminal offense. In practice, and despite their highly dubious constitutional status,[14] these statutes are employed as are the more common "public intoxication" statutes found in twenty-three other states—against the public and poor drunkard. But, at times, statutes of the "found intoxicated" type also have been employed

---

or regularly. According to anthropologist James Spradley, whose ethnographic study *You Owe Yourself a Drunk* (Boston: Little, Brown, 1970) includes a detailed discussion of the problem of terminology, the men prefer to think of themselves as "tramps," while society in general identifies them simply as "bums." But for the purposes of this discussion, both terms are inadequate. Within the criminal justice system, however, these men have been assigned a particular "legal identity." To the police, courts and jailers they are "drunks." Gradually, as they experience repeated criminal processing, the men themselves come to accept and even to adopt the designation. The opprobrium which the term "drunk" implies should not attach to the men who have been labeled, but to the system which does the labeling. The seriousness of formal labeling of "alcoholics" was recognized by the United States Supreme Court in its decision in *Wisconsin* v. *Constantinean*, 400 U.S. 433 (1971), which found unconstitutional a Wisconsin statute which allowed public officials to "post" the names of suspected alcoholics in taverns and liquor stores. In holding that the statute amounted to a denial of due process, the Court noted the stigmatic aspect which even a non-criminal label may have. The effects of the formal and informal labeling of "drunks" which occurs in the criminal justice system are equally severe.

[14] In the case of *Robinson* v. *California*, 370 U.S. 660 (1962), the United States Supreme Court ruled that a statute outlawing the "status offence" of narcotics addiction violated the Eighth Amendment's prohibition against cruel and unusual punishment; as a subject of criminal penalties, mere "drunkenness" would seem to be a status rather than a form of conduct. For a more detailed discussion of the constitutional dimensions of drunkenness, see pp. 216 ff.

to reach the passive drunk who has the misfortune to be in a private place where he simply is not wanted.

The extreme variation in the severity of penalties among jurisdictions demonstrates the absence of any coherent and consistent national statutory policy. A first offender for drunkenness gets a five-dollar maximum fine in Pennsylvania and a $500 maximum fine in Montana. In Nevada, only a second offender may be sentenced to imprisonment, and then only for a maximum of twenty-five days, but in Missouri a first offender is subject to a year in prison, and a fine of as much as $1,000. Certain states, like Maine and Nebraska, provide graduated statutory sanctions of increasing severity for recidivist drunkenness offenders, and in Vermont, the law specifically provides for a pledge of abstinence to the court as an alternative to fine or jailing:

> As evidence of my appreciation of the opportunity given me to become a sober and better citizen, in staying the fine imposed upon me this day, I hereby freely and voluntarily sign the following: PLEDGE—I will abstain from the use of intoxicating liquors of every kind and character as a beverage for the period of . . .

For most drunkenness offenders, the judge's statutory option to levy a fine rather than ordering a term of jail is a nullity in practice, because most of the criminal drunks are indigents. Before the recent Supreme Court decision limiting the judicial power to order imprisonment for the non-payment of fines, it was standard practice to levy a fine the drunk could not pay, and let him "lie out" this amount in jail at a statutory rate of so many dollars a day. Whether the Court's decisions in *Williams* v. *Illinois*[15] and *Tate* v. *Short*[16] actually have put an end to this practice is open to question; the "due process revolution" is slow in making itself felt at the lower levels of the court system. In any event, the judge's discretionary power to order a fine is of little benefit to the defendant who obviously could not pay even a minimal sum; if he cannot be jailed for non-payment, he can simply be punished by a straight sentence, and most statutes specifically authorize the jailing of a convicted drunk.

In some states, particularly those that have no statute prohibiting public drunkenness, the criminal code prohibits being "drunk

15 399 U.S. 235 (1970).
16 401 U.S. 395 (1971).

and disorderly," a crime which is often nothing more than drunken behavior or behavior annoying to others. The penalties are equivalent to those for the offense of simple intoxication.

The drunk and disorderly statute appears to be reasonable on its face. One group of commentators recently noted,

> . . . the disorderly requirement gives the appearance of a more acceptable response to the purported need of a criminal sanction for intoxication. Disorderly conduct—properly defined—undoubtedly should be subject to criminal prohibition, but there is no reason for introducing "drunkenness" as a special element. It does not appear that the person who is drunk is significantly more of a threat than other disorderly persons. Moreover, the statutes which use danger to the safety of the intoxicated person himself as grounds for conviction contain a particularly unhealthy mix of good intentions and social condemnation.[17]

State laws prohibiting public drinking, as distinct from drunkenness, are now largely a dead letter. They retain about as much vitality as the New Jersey law which sets a penalty of up to $200 and thirty days in jail for the crime of driving a horse while intoxicated. Even when a drunk is arrested with an open bottle, the evidence needed in court to support a charge for public drinking may include a laboratory analysis of the bottle's contents; it is simpler and cheaper to proceed under a general anti-drunkenness provision.

In eighteen states, laws now in force penalize "common" or "habitual" drunkards. While these states have other statutes criminalizing public drunkenness, the "common drunkard" sections tend to provide stiffer maximum penalties: In Alabama, a $500 fine and a year at hard labor; in Wisconsin, $100 or six months in jail; in Rhode Island, up to three years' imprisonment. In most jurisdictions, being a "common drunkard" is a condition punishable under an omnibus vagrancy statute, which also prohibits citizens from exhibiting an ill-assorted collection of other unpopular personal characteristics.[18] In others, habitual drunkenness has evolved into an offense in its own right, though the roots of the

---

[17] F. Grad, A. Goldberg, and B. Shapiro, *Alcoholism and the Law* (Dobbs Ferry: Oceana, 1971), p. 9. The present discussion of the statute law relating to drunkenness is indebted to the compilation of state code provisions contained in this volume.

[18] In *Papachristou* v. *City of Jacksonville*, 405 U.S. 156 (1972), the United States Supreme Court ruled that broad prohibitions of the sort contained in many vagrancy laws were unconstitutionally vague; whether this ruling

prohibition remain fixed in the history of vagrancy law. In Maine, a remarkably candid statute declares the common drunkard to be punishable as an "undesirable person."

Some of these vagrancy-related "common drunkard" laws are employed interchangeably with prohibitions against public drunkenness, without any actual inquiry into the habitual or chronic character of an accused's intoxication. The decision to employ a common drunkard law sometimes is motivated by a desire to penalize a drunkenness offender with special severity.

There has been a practical merger of theoretically distinct criminal laws relating to drunkenness, epitomized by the bizarre practice of punishing first offenders for public intoxication as common drunkards. But the drunkenness laws in general, originally intended to control lower-class inebriates, have similar uses today. Indeed, they are sometimes employed against persons who are not drunk but who are regarded as socially offensive "undesirables."

Like the general vagrancy laws which were invoked against civil rights demonstrators in the South, anti-drunkenness statutes can be a pretext for action against unpopular but otherwise law-abiding groups. But the drunks, like the vagrants of former days, are a unique "criminal class"—a segment of the American population which is regularly processed through the justice system by a society which systematically rejects them out of unreasoned fear or distaste.

ERRATIC DISCRIMINATORY PATTERN OF DRUNKENNESS ARRESTS

More than a half-century ago, after observing conditions in a city where the public drunk historically had been processed as a "vagrant-common drunkard," John Lisle decried short workhouse sentences for vagrants:

> The result is the contamination of every large city by the multitude of diseased immoral citizens, living in degradation, preying upon the charitable, breeding crime by example and inheritance,

---

would extend to the "common drunkard" provisions of vagrancy statutes—which are one degree more specific than those, for example, which forbid "being abroad at night and unable to give a good account of oneself"—is still an unresolved issue.

increasing the corrupt vote and tending to retard the advance of civilization physically, morally, mentally and hence socially.[19]

Lisle, a Philadelphia attorney, recommended a central farm colony where a long term of confinement would enable the "shiftless" to learn a trade, escape their familiar associates and recover from a "mental and physical state of degradation."

His proposal echoes the nineteenth century's misguided concept of the penitentiary as a therapeutic community. But there is another motive besides rehabilitation. Lisle noted that to put his theory into practice would cause "the loss of a large part of the electorate"—as vigorous vagrancy law enforcement and long sentences cleansed the community of undesirables.

It is inevitable that managing the men swept up in drunkenness arrests has become the priority business of many American jails. In 1965, 52.5 per cent of all persons arrested in Atlanta—reputed to have the most severe drunkenness law enforcement practices—were accused of public intoxication, and another 24.1 per cent faced related charges of disorderly conduct and vagrancy. During the same year, in Washington, D.C., 51.8 per cent of all arrests were for drunkenness, and 24.7 per cent were for disorderly conduct and vagrancy. In 1962, 51 per cent of all adult arrests in San Francisco came under a municipal public drunkenness ordinance. This pattern is clearly more a matter of policy than a crime epidemic; it can be reversed by local decision. For example, in cities like St. Louis, where in 1965 intoxication contributed only 5.5 per cent of the arrest total, police department policy and tradition dictate that a drunkenness arrest is not a "quality" arrest; individual officers have conducted themselves accordingly.

Where the local drunk court requires the attendance of the arresting officer at the trial, arrest rates also are dramatically depressed. Where arrests are not encouraged, as in St. Louis, low-visibility harassment can serve much the same purpose as a stringent arrest policy. In his recent survey of drunkenness law enforcement, *Two Million Unnecessary Arrests*,[20] Raymond Nimmer described traditional police practice in that city:

> This does not mean that St. Louis police invariably ignored the men. It indicates only that the formal drunkenness arrest was

[19] Lisle, "Vagrancy Law: Its Faults and Their Remedy," 5 *J. Crim.* 498 (1915).
[20] American Bar Foundation, 1971.

avoided. Informal methods were available and frequently used. These procedures included taking the man to his home, putting him in a cab, driving him off the patrolman's beat, pushing him into an inconspicuous corner, or dumping him at the river front.

Local arrest policy is determined by such factors as the attitudes of officers and departments toward drunks, police perceptions of community attitudes and of the purposes of drunkenness law, the design and wording of the statutes themselves, local judicial practice in processing arrests for intoxication, the priority given drunkenness enforcement relative to action against serious crime. Even the season and the weather can be important determinants.

Among the local practices documented by Nimmer is that which prevailed in Chicago's West Madison Street Skid Row district, where police, motivated by "protective" and "paternalistic" motives, arrested those derelicts who appeared to be in a "helpless" condition. They saw themselves as protecting these men from the weather, the depredations of "jackrollers" (petty thieves who relieve debilitated drunks of their few possessions), or simply from themselves. And they tended to leave "ambulatory" but obviously intoxicated men on the street, while picking up others who clearly were "sober but unconscious." The general duty "umbrella cars" and the specialized "bum squads" which police West Madison Street maintained a relatively consistent, moderate rate of drunkenness arrests.

In Chicago's other major Skid Row district, South State Street, immediately adjacent to the Loop and its prestige business and residential districts, Nimmer discovered differently motivated, more severe and less predictable police practices. Again, intoxication alone did not make a man liable to arrest, nor did sobriety render him immune. Arrests for drunkenness were motivated by police concern with "aesthetics," and by a desire to "reduce the visibility of the Skid Row colony by harassing the men out of the area." Like all police who enforce drunkenness law according to an "aesthetic" arrest policy, the officers who patrolled South State Street assumed the role of a public conscience, guided more by their own sense of propriety and their perception of society's distaste for the public drunk than by formal complaints from local residents and businessmen. The drunkenness arrest rate on South State Street was far higher than the rate prevailing on West Madison Street. Enforcement was erratic, concentrated in periodic "clean-up" drives, and sometimes involved arbitrary and brutal treatment of the arrested men.

In San Francisco, public drunks and non-intoxicated derelicts run a high risk of arrest for drunkenness only during the late afternoon, when the Skid Row district is temporarily purged for the benefit of the commuters who pass through it on their way home from nearby offices. In Washington, D.C., before the sweeping reform of drunkenness law enforcement in 1966, police concern with maintaining the image of the nation's capital for diplomats, politicians and tourists produced one of the strictest drunkenness arrest policies of any American city.[21]

In Detroit, where paternalism is the official policy, drunkenness arrests are relatively infrequent and relatively selective—from one third to one half of those taken into custody are never even formally charged, but are logged as "Golden Rule Drunks," and detained overnight to sleep it off.

Wayne LaFave's recent study of arrest practices describes what occurred when a detail of the Detroit "bum squad" stopped a staggering man and proceeded to empty his open bottle into the gutter:

> "Aw hell, boys, give me a break," the drunk pleaded, but the officers responded that he was too drunk. They added, "We will G.R.D. (Golden Rule Drunk) you if you don't have a traffic warrant, how's that?" The drunk thought that was fine.

A Detroit policeman commented on "voluntary" overnight detention:

> This was a golden rule arrest, and we usually do not make out papers on the men. It simply amounts to letting him cool off overnight. Actually, he is free to go if he wants, and we are simply furnishing him a hotel room. As a matter of fact, we usually lock the door, and it is far enough upstairs so that we can't hear him rattling the doors.[22]

The "Golden Rule" is almost never applied to "regulars," who are merely arrested. The informal lockup is reserved for men

[21] For a description of the handling of public drunks in Washington today, and of the pressures which forced the creation of a new, therapeutically oriented approach, see pp. 272 ff. below.

[22] W. LaFave, *Arrest: The Decision to Take a Suspect into Custody* (American Bar Foundation, 1965).

found drunk outside Detroit's Skid Row district, or to Skid Row drinkers who are strangers to the officers of the specialized drunk squad.

The police approach to drunkenness arrests traditionally pursued on New York City's Bowery appears to be governed by the quota system. Although the police force was under only slight community pressure to control public intoxication, as Nimmer describes it, the department felt obliged to make some gesture in the direction of enforcement. Two-man teams of so-called "condition men" were routinely assigned to conduct several daily roundups. After each filled a receiving van with available derelicts until its capacity was reached, arrests were abruptly discontinued. To accomplish their mechanical task with maximum speed and miminum inconvenience, the "condition men" adopted an unstated practice of avoiding the most severely debilitated derelicts. In meeting its quota, the squad developed a preference for ambulatory drunks, and an aversion to unconscious or seriously ill men.

Discrimination in drunkenness law enforcement does not begin with selective practices in arrest. Most well-to-do and middle-class heavy drinkers do their drinking at home, in private clubs or in familiar bars. They are known to their companions, and when they drink to excess they are labeled "sports" and bedded down to "sleep it off." The police never even impinge on their drinking habits. The poor, by contrast, drink among strangers or chance acquaintances, in districts where the police presence usually is intense. When intoxicated, they are labeled "bums"; there is no one to help them home, and often no home to which to help them. In effect, drunkenness arrest procedures serve to guarantee that a "sport" seldom will be mistaken for a "bum." They are a screening device, which winnows the "respectable" drunks from the homeless derelicts. The "respectables" will not be charged, convicted or jailed, regardless of their condition. The derelicts, drunk or sober, may be processed straight into jail.

Although most "respectable" alcoholics drink in protected privacy, those who are on a serious binge may gravitate to bars in disreputable areas. Police cannot assume that any man found drunk on Skid Row is a candidate for arrest; further screening is required. The decision not to arrest a drunkenness suspect may be made after the officer's curbside assessment of the subject's clothes and grooming. Non-arrest also may depend on the subject's ability to produce a suitable home address and enough ready cash to take a taxi to it. Sometimes, the police may deliver the respectable drunk to his respectable address, or, alternatively, to a private health facility. Or they may employ some variant of Philadelphia's "Form 80" procedure, under which selected drunkenness offenders are released at the station house to friends and relatives, who sign a waiver relieving the police of liability for false arrest.

Whatever procedures are employed, the effect is the same: drunkenness law, the contemporary equivalent and historical correlate of general vagrancy law, is systematically enforced only against a predetermined class of undesirables. And this is the result whether local arrest policy is ostensibly punitive, protective or aesthetic in its intent.

DEGRADATION IN THE TANK

The occasional affluent drinker who is processed up to the point of a formal charge is almost universally permitted to obtain his immediate release on bail. Later, he can "forfeit collateral" rather than progressing to trial. As a practical matter, his impoverished counterpart has no opportunity to "buy out" of the drunkenness law enforcement process. The economic discrimination which is built into that process, even in its post-arrest phases, is illustrated by the experience of one Seattle drunk:

> [D]uring the 21-year period from 1947 to 1968, he was convicted more than one hundred times for this crime; he received many suspended sentences and posted $165 in bail which he forfeited; and there were 74 charges of public drunkenness on which he was sentenced to jail during this period. He was given a total of 5,340 days for these convictions, or *more than fourteen years*. If he had posted $20 bail [each time] it would have cost him $1,480. In this man's experience, then, a year of his life was worth only about $100. During 1966 he received two six-month sentences which he could have avoided for only $40.[23]

For the drunk with no economic cushion between himself and the law, there will be a "trial" of sorts, and a sentence to follow. First, however, there will be jail detention.

[23] Spradley, *You Owe Yourself a Drunk.*

For the first-time drunk offender, jailing may be a startling and damaging experience; for the drunkenness recidivist, it is more familiar but not necessarily less destructive. The offender whom the police have decided to hold for trial or to keep in "protective custody" will be detained, at least overnight and sometimes for several days, in a lockup or way station jail. In some rural areas, the drunk awaiting disposition is thrown in with the general population of the county jail; in others, he is segregated from other prisoners, though often not from sentenced drunks doing time. In an urban jurisdiction, the drunk will be held in a cell or bullpen at the police precinct station, or transferred to the holding facility attached to the local court with jurisdiction over petty misdemeanors. In a court cellblock, he may have a small cell to himself, share the same tiny space with other prisoners, or be placed in a larger, segregated area set aside for drunks. But whatever its location, and whatever its physical layout, the space where he is held pending trial becomes known simply as the "drunk tank."

Few drunks delivered to a lockup will be offered or allowed a phone call; indeed, few have both the capacity to place a call and a friend or lawyer to receive it. Although a derelict seldom has the means to afford bail, and an intoxicated man with means will ordinarily never reach the lockup at all, it is still notable that lockup personnel frequently refuse to offer some drunks even an opportunity to exercise the right to immediate release on bail. The overnight lockup procedures regarding roundups of drunks or paternalistic jailings of sober derelicts are legally offensive, since they violate the principle that only probable cause should warrant arrest and detention. Custodians at these lockups often fail to observe prisoners' basic legal rights, and ignore minimum standards of procedural fairness.

Nor are minimum standards of simple decency observed. I saw this myself on visits to these holding areas. In San Francisco, for example, the men who wait in the San Francisco City Jail's drunk cells, seven floors high in the Hall of Justice Building, are pathetic rather than frightening. On one spring day in 1972, all the occupants of these abominable concrete stalls were dirty, disheveled and often bruised and cut, no doubt from falls. Many slumped and lay on the hard cell floor, unconscious or asleep. The observer is stunned and sickened by this picture of inhumane abuse. One is left with one overriding impression: the problem posed by the drunks is one of social welfare, not public safety; these men should be someplace else.

We hurt them and degrade ourselves by running such a wasteful, heartless institution. Where most of these new prisoners need care and medical assistance, we offer punishment or neglect. An offer of treatment might not cure or change them, but at least it would hurt them less and allow us to feel a little better about ourselves.

Drunk tanks ordinarily are overcrowded, unsanitary, unsafe, underserviced and unsupervised. A Washington, D.C., reporter has written of a prototypical station-house drunk tank:

> There are at least two men in each 4 x 8 foot cell and three in some. The stench of cheap alcohol, dried blood, urine and excrement covers the cell block . . . There are no lights in the cells, which form a square in the middle of the cell block . . . There are no mattresses. "Mattresses wouldn't last the night," a patrolman explains. "And with prisoners urinating all over them they wouldn't be any good if they did last." . . . "It's quiet tonight," the policeman says, "but some nights it gets so bad we have to close these." He points to two wooden green doors in front of the gate. It was on one of the noisy nights early this month that a prisoner is alleged to have beaten his cellmate to death.[24]

The problem is aggravated when untried and sentenced drunks alike are held in a single overcrowded area, sometimes in the company of other petty misdemeanants. Such drunk tanks, which exist primarily in county rather than city jails, were described by a California citizens' panel:

> [W]ooden slats are often placed on the floor so the prisoners, lying like snakes in a snake pit, will be kept partially out of their own filth, and so the deck can be hosed down from time to time. Among the features hailed as improvements in the new jails are tanks lined with plastic and other materials that are impervious to water hosing.
>
> A grand jury foreman described . . . the hold-over tank in the jail in his county, which is [meant to hold people] for a few hours and more overnight, and should by state law provide 10 square feet of floor space per man. Actually, he stated, prisoners are kept there day and night, sometimes for several months. There are no

[24] Hoagland, "Cell Block's Common Denominator: A Stench of Alcohol and Dried Blood," Washington *Post*, March 29, 1966.

beds, not even benches, and the prisoners sleep on the concrete floor. There are never enough blankets to go around and the weaker prisoners go without. This tank has 897 square feet of floor space and as many as 199 men have been confined in it at one time . . . In this tank there is one toilet and one wash bowl.[25]

In the lockup on the premises of Branch 28 of the Municipal Court of Chicago, the "Skid Row Court" which each day processes drunkenness offenders arrested on West Madison Street, one team of observers found a block of thirteen cells and a bullpen. Of these, nine cells were reserved for drunks, as was the bullpen, which housed both unconscious drunks and the regulars who were "special friends" of the officers managing the block.[26] In relative terms, the bullpen was desirable housing, since by the time a night's arrests had been completed, each of the nine small drunk cells would hold as many as twelve men. The block received a daily hosing—this was the only sanitation. The prisoners received baloney sandwiches at odd intervals—this was their only food. Yet the prisoners confined in this tank, according to the prevailing arrest policy on West Madison Street, had been arrested for their own protection.

Medical authorities on acute alcohol intoxication agree that a minimal detoxification service should provide several days of "drying out": bed rest, a high protein diet and medication to combat alcoholic withdrawal symptoms such as *delirium tremens,* which is fatal to one untreated sufferer in five. The treatment unsentenced drunks receive is a grim parody of the simple assistance acutely intoxicated men urgently require. Yet it has been estimated that in 1961 Chicago paid out $750,000 simply to finance the overnight detention of drunks, an expense which brought no commensurate benefit to either the offenders or the city.[27]

The drunkenness offender jailed pending disposition is the victim of dangerous and even deadly neglect. The symptoms of his intoxication go untreated; so do the symptoms of other more serious medical problems. What a police officer has taken for drunken behavior may be an acute disease symptom, such as an

[25] Citizens' Advisory Committee to the Attorney General of California on Crime Prevention, *California Jails* (1956), p. 22.
[26] Note, "The Law on Skid Row," 38 *Chi.-Kent L. Rev.* 22, 23, 34 (April, 1961).
[27] Ibid., p. 34.

epileptic fit or a diabetic coma. Or intoxication and deterioration may mask chronic physical complaints and recent injuries, wholly unnoted by the keepers of the drunk tank. In Washington, D.C., in 1964–65, sixteen offenders arrested for public intoxication died in their cells, from acute untreated alcoholic withdrawal symtoms or causes unrelated to alcohol use.[28] Almost every jurisdiction with any number of drunkenness arrests has a record of neglect and its fatal consequences, like that disclosed in this report of conditions in one Maryland county:

> The Prince George's Sheriff's office says it still locks up 10 to 15 drunks a night. Drunks are sent to the County hospital only if they have delirium tremens for more than four days . . . they are placed in the "tank," a bare cell with mattresses on the floor. If they were up on bunks, jailers explain, they could fall off and injure themselves.
>
> The jailers try to get hot coffee into them. When they recover, they are transferred to one of the 40-prisoner dorms where the other inmates are trusted to look after them.
>
> Two alcoholics died in Prince George's jails last year.[29]

The occasional death of a derelict in police custody is unlikely to stimulate headlines, much less substantive reform.

Alcohol withdrawal and pre-existing disease conditions are not the only threats to the safety of the drunk awaiting trial in jail; in these frequently overcrowded, unsupervised tanks, prisoners endanger one another. A Salt Lake City paper described a city jail:

> The Board of Health found that cramming 50 or 60 prisoners into an area built to accommodate 25 offered an especially dangerous potential for spreading diseases, specifically tuberculosis and hepatitis.
>
> Moreover, poor supervision of the tank is an invitation to virtual anarchy there. Salt Lake Police Chief Dewey Fillis recently told the City Commission that prisoners have been seriously injured in fights that are commonplace there, and these someday may lead to death.[30]

[28] President's Commission on Crime in the District of Columbia, *Report* (1967), p. 476.
[29] Lathan, "Drunks Still Sent to County Jails Despite Maryland Law," Washington *Post,* August 15, 1968.
[30] "Shame in Drunk Tank," Salt Lake City *Deseret News,* November 16, 1969.

The helpless drunk is the natural victim of stronger and more aggressive prisoners—or of aggressive officers. In Spradley's interviews with Seattle drunks who had experienced criminal processing, 35 per cent said they had been physically abused by police, often by the officers assigned to the lockup.[31] Such attacks allegedly often took place in the more out-of-the-way areas of the jail, like the elevator to the booking desk or the "padded drunk tank." Seeking an explanation for this apparent pattern of victimization, and for reports that Seattle police frequently taunted arrested drunks with such names as "wino son of a bitch" and "Skid Row bastard" and shook them down for cash and property, Spradley turned to a 1968 evaluation of the department by the International Association of Chiefs of Police. It was the informal practice of the department to assign officers with disciplinary problems to jail duty:

> The usual disciplinary problem of those now assigned is reported to be that of drinking. It would appear that the city jail, with the high percentage of inmates confined under conditions involving the use of intoxicants, would hardly be an appropriate assignment for sworn officers who have clearly demonstrated that they have a drinking problem themselves.[32]

Police abuse of drunks in the lockup is not unique to Seattle. Gerald Stern, head of the 1967 Crime Commission's Task Force on Drunkenness, reported the conclusion of one study:

> [S]ome of the "police brutality" observed took place while the police were attempting to book drunkenness offenders. The fact that inebriates are in no condition to stand against a counter and answer questions is foreign to the entire criminal process.[33]

The brutalities inflicted on drunkenness offenders in custody are psychological as well as physical. At the booking desk and in the tank a man finds himself labeled "drunk," a "bum" and a "criminal." Whatever tenuous sense of worth and dependence he may possess is rapidly eroded. The man in the tank soon becomes the very thing he has been labeled. Regardless of the condition in

[31] Spradley, *You Owe Yourself a Drunk,* p. 148.
[32] International Association of Chiefs of Police, *A Survey of the Police Department—Seattle, Washington* (1968), p. 476.
[33] Stern, "The National Crime Commission's Report on Public Drunkenness: Where Do We Go from Here" (NAAAP Special Report No. 40, September 18, 1967).

which he entered, after one night on a concrete floor, sometimes without enough space even to stretch out, he will emerge looking like a bum. And while most men will spend only a single night in the tank, some wait far longer; in many jurisdictions, the man arrested on Friday morning will not be brought to court until the following Monday. It is hardly surprising that drunks appear in court red-eyed, dirty, disheveled and unshaven.

A PARODY OF JUSTICE

If his night in jail is a travesty of custodial care, the drunk's day in court is an equally bizarre parody of a judicial hearing. The typical city drunk court is ominously isolated from the other departments of the municipal court. In San Francisco, it is situated in a bare room on the sixth floor of the "Hall of Justice," while the other departments are housed in recognizable courtrooms on the first and second floors. In other cities, the drunk courts are tucked away in the bowels of the courthouse. (For many years, the unmarked drunk court door in one major city had no handle on the outside; it could be opened only from within.) A spectator will often find that little or no space has been provided for onlookers. All constitutional guarantees of a public trial aside, the judicial processing of drunks is usually a private affair. Visitors are neither expected nor encouraged.

The participants on hand at a morning drunk court call generally are the same. There is the presiding official, who may be a municipal judge sitting occasionally in drunk court on a rotation basis, or a quasi-judicial officer, sometimes termed a "magistrate," or a "referee." There are the droves of drunks, many still severely intoxicated and many more demoralized and disoriented. There are the bailiffs, herding them into the courtroom in large groups. There are the police liaison officers, often in uniform, and, sometimes, "friends of the court" representing social agencies such as the Salvation Army and self-help societies such as Alcoholics Anonymous.

Defense attorneys are absent from most drunk court proceedings.[34] So are prosecutors and witnesses. In most jurisdictions,

[34] In the recent case of *Argersinger* v. *Hamlin,* 407 U.S. 25 (1972), the Supreme Court held that the Sixth Amendment guarantees misdemeanants

not even the arresting officer is expected to attend the judicial disposition of his cases.

Lack of defense counsel obviously prejudices a drunkenness offender's trial, but the absence of a prosecutor is an equally damaging feature of these exercises in routinized, assembly line justice. Deprived of the benefit of prosecutorial discretion, which ordinarily operates to screen good arrests from questionable ones, and to prevent the more doubtful cases from ever reaching trial, all drunkenness offenders who are not discharged by police or jailers will be processed, regardless of the circumstances of their arrests or the nature of the cases which can be made against them.[35] And, just as routinely, these defendants will be convicted, since trial procedures in drunk court are totally inadequate to provide any consideration of the defendants as individuals. The FBI's *Uniform Crime Reports* for 1972 show that in 3,025 reporting cities, fully 91.5 per cent of all drunkenness offenders are convicted as charged—yet only 37.7 per cent of adult defendants charged are convicted as charged of serious crimes against persons or property.

In the drunk court, the police officer designated as court liaison officer performs informal prosecutorial functions. One investigator observed in San Francisco:

> [a] court liaison officer sits at the judge's side to "show the judge the court records, and if the judge doesn't know a character, I tell him because I see them all the time." With considerable regularity, and often at the request of other officers or interested parties, court liaison officers intervene on behalf of a particular defendant. They are equally disposed to "advise" a judge to "sink this one," to "give 'em ten days to clean up," or to "give 'em 90 days probation." Indeed, when asked to compare his duties to those of the

representation by counsel—and appointed lawyers when they cannot afford their own—whenever there is a substantial risk that conviction may lead to imprisonment, however brief. If this holding were to be observed in practice, drunk court proceedings would be revolutionized. But the commands of appellate courts do not become accepted procedural law automatically in the lower trial courts; they filter down slowly, and they often meet active resistance. The right to counsel, like any other constitutional right, can be waived; the drunk courts, which historically have overlooked the requirement that a plea of guilty must be truly voluntary, may continue to do business as usual by coercing technical waivers of Sixth Amendment rights.

[35] Even in jurisdictions where a prosecutor does attend drunk court, the demands of batch processing apparently make the exercise of discretion impractical. See Spradley, *You Owe Yourself a Drunk*, p. 175.

court bailiffs, one court liaison officer replied that "they (the bailiffs) take care of the prisoners, and *we take care of the prosecution.*"[36]

The judge listens well. Law professor Caleb Foote described the interaction in Philadelphia:

> Thus frequently, when a drunkenness defendant would be called up, a police officer would interject, "Judge, this man's in here all the time. He's a regular pest." The judge would then impose sentence, and several times stressed to the writer the importance of such "cooperation" with the police.[37]

On the record, most drunkenness cases are disposed of on a plea of guilty. But, the act of pleading to the charge, an especially critical phase of an ordinary criminal trial, is debased and distorted in the context of the drunk court. It is common procedure in many jurisdictions to dispense entirely with the reading of the charge itself, apparently on the theory that the defendant either already knows well enough why he is in court or is too disoriented to understand the instruction, if it were given. In other jurisdictions, some form of charge may be read off to successive batches of ten, fifteen or twenty defendants called up as a group.

In San Francisco, batch processing is the rule, and investigator L. C. Klein's 1962 survey revealed that "Most judges open the hearings by simply asking each group of defendants if 'anyone wants the charges read,' or 'does anybody want to plead guilty?'" In Seattle, Spradley observed groups of twenty-five defendants herded into the courtroom to hear what one experienced drunk termed "the rights spiel," and then hustled back to an adjoining tank to await individual pleading and sentencing.

Even where individual defendants are individually charged, no attempt is made to determine whether a man actually understands the form of words, or the possible consequences of any plea he may enter. And, too often, the court is only slightly more conscientious in determining what plea actually has been entered. A mumbled excuse or question has been recorded as a plea of guilty, and only the most determined defendant will succeed in

[36] L. C. Klein, "The Criminal Law Process v. The Public Drunkenness Offender in San Francisco" (unpublished paper, Institute for the Study of Human Problems, October 1964).

[37] Caleb Foote, "Vagrancy Type Law and Its Enforcement," 104 *U. Pa. L. Rev.* pp. 603, 632–33 (1956).

pleading innocent, in requesting appointed counsel or in requesting time to retain private counsel.

There are also substantial practical deterrents to prevent a drunkenness offender from pleading anything other than guilty as charged. Any successful deviation from the drunk court routine ordinarily will result in the defendant's being returned to the tank to wait hours or days for further action. It also may rule out any possibility of his receiving a suspended sentence. These contingencies are enough to deter most of the defendants who might otherwise assert themselves.

But even a defendant who is prepared to plead to the charge may find himself on his way back to the tank without having been given even that opportunity. Many drunk court judges employ the continuance as an improvised, short-term sanction for defendants who eventually will receive suspended sentences, but whom they feel would benefit from additional time in the tank, either for additional drying out or as a "taste of jail."

Since the overwhelming majority of drunkenness charges are disposed of on a guilty plea—or by what Professor Foote has termed "the mere exhibition of a 'bum,'" drunk court cases seldom reach a factual issue. In the few instances where a plea of not guilty forces an inquiry into a defendant's conduct, several outcomes are possible. The defendant may be returned to the tank, with his trial date continued, only to be dismissed eventually when an arresting officer fails to appear at a later hearing. Or he may eventually be convicted, sometimes on evidence which offers only doubtful substantiation of the charge. Professor Foote has reported cases in which proof of a single incident of public intoxication has supported a conviction as a "habitual drunkard."[38] And a recent study concludes that an officer's statement that a man was talking boisterously, seemed unsteady on his feet or smelled of alcohol can be sufficient to convict him as a drunk.[39]

The judicial phase of a drunkenness offender's progress through the system is typically a mockery of justice. The Philadelphia magistrate who disposed of fifty-five drunkenness cases in a clocked time of fifteen minutes may be an extreme model

[38] Ibid., pp. 603, 608, 611.
[39] Grad, Goldberg, and Shapiro, *Alcoholism and the Law*, p. 7.

of judicial efficiency,[40] but his time is challenged daily in almost every city "drunk court." In Atlanta, the typical drunkenness "trial" averages a minute.

Most drunk court cases are not elaborate; they progress directly from the reading of the charge (if it is actually read), to the giving of the plea (if it is actually given), to the one certain and unavoidable feature of the trial, the passing of sentence. An incident Professor Foote observed in Philadelphia drunk court illustrates the essential arbitrariness of drunk court sentencing. Hurrying through a list of charged offenders, one magistrate called the name of a defendant who did not respond immediately. The following is the full transcript of that defendant's trial:

"Where are you, Martin?"
"Right here."
"You aren't going to be 'right here' for long. Three months in Correction."

Sentencing discretion in drunk court usually is fettered only by statutes which fix maximum penalties; occasionally even these limits are ignored. The exercise of discretion, however, may be circumscribed by a local rule of practice. In New York City, for example, it was standard procedure in the early 1960's to employ the suspended sentence for drunks charged under the disorderly conduct statute. In other jurisdictions, by contrast, practically every convicted drunkenness offender can expect to receive a term of confinement or a fine. In Seattle, Spradley discovered the use of a sliding scale of penalties for men with relatively good prior records, ranging from two days suspended for a first offense to up to ninety days in jail for the eighth offense within a six-month period.

The disposition of the drunk tends to depend more on the individual judge's preconceptions or whims than on the individual defendant's record or prognosis. Pre-sentence reports are nonexistent. Court records, where they are maintained, indicate little more than the number of previous appearances a defendant has made under a given name, and nothing of substance about his past or his prospects. Thus a judge who is convinced that public intoxication is a manifestation of alcoholism may regularly sentence drunkenness offenders to jail in the belief that they will benefit

[40] Foote, "Vagrancy Type Law and Its Enforcement," pp. 603, 605.

from enforced sobriety and institutional routine, or may direct that they serve their time in a medical facility when the statute gives him this authority. Another judge, equally convinced that drunkenness is a medical problem, but disillusioned with therapeutic incarceration, will suspend all sentences. Yet another, who holds the view that intoxication is morally culpable, will dispense uniformly harsh punitive sanctions.

Most drunk court judges are guided by no such clear attitudes. For them, sentencing is a matter of intuitive improvisation. A glance at the defendant, a brief look at his record card, if one is provided, a few words with a court liaison officer or a Salvation Army representative, and a sentence is pronounced.

Among the multiplicity of factors which influence this sentencing decision, the particular needs of each defendant generally are ignored. The police may be accommodated by a stiff sentence meted out to a "pest" or "steady customer." The judge may indulge an unfamiliar or relatively reputable-looking defendant with a lenient sentence. Diverse considerations such as overcrowding in the local jail or the approach of the Christmas season may trigger a series of suspended sentences. In some northern cities, the coming of winter prompts judges to commit more drunks to jail, for longer terms, as a form of "protective" safekeeping. And, in jurisdictions where "street cleaning" is emphasized, a drunk without local ties may receive a suspended sentence, contingent on his promise to get out of town. In the sentencing decision, even the condition of the drunk tank may take precedence over the condition of the drunk: some of the men at drunk call may receive a suspended sentence or an outright dismissal on the condition that they spend the morning scrubbing down the jail cells.

The closest approach to individualized sentencing to be found in the drunk courts is the occasional practice of delegating the sentencing decision to the defendant, and simply jailing the drunks who are actively seeking a respite from life on the streets. The staff of the 1967 Crime Commission's Task Force on Drunkenness found that "[i]n some cities only those offenders who request it are jailed."[41]

The general attitude of the consumers of the justice dispensed in the judicial lottery of the drunk court is summed up in their

[41] President's Commission on Law Enforcement and Administration of Justice, *Task Force Report: Drunkenness,* p. 3, n. 26.

adage "You can't beat a drunk charge." Their resentment is concentrated not against the existence and enforcement of drunkenness law, but against the depersonalized procedures by which it is administered. One municipal judge belatedly discovered this when a group of jailed drunks brought habeas corpus actions challenging their incarceration:

> In court, each was called upon to testify and, as might be expected, they didn't confine themselves to the issues of the habeas corpus action but rather proceeded to give all their grievances against municipal court treatment . . . throughout the land. Guess what they resented most? The fact that they weren't given a chance to discuss their case with the judge—that they were herded through. I was forced to admit that there was considerable validity to their complaint. When I first came on the particular bench, we had been following the practice of letting the bailiff do the arraigning before the court convened, leaving the judge only the responsibility to impose sentence. This was done with the prisoner standing in the prisoner's box with all the other prisoners and with the judge politely asking if he, the defendant, had anything to say. Very little was said, except by the most brazen and least worthy of the group. We allowed not more than one-half hour for arraigning the entire group, frequently numbering twenty to forty individuals. Obviously there was little time for individual consideration. Now, here they were in court testifying that mainly all they wanted was a simple chance to speak to the judge face to face. Since that time, I don't think any drunk has ever been arraigned in Denver who hasn't been given a chance to come up and talk to the judge as long as necessary.[42]

But Denver remains an exception. For most drunkenness offenders, the sentence they receive is the sentence of what they regard, far too often with justification, as a "kangaroo court."

Journalist Leonard Downie has described the judicial machinery of the "criminal drunkenness process" in operation:

> In Cleveland's drunk court, the judge and uniformed policemen serving as bailiffs appear untouched by the misery of the wretched men lined up along the green wall. One by one, the men are sent staggering before the judge. On a day in the spring of 1970, the presiding judge appeared to recognize at least every other face.

[42] Remarks of Judge Robert Burnett in Rocky Mountain Regional Conference of Municipal Judges, "Proceedings, Processing the Alcoholic Defendant" (1961).

"You again?" he inquired mockingly at one rubber-kneed man. "Go on home. One night in jail is enough."

Others, for one reason or another, were sent back to jail.

"You were here Monday, and you're back again?" the judge asked another derelict. "Thirty days in the workhouse."

A policeman-bailiff wrote the number "30" on a scrap of paper and pressed it into the hand of the defendant, who was pointed back toward the cellblock.

"You've been here as many times as there are stops on the Broadway bus line," the judge told another defendant and then laughed loudly at his own joke.

"I don't drink much, your honor."

Another laugh, "You live on Buckeye, and you don't drink much?" the judge said, referring to a street on Cleveland's east side. "I'm afraid that I'll have to give you fifteen days."

Another defendant said he was from out of town and intended to leave Cleveland. "You're on your way now," the judge told him. "Hurry it up."

The judge remembered that yet another defendant had promised to return to Detroit after he was last brought to court for drunkenness a week earlier. "Maybe thirty days in jail will refresh your memory," the judge said. "Take him away."

In drunk court in San Francisco, the scene is much the same, except that the drunkenness defendants are usually "tried" twenty or more at a time by the bailiff, who asks each large group, "Do any of you plead not guilty?"

Almost always, none does. "All guilty, your honor," the bailiff reports as he turns back to the judge, who then sentences the men individually.

"You don't look so good," the judge in San Francisco told one defendant. "I think we better take care of you. Thirty days in jail would do you good. Thirty days."[43]

The survival of this peculiar institution is rationalized on the ground that the drunk court provides essential services to the men who pass through it; as long as no other help exists for these men, the drunk court judge does the best he can with the means at hand.

This argument, however, overlooks the real limitations of drunk court procedures. Little good can be expected from an institution which cannot discriminate sensibly between individual offenders

[43] Leonard Downie, Jr., *Justice Denied* (New York: Praeger, 1971), pp. 55–56.

in setting a penalty. The judge may call the drunks by their first names, but he will seldom know much about their background or condition when he determines that one will be best served by a warning, another by a cautionary sentence and yet another by a spell of punitive or protective incarceration.

The essential, fatal limitation on drunk court procedures is that jailing is the only form of punishment *or* treatment which most judges can order. Data gathered in Minneapolis seemed to show that fines are more effective than jail sentences in discouraging drunkenness offense recidivism. But this finding, if it can be generalized, is applicable only to the minority of drunks who have the means to pay a fine. In most jurisdictions, for most offenders, the only real sentencing decision is between the suspended sentence and the jail commitment.[44]

The most hopeful development relating to the judicial administration of drunkenness law is the increasing restiveness of some of the judges themselves. At a recent conference of local trial judges, Denver's Judge Robert Burnett spoke about this quandary with eloquence and desperation:

> We, Judges, are prone to approach the problem of the drunk docket defendant with peculiar pessimism which only we can understand, for, day after day, we deal with the weakest and most completely inadequate segment of our society . . . the most perplexing of all of them, over these years, [are] the drunks—those sick, disheveled, zombie-like creatures frequently as much dead as alive, living in a half world of unreality, looking at the judge and the court sometimes trustingly and at other times with hostility but, most frequently, with complete disinterest and disdain.
>
> In this environment, we have been driven to extreme frustrations, in part because we have been handed the two accepted forms of criminal penalization of the fine and the jail sentence—to deal with what has appeared to us to be patently a social and medical problem. We have found ourselves dissatisfied with these tools on both philosophical and practical grounds.
>
> On the one hand, we are cast in the role of the bully trampling down and further degrading those within our society who are already the weakest and most inadequate and on the other we find ourselves frustrated by the realization that what we are doing

[44] Keith Lovald and Holger R. Stub, "Revolving Door: Reactions of Chronic Drunkenness Offenders to Court Sanctions," 59 *J. Crim. L.C. and P.S.* 525 (1968).

fails to protect society by the prevention of law violations. Little wonder we find ourselves gathering in groups such as this with the hope of gaining a fresh approach.[45]

A PATTERN OF RECIDIVISM

Complete and accurate numbers of post-sentence drunk commitments are unavailable. At the local level, jails keep only minimal records, if any. Only in exceptional jurisdictions are inmate populations systematically described by offense, length of sentence and time actually served. State and federal statistical agencies have failed both to collect what local statistics exist and to encourage local jailers to do better.

The only national census of county and city jails with an overall estimate of the proportion of drunkenness commitments to total commitments dates back to 1933; in that survey, 42 per cent of the prisoners beginning to serve sentences had been convicted of either drunkenness or disorderly conduct.

In 1945, one investigator concluded that 70 per cent of all jail inmates were simple public intoxicants.[46] A more frequently cited percentage is 50 per cent.[47]

The 1970 LEAA jail census, while it did not enumerate inmates by offense categories, did show a one-day population of roughly 67,000 sentenced adult offenders confined in 4,037 institutions.[48] Estimates of the proportion of drunks in typical jail populations would put their number at a figure in excess of 30,000 on any single given day.

In 1965, drunkenness offenders were 80 per cent of the in-

[45] Robt. Burnett, "The Responsibility of the Bench and Bar in Dealing with the Chronic Jail Offender Alcoholic," *Proceedings, The Chronic Jail Offender Alcoholic* (1964), p. 1.
[46] Benson Y. Landis, "Some Economic Aspects of Inebriety," in *Alcohol, Science and Society* (1945), pp. 201, 208.
[47] In 1962, veteran corrections expert Austin MacCormick noted that "more than half of all jail time is served by drunks." In 1967, the President's Commission on Law Enforcement and Administration of Justice repeated this conventional view.
[48] *1970 National Jail Census.* Funded by the Department of Justice and conducted by the Bureau of the Census, the survey excluded Connecticut, Delaware and Rhode Island, where the state governments administer the jails, as well as "drunk tanks," lockups and other facilities which retain persons for less than two full days.

mate population of the D.C. workhouse in Occoquan, Virginia. In 1966, sentenced drunkenness offenders accounted for 5,000 admissions—49 per cent of the total—to the Hennepin County Workhouse, the jail serving Minneapolis. In 1962, drunkenness offenders were 73.1 per cent of the admissions to the Monroe County Penitentiary, serving Rochester, New York, and 62.5 per cent of that jail's inmate population on an average day. In 1961, drunkenness offenders were 60 per cent of the sentenced population of the Atlanta City Jail, and fully 95 per cent of the sentenced prisoners held at the Atlanta jail farm (or "Stockade").

Individual jail terms are relatively brief, but the total time served by drunkenness offenders is formidable. In Washington, D.C., in 1965, 15,500 convicted drunkenness offenders were sentenced to terms of imprisonment averaging thirty-two days each. The chief judge of the Connecticut Circuit Courts estimated that during 1966, 8,000 drunkenness offenders would be sentenced to terms averaging fifteen days in county and city jails. Nationally, sentenced drunks probably serve over ten million days of time each year.

Each jail term increases the likelihood of rearrest and future jailing by diminishing the drunk's already meager chances of escape from a future of deterioration. A man with a job or family ties when he entered jail may have none when he emerges two weeks or a month later. Even an overnight detention may have serious effects. Since many potential chronic drunks rely for income on casual employment agencies whose job calls generally are held at about 6:00 A.M., a man who has been arrested the night before will miss at least one day's opportunity to work. And even a small amount of cash in hand can make a significant difference in status and in safety from arrest or harassment. The impact of a longer jail sentence is to guarantee that the offender will remain dependent and vulnerable to rearrest.

Statistics underscore the appalling recidivism rate of the unfortunate minority who are the prime targets of drunkenness law enforcement. Earl Rubington, a sociologist and authority on the indigent drunk, has estimated that "20 percent of all persons arrested for drunkenness account for between 60 and 80 percent of the total arrests."[49] Records maintained by local police departments bear him out.

[49] Rubington, "The Alcoholic and the Jail," *Federal Probation*, June 1965, p. 30.

Commenting on drunkenness offense recidivism, the 1967 presidential Crime Commission noted that:

> In 1964 in the city of Los Angeles about one-fifth of all persons arrested for drunkenness accounted for two-thirds of the total number of arrests for that offense. Some of the repeaters were arrested as many as 18 times a year.
>
> In 1957 the Committee on Prisons, Probation and Parole in the District of Columbia studied six chronic offenders and found that they had been arrested for drunkenness a total of 1,409 times . . .[50]

In city after city, the pattern is the same. In Los Angeles in 1955, 1,000 offenders were arrested on 43,709 occasions. In Atlanta in 1961, about 12,000 offenders were arrested 30,000 times out of a total of 49,000 drunkenness arrests; in a middle-sized western city, where records for 1963 were surveyed on a confidential basis, there were 16,263 arrests involving 8,954 persons, and 16 per cent of the men accounted for 42 per cent of those arrests; in 1961, in a slightly smaller eastern city, 3,185 persons were arrested 5,384 times, and 17 per cent of these men made up 42 per cent of those arrestees; in Portland, Oregon, during 1963, 2,000 offenders were arrested approximately 11,000 times.[51]

Drunkenness offense recidivism is reflected in studies of the populations of local jails. In 1951–52, for example, only 18 per cent of the drunks committed to the Monroe County Penitentiary, a jail serving Rochester, New York, were first offenders: the 82 per cent with prior records for intoxication averaged six

[50] President's Commission on Law Enforcement and Administration of Justice, *Task Force Report: Drunkenness*, p. 1.

[51] The numbers cited are drawn from a variety of sources, including the text and appendices of the 1967 Crime Commission's *Task Force Report: Drunkenness;* an unpublished report by Thomas F. A. Plaut to the Cooperative Commission Institute for the Study of Human Problems, Stanford University, reported in Sidney Cahn's *The Treatment of Alcoholics* (N.Y.: Oxford Univ. Press, 1970); Austin MacCormick's valuable survey paper "Correctional Views on Alcohol, Alcoholism and Crime," reprinted in 9 *Crime and Delinquency* (1963), and David Pittman and Duff Gillespie's "Social Policy as Deviancy Reinforcement: The Case of the Public Drunkenness Offender," in David J. Pittman, ed., *Alcoholism* (New York: J. Wiley, 1967). The failure of courts and police administrators to maintain or publish comparable figures, and the failure of scholars and investigators to gather them, are in themselves indicators of the neglect of the criminal drunk in law enforcement planning and evaluation.

drunkenness arrests each, some of these jailed as drunks on as many as 100 previous occasions. In 1955, out of 7,700 prisoners committed to the New Orleans House of Corrections as drunks, 60 per cent were repeaters on this charge.[52]

Many recidivist drunks are, in effect, serving the proverbial "life imprisonment on the installment plan." Six repeaters studied in 1957 by the Kerrick Commission in the District of Columbia had, among them, served a total of 125 years in jail. Between 1949 and 1966, the defendant in a recent test case challenging Seattle, Washington's, public intoxication ordinance had been convicted ninety-eight times and had been sentenced to jail terms totaling more than seventeen and a half years, not to mention five years of suspended sentences.[53] A typical mature drunk will have experienced tens or hundreds of arrests and received years of jail sentences.

Jailing for public drunkenness does nothing to deter recidivism; it fails to protect society since these helpless men pose no substantial anti-social threats; it fails to provide access to rehabilitative care. Instead, it confirms and supports what is publicly an expensive and individually a self-destructive and dependent way of life. As one investigator has observed: "[I]ncarceration in jail, intended as a *punishment* for public drunkenness, is a *cause* of public drunkenness."[54]

THE SOCIOLOGY OF FAILURE

Jailed drunks have common histories.[55] Surveys show that a statistically significant number have experienced broken homes

---

[52] D. Pittman and C. W. Gordon, *Revolving Door: A Study of the Chronic Police Case Inebriate* (Free Press, Glencoe, Ill. 1958), pp. 3, 44; Daniels, "The Alcoholic in Jail," *La. Rev. Alc.* no. 2 (1955): 2. The minimal records maintained by local jails severely limits any investigation of institutional recidivism as parallel to arrest recidivism on drunk charges. In some jurisdictions, jail recommittal ratios may be even higher than rates of repeated arrests.

[53] *Seattle* v. *Hill*, 435 P. 2d 692, 695 (1967). Obviously Wayne Hill had not served out each sentence in full; to have done so would have been a mathematical and human impossibility.

[54] Spradley, *You Owe Yourself a Drunk*, p. 5.

[55] Among the most comprehensive of the field surveys supporting this conclusion are Pittman and Gordon, *Revolving Door;* Rochester Bureau of Municipal Research, *Man on the Periphery* (1963); Fenny et al., "The Challenge of the Skid Row Alcoholic," *Q. J. Stud. Alc.* 16 (1955): 645; D. Kantor

and failed marriages. About half have never married, and of those who have, almost all are divorced or separated. Their first jail sentence, which prevents them from supporting their families for a time, often precipitates the breakup of already unstable marriages.

Jailed drunkenness offenders typically are older men; their average age of about forty-five years sets them apart from both the population as a whole and the population of the districts from which they are recruited. The career of a drunk is progressive and degenerative; as he grows older, more helpless and vulnerable, he is arrested more often, sentenced more often and for longer periods.

The typical jailed drunk has minimal education. His job skills are few or non-existent. The majority of such men are white, but a disproportionate number of blacks (and in some areas, American Indians) are jailed for drunkenness, the victims of a double discrimination. In *Revolving Door,* the classic study of the jailed drunk in America, David Pittman and Wayne Gordon reported that in New York State's Monroe County Penitentiary, 18 per cent of the drunks were black, compared to only 2 per cent of the county's population.

Men adopt the public drunk's life-style and eventually come to jail because they are unable to function under the pressures and demands of conventional society. Most even lack the capacity to be effective criminals—a significant and continuing criminal career is a successful, though deviant, social adaptation.

Men confined as drunks seldom are dangerous; their confinement cannot be justified on the ground of societal self-protection. Pittman and Gordon reported that the majority of jailed drunks whose police and court records they examined had never been arrested on a charge not intimately linked to intoxication. They found that 31 per cent had never been arrested on a charge other than drunkenness, not even for the often interchangeable offense of vagrancy or disorderly conduct. Another 32 per cent had at one time been charged with minor alcohol-related offenses such as vagrancy, disorderly conduct, trespassing, begging, gambling and assault. In extensive interviews, most of these men expressed

and E. Blacker, *A Survey of Bridgewater, An Institution for the Chronic Drunkenness Offender* (1958); and the as yet unpublished surveys conducted at Toronto's Don Jail by the Alcoholism and Drug Abuse Research Foundation of Toronto, Canada. The following discussion is indebted to all of these investigations.

strong disapproval of both aggressive and acquisitive criminality. Even of those in the minority, with records of other offenses, more had been charged with petty property crimes than with serious crimes against persons; even they tended to abandon their minor "criminal careers" when their pattern of arrests for drunkenness began. Jailed drunks are chiefly men who have failed at life, including the life of crime.

The few drunks who try petty crime usually take only what they need to survive—the price of a bottle or a room stolen from an unconscious fellow derelict, and perhaps the victim's shoes or trousers. In extremity, they may attempt to float a bad check for a small sum. But whatever slight threat these atypical drunks may be to other drunks, or to the businesses which feed on their condition, they are no danger to the public at large.

A recent unpublished in-depth study of the criminal histories of jailed drunks by the Toronto Alcoholism and Drug Addiction Research Foundation reported that 48.2 per cent of the drunks in metropolitan Toronto's jail (commonly known as the "Don Jail") were "pure drunks" or "petty offenders," with no significant criminal careers. Of those who had had criminal careers, almost half had given up crime. The drunks with non-alcohol-related criminal records typically had begun with assault, desertion and non-support; but these offenses had decreased as they cut adrift from their families. They had advanced to petty theft and fraud, vagrancy and trespassing—crimes primarily motivated by their alcohol use or need for money to buy alcohol.[56] They have found a new home, a makeshift community without the usual adult demands but with patterns which determine their behavior. In the free world, the men who serve jail time for drunkenness generally are residents of "Skid Row."

Skid Row is not the only American subculture which contributes significantly to drunk arrests and jailings for drunkenness. In Albuquerque, New Mexico, the many troubled and self-

[56] Alcoholism and Drug Addiction Research Foundation of Toronto, "The Chronic Drunkenness Offender: Criminal Career" (mimeographed, n.d.). The conclusions and language of this report are cited here with the foundation's generous permission. In applying those conclusions to drunks in American jails, the possibility should be considered that Canada's somewhat more discriminating approach to drunkenness law enforcement may result in sentenced drunk populations with relatively more serious criminal tendencies than their American counterparts.

destructive American Indians who travel from the nearby "dry" Navaho reservation for frequent, uncontrolled alcoholic binges are viewed as a major law enforcement problem. Drinking in bars, in the streets and even in the parking lots of strategically located package stores, these Indians are peculiarly vulnerable to arrest. On weekends, their number often exceeds the capacity of the city drunk tank, and the overflow crowd spends the night sprawled on the cement steps of the jail's staircases.[57] But while a given jurisdiction may struggle with a unique local population of chronic drunks, every community possesses some version of the Skid Row subculture. And the unfortunate drunks who are netted in masses into our jails are, in the overwhelming majority, spawned in the little worlds of American Skid Rows.[58]

The original Skid Row was Seattle's Yessler Street;[59] during the heavy logging of the Pacific Northwest, it was periodically cleared and greased, so that timber could be skidded along its length from the high ground to the water. Because log loading was seasonal employment, it attracted unskilled transients and aimless men, often on the move and often returning to Yessler Street's bars and

[57] Calvin Trillin, "U.S. Journal."
[58] There is an extensive sociological and popular literature on Skid Row. Among the most valuable recent volumes are Donald Joseph Bogue's *Skid Row in American Cities* (1963), an empirical Skid Row "census," with special emphasis on Chicago, and Samuel Wallace's *Skid Row as a Way of Life* (Totowa, N.J.: Bedminster Press, 1965), which conveys much of the Skid Row "insider's" perspective on his condition. James P. Spradley's previously cited *You Owe Yourself a Drunk* (Boston: Little, Brown) contains unique information on the accommodations with society reached by both "home guard tramps," the typical urban Skid Row men, and the homeless migrants who drift from one major Skid Row to another. His investigation documents both the misery and the resourcefulness of the Skid Row population.

Discussions of the special problems of Skid Row and urban renewal are contained in various publications of the Chicago Tenants' Bureau and the Philadelphia Diagnostic and Relocation Service Corporation. General sociological studies with special relevance to the problems of Skid Row men include Howard Becker's *Outsiders* (London: Free Press of Glencoe, 1965), and H. Behr's *Homelessness and Disaffiliation* (1968). Michael Harrington's *The Other America* (New York: Macmillan, 1962), includes a personal but well-documented account of Skid Row as an American "culture of poverty."

The bibliography of informative articles on Skid Row is immense. Joan Jackson and Ralph Conner's "The Skid Row Alcoholic," 14 *QJSA* 468 (1953) is especially interesting. Others will be specifically cited.
[59] See Spradley, *You Owe Yourself a Drunk,* p. 7; D. Pittman, "Public Intoxication and the Alcoholic Offender in American Society," in President's Commission on Law Enforcement and Administration of Justice, *Task Force Report: Drunkenness,* p. 11.

lodging houses. They were literally and figuratively "on the skids." In almost every large town or city a local "Skid Row" district is, in a sense, assigned to men caught in purposeless, progressive and apparently irresistible downward drift. These districts are crowded with decayed boarding houses, cheap bars and restaurants, employment agencies and pawnshops, package stores, secondhand emporia, shelters, missions, cubical hotels and tourist-oriented honky-tonks. Most of their inhabitants are men. Women are an insignificant element in the Skid Row problem, making up no more than 10 per cent of a typical Skid Row population, and contributing only about 7 per cent to the total of all drunkenness arrests.[60]

In some cities, especially those undergoing intensive urban renewal, the Skid Row population may have been dispersed geographically; in most, it is still concentrated in one or more distinct areas, often contiguous to a downtown central business district. Sociologist Donald Joseph Bogue concluded that almost every American city of 500,000 or more has a Skid Row neighborhood, and that cities with 175,000 or more residents are developing such neighborhoods. For 1950, Bogue estimated that thirty-seven American cities had a concentrated Skid Row population of more than 1,000, led by Chicago, with 20,800; San Francisco, with 18,500; Los Angeles, with 16,000; and Detroit, with 13,000.[61] Where towns are too small to support a full-blown Skid Row district, substitutes are found—a discreted block or a town square.[62] Finally, the only common factor of all Skid Rows is a public street, the only space to which the homeless poor can expect free access. It is no accident that police roundups of drunk offenders are oftentimes "street-cleaning" operations. In its essence, drunkenness law enforcement is primarily a prolonged and inconclusive battle over the use of public space.

Skid Row is not just a demographic concept. The term also signifies a system of institutions, which bind men and women to

[60] In many cities, female drunks are tried separately from their male counterparts, and are less likely to be jailed. Even when they are jailed, their situation has more in common with that of other female misdemeanants than with that of male drunks.

[61] D. Bogue, *Skid Row in American Cities,* pp. 5–17. He used 1950 census data.

[62] Irwin Deutscher, "The Petty Offender: Society's Orphan," *Federal Probation,* June 1955, p. 12.

a particular way of life, and which may exist even where the homeless population is physically dispersed. Charity missions, public shelters and borderline businesses attract and hold their clientele by providing supportive services at little or no cost. They serve and breed dependency, appealing to simple, urgent needs. Exploitative Skid Row institutions—like the casual employment agencies to which Skid Row men pay unconscionably high commissions for low-paying work assignments—foster dependency and profit from it. The employment agencies, like the Skid Row liquor stores and some of the more "efficient" lodging facilities, are lucrative enterprises. Their proprietors have a considerable financial stake in the maintenance of Skid Row. A merger of personal, institutional and economic interests has maintained the vitality of Skid Row in the face of urban change.

Skid Row society appears to be anarchic, open-ended and, in the favorite term of some academic observers, "non-demanding." In fact, it is an ordered, stratified organization with defined standards and values. Its members are not individualistic "loners" as depicted in some portraits of Skid Row life; rather they are abandoned, lonely persons with unfulfilled needs that only a coherent alternative society can satisfy.

Michael Harrington described the men who live in New York City's principal Skid Row district, the Bowery, as "different from almost all the other poor people." He viewed the Bowery as integrating refugees "from every social class, every educational background to be found in the United States . . . This is the one place in the other America where the poor are actually the sum total of misfits from all of the social classes."[63] Like the writers who continue to celebrate the unfettered life of the hobo, Harrington may be perpetuating romantic myth. The defrocked priest and the fallen professional can still be found on Skid Row, but they are scarce. Most of the men on Skid Row come from lower and lower-middle-class backgrounds, and have never experienced real hopes of upward mobility or social attainment.

Skid Row does, however, assimilate individuals with diverse life histories readily and thoroughly. Their origins may be similar or dissimilar, but their fates on the Row will be much alike. To the Skid Row subculture, they bring their failure; they bring their

[63] Harrington, *The Other America* (Macmillan, 1962), p. 100.

financial dependence on institutional charity, pension and welfare payments, or private handouts; they bring their psychological dependence on group support. From that subculture, they receive support and indoctrination.

The raw recruit learns quickly to make do by cadging, begging and occasional petty thievery. He absorbs the Skid Row community's sense of self-disdain. He learns to shelter himself in an alley or a hallway when he has no cash for a "flop." He adapts to official harassment and private exploitation while he learns the simple social ethic of the Skid Row community: don't ask questions, share your good luck, never protest authority. He assumes patterns of behavior that may bring him to the repeated attention of the police, and habits of mind which will make him an easy mark for arrest, prosecution and jailing. Even on Skid Row there is a caste system of sorts. Although all Skid Row men are potential targets of drunkenness law enforcement, only the heavy drinkers there—an estimated 45 per cent—are likely to be marked as chronic criminal drunks. Bogue has estimated that 35 per cent of Skid Row drinkers—light, moderate and heavy—have never been arrested for drunkenness, and that fully two thirds of all Skid Row drinkers have never been jailed for this offense.[64] Nor are all the Row's heavy drinkers equally liable to arrest and prosecution as drunks; those with relatively higher status and relatively greater means will frequently escape police attention.

According to Bogue, "there seems to be more status in being a periodic drinker than a common perennial drunk."[65] A "lush," one of the clannish elite of Skid Row alcoholics with a preference for hard liquor, may drink compulsively but not constantly. The relative infrequency of the lushes' alcoholic binges is one factor which makes them unlikely targets for drunkenness law enforcement.[66] Another is their relative affluence; and because most lushes have some regular source of income—small pension or disability payments, for example—they can afford to drink in the private space of bars or rented rooms. The burden of enforcement falls instead on Skid Row's low-ranking "winos," who use cheap wine or crude spirits such as sterno. Unlike the lushes, the winos

[64] Bogue, *Skid Row in American Cities.*
[65] Ibid., p. 275.
[66] For a discussion of social stratification on Skid Row, see E. Rubington, "The Chronic Drunkenness Offender," *Annals* 315 (1958), pp. 65, 68–70.

drink frequently, but not compulsively, foregoing the quick "knockout" for the prolonged mild "high." In response to their "sharing ethic," however, they usually drink in large groups (the so-called "bottle gangs").[67] And because they are less affluent than the lushes, they are likely to have no private place to drink. The poorest of Skid Row men, the winos appear most disreputable and disheveled; even more than other Skid Row men, they live and drink in public. Their free access to public space is constantly challenged and defeated by the law.

It is more because they are chronic losers in a continuing battle for space than because of the severity of their drinking problems, that Skid Row's winos become the jail's drunks. The social structure forces their behavior out into public, and hence under the eyes of the law. Because low-ranking Skid Row men have developed a high degree of the passivity, they are unlikely to protest arrest or to offer resistance to the police. And because they are the poorest and most dependent of the homeless population, they have no way—and sometimes no desire—to resist repeated jailing.

The typical jailed drunk is the extreme type of the Skid Row man. In comparison to his more fortunate fellows, he is more dependent, more vulnerable, poorer and sicker. And of Skid Row men in general, Dr. Ruth Fox, an authority on the treatment of alcoholism, has written:

> There is probably no sicker group anywhere in the United States . . . Most of them have liver damage, many have heart disease, others have tuberculosis, almost all are grossly undernourished, and some are brain damaged and grossly below normal.[68]

Bogue's systematic interviews among Chicago's Skid Row population revealed that, in general, its inhabitants are physically deteriorated. Among the many chronic ailments reported, one man in eight suffered from arthritis or rheumatism, one in four from other bone and muscle diseases, and one in ten from chronic digestive disorders. Many of the men had permanent, uncorrected physical disabilities: one in four had lost an arm or a foot.[69] In

---

[67] The best discussion of the limited but nonetheless self-destructive alcohol use which characterizes these men is, Raymond G. McCarthy and Robert Straus, "Non-Addictive Pathological Drinking Patterns of Skid Row Men," 12 *Q. J. Stud. Alc.* (1951), p. 601.

[68] Bogue, op. cit.

[69] Ibid., p. 207.

general, "the rates of chronic illness were almost unbelievably high, even among younger men." Surprisingly, the middle-aged Skid Row men—and the largest proportion of the population of jailed drunks is middle-aged—showed even higher rates of illness than their older fellows.

A medical screening of men appearing in Atlanta's drunk court found a TB incidence about ten times that of the general population. Many of these persons had been housed in the past at the City Prison Farm: "as such, they constitute a health hazard for their fellow inmates."[70]

Another detailed medical screening of Skid Row men, involving the first 200 patients rescued from the streets—and the criminal process—by the Vera Institute's Manhattan Bowery Project in 1967, confirms the findings of earlier investigators. The project's medical staff regarded this sample as an atypically healthy one: nevertheless, more than 23 per cent had neurological diseases, about the same number had chronic complaints of the liver or skin diseases; more than 63 per cent had lung diseases; about 9 per cent had gastrointestinal conditions, and another 9 per cent suffered from chronic heart or circulatory diseases. In an ordinary jurisdiction, many of these men would have been destined for the local jail.[71]

Some of these diseases are directly related to alcohol abuse,[72] but many more are the direct and simple consequences of the poverty, exposure and self-neglect which are inseparable from the Skid Row way of life. A report of the Chicago Tenants' Bureau sums up the implications of this evidence: "At most ages, Skid Row inhabitants may expect to live less than one-half as long as the general population of the same age."[73]

The psychological health profiles of Skid Row men, in general, and jailed drunks in particular, are no more encouraging. A study of chronic drunkenness offenders confined in the Washington, D.C., workhouse in the early 1950's concluded that 88 per cent

[70] Alcohol Project of Emory University Department of Psychiatry, "Report," in President's Commission on Law Enforcement and Administration of Justice, *Task Force Report: Drunkenness,* pp. 82, 91–92.
[71] Vera Institute of Justice, "First Annual Report of the Manhattan Bowery Project," (1969), pp. 56–57.
[72] Cirrhosis and other forms of liver damage, and such neurological complaints as Korsakoff's syndrome and polyneuritis are notable examples.
[73] Vera, loc. cit.

were of average or higher intelligence, but that 48 per cent were psychotics or borderline psychotics, and an additional 10 per cent suffered chronic brain syndrome without psychotic complications.[74] The Manhattan Bowery Project screening discovered high proportions of seriously disturbed Skid Row men, including 33 per cent schizophrenics, 38 per cent with personality disorders, and 35 per cent with chronic brain syndrome.[75]

These are the men condemned as dangerous to society and discarded into the jails of the country. The criminal justice system has assumed or has been assigned to deal with men who generally are not criminals, in the sense that they pose any danger to others. The treatment they receive is neither just nor humane. Nor is it effective in arresting their condition.

IS ALCOHOLISM A DISEASE OR A MORAL WEAKNESS?

In most discussions of the problems of Skid Row men—and of jailed drunks—it is assumed that their most critical unmet need is treatment for the disease of "alcoholism." Granted, however, that these men need care, two questions remain: Is there a disease called "alcoholism," in the sense that there is a disease called "cancer" or one called "schizophrenia"? If so, is the criminal drunk an alcoholic?[76]

[74] Fenny et al., "The Challenge of the Skid Row Alcoholic."
[75] Vera Institute of Justice, "First Annual Report of the Manhattan Bowery Project," pp. 58–59. Other complaints included anxiety neuroses, seizure history, alcoholic hallucinosis, delirium tremens and drug addiction.
[76] The classic work in this area is E. M. Jellinek's *The Disease Concept of Alcoholism* (Rutgers Center for Alcohol Studies, Rutgers State U. Press, New Brunswick, New Jersey, 1960), an invaluable compendium of historical scholarship, medical analysis and responsible advocacy by the man who is generally credited with stimulating a revival, in the early 1940's, of the notion that alcoholism is a distinct, medically cognizable and treatable illness. Jellinek was not a physician. Indeed, the "disease concept" has been sponsored and advanced primarily by sociologists, medical researchers and psychologists. A large number of clinicians practicing physical medicine have doubted or denied its validity. This has created an abiding problem, since, as Jellinek recognized, "a disease is what the medical profession recognizes as such."
A useful summary of early responses to the disease concept of alcoholism in America is Raymond G. McCarthy's "Alcoholism: Attitudes and Attacks, 1775–1935," in *Understanding Alcoholism*, Vol. 315 of *The Annals of the American Academy of Political and Social Science* (1954).
The development of the disease concept in recent years can be traced in

In the late eighteenth century, two physicians, Dr. Thomas
Trotter, a Scot who had had firsthand experience with the problem
of "inebriety" as a surgeon with the British merchant marine, and
Dr. Benjamin Rush, an American who had served as physician-
general of the Colonial Army in the Revolutionary War, argued a
similar thesis: self-destructive overindulgence in alcohol was not
primarily a damnable moral fault to be corrected by preachments
and prayer, but a medical affliction. Trotter complained:

> Mankind, ever in pursuit of pleasure, have reluctantly admitted
> into the catalogue of their disease, those evils which were the im-

the pages of the principal organ of its advocates, the *Quarterly Journal of
Alcohol Studies,* a publication of the Rutgers (formerly Yale) Center for
Alcohol Studies. In the journal are to be found studies of alcohol metabolism,
presentations of theories of causation for disease alcoholism and contributions
to the debate.

A recent volume which gathers much of the best writing on disease alcoholism, along with other scholarship of alcohol use, is *Society, Culture and
Drinking Patterns* (1962), edited by David Pittman and Charles Snyder. Of
particular interest in the present context are its sections IV and V, "The Genesis and Patterning of Alcoholism," and "Responsive Movements and Systems
of Control."

The last decade of scholarship is summarized in the U. S. Department of
Health, Education and Welfare's *First Special Report to the U. S. Congress
on Alcohol and Health* (1971), in Chapter II, "Extract and Pattern of Use
and Abuse of Alcohol," Chapter V, "Theories about the Disease of Alcoholism," and Chapter VI, "Treatment of Alcoholism."

Some of the most interesting recent objections to the disease concept are
discussed in *Alcohol Problems—A Report to the Nation by the Cooperative
Commission on the Study of Alcoholism* (1967), prepared by Thomas F. A.
Plaut. Like much of the recent alcohol literature, this study avoids a simplified
stereotyping of alcoholism as a disease, and emphasizes instead a "comprehensive health view" embracing a wide variety of "drinking problems."

Dr. Thomas Szasz's article "Alcoholism: A Social-Ethical Perspective," in
Vol. 6 of the *Washburn Law Journal* (1967), like his attacks on the concept
of "mental illness," stresses the view that to designate a personal condition
as a disease is to absolve those who suffer from it of their responsibility to
change that condition, or deprive them of their freedom to continue to
suffer.

The most comprehensive recent attack on the intellectual integrity of the
disease concept as formulated by Jellinek is Herbert Finagretti's "The Perils
of Powell: In Search of a Factual Foundation for the Disease Concept of Alcoholism," published in Vol. 83 of the *Harvard Law Review* (1970). This
discussion has special relevance to the problem of the drunkenness offense,
since it concerns the relation between the disease concept and the "alcoholism
defense."

A thoroughgoing and dispassionate survey of both sides of the argument
is A. E. Wilkerson, Jr.'s, "A History of the Concept of Alcoholism as a
Disease," (196?), a doctoral dissertation prepared at the University of
Pennsylvania. The following discussion is indebted to Wilkerson's research,
and especially to his investigations of the disease concept.

mediate offspring of their luxuries . . . Hence in the writings of medicine, we find drunkenness only cursorily mentioned among the powers that injure health, while the mode of action is entirely neglected and left unexplained.[77]

Even these early "disease theorists," however, were prone to relapse into moralism. Rush, for example, recommended a series of practical-minded, somewhat harsh treatments for what today is termed auto-intoxication: inducing vomiting, immersing the drunkard in cold water, causing a fright and, in extreme cases, bleeding. Some of his suggestions for the treatment of the "disease of intemperance," by contrast, seem most unmedical: instilling belief in Christian principles (today, the "first step" of the Alcoholics Anonymous program), causing sudden shame and compelling the patient to witness the death of another drunkard, are examples. Still other treatments favored by Rush—creating disagreeable association with drink (as by the simultaneous administration of an emetic—an interesting anticipation of modern behaviorists' "aversion therapy"), prescribing a vegetarian diet, applying an ankle blister, and exposing the patient to another serious illness (such as yellow fever)—represent serious accommodations between medicine and moralism.

Along with the growth of a "physicians' temperance movement" stressing sensible alcohol use, rather than total abstinence, the first half of the nineteenth century saw the establishment of a number of specialized asylums for the non-punitive medical treatment of chronic inebriates. Despite these beginnings, however, the disease concept failed to take firm hold in America. Instead, an uncompromisingly moralistic popular religious temperance movement arose and inebriate homes declined. Some, like the New York State Inebriate Asylum, where Dr. Edward Turner's enlightened therapy had eliminated pledges and exhortations, were hounded out of existence by a confused and hostile public. Others merely lapsed into desuetude, surviving in name while their buildings were devoted to other uses. Today, some local jails still bear the mockingly anachronistic name "County Workhouse and Inebriate Asylum."

[77] The quotation is from Trotter's *Essay, Medical, Philosophical and Chemical on Drunkenness* (1778), the first major entry in the library of "alcohol literature." Rush followed suit shortly thereafter with *An Inquiry Into the Effects of Ardent Spirits on the Human Body and Mind* (1784), a work widely reprinted in early nineteenth-century America.

Not until the 1940's did substantial medical interest in the "disease of alcoholism" emerge again with studies by E. M. Jellinek, Dr. Howard M. Haggard and their colleagues at Yale University. The new movement gathered scientific data on the sociology and physiology of alcohol use, normal and abnormal, and devoted its energy and prestige to popularizing the idea that alcoholism was a true disease—a pathological condition characterized by an individual's "loss of control" over his drinking behavior.

John Seely, a leading figure in modern alcohol studies, has written that, after definitions of alcoholism as "crime" or "sin" are rejected, "disease" appears as the only hopeful "experimental" alternative in an effort to influence social policy. He also stresses the risk of creating the false expectation that a pill, an injection, or a course of psychotherapy will "cure" compulsive drinking. As far as public communications is concerned . . . the bare statement that "alcoholism is a disease" is most misleading since (a) it links up with a much too narrow concept of "disease" in the public mind, and (b) it conceals what is essential—that is, that a step in public policy is being recommended, not a scientific discovery announced.[78]

For Dr. David J. Myerson, the revival of the disease concept represented a practical step, rather than a medical breakthrough:

> You want to get hospitals to take in alcoholic problems, but to do so, you have to hammer them on the head, to get them to accept it as a disease. So I would agree that we should call it disease . . . In this very refined academic atmosphere where we can be "up in the clouds," you know. It is a pragmatic definition. It has useful consequences, and I think that justifies the philosophical point.[79]

Unfortunately, the useful consequences are coupled with dangerous ones, particularly the problem of false expectations. If alcoholism is a disease, then it can and should be treated. As more and more policy makers come to believe that medical management is the solution to problem drinking, advocates of the non-criminal handling of public intoxication cases are stressing a conviction that

[78] Seely, "Alcoholism is a Disease: Implications for Social Policy," in Pittman and Snyder, *Society, Culture and Drinking Patterns,* p. 586.
[79] David Myerson and Joseph Mayer, "Origins, Treatment and Destiny of Skid-Row Alcoholic Men—Comments" 19 *S. Car. L. Rev.* 348 (1967).

what the criminal drunk really requires is treatment for the disease of alcoholism. But the medical profession has yet to accept the responsibilities which are being urged upon it. In part, no doubt, its reluctance is due to residual moralism; as recently as 1970, Dr. Morris Chafetz, who now heads NIMH's National Institute of Alcoholism and Alcoholic Abuse, scored the "ignorant, moralistic and punitive attitude" which "thrives among the caretaking professions."[80] But continuing confusion over the causes and treatment of disease alcoholism is also a factor.

For the acute symptoms of alcohol abuse, medical science has developed a well-proven, safe and inexpensive system of detoxification treatment. But for long-term treatment of chronic alcoholism, medicine has fewer answers, and the founders of the new science of alcohol studies have reached no consensus about the causes of the disease or the most fruitful therapeutic strategies.

Is alcoholism the result of a latent allergy, a metabolic imbalance, a glandular disorder, the result of unhappy childhood? There is no agreement. Whatever alcoholism may be, is it best treated by conventional psychotherapy, group therapy, behavioral conditioning, drugs or some combination of these tactics? To this key question there are as many answers as there are experts.

Recent experiments have cast doubt on even the essential element of most definitions of disease alcoholism, the alcoholic's "loss of control" over his liquor intake. One group of addictive drinkers, hospitalized under what they believed to be a regime of enforced abstinence, received a secret daily dose of vodka. The subjects had been asked to report any compulsive "craving" for drink they experienced during their hospital stay, but none did so.[81] Many alcohol researchers dispute such results, but others find them deeply disturbing. Indeed, Dr. Jack Mendelson, speaking as chief of the NIMH's Center for the Prevention and Control of Alcoholism, has rejected the notion that disease alcoholism exists when "once an individual has one drink . . . he can't control his alcohol consumption."[82]

[80] Chafetz et al., eds., *Frontiers of Alcoholism* (New York: Science House, 1970).
[81] Merry, "The 'Loss of Control' Myth," *The Lancet* 1 (1966), p. 1257.
[82] U. S. Department of Health, Education and Welfare, *Social Welfare and Alcoholism* (Washington, D.C.: Govt. Printing Office, 1967), p. 21.

According to Harold Mulford, who has conducted detailed investigations of public attitudes toward alcohol use:

> Alcoholism has not been defined in terms that tell a physician what to do about it. . . . Physicians can hardly be expected to apply a nonexistent treatment to an undefined disease in a population that denies the disease and rejects the treatment.[83]

The medical profession paid lip service to the disease concept in the American Medical Association's belated House of Delegates resolution of 1956, which declared that "Alcoholic symptomology and complications . . . come within the scope of medical practice," and the American Hospital Association's 1957 statement urging its member institutions to "develop a program of care for alcoholics and . . . to base the decision as to admission . . . upon the condition and needs of the individual patient."

The reluctance of private physicians to accept alcoholics as private patients is notorious. The disparity between the pronouncements of the American Hospital Association and the practices of its member hospitals is more surprising. Researcher Robert Straus has reported that alcoholic patients in general hospital wards were usually admitted because of "more medically acceptable symptoms."[84] A 1964 survey of general hospital admission policies in Connecticut confirmed the unwillingness of administrators to accept patients under a primary diagnosis of alcoholism.[85]

Convincing pilot studies[86] demonstrate that alcoholics and even Skid Row drinkers can be detoxified and housed among other patients without any special expense or danger. Yet the general hospitals continue to turn away or discourage such patients. And one recent survey, which praises the development of specialized alcoholism wards and programs in public mental hospitals, nevertheless notes that "there are few lower-class alcoholic patients in the specialized wards. For this social class, the jails are the 'treatment' agencies."[87] For the middle-class drinker of modest means,

---

[83] "Directory of Alcoholism Resources in Connecticut," quoted in E. Lisensky, *The Chronic Drunkenness Offender* (1967), p. 48.
[84] Straus, "Medical Practice and the Alcoholic," in Jaco, ed., *Patients, Physicians and Illness* (New York: The Free Press, 1958).
[85] "Directory of Alcoholism Resources in Connecticut," quoted in E. Lisensky, *The Chronic Drunkenness Offender*, p. 48.
[86] See, e.g., Barke et al., "A Study of the Nonsegregated Hospitalization of Alcoholic Patients in a General Hospital" (AHA Monograph No. 7, 1959).
[87] Cahn, *The Treatment of Alcoholics*, p. 75.

obtaining professional medical care—in an emergency or on a long-term basis—may prove difficult. For the Skid Row man, it is a near impossibility.

Indigent, homeless drunks are seldom insured, they are suspected of posing special disciplinary problems in a hospital ward, they have poor prognoses for full recovery and they lack "motivation." Lack of motivation, a vague concept often employed in discussions of alcohol therapy, appears to be an updated code word for the unscientific and moralistic concept of "lack of will power."[88]

Even assuming that the medical profession was able to define and willing to treat alcoholism, could such treatment serve the jailed drunk? The winos of Skid Row are by no means clear-cut clinical alcoholics. The men repeatedly arrested and jailed for public intoxication often are in conspicuous control of their drinking. For many, alcohol is a scarce resource to be conserved and rationed, and a frequent, mild alcoholic "high" is more desirable than periodic severe intoxication. Their drinking is a secondary problem and a social adaptation, not the root cause of their distress. Indeed, some authorities believe that "no more than 8 per cent of all the problem drinkers on Skid Row are clinical alcoholics."[89] Investigators who have studied the needs and habits of the winos have cautioned strongly against devising treatment programs that assume these men to be chronic alcoholic addicts. The drinking of these Skid Row men, they noted, is distinctly different from that more often observed in members of Alcoholics Anonymous, in patients treated at alcoholism clinics and in those who may respond in part to the services of "drying out" facilities.

JAILING: THE ANTITHESIS OF TREATMENT

Alcoholism therapy may not rank first among the jailed drunk's needs. Rehabilitation services to the drunk must be addressed to the poverty, deterioration and social isolation which are the causes

[88] See Muriel W. Sterne and David J. Pittman, "The Concept of Motivation: A Source of Institutional and Professional Blockage in the Treatment of Alcoholics," 26 *Q. J. Stud. Alc.* (1965), 41.
[89] Rubington, "The Chronic Drunkenness Offender," pp. 65, 67, citing Wellman et al., "Private Hospital Alcoholic Patients and the 'Typical' Alcoholic," 18 *Q. J. Stud. Alc.* (1957), 401.

of his condition, as well as the drinking behavior which is its
symptom. The penal handling of the drunk addresses neither.

Unlike many other newly committed jail inmates, the drunk has
an urgent need for a particular form of short-term medical care—
scientific detoxification, bed rest, tranquilizing drugs and a high
protein diet. Generally, this need goes unfulfilled.

According to the *1970 National Jail Census,* the administrators
of almost half the 1,627 local holding institutions serving counties
or cities with populations of more than 25,000 reported that they
had no medical facilities whatsoever. A recent survey by the National Council on Crime and Delinquency concluded that only
about 7 per cent of the nation's jails have anything which could
be called an "alcoholism treatment program," even one as casual
as a weekly Alcoholics Anonymous counseling session.[90]

Even the most adamant opponents of jailing for public drunkenness concede that the relatively clean cells and adequate meals
provided by the more exemplary jails occasionally can be life-
saving services for the most unfortunate of the drunks, whose
only alternatives are continued exposure and malnutrition.
Peter B. Hutt, an attorney who played a prominent part in a series
of test cases challenging the foundations of drunkenness law,
commented that some of the derelicts who died in the streets in
the wake of a court decision drastically modifying police practice
in Washington, D.C., "might have lived had they been sent to
jail," but that, "the only way we in Washington could get help was
to create the mess which we did create."[91] Harvard Medical
School's Dr. David Myerson has recently been quoted for the
proposition:

> Haphazard but necessary disposition of the destitute alcoholic to
> the jails is probably the only resource we have at our disposal
> for what really amounts to a public health problem.[92]

But experts also concur that the jail is a dubious resource at
best, where the real need is for emergency medical care. The
life-saving function of the jail is unplanned, unfocused and, in

[90] NCCD, "Corrections in the United States," 13 *Crime and Delinquency*
147 (1967).
[91] Quoted in Peter Barton Hutt, "Modern Trends in Handling the Chronic
Court Offender," 19 *S. Car. L. Rev.* 305, 313 (1967).
[92] Ralph Slovenko, "Alcoholism and the Criminal Law," 6 *Wash. L. Rev.*
269, 283, citing *The Medical Tribune,* October 30–31, 1955, p. 7.

terms of the numbers of drunks actually affected, wholly inadequate in scope. There is reason to suspect that there are drunks who die in jail of simple neglect when they might have survived outside, as there are men who survive in jail but might have succumbed in the streets.[93]

The paternalistic arguments advanced for the perpetuation of the system of drunkenness law enforcement must be critically re-examined in terms of the jailed drunk's real experience, which too often is characterized not only by neglect, but by outright victimization. Weakened, debilitated and passive by habit, the jailed drunk is easy prey for healthier, more aggressive fellow-inmates. The "free flop" which the jailing system offers may be an illusory benefit.

JAIL, LIKE SKID ROW, A DEPENDENT SOCIETY

Even if jailing sometimes is of marginal physical benefit to the drunk, it inevitably damages self-esteem and weakens the capacity to survive. Jail becomes, David Pittman and Duff Gillespie say, an instrument of "deviancy reinforcement," and the drunk who is continually jailed cannot keep a marriage together or find and keep a job. "Constantly labelled as a public drunk, he begins to see himself as a public drunk; the jail becomes little more than a shelter to regain his physical strength."[94]

Intake is a dehumanizing experience for any inmate. For drunks, who are suspected to be unclean and assumed to be degraded, its effects can be especially profound. In the delousing procedure of the Seattle City Jail, which most drunks regarded as "the worst part of making the bucket," men are crowded together naked in groups of forty or more, while their clothing is processed in batches. A man who entered the tank with reasonably good

[93] The only systematic study to have addressed the question of the jail's impact on the physical condition of the drunks concludes that *frequent and repeated* jailing may make a measurable positive contribution to health, by removing an offender from the risks of Skid Row life for long periods. The study, based primarily on Canadian data, does not deal with the relativity of risk between incarceration and freedom where a man is jailed only occasionally. See J. Olin, *The Chronic Drunkenness Offender: Physical Health* (Alcoholism and Drug Addiction Research Foundation, 1968).

[94] Pittman and Gillespie, "Social Policy as Deviancy Reinforcement," in Pittman, *Alcoholism*, pp. 106, 118.

clothes may leave with them torn, shrunken or burned by the
delousing machinery. A man who cared for himself in the streets
will pick up the lice carried by other inmates. "The entire process
of delousing is utterly degrading and makes men begin to feel
that they are no longer human beings."[95]

Every jail has its own ways of branding inmates. Drunks must
endure the verbal abuse and crude wit of jailers and the disdain
of other inmates. Often, they will be housed in a segregated
wing or cellblock reserved for drunkenness offenders.

Once they have become accustomed to such a life, drunks can
become dependent on jail, as they have been on the institutions
of Skid Row. Even the facilities may be similar, if a "fireproof
cubicle hotel" on Chicago's Madison Street (eighty-five cents a
night with a window, and seventy-five cents without) is a typical
Skid Row accommodation:

> [Built] before 1900 [it has been converted] by dividing the floor
> space into cubicles with thin partitions. Each cubicle measures
> approximately 5′ x 7′, and most of this space is occupied by a
> simple iron bed with a thin mattress, 2 sheets, a blanket and a
> pillow. The bed occupies so much space that it is impossible to
> open fully the door to the cubicle. The rest of the furniture con-
> sists of an iron locker and a wooden chair . . . In order to facili-
> tate ventilation, the cubicle is covered with chicken wire netting
> above which a dim light bulb provides illumination.[96]

One cell is exchanged for another for the arrested drunk.

Eventually, the criminal drunk may adapt and come to need
the society of the jail as much as he needs the society of Skid
Row. He may come to welcome the jailing.[97] His migrations between these two shadow-worlds become more frequent and less
traumatic, and the dependent drunk is regarded by his jailers as
"a very good prisoner . . . who abides by jail norms."[98]

The jail may become a meeting place for Skid Row men, and a
clearinghouse for communications about old associates, the police

[95] Spradley, *You Owe Yourself a Drunk*, pp. 211–12.
[96] Note, "The Law on Skid Row," 38 *Chi.-Kent L. Rev.* 22, 26 (1961).
[97] For one account contrasting the way in which some drunks tolerate and
even welcome jailing with the attitudes of other inmates, see M. Amir, "Sociological Study of the House of Correction," 28 *Am. J. Corr.* 20 (1966).
[98] Rubington, "The Alcoholic and the Jail," *Federal Probation*, June 1965,
pp. 30, 31.

and the drunk courts. "Jail socialization" is the reconstruction of a Skid Row society inside the walls of the penal institution.

The younger drunks learn from older men the workings of the jail black market in cigarettes, food and clothing. The techniques of cadging necessities without money are useful in jail and on the streets.

And as Spradley has noted:

> After being in jail and learning to bum, a man will never again feel threatened when he is alone on the street without a penny in his pocket for he has discovered that there is a spirit of reciprocity with the world of tramps, something he may not have known before but which now draws him into that world, where it helps him to survive.[99]

Even in jail, the process of indoctrination into the Skid Row way of life continues.

IMPRESSED, AND UNPAID, LABOR

All total institutions—particularly penal institutions and most particularly jails—may be said to be run for the convenience and benefit of the staff and administrators, rather than the welfare of the inmates. Where the relationship between the ordinary misdemeanant and his jailer-employer often is one of exploitation, the relationship between the jailed drunk and his taskmaster is perversely symbiotic. The jail administrator who drafts prisoners as servants gets free labor; the drunk finds he is needed temporarily. Despite the verbal abuse he receives from some quarters, the drunk's status in jail is high. A medium- or large-sized jail requires kitchen help, laundry workers, groundkeepers and other staff. The drunk makes a passive non-rebellious worker. And among the inmates with whom a drunk identifies, status in jail society is largely a function of the job assignment.

A job that is useful, that is physically undemanding, that carries responsibility and implies the trust of jail authorities; a job that provides extra or special food, reading matter, additional tobacco rations, more freedom of movement—that job has status in jail. Such jobs are precisely those to which confined drunks

[99] Spradley, *You Owe Yourself a Drunk*, p. 242.

are likely to be assigned. I remember being shown around one jail by a proud warden. When we got to an empty immaculate kitchen, he pointed with pride to a shiny, polished chrome stove. "We've got an alky," he told me, "who is in here every month. Whenever he comes, his project is that stove. He loves it and keeps it in that shape for us."

The population of jailed drunks, and particularly its older and more familiar members, provides a valuable labor pool for the management and maintenance of otherwise underfinanced and understaffed institutions. The typical drunk is sentenced with dependable regularity and often for increasingly long terms; he submits readily to authority and responds positively to insignificant rewards; he seldom is troubled by sexual deprivation, since active sexuality has ceased to be a focus of his free existence; and—since he is not a clinical alcoholic but a chronic drunk—he is little troubled by enforced sobriety after the first few days of his sentence. He is a prized asset. The more often he is sentenced, the closer he comes to being the ideal jail laborer; the younger drunkenness offender must work his way up the job-status scale.

The Toronto Alcoholism and Drug Addiction Research Foundation's study of its local jail disclosed a highly elaborate caste system and jail hierarchy based on occupational prestige.[100] Jobs assigned to drunks ranged from the highly desirable positions of the "Governor's men" (the warden's houseboys), the "tea room gang" (men assigned to serve the guards), and barbers; through positions of intermediate desirability, such as the clothing details and the garden gang; down to the lowly garbage detail. The best jobs, and most of the fringe benefits, went to the most thoroughly confirmed recidivist drunks.

In the Seattle City Jail, drunks compete for especially desirable job assignments:

> It was discovered that there were about 60 categories (of "trusties") who work at an enormous number of jobs: they staple targets and mow lawns, mop floors, clean boats, clean toilets, make coffee, usher in the court, care for the sick, make pastries, wait on bulls, carry messages, wash pots, run elevators, cut hair

[100] Alcoholism and Drug Addiction Research Foundation of Toronto, "The Chronic Drunkenness Offender: The Jail" (Research Report No. 6, unpublished, n.d.). The findings of this study, conducted during 1960–61, are cited here with the kind permission of the foundation.

and a variety of other tasks. In this jail, which has a capacity for approximately 500 inmates, nearly 150 trusties are required each day to work. It was estimated by one police official that 80 percent of the inmates at any time are those charged with public drunkenness and that these are the men chosen to become trusties . . .[101]

Such exploitation of free labor sometimes extends to a form of "recruitment":

Penal officials like police officers don't consider public drunkenness offenders as serious criminals. It is simple enough to observe that many of the men when sober are steady workers . . . Much of the janitorial work in the jails is assigned to them. There are many instances where especially good workers with skills needed by the jail system are picked up by the police specifically to fill the jail's "need."[102]

The drunks Spradley interviewed in Seattle told of being shanghaied in this manner in jurisdictions through Washington and California. One man, while working in the kitchen of the Seattle Jail, "overheard the cook ask an officer where a certain man was who had been a good cook. The officer replied that they knew his whereabouts and would pick him up in a few days."[103]

A 1970 survey of California county jails found that the general view that drunks should be removed from the penal system was tempered by administrators' reliance on these dependable—and dependent—prisoners:

[E]ven when faced with the obvious problem of handling and caring for these individuals, a few sheriffs were reluctant to suggest removing all such persons from their jurisdictions. They based their opposition on their present needs for trustees to do custodial, maintenance and kitchen duty. Experienced jail supervisors know that the older alcoholics are docile, amiable and obedient workers when sober, as well as experienced in the ways of an institution. Some of these same supervisors are reluctant to change the system which provides such workers when no alternative sources of labor are available.[104]

[101] Spradley, *You Owe Yourself a Drunk,* p. 84.
[102] Cahn, *The Treatment of Alcoholics,* p. 47.
[103] Spradley, *You Owe Yourself a Drunk,* p. 85.
[104] California State Board of Corrections, "A Study of California County Jails" (April 1970), pp. 129–30.

The work drunks do in the jail cannot be rationalized as a kind of improvised vocational rehabilitation. Any correspondence between the labor needs of a jail and the demands of the job market is accidental. Like every other facet of the drunk's experience as an inmate, his institutional work prepares him for only one career —chronic recidivism.

A LIMITED ALTERNATIVE: SPECIAL SENTENCES FOR SELECTED OFFENDERS

Sheriffs and jail administrators frequently admit that the present system of jailing drunks simply does not work. Sheriff Robert H. Jamison, past president of the National Jail Association, echoed the feelings of the vast majority of his colleagues when he said,

> I feel that the jailing of alcoholics is definitely a serious problem, and one which should be stopped. These people are not criminal and should be treated by society as a medical and social problem.[105]

Even the rudimentary attention received by drunks on intake seems to correction officials to be intolerably costly, time-consuming and disruptive of institutional routine. The sheer size of the drunk population—40, 60 or even 80 per cent of all sentenced prisoners—threatens to overwhelm the jails' capacity.

The majority of California county jail administrators surveyed recently recommended a shift to "civil" handling of criminal drunks. One bluntly honest California official said, "The jails are loaded with drunks, therefore making it hard to have room for the real criminals."[106]

Among the simplest, most widely tested and ultimately most limited alternatives to the jailing of drunks is the "court school," "court clinic" or "honor class." Under this scheme individual judges, working with the aid of local social service agencies, screen men convicted of drunkenness and offer to a few, as a condition

[105] Sheriff Jamison's remarks are quoted in D. Goff, "Corrections and the Alcoholic," in U. S. Department of Health, Education, and Welfare, *The Court and the Chronic Inebriate* (Washington, D.C.: Government Printing Office, 1965).
[106] California State Board of Corrections, "A Study of California County Jails" (April 1970), pp. 125, 126.

of probation, attendance at a series of educational or therapeutic sessions. Such programs have existed in Europe for decades; the earliest American experiments began in Washington, D.C., in 1946, and in Stoughton, Massachusetts, in the early 1950's.[107] In Washington, men were released to the program after a three- to five-day drying-out period in the D. C. Jail, and participated in meetings strongly influenced by the principles of Alcoholics Anonymous. In Stoughton, candidates were referred directly from the court to a ten-week routine of group therapy and individual counseling. Both programs reported encouraging results, but neither affected more than a fraction of the convicted drunks in the jurisdiction.

Such experiments in post-trial "diversion" from jail have proliferated. Tests in specialized sentencing for drunkenness offenders have been conducted in San Francisco, California; Des Moines, Iowa; Denver, Colorado; Hartford, Connecticut; and Miami, Florida; among other cities.[108] Some imitate the "traffic school," with illustrated lectures on the dangers of drink; some stress the informal, confessional atmosphere of an AA meeting; some emphasize individualized supervision; and others offer simplified group psychotherapy.

Participants are selected by the court, on the basis of apparent sincerity and treatability. First offenders and the "respectable" drunks who occasionally are caught up in the criminal justice mill by accident are regarded as having the most potential. Participants return to jail less frequently and some make progress toward sobriety. But hard cases—confirmed criminal drunks—are usually excluded.

When more typical drunkenness offenders are admitted to a court-sponsored alternative sentencing program, the results are less encouraging. After a recent experiment, the San Diego Municipal Court concluded that for chronic drunks, even a form of

[107] Edward W. Soden, "How a Municipal Court Helps Alcoholics," *Federal Probation,* September 1960, p. 45; Brunner-Orne et al., "A Court Clinic for Alcoholics," 12 *Q. J. Stud. Alc.* 217 (1951).
[108] Levin, "San Francisco Court School of Alcoholism Prevention," 53 *A.B.A.J.* 1043 (1967); Burnett, "Remarks" in *Proceedings: The Alcoholic and the Court* (Oregon, May 23–25, 1963); Lisensky, *The Chronic Drunkenness Offender,* p. 36; Pinardi, "The Chronic Drunkenness Offender; What One City Is Doing About the Revolving Door," 12 *Crime and Delinquency,* 339 (1966).

intensive probation, with counseling and supervision by Alcoholics Anonymous members or medical personnel, had no demonstrable effects on rates of recidivism.[109] Apparently, the drunks need more than the meager social services which the courts can provide through variations in sentencing practices.

IN-JAIL TREATMENT: ALCOHOLIC THERAPY BEHIND BARS

Counseling and self-help programs conducted within short-term penal institutions are few in number. Even the rare and best ones, however, are palliatives rather than solutions. Beginning with the assumption that alcohol use is the jailed drunk's primary problem, they ignore the milieu from which the drunk comes and to which he will return.

AA meetings in jail are well attended; but attendance is not a measure of future success, or of motivation. In one jail, such a gathering was announced by a guard bellowing, "All right, all 'winoes,' fall out for A.A."[110] Also, the meetings provide variety in the jail routine, an opportunity to meet friends confined in other parts of the jail, free AA coffee and doughnuts. In the most successful programs, the visitors offer tobacco to supplement the meager jail ration.

Unlike the AA chapters which operate with some apparent success in long-term penal institutions, groups in jail cannot develop into self-sustaining units with regular membership and a stable organization because the jail inmate population is constantly shifting.

AA, with its uncompromising emphasis on sincerity, personal motivation and self-help may impose an extra burden on the drunk in jail.[111] The AA credo insists that before a drinker can begin to reclaim himself, he must admit that he is, first and foremost, an alcoholic. Most criminal drunks are not alcoholics or, if they are, able to say so.[112] AA has an impressive and well-documented

109 Ditman et al., "A Controlled Experiment on the Use of Court Probation for Drunk Arrests," 124 *Am. J. Psych.* (1967), 2.
110 Rubington, "The Alcoholic and the Jail," *Federal Probation,* June 1965, pp. 30, 33.
111 See "Alcoholics Anonymous in Prison," *Federal Probation,* December 1954, p. 17. (Authored by anonymous AA member.)
112 As has already been indicated, the best evidence suggests that only a

record of success among middle-class alcoholics. It does not address the serious handicaps of lower-status men.[113]

The effectiveness of referrals to AA groups on the outside for follow-up after release, which are potentially the most constructive feature of the organization's in-jail programs, depends on the outside group's receptiveness to Skid Row men and on the willingness of the men to seek them out. Here, too, the fact that AA is a predominantly middle-class organization, with middle-class concerns for punctuality and personal hygiene, discourages the Skid Row drunk, who is acutely sensitive to social rebuffs. Few local chapters of AA are composed predominantly of former and present Skid Row men. An ordinary chapter may not reject the drunk if he appears without a shave and a clean shirt, but he is unlikely to put the matter to the test.

Specialized professionally staffed alcoholism rehabilitation programs operate within a few of the nation's most progressive and best-financed local jails. Two notable examples are the Santa Rita Rehabilitation Center, near Oakland in California's Alameda County, and the Westchester County Penitentiary at Valhalla, New York.[114] At both, the program is a mix of scientific detoxi-

---

minority of criminal drunks are clinical alcoholics. But all problems of medical definition aside, Skid Row men and criminal drunks do not regard or identify themselves as "alcoholics." When a sample of Chicago's Skid Row drinkers were questioned as to why they drank, only 27 per cent referred to any concept of compulsion or addiction. Bogue, *Skid Row in American Cities*, p. 288 (1963). In Seattle, a sample of criminal drunks had all heard the term "alcoholic" and had been in one or more alcoholism treatment centers, yet this identity was not too significant to many of them. Spradley, *You Owe Yourself a Drunk*, p. 66.

[113] For an early and optimistic account of AA's potential role in the jail, see Howard B. Gill, "The Alcoholic in the Penal Institution," 6 *Q. J. Stud. Alc.* (1945): 233. For the recent description of an AA jail program in operation, see Alcoholism and Drug Addiction Research Foundation of Toronto, "The Chronic Drunkenness Offender: The Jail."

[114] The Santa Rita Center's program is described in some detail in Mac-Cormick, "Correctional Views on Alcohol, Alcoholism, and Crime," 9 *Crime and Delinquency* 15, 22–23 (1963). For the program of the Westchester Penitentiary, see Alvin R. Yaplater, "Rehabilitation Program for Alcoholic Inmates at the Westchester County Penitentiary" 65 *N.Y. St. J. Med.* (1965): 1003. A former warden of the Westchester facility describes the history and development of that program in Paul R. Brown, "The Problem Drinker and the Jail," 16 *Q. J. Stud. Alc.* (1955): 474.

The NCCD survey "Corrections in the United States," 13 *Crime and Delinquency* 147 (1967), indicated that only 7 per cent of the jails studied had any program for alcoholics. Even at exemplary institutions like Pennsylvania's Bucks County Jail, alcoholism treatment within the jail itself is far more

fication, intensive medical care, group and individual psychotherapy, tranquilizing and alcohol-reactive medication, and vocational and academic training. Films, lectures, pre-release counseling, and Alcoholics Anonymous sessions also are employed, in an attempt to prepare jailed drunks for a future of sobriety. But even these well-staffed and humane institutions assume that jailed drunks can be helped permanently by medical management of their drinking problems. Their more critical problems, however, cannot be addressed in an isolated, institutional setting.

Enlightened institutional care programs do show positive results on paper, primarily because participants have been pre-screened from the jail's drunk population on the basis of their prognosis for recovery. For the alcoholic offender who is not a confirmed Skid Row drunk, alcoholism therapy may have real value. For the typical jailed drunk, however, the critical moment occurs when he is released back to the streets, and is confronted once again by the evidence of his inadequacy. For him, alcoholism therapy becomes irrelevant; the absence of friends, family, work opportunities and other practical contacts in society at large is paramount.

RE-ENTRY PROGRAMS

No programs operating either in a short-term penal institution or through courts' probation and parole officers have succeeded in preparing many confirmed drunks for re-entry into society. None provides the critical, sustaining, comprehensive "aftercare" services uniquely required by their constituents.

Specialized halfway houses can provide uniquely valuable aftercare services for drunks discharged from the courts and the jails, providing them with a sure residential base in the community while they find work, permanent housing and social contacts, and

---

limited than that provided by the Santa Rita and Westchester County facilities.

In several cities, including San Francisco and Seattle, the court may order a few drunks to serve their time in an independent treatment center, but no services are offered within the jail itself. For an account of one interesting program, now defunct, see Jackson, Fagan, and Burr, "The Seattle Police Department Rehabilitation Program for Chronic Alcoholics," *Federal Probation*, June 1958, p. 36. Under this plan, jailed drunks volunteered for treatment at a separate facility emphasizing work-therapy and quasi-military discipline.

eliminating the stress which attends rapid re-entry into society.[115]

In 1965, there were between fifty and seventy-five transitional residences on or near American Skid Rows, and many of them had some residents referred from the courts and the jails. But few of these houses have served the chronic criminal drunk. In the many houses operated by the Salvation Army's Harbor Light agency:

> Most of the men referred or selected for the residence are not Skid Row public drunkenness offenders but men of higher status who are one-time or infrequent offenders. Like other agencies, the Salvation Army seeks "motivated" alcoholics, and the concept of motivation is a sieve which sifts out the chronic Skid Row alcoholic.[116]

The Connecticut Department of Mental Health's Compass Clubs in Hartford and New Haven have made more serious efforts to reach the typical drunk.[117] And the record of the work-oriented halfway house for Skid Row men at Boston's Long Island City Hospital demonstrates that a program with flexible goals and a realistic concept of "rehabilitation" can make real progress.[118] In a ten-year follow-up study, all the residents traced were former chronic criminal drunks and many were middle-aged or older. All originally had entered the hospital for alcoholic detoxification, and stayed on voluntarily in the residential program, which emphasized neither eternal sobriety nor a quick transition to complete self-sufficiency, but gradual progress. Their temporary relapses had been expected and accepted. Of the 100 men whose careers were followed, twenty-two had re-entered society successfully, twenty-four were "partial" successes, depending on the halfway house and hospital for occasional care and assistance, and fifty-four were judged failures.

The successes of private and public halfway houses operated outside the criminal justice system have encouraged some local

---

[115] For a detailed account of the halfway house rationale, and an account of a successful British program, see Pollack, "Rathcole—A Residential House for the Skid Row Alcoholic," in Timothy Cook, Dennis Gath, and Celia Hensman, eds., *The Drunkenness Offender* (Elmsford: Pergamon 1969).

[116] Cahn, *The Treatment of Alcoholics*, p. 161.

[117] See generally, Lisensky, *The Chronic Drunkenness Offender*, pp. 49–52.

[118] For the program and record of the Long Island Hospital facility, see Myerson and Mayer, "Origins, Treatment and Destiny of Skid Row Alcoholic Men," 19 *S. Car. L. Rev.* 332 (1967).

courts and correction departments to make transitional residences for drunks a part of their official program. A facility called Reception House recently has been established in Rochester, New York,[119] to house a small number of alcoholic men who would otherwise be sentenced to jail. In Bucks County, Pennsylvania, the jail complex itself includes such transitional housing.

One dramatically successful halfway house program for criminal drunks is Arlington County, Virginia's, Alcoholic Rehabilitation, Inc. (ARI),[120] a private organization which takes court referrals. These are men whose cases have been continued on the condition that they enter the ARI program. If they succeed in that program, the charges are dismissed, and all references to prior alcohol-related offenses are expunged from their criminal records. Thomas Dodge, chief judge of the county courts, says that "Arlington's alcoholic recidivism problem has actually been brought under control [by drying up] the reservoir of hopeless drunks who used to turn up in court again and again."

A drunk in ARI spends three weeks on an isolated and somewhat dilapidated farm, which strikes a delicate balance between comfort and hardship according to the program's director: "If it were nicer, the men would retire here. If it were nastier, they couldn't stand it." The drunk then is transferred for an indeterminate stay at one of five urban halfway houses, from which they graduate into the community. Many relapse and return repeatedly to the house to make a fresh start, but ARI officials maintain that of the 1,300 men who have passed through the program in the last ten years, more than 900 have achieved "success," defined as a full year of complete voluntary abstinence. The participants are volunteers, but they also are primarily what one county judge describes as "your classic Skid Row types . . . my toughest cases."

Among halfway house programs, it is rare to find one which displays no bias against the confirmed drunk whose resistance to change can mar a program's success record and depress staff morale. The ARI staff of former alcoholics seems prepared to deal patiently with the hard cases. But financial support for similar projects is unlikely to be forthcoming from a society which prefers

[119] Pittman and Gillespie, "Social Policy as Deviancy Reinforcement," in Pittman, *Alcoholism,* pp. 106, 122.
[120] Burchard, "At Last, a Drunk Farm That Works," Washington *Post,* January 27, 1972.

its drunks out of sight and out of mind. Even in Arlington, this tried and tested halfway house program is at the point of bankruptcy. ARI can maintain a program participant for eighty-four cents a day, in contrast to the seven-to-eight-dollar daily cost of warehousing a man in the Arlington County Jail. Although it receives some public support, it survives on private donations and the income its founder-director earns driving a cab in off hours. Fiscal anomalies like that just cited suggest one simple solution to the problem of financing care for the Skid Row drunk: a small additional tax levy on all sales of beverage alcohol, to be reserved in a special fund, just as some gasoline taxes are allocated for transportation expenditures. For most Americans, drink is a desirable luxury. For the Skid Row men, it is a symbol of failure and neglect. It seems only appropriate that the vast majority should contribute to the salvation of these victims. A liquor tax of the sort proposed also would be a dependable revenue source.

REFORM OF DRUNKENNESS LAW

The 1967 presidential Crime Commission recommended that: "Drunkenness in itself should not be a criminal offense." The suggestion was by no means new. As Seldon Bacon, a scholar of alcoholism, has noted, similar task forces have made similar proposals repeatedly for a century or more. Even in the early 1820's, the Connecticut legislature recommended non-criminal handling of drunkenness. By the late 1960's, task force reports had ceased to provide new solutions; resort to them had become part of the problem, in fact. They did signal, however, a growing urgency in the criminal justice system's dissatisfaction with the dirty and unrewarding business of processing drunks into jail. As Bacon observed:

> The medical profession and its various administrative branches (hospitals, private offices, clinics, disease recording systems, training schools) long ago came to the same conclusion. Social and welfare agencies made this discovery and established their position of getting and staying "out" . . . Now, at long last, criminal justice and law enforcement "want out." But to whom will they hand this very large mess?[121]

[121] Bacon, "Alcoholism and the Criminal Justice System," 2 *Law & Soc. Rev.* 489, 492 (1968).

A rational, orderly transfer of official responsibility for the processing of public drunks appears to be a near impossibility.

The mid-1960's saw a drive in the courts to take some drunkenness offenders out of the criminal justice system altogether. The objective was to establish the disease of chronic alcoholism as an absolute defense to a charge of public drunkenness—and thus to force the caretaking professions into action.[122]

The reformers who sought to shake the legal foundation of drunkenness law enforcement through test litigation faced formidable obstacles.

An almost unbroken line of decisions, highlighted by *State* v. *Potts,*[123] a North Carolina case of 1888, had held that "involuntary intoxication" was no defense to a charge of criminal conduct. In the 1962 case of *Robinson* v. *California,*[124] however, the United States Supreme Court reversed a criminal

[122] The history of this extraordinary campaign is recorded in the publications of Peter Hutt and Richard Merrill, two attorneys who became advocates for homeless men. See, for example, Hutt, "Recent Forensic Developments in the Field of Alcoholism," 8 *W. & M. L. R.* 343 (1967), and Merrill, "Drunkenness and Reform of the Criminal Law," 54 *Va. L. Rev.* 1135 (1968), a fascinating look into the practical difficulties involved in constructing an ideal test case. Of special interest are Hutt's informal remarks in "Comments on 'Institute on Modern Trends in Handling the Chronic Alcoholic Offender,'" 19 *S. Car. L. Rev.* 305 (1967).

A number of articles provide valuable background on the "alcoholism defense" and its roots in English and American criminal jurisprudence. Both R. U. Singh, "The Defense of Drunkenness in English Criminal Law," 49 *L. Q. Rev.* 558 (1933) and Prof. James Starrs, "The Disease Concept of Alcoholism and The Traditional Criminal Law," 19 *S. Car. L. Rev.* 349 (1967) analyze complex legal concepts with admirable clarity.

Some of the implications of the alcoholism defense are explored in Hutt, "Is the Alcoholic Immune from Criminal Prosecution?" 25 *Legal Aid Brief Case* 70 (1967). His answer, it may be noted, is in the negative. And the progress, or lack of progress, in judicial drunkenness law reform since the United States Supreme Court's rejection of the alcoholism defense is surveyed in Leo Hollister, "Alcoholics and Public Drunkenness—The Emerging Retreat from Punishment," 16 *Crime and Delinquency* 239 (1970). Recent developments in drunkenness law reform generally are summarized in the U. S. Department of Health, Education, and Welfare's *First Special Report to the U. S. Congress on Alcohol and Health,* Chap. VIII, "The Legal Status of Intoxication and Alcoholism."

The most persuasive attack on the legal and medical underpinnings of the alcoholism defense is Finagretti, "The Perils of *Powell.*"

For a concise summary of all the legal aspects and complications of problem drinking, see F. Grad, A. Goldberg, and B. Shapiro, *Alcoholism and the Law.*

[123] 100 N.C. 456, 6 N.E. 657.

[124] 370 U.S. 660 (1962).

conviction under a statute outlawing narcotics addiction. Any penalty for a "status offense," involving a disease condition over which the sufferer had no control, was ruled impermissible as an unconstitutionally "cruel and unusual" punishment. Law enforcement officials regarded *Robinson* as a revolutionary and potentially dangerous decision. Its effects, they feared, might be to leave the addict immune from prosecution for the sale of narcotics, or to excuse the arsonist who advanced pyromania as a defense.

Nevertheless, reform-minded lawyers hoped to extend the rule of the *Robinson* case from drug addiction into alcoholism, and to establish the principle that what were technically punishments for the conduct of appearing drunk in public amounted to penalties on the status of alcoholism. If it was impermissible to punish having a compulsive disease, they argued, the bar against prosecution should extend to the immediate symptoms of the disease as well. This constitutional point was the first element of the reformers' two-part case against drunkenness law enforcement.

Their second point was an argument based on the common law principle that a criminal act must be done with wrongful intent. The reformers contended the chronic alcoholic who had lost control over his drinking could not be held criminally responsible for the immediate consequence of that drinking—public intoxication. Their contention ran directly counter to the role of *State* v. *Potts*. Even though an alcoholic may have no present control over his drinking, the cases held, he has not always lacked such control; therefore, the conventional reasoning ran, if an alcoholic became drunk and violated the law while under the influence, his act must be interpreted as the final outcome of a course of conduct voluntarily undertaken. In effect, the reformers faced the task of rebutting a well-entrenched legal fiction.

In December 1963, Joe B. Driver, an impoverished, chronic alcoholic from Durham County, North Carolina, was convicted for public drunkenness in the local superior court and sentenced to two years in jail, his fifth conviction within a twelve-month period, and his 209th overall. He testified at his sentencing that he was fifty-eight years old, that he was first arrested for drunkenness at twenty-four and had since spent two thirds of his life "on the roads for drinking." The judge told Driver, "you are an alcoholic if I ever saw one."

"Yes, sir, I consider myself an alcoholic," he testified. "I want to do something about it but it don't look like I can. For seven years I have been rated totally disabled." Medical testimony corroborated that Driver was a chronic alcoholic.

The North Carolina Supreme Court affirmed the conviction and sentence in May 1964,[125] held that imprisonment without medical or psychological treatment was proper and rejected the argument of the defense that such handling of a sick man was wrong. So long as society approved drunkenness laws and the legislature adopted them, it reasoned, the criminal courts should not decline to enforce them.

Driver's lawyers appealed his case to the federal courts with the aid of Washington attorney Peter Hutt, an expert in this field who had been retained by the ACLU and who was trying an analogous case in Washington, D.C.[126] They argued that the imprisonment of an alcoholic violated the Eighth Amendment's prohibition of cruel and unusual punishment. Seeking habeas corpus release from the state court ruling,[127] Driver's lawyers relied on the Supreme Court's ruling in *Robinson*.[128]

Driver argued that it was as wrong for North Carolina to punish the anti-social symptoms of his disease as it had been for California to punish the fact of an addict's sickness itself. The Federal District Court in North Carolina said that to expand the California ruling would be mischievous and improper. Driver's sentence was conventional (accomplished by no unusual means, and within the limits set by the public drunkenness statute). The provision for punishment without treatment was considered proper. In sentencing, the court held, only relative decency—not wisdom or rationality—was necessary. Specialized, individualized rehabilitative treatment of offenders while "politically, socially and economically desirable, is hardly a constitutional requisite."

Driver appealed further and took his case to the United States Court of Appeals.[129] Relying on the definitions of chronic alcoholism employed by the National Council on Alcoholism, the American Medical Association and World Health Organization—

---

[125] *State* v. *Driver,* 262 N.C. 92, 136 S.E. 2d 208 (1964).
[126] *Easter* v. *District of Columbia,* the companion case, is discussed below.
[127] *Driver* v. *Hinnant,* 243 F. Supp. 95 (1965).
[128] *Robinson* v. *California,* 370 U.S. 660 (1962).
[129] *Driver* v. *Hinnant,* 356 F. 2d 761 (1966).

which describe the alcoholic as a person "who is powerless to stop drinking" and so dependent on alcohol that his "social and economic behavior" is impaired—this court agreed that Driver had no willpower to resist drunkenness, and thus no volition to commit the crime of intoxication. His acts were not crimes but involuntary exhibitions of an infirmity.

Driver had been convicted twice again of public intoxication while on bail pending his appeal. The court held that his conduct did not include that evil intent or consciousness of wrongdoing which the law considers "indispensable ingredients of a crime." Thus it concluded that to punish Driver's drunkenness was unconstitutionally "cruel and unusual." It confined its ruling to the involuntary drinker, who was like "an imbecile or a person in a delirium of a fever." However, the court noted that "nothing we have said precludes appropriate detention of him for treatment and rehabilitation so long as he is not marked a criminal."

Also in early 1965, and before Driver's ultimately successful petition of habeas corpus had been filed, attorney Peter Hutt had appealed the conviction of DeWitt Easter under the District of Columbia's public intoxication statute, and his suspended sentence to ninety days in jail. The D. C. Court of Appeals had upheld the conviction,[130] reasoning that drunkenness is no defense to a prosecution where specific intent is not an element of the offense charged, and no issue of insanity is raised.

Easter had been a familiar local alcoholic who had drunk intemperately for over thirty years. His arrest record documented more than seventy similar offenses. Many times he had been intoxicated but not arrested. His drinking had led to "a broken home life, recurrent hospitalization and loss of steady employment." He had been referred to clinics for rehabilitation. To his argument that medical facilities at the jail were inadequate, the court responded that it was "without means of solving the problem," and deferred to the legislature for the appropriate solution.

The District of Columbia court distinguished the *Robinson* rule with this less than edifying rationale: Easter "was not punished because of his addiction to alcohol. He was convicted for being intoxicated in public."

The United States Court of Appeals for the District of

---

[130] *Easter* v. *District of Columbia,* 109 A. 2d 625 (1965).

Columbia was more sympathetic.[131] Concluding as its North Carolina colleagues had that the evidence is quite clear that chronic alcoholism is a disease precluding the intent essential to the categorization of an act as a crime, the full court ruled unanimously that Easter's conviction must be reversed; half its members went farther and concluded in addition that the conviction was an unconstitutionally cruel and unusual punishment. The court reasoned that if suffering from a sickness is not a crime, manifesting it in a public place cannot be either. "The very nature of the sickness goes where its victim goes." The court followed its view of Congress' intent to treat chronic alcoholism through civil, not criminal, processes by relying on a local statute establishing a program for rehabilitation of alcoholics through "medical, psychiatric and other scientific treatment."[132]

During 1967, the Superior Court of Fulton County, Georgia, in *Dunlap* v. *City of Alabama*,[133] the Pennsylvania Court of Common Pleas in Philadelphia, in *Lee* v. *Hendrick*,[134] and the Circuit Court for Montgomery County, Maryland, in *State* v. *Ricketts*,[135] all held that chronic alcoholism constitutes a defense to charges of public intoxication, on common law and constitutional grounds.

The progressive and enlightened trend of these rulings was set back in 1968 when the United States Supreme Court delivered its decision in *Powell* v. *Texas*,[136] an appeal from the public drunkenness conviction of an Austin, Texas, bootblack. Leroy Powell was a benign but chronic, uncontrollable and impoverished alcoholic; he had been fined fifty dollars for this, his hundredth such conviction.

In response to the same points Driver and Easter had raised, Associate Justice Thurgood Marshall, author of the Supreme Court's prevailing opinion (joined by Justices Warren, Black and Harlan), said that the definition of an alcoholic generally is too

[131] *Easter* v. *District of Columbia,* 361 F. 2d 50 (1966) (*en banc*).
[132] D. C. Code, 24-501.
[133] No. B-29126 (July 17, 1967), reprinted in 113 Cong. Rec. H-11089 (August 23, 1967) (daily ed.).
[134] No. H. C. -0075 (August 31, 1967), reprinted in 113 Cong. Rec. H-15368 (November 15, 1967) (daily ed.); 1 *Crim. L. Nqtr.* 2364.
[135] Crim. No. 8787 (October 25, 1967), reprinted in 113 Cong. Rec. S-15974 (November 7, 1967) (daily ed.).
[136] 392 U.S. 514.

uncertain and that the specific expert testimony in this case provided too inadequate a predicate for the broad constitutional finding the Court was asked to make. The record did not adequately demonstrate whether Powell was both initially unable to abstain from drinking and out of control once he began.

"It would be tragic to return large numbers of helpless, sometimes dangerous and frequently unsanitary inebriates to the streets of our city without even the opportunity to sober up adequately which a brief jail term provides," Marshall stated. And, he continued, there is no evidence that any compulsory treatment scheme "would provide anything more than slightly higher-class jails for our indigent habitual inebriates. Thus, we run the grave risk that nothing will be accomplished beyond the hanging of a new sign —'hospital'—over one wing of the jailhouse."

> One virtue of the criminal process is, at least, that the duration of penal incarceration typically has some outside statutory limit; this is universally true in the case of petty offenses, such as public drunkenness, where jail terms are quite short on the whole. "Therapeutic civil commitment" lacks this feature; one is typically committed until one is "cured." Thus, to do otherwise than affirm might subject indigent alcoholics to the risk that they may be locked up for an indefinite period of time under the same conditions as before, with no more hope than before of receiving effective treatment and no prospect of periodic "freedom."[137]

Justice Marshall reasoned that the penal sanction may not be "utterly lacking in social value," and until practical alternatives offered effective rehabilitation, it ought not to be abandoned lightly. Harsh penal sanctions may have a deterrent effect, if not on the chronic drunk, then on the many American alcoholics who conceal their affliction. The "validity of the deterrence justification," remaining a matter of lively debate, was not resolved in the *Powell* decision.

Justice Marshall—and the three justices concurring in his opinion—refused to interfere with the power of the states to experiment locally with social policy through criminal laws consistent with evolving religious, moral, philosophical or medical views; they also refused to fashion an insanity defense of constitutional proportions by excusing every compulsive crime.

[137] Ibid., p. 529.

Justice Hugo Black's preference was to make moral blame-worthiness an integral part of all crimes. Nevertheless, he agreed as to the Court's lack of expert qualifications to answer questions about the status of alcoholism, the therapeutic and deterrent value of jailing drunkards and the precipitous nature and social stigma of alternate civil commitment procedures.

Thus the Court split four to four on the major constitutional and common law questions raised by Leroy Powell's case. Justice White, concurring in Justice Marshall's conclusion, but not in his reasoning, cast the deciding vote in favor of affirmance. His own opinion stressed that the essence of Powell's offense was the public nature of his intoxication, and that without evidence that Powell was compelled not only to drink but also to drink in public, the rule of *Robinson* could not be extended to his case.

Read together, the opinions of the justices in *Powell* do not form a coherent whole. Although the Court disposed of the case of one Texas bootblack, the larger implication of its opinion for the future of drunkenness law enforcement remained uncertain. It has been argued that Powell's appeal failed only because he was not a "homeless" Skid Row alcoholic and that a majority of the justices in fact agreed that "a homeless alcoholic is not accountable for his act."[138] But the Court did not so hold. How it would have weighed the case of a drunkenness offender more typical than Powell remains a matter of speculation, until such a case is presented for its decision.

Justices Douglas, Brennan and Stewart joined in a dissent written by Justice Fortas. The dissenters urged that medical evidence adequately establishes alcoholism as a disease; the facts in the record in this case adequately showed that Powell was an alcoholic and that being drunk in public was "a characteristic part of the pattern of his disease." Furthermore, they argued, the jailing was a punishment since it could serve no therapeutic or deterrent purpose; in fact, it could only be part of a destructive and wasteful revolving door process of arrest, incarceration, release and re-arrest. Since Powell was powerless to change his condition, the minority felt it would be cruel and unusual punishment to exact criminal penalties.

[138] See John N. Mitchell, "Alcoholism—To Heal, and Not to Punish," in U. S. Department of Health, Education, and Welfare, *First Special Report to the U. S. Congress on Alcohol and Health,* pp. 119, 120.

Whatever its real legal significance, in practice the *Powell* decision stalled the drive for judicial reform of drunkenness law. Even before *Powell* the Supreme Court of Michigan had refused to reverse a ruling which held that voluntariness was not an issue in a public drunkenness prosecution because the statute involved was in the nature of a police regulation and did not require criminal intent.[139] After *Powell,* the Supreme Court of Georgia rejected the defense of chronic alcoholism, in part because it feared opening what it termed the "Pandora's box" of a defense based on compulsion ("And why not accept a plea . . . of nymphomania from a prostitute, or a similar plea of impulse and non-volitional action by a child molester?")[140]

The Supreme Court of Washington also rejected the defense of chronic alcoholism.

> Alcoholism is a terrible thing . . . its victims should be treated with compassion . . . Among its consequences too are the pain and suffering, the humiliation and deprivation inflicted upon [the alcoholic's] family; and not to be overlooked is the fact that alcoholics have been known to commit serious crimes.
>
> If we were to condition this rule [of responsibility for voluntary acts] by relieving chronic alcoholics of responsibility for public misconduct while drunk, we would inevitably, under the same reasoning, be forced to relieve them of the legal consequences of other crimes committed while under the influence of voluntarily consumed intoxicants.
>
> Suppose this court, as a matter of public policy, were to strike down Seattle's ordinance prohibiting public drunkenness. What then are the alternatives? The courts levy no taxes, appropriate no moneys, employ no doctors, nurses, social workers and attendants, operate no hospitals, clinics, detoxification centers, and hire no personnel or facilities under their direction for the care and treatment of chronic addictive alcoholics or for the protection of society from their behavior. Having created the vacuum, the courts have no means to refill it.
>
> And what of the alcoholic himself? Is the Seattle ordinance against public drunkenness completely insensitive to him? Defendant's frequent periods of internment in the city jail, away from liquor and with nourishing food, undoubtedly have done

---

[139] *People* v. *Hoy,* 3 Mich. App. 666, 143 N.W. 2d 577 (1966).
[140] *Burger* v. *State,* 118 Ga. App. 328, 163 S.E. 2d 333, 334 (1968). One possible response to the court's rhetorical inquiry is that, unlike sex offenses, public drunkenness is "victimless crime" in its purest imaginable form.

much to keep him alive and in good physical health. Better a clean
warm jail on a rainy, winter night than a miserable wet gutter.[141]

In 1969, the Supreme Court of Minnesota noted that chronic
alcoholism *was* a good defense in a prosecution under a statute
which specifically forbade "voluntary intoxication,"[142] since
medical evidence had established beyond question that the alcoholic has lost voluntary control over his drinking. But the Supreme
Court of Alaska, in the same year, reached the opposite conclusion.[143] The alcoholic's compulsion to drink, the Alaska court
held, was not "so completely overpowering" as to excuse the
prohibited conduct. More generally, it reasoned that acceptance
of the defense of involuntariness "would tend toward a virtual
abandonment of the criminal law."

Efforts to reform drunkenness law through the courts ground to
an inconclusive halt. As long as state appellate courts steer by the
dim beacon of *Powell* v. *Texas,* it is unlikely that they will provide much more relief to the criminal drunk. The perspective of
the frontline judges of the municipal and county courts, who con-
front the problem of the drunk every morning in all its noisome
immediacy, is different from that of the more detached appellate
judges. One of the remarkable features of drunkenness offender
Wayne Hill's trial *de novo* before the full Supreme Court of
Washington was the eloquent testimony of Municipal Judge
Charles Z. Smith for the defense. But Judge Smith's portrait of
the cruel and irrational revolving door did not impress a majority
of the appellate court. Wayne Hill went back to jail and Judge
Smith returned to his bench—each a prisoner of the futility of
drunkenness law enforcement and the immobility of the high
courts.

The extent of the setback administered by the Supreme Court
in *Powell* should not, however, be exaggerated. The courts are
not the only arena through which reform in drunkenness law has
been sought, and after *Powell,* efforts to win legislative and administrative changes have continued. In the main, these efforts
would have been necessary in any event. Indeed, even if the drive
for judicial law reform had succeeded altogether the reform
movement would still have faced two dilemmas: the limited avail-

---

[141] *Seattle* v. *Hill,* 435 P. 2d 692, 697, 702 (Wash. 1967).
[142] *State* v. *Fearon* 166 N.W. 2d 720 (Minn. 1969).
[143] *Vick* v. *State* 453 P. 2d 342 (Alaska 1969).

ability of the alcoholism defense and the limited immediate prospects for working alternatives to jail or neglect.

The first of these dilemmas may be more daunting in theory than in practice. Technically, even a decision taking the position of the *Powell* dissent would not eliminate drunkenness law or all the injustices of its enforcement. The drive for judicial law reform had sought only to provide an absolute defense for those arrested drunks who could qualify as chronic, addictive drinkers who had lost control of their alcohol intake. The test defendants whose cases had been selected for appeal met the narrow definition of "clinical alcoholics." But, as has already been noted, there is formidable evidence to suggest that many of America's Skid Row drunks are not suffering from the disease of alcoholism, in this sense.

How would general judicial recognition of the alcoholism defense have affected the "winos"—the "nonaddictive pathological" homeless drinkers? If the courts were to have interpreted the defense stringently, well over a half of today's criminal drunks might have found themselves still caught in the revolving door, repeatedly arrested and jailed without offense to constitutional or common law principles. But given the existing dissatisfaction of many officials with their roles in drunkenness law enforcement, the provision of a convenient defense to some chronic criminal drunks would probably have benefited all the drunks, alcoholics and nonalcoholics alike. In itself, the obvious inconvenience of making the nice discriminations among drunks under a new rule of responsibility would have been enough to make a dead letter of existing prohibitions against public intoxication.

The problem of alternative management in the wake of a decision recognizing the alcoholism defense could not resolve itself so easily. The leaders of the drive for judicial law reform believed that as significant numbers of drunks were removed from the criminal process, the caretaking professions would at last be shocked out of their complacent reliance on the jail as a treatment facility; provision of services to these homeless men, ranging from scientific detoxification to vocational rehabilitation, would have become a matter of urgent and unavoidable necessity.[144] But the reformers also recognized that the caretaking professionals, with

---

[144] Hutt, "Comment on 'Institute on Modern Trends in Handling the Chronic Alcoholic Offender,' " 19 *S. Car. L. Rev.* 305 (1967).

their historic aversion to dealing with the drunk, might counter with new, and potentially even more dangerous, evasions. They risked provoking a medical-legal response that substituted long-term compulsory inpatient "treatment" for the evils of revolving door jailing.

One California legislator, discussing a bill which would have authorized widespread civil commitment of chronic public drunks, articulated the fear of treatment rationales: "It's better to be arrested as a drunk than (confined) as an alcoholic."[145] As Justice Marshall noted in his opinion in *Powell,* men who were able to avoid public drunkenness convictions by asserting an alcoholism defense, might find themselves subject to "civil commitment."

In their legal arguments supporting the alcoholism defense, the attorneys for the test defendants attempted to draw a careful conceptual distinction between an alcoholism defense and an insanity defense, since an insanity defense, when successfully asserted, leads almost inevitably to an indeterminate therapeutic commitment.

Proposals for involuntary commitment as an alternative to the criminal processing of drunks are hardly new. In 1910 and 1911, the New York legislature enacted a series of laws creating an elaborate non-judicial system to deal specifically with public intoxication. First offenders would be paroled under close supervision, but those who repeated within a twelve-month period, would be confined for up to three years at a special state hospital and "industrial colony." The facilities were built, a Board of Inebriety commissioned, and a number of drunks actually committed under the acts before the procedure was abolished in 1920, as overly elaborate and expensive. Today, the buildings of the one-time inebriate colony function as a local jail, the Erie County Penitentiary.

Persuasive policy arguments can be made against the long-term involuntary hospitalization of alcoholics. The foremost is that medical science has demonstrated no ability to treat this "disease" successfully. Nevertheless, twenty-one states presently have laws authorizing the involuntary commitment of non-criminal alcoholics to inpatient treatment programs, and though some statutes authorize only a relatively short initial holding period, the recommit-

---

[145] Quoted in 25 *Q. J. Stud. Alc.* (1964).

tal rates for court-adjudicated alcoholics are uniformly high.[146] Ironically, it is because drunkenness remains criminally punishable that commitment laws pose no great threat to the freedom of Skid Row men.

The long-term involuntary commitment of chronic Skid Row drunks does continue to command considerable support as a strategy. Donald Goff of the Correctional Association of New York[147] supports commitment because it is humane; he ignores the dismal record of failure accumulated by quasi-correctional experiments initiated in the name of treatment.

Opponents of commitment have raised substantial questions as to the constitutionality of any proposal in this vein. Hutt, for example, has contended that drunks should be analogized not to non-dangerous insane, who are committed on the presumption that they lack the capacity to choose between treatment and sickness, but to other varieties of healthy "risk takers," who are not institutionalized for their own good. Hypertensive heart patients are allowed to continue working under stress, racing drivers are not restricted from pursuing the lure of the track:

> In what way, then, is the alcoholic different? It may be that De-Witt Easter and Joe Driver fully appreciate that the constant imbibing will shorten their life expectancies. It may be that they prefer this way of life to any other. And it may well be that, as a result, they want no part of rehabilitative treatment, however enlightened it may be.[148]

Certainly, medical warehousing of drunks is a questionable substitute for penal confinement. But when and if conventional drunkenness law enforcement finally is discredited, judicially or legislatively, nice constitutional arguments are in jeopardy of falling before the impetus to substitute medical "street cleaning" for its criminal predecessor.

[146] For a discussion and tabular summary of these provisions, see F. Grad, A. Goldberg and B. Shapiro, *Alcoholism and the Law* 66–98, 250–66 (1971).
[147] See, e.g., Goff, "The Legal Position in the United States," in Cook, Gath, and Hensman, eds., *The Drunkenness Offender;* and D. Goff, "Corrections and the Alcoholic," U. S. Department of Health, Education and Welfare, *The Court and the Chronic Inebriate,* pp. 21–24. The present discussion is indebted to the latter article for the details of the 1910–11 New York commitment legislation, which Goff regards as an historic model rather than an item of well-intentioned folly.
[148] Hutt, "Recent Forensic Developments in the Field of Alcoholism," 8 *W. & M. L. Rev.* 343, 355 (1967).

DETOXIFICATION AND DECRIMINALIZATION

The battle for drunkenness law reform in the middle and late 1960's was fought on several fronts. The ferment about judicial reform impelled a number of localities to adopt comprehensive legislative and administrative reforms for the handling of drunks. In St. Louis, Missouri, Washington, D.C., and New York City, constructive changes short of unqualified decriminalization of public intoxication were instituted.

In his book *Two Million Unnecessary Arrests,* Raymond Nimmer evaluated the performance of these three metropolitan ventures into the modification of drunkenness law enforcement. He characterized the St. Louis experience as being, "less a demonstration of the proposition that the criminal process can be reformed via the police-initiated detoxification scheme, than a demonstration of the difficulties that inhere in this approach to reform."[149]

The St. Louis Police Department in 1966 opened the nation's first operating "civil detoxification center." A federal demonstration grant provided the financing; a standing order from the chief of police codified the new procedure. An arrested drunk was offered the choice between criminal processing and "voluntary" detoxification.[150]

If a qualified offender chose detoxification (a man requiring hospitalization for a physical disease did not qualify; neither did a man charged with other, more serious crimes), he was transported to the detoxification center for a seven-day stay. A summons charging the new patient with public drunkenness and setting a court date was left with the staff. If the patient completed the seven-day program, the summons was quashed on his release. If he left against medical advice, the criminal process, from which he had been temporarily diverted, was resumed. He was subject to prosecution for drunkenness.

[149] Nimmer, *Two Million Unnecessary Arrests,* p. 98; the following discussion of the St. Louis program is based on Nimmer's evaluation, and on St. Louis Metropolitan Police Department, "The St. Louis Detoxification and Diagnostic Evaluation Center, Final Evaluation Report" (1969).
[150] Given the nature of the two alternatives and the drunken man's limited capacity for choice, however, the voluntariness of the elections made was open to some question.

The St. Louis program continues to operate under these guidelines. It offers some drunks emergency medical care of the highest quality. However, it reaches only a fraction of the men who could benefit from it and provides no effective aftercare to the patient-offender after detoxification.

The St. Louis program's intake program is controlled by a police department whose traditional policy was to overlook drunks. Members of the force generally have refused to involve more drunks under the new program, even in the face of departmental directives urging change. Their initial recalcitrance, attributable to long "booking" time at the medical facility and to ingrained administrative habit, was to become more pronounced. As federal funding began to run out, the center was transferred from a center-city hospital to a ward in a state institution inconveniently located a half hour drive from the St. Louis Skid Row districts.

Nimmer has observed several procedures adopted by the St. Louis police to evade using the detoxification procedure: some drunkenness offenders are ignored, others are taken into custody under anti-loitering laws and processed as criminals, while still others simply are removed from the streets and dropped at the river front. The detoxification center is seriously underutilized; many of its beds are empty.

The St. Louis program has succeeded in conserving court time and jail space. But what impact has it had on the lives of the program participants? If improvement is to be measured by short-term recidivism rates, they have apparently received some benefit. Program participants averaged one arrest each in the three months preceding their detoxification, and only 0.3 arrests in the three months following; 46 per cent had been charged with drunkenness in the three months before the arrest which brought them to the center, but only 13 per cent were arrested in the three months after discharge.

The project's 1970 evaluation reports no statistics measuring the longer-term recidivism of detoxification patients.[151] The implications of other information in that report are that their prospects are poor. An evaluation of 160 male participants interviewed four months after their release, determined that, in the subjective

[151] U. S. Department of Justice, Law Enforcement Assistance Agency, *The St. Louis Detoxification and Diagnostic Evaluation Center* (Washington, D.C.: Government Printing Office, 1970).

judgment of the project staff members who conducted the interviews, 47 per cent had "improved" in drinking behavior, 53 per cent showed either no change or had "deteriorated." The health of 49 per cent had "improved"; but only 15 per cent had found better housing. In employment, 18 per cent had improved, and 82 per cent were unchanged or had deteriorated, 16 per cent were earning more, and 13 per cent less.[152]

"Improvements" in drinking behavior and health are the inevitable short-term effects of high-quality medical detoxification; the men surveyed had been contacted soon after their release from the program's clinic. The lower improvement rates for employment, income and housing—all major indices of social stability—are more significant. Little had occurred to change life patterns. Without such changes, they are destined to come into conflict with drunkenness law again.

The failure of the St. Louis detoxification program to intervene successfully in the degenerative, repetitive life cycles of most of its Skid Row patients probably is traceable to ineffective aftercare referrals. Attempts are made to direct discharged patients to appropriate social service agencies for assistance; but of 1,122 patients discharged in 1967, only one in four actually accepted employment referrals, and less than one in five took housing referrals. The staff made no consistent effort to see that referrals made were actually followed through, and it is possible that few of the minority referred appeared at the agencies.

Nevertheless, the St. Louis experiment has had its limited successes. It has discouraged criminal arrests for drunkenness, provided some medical treatment in place of criminal processing, and has effected, at least marginally, the continuing conduct of a minority of the city's chronic drunks.

The experience of the Washington, D.C., detoxification experiment generally has been similar to St. Louis's, with some marked differences. Both programs suffer because they rely on police pickups for primary intake and because they provide inadequate aftercare services to program participants. But where the St. Louis program was initiated by the police, and conducted within the framework of existing criminal drunkenness law, the Washington

[152] The 160 men actually interviewed were part of a designed sample of 200; the other forty could not be located; no doubt many had reverted to their previous condition altogether.

program was designed by public health authorities, in response to a major court decision and an act of Congress which altered the system of legal prohibitions and sanctions against public drunkenness.[153]

Washington's first detoxification center was established in 1967, as a direct response to the decision in *Easter* v. *District of Columbia;* it had special federal funding. A good deal of confusion prevailed as to who could be arrested for public drunkenness after the *Easter* decision; still, it was clear that some identifiable chronic alcoholics would require non-criminal handling if they were to be processed in any way.[154] Many police officers believed that only consenting drunks could be transported to the "Detox." And the center was underused in the beginning. Despite later clarification of the scope of police authority, this pattern persists. But, unlike the St. Louis center, Washington's "Detox" accepts self-referred patients as well as police pickups; recently, the ratio in the facility's population has been one walk-in to every pickup. The center now operates at capacity level.

Official clarification of the scope of police power and the relation of the detoxification center to the criminal justice system came with the Alcoholic Rehabilitation Act of 1968,[155] which proclaims that "all public officials in the District of Columbia shall take cognizance of the fact that public intoxication shall be handled as a public health problem rather than as a criminal offense." Police are empowered to transport any person found intoxicated in public to his home, to a private hospital or to the detoxification center. Once admitted to the center as a police pickup—or as a walk-in—a person guilty of no offense can be held against his will, "until sober and no longer incapacitated," for up to seventy-two hours. A person brought to the detoxification center as a violator of criminal prohibitions retained by the act, which apply to anyone "who shall be intoxicated and endanger the safety of himself or of any other persons or property," can be held longer—as long as is "reasonably necessary" for diagnosis. Medical evaluation may lead to the offender's adjudication as a "chronic alcoholic," which will supply a defense to the criminal charge and

[153] Alcoholic Rehabilitation Act, D. C. Code Ann. 24–501 et seq. (1968).
[154] See R. Nimmer, "The Public Drunk: Formalizing the Police Role as a Social Help Agency," 58 *Geo. W. L. Rev.* 1089, 1099–1101 (1970).
[155] D. C. Code Ann. 24–501 et seq.

also may result in short- or medium-term civil commitment: thirty days on a first-term commitment, and ninety days for repeaters.

In practice, almost all "Detox" admissions initiated by police are routine, non-criminal pickups. Simple public drunkenness technically has been decriminalized in the District of Columbia, but police have been given new and absolute authority to make protective arrests and conduct "street-cleaning" operations. Some younger officers are enthusiastic about the detoxification procedure and their new role in a process which stresses rehabilitation over punishment. Despite Washington's tradition of strict drunkenness law enforcement, however, many police now share the view of one patrolman interviewed by Nimmer: "It's no longer our problem. The bill takes it out of our hands." Even under the Rehabilitation Act, many officers also remain uncertain whether they have authority to pick up a non-consenting drunk without risking liability for false arrest. And, in some Washington precincts, where officers are evaluated by "scandal sheets," which record their arrest totals and other measures of performance, there is an additional disincentive to assisting non-criminal drunks. Before the Rehabilitation Act, an arrest for drunkenness had the same weight as any other misdemeanor arrest, but after the act, a "Detox run" has no place in the daily log. An officer can receive some credit on his record for reporting a malfunctioning traffic signal; he gets no points for helping a drunk to the "Detox."

In Nimmer's view, another factor in the reluctance of Washington police to use the detoxification alternative is their conviction that:

> The longer term model [of thirty-day sentences for public drunkenness] was functional in removing the men from the streets for long periods. It was also interpreted as being beneficial for the men by giving them time to dry out, recuperate from extended drinking, and rebuild their physical condition. Now, the police derisively observe, the men are back on the streets the next day.

This is not a complete exaggeration. Although the District of Columbia Detoxification Center is authorized to hold patients up to seventy-two hours, it is geared to provide only basic drying-out services. After twenty-four hours some men who need more care are shipped to an inpatient facility in rural Virginia for another two days of treatment. Many others are released back to the streets.

For many drunks Washington's detoxification procedure has become a non-criminal version of the familiar "revolving door" cycle. And as patrolmen encounter these "regulars" again and again, they are less inclined to transport them to the "Detox" and more inclined simply to order them to "move on."

Not all of Washington's former criminal drunks are served by the "Detox." Some who are overlooked by the police may come as walk-ins; more simply avoid all contact with the official program. The staff of SOME (So Others Might Eat), a volunteer organization providing food and clothing to all comers in the heart of one of Washington's Skid Row districts, say that many of the derelicts who gather daily at their center are men who were once abused as criminal drunks, and who today are the victims of simple neglect.

There are no recidivism statistics by which to gauge the impact of the new approach to public drunkenness on the life patterns of Skid Row men. Some men are detoxified with mechanical regularity, others are left to their own devices so long as they avoid particular streets and parks. Hence it would be unrealistic to conclude that the Washington experiment has made much progress toward meaningful rehabilitation of its alcoholic population.

As every patient completes emergency treatment, an attempt is made to provide him with a written referral to another agency, such as a hospital outpatient clinic, a Salvation Army program, or the Public Health Department's Rehabilitation Center for Alcoholics. But the overworked detoxification staff has no way of ensuring that a patient reaches the referral agency; the little information available suggests that few referrals are actually followed up.[156]

The principal referral agency for men leaving detoxification is the Rehabilitation Center for Alcoholics at Occoquan, Virginia, the site of the defunct District of Columbia workhouse, where criminal drunks once served their time. In theory, a patient volunteering for the ninety-day RCA rehabilitation program is provided with psychotherapy, job training, medical attention and counseling to prepare him for social reintegration. In fact, the program is underfinanced and understaffed, offering participants

---

[156] See Nimmer, *Two Million Unnecessary Arrests*, p. 122. Almost 1,300 referrals to one aftercare facility were made in the first six months of 1969; and only sixteen of the men entering there during that period treatment were identified as men following up on referrals from the detoxification program.

little more than nominally non-punitive warehousing under the supervision of a sympathetic but frustrated staff. In a recent interview RCA's director, Dr. Paul Trevis, commented on recent budget cuts and the future of the institution. He noted that overcrowding had become a threat to the health and safety of the patients, 62 per cent of whom are recidivists in the RCA program, and that the care was not truly rehabilitative: "I'll probably be fired for saying some of these things, but if this is going to be a custodial institution, I don't want to be here."[157]

His grievances have much in common with the complaints of jail officers about their drunk inmate populations. The men released from the RCA clinic tell the same sad story as released drunks throughout the United States. At the end of ninety days, a bus sets them down in the middle of the city, without money, jobs, friends or contacts outside Washington's Skid Row, and without the support they need to make these contacts. The tenuous purchase of physical health they may have gained at RCA will soon slip away, as these men make their rounds, seeking a "feed and flop." The missions, soup lines and the streets will reclaim the majority. In the crowd of worn and hopeless figures who crowd the courtyard outside SOME's free dining room every afternoon, waiting for their two-thirty meal, it is impossible to distinguish recent RCA graduates from men who have survived the last months on the skids.

Washington's experiment in the alternative handling of public drunks has had one dramatic success: it ended the jailing of Skid Row men as simple drunks, and dramatically reduced the number of harmless derelicts who are treated as criminals. It has substituted a promise of voluntary aftercare for compulsory incarceration; if this promise were to become a reality, the program might become a model. Until it does, the Washington experiment serves as a reminder that legislative fiat without administrative reforms will not necessarily succeed in diverting public drunks into constructive rehabilitation.

New York City's Manhattan Bowery Project, a new model program for public drunks operated by a private organization with

[157] Claiborne, "D. C. Alcoholics' Unit Deteriorates Quickly," Washington *Post,* April 16, 1972.

official co-operation provides an effective contrast.[158] The Bowery Project provides needed short- and long-term services to large numbers of homeless men; by moving a substantial number of these men out of the typical Skid Row life cycle it has managed to put them beyond the reach of New York's public drunkenness law.

In 1966, as the New York City Government pondered its response to the *Driver* and *Easter* decisions, Mayor John Lindsay invited the Vera Institute of Justice to suggest an alternative to the criminal processing of chronic drunkenness offenders in Manhattan's major Skid Row district. The Institute proposed a program designed to supplement traditional drunkenness law enforcement by offering voluntary medical detoxification and effective referrals for longer-term rehabilitative aftercare. It was hoped that without making drunk arrests legally impossible, the new approach would reduce or eliminate the call for such arrests.

The Bowery Project's designers recognized that some of the clients who would arrive at the converted space at the old Men's Shelter on the Bowery (provided by the city Department of Social Services) would be regulars, men too isolated and too dependent to escape the Bowery; others would be capable of responding more positively to care.

The project was prepared to provide periodic detoxification services to all the men who desired it. The regulars were not to be considered as hopeless recidivists who had exchanged one revolving door for another, but as an element of the client population which needed continuing services. By tailoring its services for repeaters, the project intended to improve their lot, even if it could not change their status.

For the men whose lives could be materially affected by effective aftercare, hopes were higher. Relapses were to be expected, but the project was designed to identify the men with a potential for social reintegration, and to direct them to medical facilities, and jobs, housing opportunities—referrals that might gradually make them truly independent of the project, the Bowery and the criminal justice system.

Some participants are walk-ins. Others have been contacted on the street by the project's regular patrol, a small van operated by

[158] The following account of the project is indebted to Nimmer's *Two Million Unnecessary Arrests,* and to Vera Institute of Justice's "Annual Report of the Manhattan Bowery Project" for 1969, 1970 and 1971.

a "rescue worker," himself a former alcoholic, and a plainclothes policeman, on hand solely to manage the rare man who proves belligerent or menacing. The rescue teams have nothing to do with what Nimmer calls the "voluntary-or-else" approach of Washington and St. Louis; a man in trouble receives an offer of help and transportation. He is free to reject it, as 33 per cent of the men contacted in the project's first year did. Once a man has embarked on the project's five-day detoxification schedule, he may leave at any time. Only about 3 per cent of the men entering in the first year actually left against medical advice.

According to the project's 1969 annual report:

> Rehabilitation for many Bowery men cannot be measured in absolute terms of permanent sobriety and of acquisition of jobs, families, property, and other social ties . . . [T]here are many relatively substantial forward steps a Bowery man can make on a less absolute scale. He can lengthen his average time between benders from a few weeks to a few months. He can obtain better paying jobs for longer periods of time. He can make better use of the City's health resources and obtain regular medical and dental attention. He can, through use of medically prescribed tranquillizers and other drugs, combat periods of stress by means other than alcohol.[159]

The unique approach of the Bowery Project to the homeless dictates the range and quality of its provisions for aftercare. The staff designs individualized programs for all discharged men, drawing on more than forty public and private medical and social service agencies, including a special clinic created by the project itself to accommodate men requiring continuing outpatient medical care.

This Out-Patient Department (OPD) now is the second most important referral resource—in terms of numbers of referrals, made and completed—on which the project's recently detoxified patients rely.[160] Staffed by two full-time caseworkers and three nurses, and served by three part-time psychiatric residents, it carries about 100 active patients on its rolls. A new and notable feature of the

[159] Vera Institute of Justice, "First Annual Report of the Manhattan Bowery Project," pp. 39–40.
[160] In terms of absolute numbers of referrals made, the project reports that its largest single referral resource is Camp La Guardia, a city-run recovery barracks for destitute alcoholic men located away from the Bowery, where men can recover in "a relaxed environment."

OPD's medical service is the administration of Antabuse (disulfiram); in itself the drug is benign, but in combination with alcohol it produces a highly unpleasant reaction. Widely employed in "aversion therapy" for millions of middle-class alcoholics, Antabuse is now being used with good effect by homeless drinkers. The Bowery Project reports that "nearly all OPD patients" participate in Antabuse treatment, and the staff credits its success to its effect in reducing the number of hard decisions a Skid Row drinker must face on the streets. For recently detoxified Skid Row drinkers, every day presents multiple opportunities to drink—or to remain sober. For a man on Antabuse, control over drinking involves only one choice daily—to report for medication. Antabuse, they emphasized, is not a panacea; its use, however, does free patients to trust themselves in solving their difficulties.

As an additional referral resource for a limited number of inpatients and outpatients from the Bowery Project, the Vera Institute has organized "Project Renewal," a work-oriented halfway house located in Brooklyn and managed by its ten residents. These are men who have maintained sobriety for a month or more after detoxification, also agreeing to use Antabuse throughout their first six months in the house. They work as employees of New York City in parks, doing repairs and maintenance; a part of their salaries goes to cover house expenses. Modest in scope, Project Renewal is in design stages. In the two years following its establishment in June 1970, about ten of the house's residents "graduated." They continue to use new skills on city jobs, but have made their own living arrangements; all remain sober.

With time, the project staff is becoming increasingly skilled at convincing detoxification patients to give the referrals a serious try. By January 1969, 57 per cent of the men discharged were doing so, a marked contrast to the negligible number of effective referrals accomplished in St. Louis and Washington.

No detailed follow-up studies have been conducted with the project's participants. In 1969, a "very preliminary study" showed that three months after discharge, 17 per cent of the men were "known to be sober and either working or in some organized program." But there are other indications that, even in its first year, the project has had successes not even reflected in this statistic.

The program apparently has made contact with most of the

Bowery men in need of help. An entry in a rescue worker's journal describes the range of service:

> Filled out daily tab sheet. Total for both teams 8—3 Negroes, 4 Whites, 1 Puerto Rican. Four virgins, four readmissions. Getting hard to find first-timers.[161]

Despite the New York police tradition of coping, at least symbolically, with homeless men, the force agreed early in the project's history to terminate roundups on the Bowery. Since then, it has been willing to abide by that agreement. The Bowery Project is serving the men who were the chronic criminal drunks capably enough to take them out of the category of law enforcement problems. It also is building its reputation among the drunks; during 1970–71, only about 20 per cent of the men approached on the street refused the project's assistance.[162]

On a recent visit to the Bowery Project's detoxification and outpatient clinics, one of my researchers observed the intangibles which have contributed to their success. The physical setting is unprepossessing. The huge, bare and dilapidated former Men's Shelter structure is a sharp reminder of times past, when the best a drunk could expect was a "flop" at public expense. But the rooms which have been converted into treatment areas are a total contrast; they are clean, bright and well organized—clean but not aggressively medical in atmosphere. Although the inpatient detoxification clinic's fifty-bed capacity is always filled, there is no sense of hurry and crowding; the medical routine and the counseling, which accompany it, are conducted with individualized concern and complete professionalism. The project's medical staff take time to stop and visit informally with their patients. Ambulatory patients—and most are ambulatory after a few days of bed rest—use the clinic's dayrooms and activity areas.

It becomes obvious that the staff is the Bowery Project's unique asset. They have mastered the refinements of detoxification treat-

---

[161] Vera Institute of Justice, "First Annual Report of the Manhattan Bowery Project" (1969), pp. 37, 54.

[162] Notably, the blacks and Puerto Ricans who are a small but growing element of the Bowery population are most likely to refuse aid. The project observes that their low acceptance rates may be explained by "a greater suspicion of arrest and/or of institutional contact" and "by the fact that they tend to be younger than the whites and appear less debilitated" (Vera Institute of Justice, "Annual Report of the Manhattan Bowery Project, July 1, 1970–June 30, 1971" [mimeographed, 1971], p. 2).

ment so completely that medical emergencies and acute alcohol withdrawal reactions are almost unknown. They have introduced new medical techniques which are being widely imitated. Even more important, they have pioneered a new, constructive and unpatronizing approach to public drunks as men. Gradually, as Bowery Project staff members transfer to new programs in other cities, this approach is spreading. In Rochester, New York, for example, a former Bowery Project staff nurse is the nursing director of the new hospital-based "Community Alcohol Outreach Service." Like the Bowery Project, it is designed to intervene in the lives of homeless drinkers before arrest, and to make drunkenness law enforcement simply unnecessary. Another veteran of the Bowery Project nursing staff has taken her experience to Boston, where there is a detoxification program of similar design.

Not every community with a serious drunkenness law enforcement problem and a large jail population of drunks has the range of referral agencies which make the Bowery Project's approach to aftercare possible. Still, the essential design of its project is adaptable to the need and resources of cities and towns throughout the United States. Any locality can easily establish the one vital referral resource which the Bowery Project's reports note is generally lacking in New York City: halfway houses for men discharged after detoxification.[163] Such havens undoubtedly would reduce the problem of multiple referrals.

Expense is the main obstacle to the establishment of any designed institutional alternative to criminal processing and jailing of drunks. The Bowery Project runs at an average cost of about $38.00 per patient-day. No equivalent figure is available for St. Louis, but, given the high quality of the medical services provided, it would almost certainly be as great. In Washington, the daily cost of detoxification treatment is estimated at more than $20.75. Since the jailing of a drunk may cost no more than $5.00 per day, hopes of short-run cost savings from medically oriented alternative programs probably are illusory. Nimmer notes that while the St. Louis detoxification program is estimated to have conserved police and court time valued at $50,000 annually, the

---

[163] Vera Institute of Justice, "First Annual Report of the Manhattan Bowery Project," pp. 40–42. Project Renewal represents a first step toward making up this deficiency in the New York City area.

program itself is budgeted at $200,000.[164] The real cost saving
promised by alternative processing is long-term; a Bowery Project
report concludes that "Insofar as society is prepared to provide
these programs . . . the problems of homeless alcoholics could
be mitigated, and Skid Rows themselves would gradually disappear."[165]

Most states which have taken the step of abolishing the drunkenness offense by legislation have simultaneously created a medical
substitute for criminal processing. In Hawaii, the new "civil treatment program" is nothing more than the old involuntary commitment scheme for chronic alcoholics. But other states have at best
made gestures toward establishing new facilities for short-term
voluntary and semi-voluntary detoxification. Maryland moved by
legislation in 1968; several years after the abolition of the drunkenness offense, however, drunks were still being held in the state's
jails because bed space in civil detoxification facilities was not
uniformly available. In North Dakota, where the offense of intoxication was legislated out of existence in 1969, the new act
expressly provided that twenty-four-hour jail detention—for detoxification purposes—was to be permitted. Simple intoxication also
has been abolished as an offense in Connecticut, Florida and
Massachusetts; in each state, attempts are under way to provide an
organized statewide system of public civil detoxification facilities,
to which police will be able to deliver non-criminal drunks. Of the
states which have tied abolition of the drunkenness offense to the
provision of special detoxification services, California's position is
the most extreme. The net effect of the 1969 reform legislation of
that state was to decriminalize simple drunkenness—but only in
those counties which had established state-approved seventy-two-
hour treatment centers to which police can convey drunks.[166] The
approach to drunkenness law reform which substituted short-term
custodial treatment for arrest and jailing has been endorsed by the
National Conference of Commissioners on Uniform State Laws
in its 1971 draft "Uniform Alcoholism and Intoxication Act"
(which has not yet been enacted into law in any jurisdiction). It

---

[164] Nimmer, *Two Million Unnecessary Arrests*, p. 96.
[165] Vera Institute of Justice, "First Annual Report of the Manhattan Bowery
Project," p. 48.
[166] Cal. Penal Code §§647 (F) & (FF); Cal. Welfare and Institutions Code
§5170.

provided for establishment of civil detoxification facilities and empowered police to make use of them. Implementation of the approach is being encouraged by the federal government. Under the
Alcoholic Rehabilitation Act of 1968, and the Community Medical
Health Centers Act amendments of 1968 and 1970, funding assistance is available—through the new National Institute of Alcoholics and Alcohol Abuse—for treatment programs designed to
reach the "public inebriate."

Nevertheless, it remains likely that many communities with
substantial jailed drunkenness offender populations may be unable, if not unwilling, to adopt relatively costly alternatives to
criminal processing. This prospect raises an important question:
Are alternative programs necessary? How many of the evils of
the present system can be cured by decriminalizing public drunkenness? From his analysis of detoxification programs, Nimmer
concluded that the abolition of the drunkenness offense need not
be co-ordinated with service programs:

> The question of relieving the burden upon the criminal process
> is separable from that of providing service to the skid row men
> . . . To view a treatment service as a necessary replacement for
> an arrest process which does nothing but harass the skid row men
> borders on the absurd.[167]

In the opinion of one legal scholar, the late Herbert Packer, any
argument that the decriminalization of public intoxication must
wait on alternative services is fallacious:

> One question which must be asked is why the elimination of
> drunkenness as a crime should have to wait upon the provision
> of facilities that, however desirable, are going to call for increased
> public expenditures and therefore are not going to be provided on
> an adequate scale very soon. Is it because the public welfare re-
> quires some form of short-term handling of the inebriate? And
> does that in turn mean that compulsion should be used to require
> people who are drunk to undergo short-term detoxification? This
> seems an overly broad proposition at best; at worst it is a down-
> right dangerous one.[168]

In Packer's view, "drunkenness is the paradigm case of an im-
provident use of the criminal sanction," and any civil or criminal

[167] Nimmer, *Two Million Unnecessary Arrests*, p. 153.
[168] Herbert L. Packer, *The Limits of the Criminal Sanction* (Stanford: Stanford Univ. Press, 1968), p. 346.

compulsion applied to the drunk is offensive to the concepts of individual liberty and effective social regulation.

There are other arguments for abolishing the revolving door jail for alcoholics by the simple decriminalization of public drunkenness. In the aftermath of decriminalization, services truly necessary to homeless men might develop. By eliminating institutions central to their dependent way of life, decriminalization alone might force a certain number of men to choose social reintegration over the bleaker alternatives of death and permanent hospitalization. · Decriminalization of drunkenness today might help prevent the development of a new generation of homeless men.

The efficacy and humanity of simple decriminalization are being put to the test in Minnesota, where, as of July 1, 1971, all statewide prohibitions against public drunkenness were repealed by a statute which provides that:

> Notwithstanding any provision of local laws or ordinances no person shall be charged with or convicted of the offense of drunkenness or public drunkenness.[169]

As of January 1972, there was only one detoxification center in Minnesota, serving Minneapolis and all of Hennepin County. Others were planned, not as part of a statutory scheme to reform drunkenness law, but as a natural response to need. Hospitals in some Minnesota counties have been accepting acutely intoxicated indigent men.

Before the state's decriminalization, drunkenness had accounted for about 2,800 of an annual total of 12,800 jail sentences in Minnesota. Repeal made a real impact on the state's jails. By January 1972, the jail population had been reduced by an estimated 10 per cent; the rate of jail commitments was down about 20 per cent. Public reaction was positive, and law enforcement personnel generally were pleased to be relieved of a role they regarded as "baby-sitting for a bunch of drunks."[170]

For the vast majority affected by the change, decriminalization of drunkenness seems to be a marked improvement over repeated jailing. The Minnesota experiment must be weighed; drunkenness

[169] Minn. Stats., Ch. 340.961.
[170] Letter from Dr. David Fogel, Minnesota commissioner of corrections, December 28, 1971, on file at Goldfarb and Singer, Washington, D.C.

permits local innovation in alternative care systems. If, with time, the action taken in these jurisdictions proves successful, it will be the model for an inexpensive and eminently practical way of ending the vice of jailing drunks. The overburdened jail system will be relieved. And the individuals previously trapped by the system will be more likely to escape into a life of productivity and meaning. The dual system of care, which guaranteed inferior treatment for lower-status, poor persons, should be abolished in favor of a unitary system of voluntary rehabilitation for all persons who have used alcohol self-destructively.

6

JUVENILE JAILS

An Adolescent Girl: *Sometimes it's slapped in the face, and sometimes it's the paddle. Like up in detention they usually give you the paddle before they slap you . . . When they hit you, they make sure it hurts. They try their best to knock you across the table when they hit you . . . When you're in an institution with all girls, and there's no males around, I mean lot of girls have low, high sex.*

Dr. Karl Menninger: *If people have enough money of course they never go to jail, you know that. Jails are for poor people. Jails are for black people. And jails are for children.*

Moderator: *In Iowa a girl is thrown into jail because she runs away to get married: she hangs herself. She is sixteen years old.*

In the Children's Detention Center in New York, four children attempt suicide within ten days.

In Missouri, a seventeen-year-old is homosexually assaulted and kicked to death by jail cellmates.

Another seventeen-year-old is murdered in a Miami jail.

Cook County Jail, copied from a nineteenth-century French prison, was built to hold 1,300 people. It now holds almost twice that number. Three hundred are juveniles accused of serious crimes. None of them has been convicted. Some of them have remained behind these bars as long as two years, getting a glimpse of their parents only on infrequent visiting days. Juveniles in Cook County Jail are certain to be poor and almost certain to be black. They are crowded into prison just as they were crowded in Chicago's crime-ridden ghettos. They have in fact changed one ghetto for another.

Legal Aid Attorney: *I can think of two cases, for instance, involving two children, one from an area called Uptown here in Chicago, which is primarily a white Appalachian area, and another from the West Side black ghetto . . . They both ended up at Elgin State Hospital. Recently they were both caught in consenting homosexual conduct, they both being about thirteen now. Now it may be wrong to do this, it may not be. I'm just a lawyer, I can't make moral judgments; however, the people at the hospital did, and they bound them to their beds for a period of seventy-seven and one half hours, and they tied their hands and their feet to the bedposts, and spread-eagled them to the beds in such position that the boys could only move their hands about three or four inches in each direction. They were allowed up only to shower. In seventy-seven and one half hours.*

Hospital Official: *We're not using punishment over here. We are using a multiplicity of treatment in order to change the behavior of the person.*

Interviewer: *Nonetheless, tying a child to a bed for seventy-seven hours sounds to me like punishment.*

Hospital Official: *Okay. Well, that's a matter of opinion. We are trying to provide here in this institution to some of the kids some kind of therapeutical, um ah, behavior modification, and some kind of disciplinary approach to the patient.*

Interviewer: *In other words, tying a child to a bed for seventy-seven hours does not create any physical pain?*

Hospital Official: *This kind of kid; no.* [Excerpts from "This Child Is Rated X," an NBC News White Paper on juvenile justice, broadcast May 2, 1971.]

CHILDREN IN JAIL

Children have been held in jails intended for adults ever since those jails were built. Before the rise of the juvenile courts in America, there were few practical alternatives. But, even after reform, children still went to jail, and most of them had had no trial and had been convicted of no crime. It is still true. The National Council on Crime and Delinquency has estimated that 100,-000 children, aged seven to seventeen, are detained in county jails and police lockups every year.[1] The estimate has been constant for the last decade.

Most states have statutes providing that a child brought before the juvenile court or apprehended by the police shall be released to his parents pending trial unless he must be prevented from running away, must be restrained from endangering himself or others, or must be held for another jurisdiction.[2] But these statutes are broadly worded, and broadly interpreted. The NCCD said that about two out of three apprehended children did not go home after being picked up but were being held either in jails or in detention homes.[3]

Despite the noble assertions of state statutes, 400,000 children were in detention facilities at some time during 1965.[4] About three quarters of these locked-up children were held in 243 special juvenile detention homes; more than 100,000 others were in local jails or police lockups.[5] The rate of juvenile offenses, and the numbers of juveniles apprehended, have increased steadily. According to the report of the 1970 White House Conference on Children,[6] since 1963, juvenile delinquency (crimes by ten- to seventeen-year-olds) has been increasing at faster rates than the corresponding rises in the juvenile population, with urban rates more than triple the rural rates.

Yet, a U. S. Department of Health, Education, and Welfare report recognized that, "with few exceptions, individual counties do not have a sufficient number of detention cases to justify maintaining a detention service";[7] 93 per cent of the country's juvenile court jurisdictions, serving 44 per cent of the overall population, have no special facilities to detain children. Inadequate facilities

---

[1] Cf. NCCD, *Standards and Guides for the Detention of Children and Youth* (2d ed., 1961), p. xxi, and NCCD, "Correction in the United States" (1966), p. 16.

[2] See National Council on Crime and Delinquency, *Standard Juvenile Court Act* (6th ed., 1959), Article 4 §17.

[3] NCCD, "Correction in the United States," p. 15.

[4] NCCD, *Standard Juvenile Court Act.*

[5] NCCD, "Correction in the United States," p. 13 (Survey for the President's Commission on Law Enforcement and the Administration of Justice, 1966) (hereafter cited as NCCD Correction Survey).

[6] White House Conference on Children, 1970, *Profiles of Children* (Washington, D.C.: Government Printing Office, n.d.), p. 78.

[7] J. Downey, "State Responsibility for Juvenile Detention Care" (Youth Development and Delinquency Prevention Administration, U. S. Department of Health, Education, and Welfare, 1970), p. 1.

and staffing frequently make separation from adult prisoners impossible. Nine states have laws that forbid placing children in jail at all, but, in fact, only in Connecticut, Vermont and Puerto Rico are children never jailed. In most states statutory exceptions allow the use of jails for holding some children. In nineteen, juveniles may be jailed only if segregated from adult prisoners; in others, statutes allow jail detention of young people who are charged with serious offenses or present special custodial problems.[8]

Counties without local jails or special juvenile detention facilities may send all their children to adult penal institutions for temporary custody. As of mid-1969, Goochland County, Virginia, which lacked a local jail, held all its pretrial detainees at a maximum security cellblock within the Virginia State Farm, an institution for adult convicts ranging from vagrants to murderers. Juveniles, untried and unconvicted, were forced into the most hazardous and repressive of penal environments. Attorney Philip Hirshkop described the consequences to a congressional committee:

> [A] fifteen year old boy, Bobby Lee Taylor, awaiting trial at Goochland, was held in this maximum security block and was tear gassed twice by having tear gas shot in his face from a tear gas cannister, while he was locked in his cell. Both tear gassing attacks on him by a guard were made because he was calling to the guard for medical assistance for another prisoner. On one occasion it was to assist a prisoner who was deaf and dumb and appeared to be in physical agony.[9]

Data describing juveniles in jails is sketchy and inadequate. Few surveys or systematic studies have dealt with this problem. According to a survey of Illinois jails in 1970, only one in three of the 160 lockups could supply monthly prisoner totals broken down by age or sex; another one in three could supply only gross monthly totals. Only about 10 per cent had records on the legal status of inmates—sentenced, pretrial or other. Five jails kept no inmate records at all.[10] Yet, ironically, the Illinois survey is the most thorough to date.

[8] NCCD Correction Survey, p. 16.
[9] Testimony of Philip Hirshkop, Hearings before the Subcommittee to Investigate Juvenile Delinquency of the Committee on the Judiciary, U. S. Senate, 91st Cong., 1st sess. (1970) at 5010–11 (hereafter 1970 Senate Hearings).
[10] Mattick and Sweet, *Illinois Jails*, pp. 30–35.

The U. S. Bureau of the Census is now conducting two inter-related sample surveys of jails and their inmates; but the responses requested are sketchy and will shed little additional light on the condition of the forgotten children in jails.[11] Investigators now must rely on one-day head counts and multiply to obtain estimates of longer-term confinement. They also must depend heavily on detention administrators' impressions of what is "average" or "normal" in their institutions.

Problems of definition complicate the data search. "Jail" is used loosely. Some take it to mean prison. Others interpret it as including special juvenile facilities. Therefore statistics must be read with their limitations in mind. Definitions of "juvenile" status also vary widely from state to state, and even within particular states. In Maryland, for example, until 1971, juveniles were persons under eighteen years of age except in Baltimore City, where the maximum age was sixteen. As a result, sixteen- to eighteen-year-olds were routinely detained in the Baltimore City Jail, but classified as "adults." Definitions also vary with the crime. In most jurisdictions, children under eighteen who are charged with certain serious offenses can be waived from the juvenile court jurisdiction. Thereafter, they are processed like adults, detained in adult jails and often enumerated as adults in local criminal justice statistics. But despite the inadequacy of statistics, the picture that emerges is not blurred but clear; and it is shocking.

The recent LEAA jail census found seventy-three "juveniles" in Minnesota adult jails on a single day, March 15, 1970,[12] but a Minnesota state report said that 6,500 children were held in adult jails during the year 1969.[13] From interviews with Nebraska jailers, it appeared that a minimum of 2,136 persons eighteen years old or younger were booked into the state's local adult jails during a twelve-month period in 1968 and 1969.[14]

The Census Bureau's 1950 review found about 7,000 young men and women under twenty in jails and workhouses in the United States as of the date surveyed. By 1960 there were more

---

[11] Mattick and Sweet, op. cit., p. 92.

[12] *1970 National Jail Census,* p. 10.

[13] Minnesota Department of Corrections, *A Comprehensive Plan for Regional Jailing and Juvenile Detention in Minnesota* (January 1971), p. 4.

[14] Nebraska Department of Economic Development, "For Better or Worse: Nebraska's Misdemeanant Correctional System" (n.d.), p. 10.

than 13,000, an increase of almost 90 per cent.[15] During the same decade, the number of Americans under twenty-one years of age grew only about 61.5 per cent.[16]

Equivalent returns from the 1970 Census of Institutions were not yet available as of this writing, but a special LEAA jail survey said that on a single day surveyed, March 15, 1970, 7,800 juveniles were held in about 4,000 adult jails.[17] (Since the survey excluded the jails of several states and all lockups lacking authority to hold over forty-eight hours, an inclusive total would have been substantially larger. The many youngsters in other detention facilities were not counted.) Two thirds of the 7,800 juveniles in adult jails, according to the LEAA survey of March 1970, were being held before trial; the other third were either serving sentences, were being held for officials of other jurisdictions (a common status for young runaways), were waiting transfer or were being held because they were neglected and as is often said, there is no place else to keep them. Only a minority had been convicted and sentenced.

CHILDREN IN DETENTION

The children in adult jails are only a small and highly obvious component of the dilemma of juveniles in trouble. The children now held in other specialized pretrial centers represent a far larger and far more complex population.

A number of state legislatures have given formal recognition to vast practical differences which exist between individual juvenile offenders, in part to remove the stigma associated with an adjudication of delinquency. Delinquents are more serious offenders—or are charged with such offenses. Truants, curfew violators and incorrigibles are designated not as "delinquents," but as "predelinquents," "persons in need of supervision" (PINS); or as

15 U. S. Bureau of the Census, *1950 Census, Special Report: Institutional Populations,* and *1960 Census, Special Report: Inmates of Institutions* (Washington, D.C.: Government Printing Office).
16 U. S. Bureau of the Census, *Pocket Data Book, U.S.A. 1971* (Washington, D.C.: Government Printing Office, 1971).
17 *1970 National Jail Census,* p. 10.

"children in need of supervision" (CINS); or as "minors in need of supervision" (MINS). These children, in turn, are distinguished from dependent and neglected youngsters.

In New York State, a statute now specifically prohibits detention of PINS children prior to the filing of a petition with the juvenile court, and even limits the number of days they can be held in detention after the filing of a petition. But the state Department of Social Services' director of detention services has said, "I have yet to learn of a juvenile detention facility in this State which has not contained children in violation of this statute!"[18] In Maryland, CINS children may be detained; the only protective requirement of the new law is that they be segregated from accused delinquents. In New Mexico, while CINS children cannot be committed to state training schools after adjudication, they may legally be detained pending trial. Reclassification of juvenile offenses may discourage some unnecessary detention, but reclassification alone cannot prevent such detention.

Today, children-only offenses account for more than half the caseload of the juvenile courts.[19]

The number of children in detention homes has risen even more steeply than the number in jails, though from a lower base. From about 2,500 in 1950, it had quadrupled by 1960, to almost 10,000.

Not every local jurisdiction or court district has a juvenile detention facility; all but ten states have some such institutions.[20] According to the one national survey on this subject, the 242 publicly run juvenile detention facilities in the United States housed 10,216 children; six private homes housed 659. The smallest facilities housed fewer than five children; the largest housed

[18] Bruce R. Fox, "Juvenile Detention—The Name of the Game," Address presented at the Frederick A. Moran Memorial Institute, St. Lawrence University, Canton, New York, June 23, 1969.

[19] S. Norman, *The Youth Service Bureau* (National Council on Crime and Delinquency, 1972), p. 1.

[20] The most recent, and the most thorough study of children's detention facilities forms part of the *Census of Children's Residential Institutions in the United States, Puerto Rico and the Virgin Islands: 1966,* conducted by Donnell M. Pappenfort and Dee Morgan Kilpatrick; Vol. 1, *Seven Types of Institutions;* Vol. 7, *Detention Facilities* (Social Service Monographs, 2d Series, School of Social Service Administration, University of Chicago, 1970) (hereafter cited as Pappenfort Census). Pappenfort Census, Vol. 7, Table 1, p. 2.

more than 500.[21] The few large institutions together held over half of all children in specialized detention facilities.

DUMPING GROUNDS FOR TROUBLED CHILDREN

Children go to jails or counterpart institutions for reasons which never would land an adult in jail—truancy, "incorrigibility" and wrongs of their parents or their own which are neither criminal nor necessarily dangerous to others. Children may be in jail simply because they were abused by their parents or because they are witnesses to crimes. Yet, even for these "crimes," most of those in jail have not been tried or sentenced. The courts and police procedures which govern children were designed to be paternalistic and benign. In practice, they are punitive and prejudicial.

Jails are used in some jurisdictions to relieve overcrowding in juvenile facilities or to handle children who are considered too tough or too troublesome. In March 1972, the superintendent of the Marion County Juvenile Detention Center in Indianapolis, Indiana, told one of my researchers that he had sent several "uncontrollable" children to the local jail that month. Usually, he said, these were older children, but along with two seventeen-year-olds transferred a few weeks before had gone a thirteen-year-old. "But that kid was big," the superintendent explained. Almost every juvenile detention supervisor I interviewed, even the most progressive and reform-minded, admitted sending some of their tough cases to local jails.

I have a vivid impression derived from countless walks through countless usually smaller and average-sized jails and the sight of countless youngsters behind bars. Many of these children looked sick, all were poor and socially deprived and most could have been somewhere else with little risk or cost to society. A few had been charged with serious offenses. Most had not. They sat in their bleak cells, sullen, wasting, mournful.

The scene was always the same: a dank, dark, odored, filthy cell; a lone adolescent or young man sitting at a table playing with a tattered deck of old cards or reading a comic book, inevitably smoking (his pack of cigarettes sitting on the cross bar);

[21] Pappenfort Census, Vol. 1, Tables 21 and 22, pp. 30–31; Vol. 7, Table 2, p. 4.

dressed in crumpled institutional-issue colored trousers and a rumpled white undershirt, often with epithets crudely inked on his hands and arms; an estranged look in his eyes, an air of depression and fatality.

Even at the least jail-like facilities I have seen—the relatively open sprawling residential complexes of California's "juvenile halls"—the children know they are locked in. One California administrator who tried to counteract the sense of confinement, said: "I show them where the fence is and how to get over it. I would rather have an escape valve than that they hurt somebody here trying to get away."

A poorly informed and unconcerned public in most jurisdictions allows far too many of its children to be dumped into jails and other catchall detention facilities. Thus, nearly half the detention facilities, in addition to holding juveniles charged with offenses, also house pre-delinquents, dependent and neglected children who could be kept at home, emotionally disturbed children who need medical care, or victims of abuse or neglect who need foster homes or group homes. Most detention homes have residents who belong in group homes or other institutions, but cannot be placed. Only 3 per cent refuse to take children already labeled as delinquent.[22] More than 70 per cent house children who are there only because appropriate foster homes cannot be found for them.[23]

Of the 1960 total of children recorded by the Census as in jail or workhouses, more than 90 per cent were boys, and about 63 per cent were white, 37 per cent non-white. Thus males and non-whites receive special and prejudicial treatment at the hands of the juvenile "justice" system, as they do in the adult system.

Detention homes clearly are in danger of becoming for poor juveniles what jails are for poor adults: catchall institutions for troubled, difficult and unwanted people, where attempts at real programming and assistance are few and often futile.

[22] The children's jails of Detroit, Miami and Roslindale are described in Bagdikian, "Juvenile Prison: Society's Stigma," Washington *Post,* February 3, 1972, p. A-12.
[23] Pappenfort Census, Vol. 7, Tables 104–6, pp. 111–13.

INFANTS, CHILDREN, YOUTH

In 1960, the Census found 33 children under 5 in jails or work-houses on a single day; 13 were aged 5 to 9; about 550 were aged 10 to 14; and more than 12,000 were between 15 to 19 years of age. The 1960 Census data on children in institutions showed that children in jails and workhouses were predominantly 15 years of age or older; detention homes had a greater proportion of younger children. Half the children in these special juvenile detention facilities were under 15, and 8 per cent were under 10.[24]

In some jurisdictions, the common law presumes that a child younger than seven cannot commit a crime; in others, statutes set minimums between eight and twelve years; there are no lower limits at all in some states. Maximum ages for treatment as a juvenile also vary—anywhere from sixteen to twenty-one years.

Yet the facts of jailing are more shameful than the law. Joseph Egeberg, the Maryland state chief jail inspector, has told of finding a three-year-old child being "held" in Baltimore's Pine Street jail. When the police officer in charge unlocked the cell and went in, the child ran to him and threw his arms around the officer's neck; when the officer left a few minutes later and locked the door on the lonely child, the three-year-old cried. "The officer found it difficult to leave the child. But he had no alternative."[25] The system apparently had no alternative to keeping this youngster—a victim of parental abuse—locked in a tiny barred cell.

In 1966, almost 1 per cent of children in juvenile detention facilities were infants under two years of age; another 1.7 per cent were aged two through five. Most of these tiny children were being held in the larger institutions—those with more than seventy-five residents. Six- to eleven-year-olds account for 8.5 per cent of the children in detention homes; two thirds of these are also in the larger facilities. The largest age group in the detention population—60.2 per cent—is made up of twelve- to fifteen-year-

[24] S. Low, *America's Children and Youth in Institutions, 1950-1960-1964: A Demographic Analysis* (Children's Bureau, U. S. Department of Health, Education, and Welfare, 1965), p. 6.
[25] 1970 Senate Hearings at 5222.

olds, over half of whom are detained in the larger institutions.[26]
The youngest children, who would benefit most from a truly
"homelike" detention setting, are, in fact, most likely to be held in
mass facilities, some with 500 or more children—"homes" in name
only.

Yet, experts agree that very young children whether charged
with crimes or not, do not need "secure" detention, and can suffer
great harm if they are locked up with older, seriously disturbed
children. Yet more than 10 per cent of the children in detention
are under twelve years of age.[27] For a troubled preschool child,
confinement in a strange institution is not only terrifying but
an apparent confirmation of his own sense of worthlessness and
evil.

And, although most children stay in these cells and other institutions for relatively brief periods, some of their stays were
shockingly long. Of the more than 13,000 jailed youths recorded
in the 1960 Census, 4 per cent had been jailed for periods ranging
from 1.25 to 2.5 years; another 4 per cent between 2.5 and 5
years; over 3 per cent were incarcerated between 5 and 10.25
years; and 3.8 per cent—505 children—had been jailed *10.25 years
or more!* Thus one in about six or seven were jailed more than a
year.[28]

The average child in detention facilities, in contrast with jail,
stays less one month; in about 12 per cent it is from one to
three months; and in 1.2 per cent it is six months to a year. But
most of these children have had no trial. Many are accused of no
crime except the "crime" of having been rejected.

The NCCD long has recommended that detention should average no more than ten to fourteen days,[29] the time ordinarily
required to prepare a juvenile case for court.

There are dramatic disparities in treatment. During 1966, in
Washington, D.C., about half the approximately 3,200 children
detained were held less than a week. The first week was crucial;
children not released during that time remained, on an average,

26 Pappenfort Census, Vol. 7, Table 4, p. 7.
27 Ibid., p. 8.
28 U. S. Bureau of the Census, *1960 Census, Special Report: Inmates of Institutions.*
29 NCCD, *Standards and Guides for Detention of Children and Youth,* p. 29.

for more than a month.[30] About 35 per cent stayed between one week and one month; roughly 15 per cent stayed for up to three months; and more than 1 per cent stayed longer. In Albuquerque, New Mexico, during the last six months of 1971, approximately half the children were detained for one day or less but more than 7 per cent stayed beyond the NCCD recommendation of fourteen days and about 2 per cent more than a month.[31] During a recent visit, one of my researchers was told that stays in the Marion County (Indianapolis), Indiana, detention home range from a few hours up to three months. And, although the average length of stay at the Northern Virginia Juvenile Detention Home is two to three weeks, some children remain there *over a year*.[32]

"WISE PARENTS" AND "WAYWARD CHILDREN"

An historic ruin in Rome's busy Piazza di Porta Portese, called "Clementina," was built to handle fourteen-to-eighteen-year-old boys during the reign of Pope Clement XI. San Michele (its formal name) is still in use. This old stone building, with its narrow, high-ceilinged cells, and its stone central courtyard for minimal recreation, looks like many American facilities for children today.

Crude workhouses and detention centers housed poor offenders of all ages before the system of prisons and jails developed in the United States in the eighteenth and nineteenth centuries. The system made no provisions for housing youthful offenders separately either before trial or after conviction.

The American "child-saving" movement of the late nineteenth century in this country which fought slum conditions and abusive child labor practices and tried to cope with the problems of homeless and errant youth, led to special juvenile court systems and establishment of training schools, reform schools, houses of refuge and other institutional alternatives to the wretched urban

[30] President's Commission on Crime in the District of Columbia, *Report* (1967), p. 641.
[31] Bernalillo County Detention Home, unpublished statistical review prepared by Director Nestor J. Baca.
[32] Burchard, "Two Alternatives in Youth Detention Problems—Virginia Keeps Admissions Low, But Result Is Use of Jail," Washington *Post,* November 21, 1971.

environments in which so many youngsters lived. One early juvenile court judge said the state was to act through its new courts and institutions "as a wise parent would deal with a wayward child," and cease continuing to criminalize children "by the very methods it used in dealing with them."[33]

America's first state-funded facility for youthful convicts had opened in Massachusetts in 1847; in 1869 Massachusetts moved to distinguish criminal court proceedings involving young people from those involving adults.[34] The new institutions for juveniles were designed to be "training schools" and "reformatories." They trained and reformed few. Most were merely junior versions of jails.

Offenders were not to be stigmatized by being called criminals, but were to be classified as "juvenile delinquents." Procedures were to be informal and non-adversary, treatment was to be non-penal and humane. The juvenile court would dispense with the traditional procedures of the criminal trial; the juvenile justice proceeding would address the welfare of the young "wards" of the courts. The priority was not to determine that a youngster had committed a crime and to punish him for it, but to decide what care he needed and to see that he got it.

The Standard Juvenile Court Act provides:

> Each child coming within the jurisdiction of the court shall receive, preferably in his own home the care, guidance and control that will conduce to his welfare and the best interests of the State. . . . When he is removed from the control of his parents the court shall secure for him care as nearly as possible equivalent to that which they could have given him.

Yet, by 1966, in the U. S. Supreme Court's famous *Kent* decision, Justice Abe Fortas noted that, under the prevailing juvenile justice system, "the child receives the worst of both worlds . . . he gets neither the protections accorded to adults nor the solicitous care and regenerative treatment postulated for children."[35]

The philosophy as stated but not as practiced has been that children are malleable and, hence, their criminal tendencies could be curbed by benevolent intervention. The state-as-a-parent

[33] Julian Mack, "The Juvenile Court," 23 *Harvard L. Rev.* 104 (1909).
[34] Tenny, "The Utopian World of Juvenile Courts," 383 *Annals* 101, 103 (1969).
[35] *Kent* v. *United States,* 383 U.S. 541, 556 (1966).

er what her background, if she doesn't get along with her parents,
she will be put in an institution.[37]

Families with means and influence, thus avoid the system—
especially in cases involving morals more than criminal offenses
—by private conciliation, restitution and treatment.

In 1970, there were 2,662 juvenile courts in the United
States.[38] The proliferation had made little difference to thousands
of neglected children.

[36] U. S. Department of Health, Education, and Welfare, *Juvenile Court Statistics—1970* 6 (Social and Rehabilitation Service 1972).
[37] Testimony of Patrick T. Murphy in "Juvenile Confinement Institutions and Correctional Systems," Hearings before the Subcommittee to Investigate Juvenile Delinquency of the Committee on the Judiciary, U. S. Senate, 92d Cong., 1st sess., 197 (1971).
[38] Children's Bureau, U. S. Department of Health, Education, and Welfare, *Juvenile Court Statistics—1970* (1971).

Of the jails where children are housed, less than 20 per cent have been rated by the federal Bureau of Prisons as suitable, even by its rather expansive minimum standards of decency for adult federal prisoners.[39]

Although the purpose of separate detention facilities for children, as stated forty years ago, was "to keep the child from the evils of jail . . . [and to care for him] as a wise father would care for his children,"[40] a recent federal report written to urge states to accept responsibility for providing regional detention facilities, noted that makeshift detention homes often are "virtually child jails . . . [consisting] of a barred room in a county court house, or home for the aged or in other institutions."[41]

Joseph Egeberg, a Maryland jail inspector, told Congress that thirteen of twenty-three county jails in his state should be closed; "Conditions are such that in some cases sheriffs have pleaded with me, off the record, to close up, and in effect condemn their own jails."[42]

In Illinois, where 142 of the state's 160 jails house juveniles, most jails average forty-five square feet or less per bed (including space occupied by the bed), 35 per cent have twenty-five square feet or less per bed. The American Correctional Association has recommended a seventy-five-square-foot minimum in usable space for every inmate.[43] Lack of space and crowding is especially damaging for children, who are naturally more active than adults.

The conditions in jails and detention centers not infrequently lead to tragedy.

The President's Crime Commission was told of four teen-age boys, jailed on suspicion of stealing beer, who died of asphyxiation from a defective gas heater, after being left alone for eleven hours in an Arizona jail. In Indiana, a thirteen-year-old boy veteran of five foster homes drove his current foster father's car to the county jail and asked the sheriff to lock him up. The child was segregated from adults, pending a hearing for auto theft. A week

[39] NCCD Correction Survey, p. 16.
[40] F. Wagner, *Juvenile Detention in the United States* (Social Service Monographs No. 20, University of Chicago Press, 1933 [jacket]).
[41] J. Downey, "State Responsibility for Juvenile Detention Care," p. 2.
[42] 1970 Senate Hearings at 5219.
[43] American Correctional Association, *Manual of Correctional Standards* (3d ed. 1966), p. 49.

later his body was found hanging from the bars of his cell; a penciled note nearby read: "I don't belong anywhere."[44]

In a 1971 television exposé of juvenile justice,[45] a girl explained that she had been placed in an Indiana orphanage after her parents had signed her over to the state. She had run away from the orphanage, and ended up in jail: "There were prostitutes . . . and then there were two, I think, that was in there for murder. And it really was a scary feeling to be around such people."

A New York *Times* story about Riker's Island Remand Shelter reported that "Last year [in 1971], four inmates of the [Riker's Island] remand shelter [in New York City] hanged themselves. In the last two years, two correction officers have been indicted for selling heroin to their teenage prisoners. On the average, it has probably been the most overcrowded of all the overcrowded city detention facilities."[46]

Gertrude Samuels described consequences of confinement in two New York juvenile centers:

Perhaps most appalling is the high rate of attempted suicide found among these hostile, fearful, cooped-up children. A combined survey of the Spofford and Manida Juvenile Centers for the six-month period from November, 1970 to last May, discloses a total of 45 such attempts. . . .

Because these attempts seldom "succeed," many staff members are likely to consider them as nothing but gestures to get attention. Yet the attempts are serious enough. Kids slash their wrists with pieces of glass, try to hang themselves by their belts from light fixtures, or attempt to overdose themselves with tranquilizers saved up from the infirmary.[47]

For such children there is no "reform," no "shelter," no "home" in the nation's jails and detention centers. For some, death seems a preferable answer.

[44] Presidential Commission on Law Enforcement and Administration, Task Force Report on Correction at p. 121. Government Printing Office.
[45] "This Child Is Rated X," an NBC News White Paper on juvenile justice, broadcast May 2, 1971.
[46] Emory, "Riker's Island Prison Known as Monstrosity," New York *Times,* February 29, 1972, p. C-23.
[47] Samuels, "Children and the Law," *New York Times Magazine,* December 5, 1971.

UNNECESSARY DETENTION

Juvenile detention administrators know their facilities are over-crowded dumping grounds for all types of troubled children. The heterogeneity of the juvenile detention population makes it impossible to program adequately for any center's young inmates; most staff time must be devoted simply to keeping aggressive children from preying on weaker ones, to protecting neglected preschoolers from seasoned adolescent delinquents.

Most detention homes have no authority to refuse children assigned to them. They must take every child referred by the police or court, and hold him until the court orders his release, regardless of the staff's evaluation of the child's need. Detention administrators, at a national conference, complained most frequently of their practical inability to shape detention practices by controlling admissions.[48]

The NCCD has said that, even of the juvenile offenders—excluding the many who are simply neglected and troubled children —no more than 10 per cent need be detained, at all.[49] The rest are no real danger to anyone, and would appear for juvenile court hearings when required. Detention rates vary from place to place. In some, all children are held in jail or detention centers; they are committed not by a court but by police; none are sent home to wait for judicial action.

In Salt Lake County, Utah, during 1969, 44 per cent of the children referred to juvenile court for delinquency hearings were detained. About 40 per cent were detained "inappropriately"; they were children who did not require institutionalization and could have been returned to their homes. Ultimately, 95 per cent of all children detained at the Salt Lake Detention Home were released to their families and only 5 per cent were committed to the State Industrial School or to foster or group homes.[50] In jurisdiction after jurisdiction, police, youth services workers and judges are

[48] Delinquency Study and Youth Development Project, "National Institute for Juvenile Detention Home Administrators" (Southern Illinois University, 1968).
[49] NCCD, *Standards and Guides for Detention of Children and Youth*, p. 18.
[50] Utah State Law Enforcement Planning Agency, *Utah Youth Services Planning Project 1972*, pp. 25, 67, 69.

willing to deprive youngsters of their freedom pending a court hearing, and they often have nearly unfettered authority to do so. Only later, after these children have spent days or weeks in detention, is it decided that most of them are not appropriate candidates for institutional confinement after all.

But such excessive control is not uniform. In many small towns and rural jurisdictions, where youthful offenders are known to arresting authorities, juvenile detention is restricted; some large cities also have low rates of detention. In Minneapolis, one thirty-bed detention facility serves a population of more than 923,000; in 1965 the average daily population was only twenty-four children.[51] In Albuquerque, detention administrators recently said that their facility is used to house only about 5 per cent of all children picked up by police.

The role of the police is always crucial in all jurisdictions. It is the police who make most initial referrals to detention, and who have the power to release a youngster back to his parents, formally or informally. Many police departments do give new recruits special training in handling juveniles, but not enough. In Salt Lake City, out of 240 hours of police training, only eighteen deal with juvenile matters; of the forty hours of in-service training required of each officer, two hours concern juveniles—yet one third of all persons arrested and charged in Salt Lake City are juveniles.[52]

Many large police forces have specialized "youth divisions." When a uniformed officer in such a department picks up a child, he must turn the child over to the youth division. A trained officer then determines whether the child should be detained. Such specialization should decrease the use of detention; sometimes, however, it has the opposite effect. In Marion County, Indiana, where special juvenile division officers alone determine whether to detain children who are picked up, after these officers go off duty at 11 P.M. juveniles are held routinely at the detention facility until the next day, when they are interviewed by a police specialist. Many are released, but they have been kept behind bars unnecessarily overnight. There are strong arguments in favor of allowing every officer discretion to release suspected delinquents to their parents immediately after arrest.

[51] A Report on the Status of County Jails.
[52] Utah State Law Enforcement Planning Agency, *Utah Youth Services Planning Project 1972*, pp. 145–46.

After the police have made their initial determination, other officials—a judge, a court-designated social worker, a juvenile probation officer, or a detention home administrator—review the decision to detain. The result is always to thin the ranks of the detainees dramatically. In most jurisdictions more than half the children initially referred to detention by police are released within days—prior to any juvenile court hearing on the pending charges themselves. In Indianapolis, one of my researchers was told that 20 per cent of all children detained are released within twenty-four hours, and 19 per cent more within forty-eight hours. Within four days, one of every two children detained is free again. Such statistics, as much as they may reflect flexible or humane release policies, also evidence an initial mistake—many of the children detained should never have been held in the first place. These children are the victims of poor screening and administrative insensitivity.

The courts are not without blame. Most detention facilities are directly or indirectly controlled by local juvenile courts, which have the power to limit the use of detention, and to require that all decisions to detain be made in strict compliance with statutory criteria. The judges seldom exercise that power.

The juvenile courts can assure such compliance by providing the services of a professional intake unit available to police and detention facility staffs. When all questionable cases are routinely referred to such a unit, those that do not require court attention can be settled informally or dropped. Children whose cases may need court attention, but not pretrial detention, can go home. The NCCD reports that the introduction of comprehensive intake screening in New York City cut delinquency referrals to the court by 37 per cent and the population of boys in detention by almost half.[53]

In Seattle, Washington, juvenile probation officers staff an intake unit from 7 A.M. to 12 P.M. During 1970, half the children they considered as candidates for detention were released immediately; another 8 per cent were detained at first, but released by the intake staff prior to any judicial detention hearing.[54] A professional intake staff does more than routine diagnosis and evaluation. It contacts the parents of children in trouble to deter-

[53] NCCD Correction Survey, p. 32.
[54] King County Juvenile Court, "Annual Report—1970," p. 1.

mine whether home release is appropriate, and arranges for parents to pick up their children from custody. When parents are reluctant to take responsibility during the pretrial period, intake workers strive to persuade them, or seek alternative non-institutional placements for the children. Thus, even the children who cannot be spared all detention may benefit from the services of a professional intake unit.

The Albuquerque probation department has a novel arrangement with the police. Parents of children apprehended as minor offenders—runaways, truants, curfew violators or misdemeanants —are called by the police and asked to come to the place of the arrest. Most children are apprehended near home, and the parents who could not or would not report quickly to the police or the detention facility get there quickly. Parents are also more likely to respond before their child is taken into formal custody.

One widespread but controversial strategy is "informal supervision," the practice of releasing youngsters on condition that, if they obey certain strictures set down by the intake staff, no petition will be filed. Advocates concerned with the legal rights of accused juveniles disapprove the practice. The child, after all, has been charged with and convicted of nothing. Proponents of "institutionalized non-adjudicatory procedures,"[55] argue that it nevertheless may prevent a child from institutional placement.

ADULT PRISONERS AND CHILDREN TOGETHER

Jailed children frequently are housed with sentenced adult criminals. Although most states have laws forbidding the use of jails for juvenile detention, or requiring that juveniles be held separate from adults, the LEAA 1970 National Jail Census said that in forty-seven states and the District of Columbia, some jails do, in fact, hold juveniles.

Statutes mandating segregation of juveniles from adult offenders

[55] For a full discussion of the argument, see Elyce Ferster, Thomas Courtless, and Edith Snethen, "Separating Official and Unofficial Delinquents," *55 Iowa L. Rev.* 864 (1970). Some of the most enthusiastic recent advocacy for a variety of informal non-adjudicatory dispositions is to be found in President's Commission on Law Enforcement and Administration of Justice, *Task Force Report: Juvenile Delinquency and Youth Crime* (Washington, D.C.: Government Printing Office, 1967), pp. 21–22.

are frequently disobeyed. In the St. Marys County Jail, in Maryland, where the physical design would permit segregation, the lack of adequate supervisory personnel makes segregation impossible; adults, mentally ill, sick and juveniles all are mixed together in the same jail.[56] A report on Washington State jails noted that "[i]n one jail, when juvenile boys must be housed, they are placed with the adult first offender."[57] This jailer was trying—and failing—to maintain a semblance of segregation. But an Illinois county jail administrator deliberately places juveniles with adults so that the older prisoners can "straighten out" the youngsters.[58]

Milton Rector, director of the National Council on Crime and Delinquency, recently told Congress that 90 per cent of the nation's juvenile courts, serving 44 per cent of the population, have no separate juvenile detention facilities.[59]

In the 1967 survey of Illinois jails that estimated 10,251 juveniles incarcerated in 142 of the 160 adult jails that year, only nine reported that they did not segregate them from adults. Yet inmate self "segregation" occurred unofficially:

Over one-third of the jails have one area normally used for adult male inmates and one other usually smaller area reserved for any of the other age—sex categories of inmates. When only adult males are present, jails may alleviate overcrowding by using this reserved space; however, when a female or juvenile prisoner is detained, this cannot be done. When both a female and a juvenile are handled, the jails either place the juvenile in with the adults or they take them to other jails.[60]

In Kentucky, of the 72 per cent of the state's 170 local jails that detain juveniles, 19 per cent make no provision to separate them from adults; less than half have reserved juvenile cells, and only about a third hold young people in a separate part of the jail building.[61]

[56] Maryland Department of Correctional Services, "Reports of Inspection" (mimeographed; Howard County Jail, May 6, 1968; St. Marys County Jail, n.d.).
[57] Washington State Department of Institutions, Jail Inspection Report—1968, p. 16.
[58] Mattick and Sweet, Illinois Jails, p. 120.
[59] 1970 Senate Hearings at 5742.
[60] Mattick and Sweet, Illinois Jails, p. 92.
[61] Kentucky Commission on Law Enforcement and Crime Prevention, Kentucky Jails (1969), p. 9.

In New Mexico, juveniles are required by law to be segregated from adults, but one of my researchers recently was told that segregation in local jails is nominal. An Albuquerque probation supervisor said adults and children are held in close proximity in jails throughout the state; they can hear, see and touch each other—but because there are bars separating them, the jailers are in compliance with law.

In North Carolina's juvenile system, Duke University researchers found in 1969 that only seven counties provided youth detention facilities. The rest must borrow space in one of these special facilities, or use the ordinary local jails. Under North Carolina statutes, private resources are to be used if a county has no detention facility. But if a child needs "secure custody," then the judge may order that the child be detained in the county jail. The researchers found that "[d]etention frequently is employed as a 'scare tactic' or 'threat' by a perplexed counsellor."[62]

In Mississippi, where 85 of the state's 98 jails receive juveniles, 5 of the 79 for which data is available house adults serving sentences up to 2 years; 56 house adults serving sentences up to one year. All but 10 segregated young people from adults, but since all are poorly staffed, the quality of the segregation actually in force is open to question.[63]

Even if there were segregation of children from adults, it would be no panacea. If there is only one child in a separated section, he may, like the three-year-old child in Baltimore's Pine Street jail, be totally isolated from human contact; if there are several, the younger or smaller children may be brutalized by the older children.

In Maryland, where some juveniles are held in jails and are mixed in with adult prisoners, those who are segregated are held in stricter confinement. Thus in the Howard County Jail adults eat in a dining room. Women, security cell inmates—and juveniles—are deprived of this minor diversion. They are fed in their cells.

---

[62] "A Report on the North Carolina Juvenile System: Courts, Correction and Aftercare" (Duke University, mimeographed, n.d.), pp. 37–38.
[63] "Survey of Jails in Mississippi" (mimeographed, n.d.). This data, obtained from the Law Enforcement Assistance Division of the State of Mississippi, was prepared in conjunction with LEAA's one-day national jail census, on March 15, 1970.

CHILDREN WITHOUT SCHOOL OR PLAY

In the 1970 LEAA survey, 86 per cent of all the jails reported that they had no exercise or recreation facilities for any prisoners; nearly 90 per cent of the jails had no educational facilities; slightly more than half had no medical facilities and one fourth had no visiting facilities.[64] These conditions, bad in any case, are especially intolerable with respect to the children in those jails.

In New Jersey, for example, where 19 of the 20 county jails participating in a state-run study were holding juveniles, only 5 had any formal educational program; 4 had vocational training programs; 14 had social services available, 13 reported had psychological services in special situations only. Only 9 reported any community aftercare services.[65]

Low budgets lead to bleak confinement. In the 79 Mississippi jails housing juveniles, where 3 had annual budgets over $40,000; 42 had budgets under $10,000; and one had a budget of $1,100, only one had recreational facilities and only one had educational facilities. (Two did not even have operating flush toilets.)

Inspectors' reports of Maryland jails state most have no programs of any kind, not even for recreation or education. Children who are kept in detention homes pending court dispositions also are rarely given anything to do. Fewer than half the detention homes have school programs conducted by professional educators; fewer than half have the services of psychiatric counselors or social workers or recreation specialists.[66] Fewer than 22 per cent of all detention homes test and evaluate new admissions.[67]

In the Adolescent Remand Shelter on Riker's Island, described as "the worst prison in [New York City],"[68] inmates are less well off in many ways than prisoners in the city's adult jails.

[64] *1970 National Jail Census,* pp. 18–19. According to the text, "the definitions of these items were left to the interpretation of the respondent." As LEAA staffers explained, jail administrators whose institutions contained a small library or a few tattered books could have checked "Yes" for "educational facilities" on the survey questionnaire.

[65] State of New Jersey Law Enforcement Planning Agency—Informal Survey of New Jersey Jails.

[66] NCCD Correction Survey, p. 19.

[67] Pappenfort Census, Vol. 1, p. 89.

[68] New York City Board of Corrections, *Crisis in the Prisons* (1971 Annual Report to the Mayor and Commissioner of Corrections), p. 28.

Juvenile pretrial defendants at the Riker's Island Adolescent Remand Shelter are locked either in their cells or cell blocks virtually all day except for meals. In contrast, the lock-in regimen at the Tombs has been relieved at the prodding of the Board of Correction, to the extent that most prisoners there are now locked *out* of their cells for six and one-half hours per day, excluding meals.[69]

The only activity designed specifically for Spanish-speaking juveniles, who make up 20 per cent of the population, is a Bible class.[70]

One would have supposed that juvenile detention facilities would make every effort as "wise fathers" for their children to supply what these neglected children lack. For example, most of the children in trouble are far behind average in educational achievement:

> [I]f there is any one common characteristic about a delinquent kid . . . it is they are educationally retarded. We get a kid and we give him an intelligence test. He scores in the average or above-average range; he is in the ninth grade, and he reads on the fourth or fifth grade level.[71]

Detention home supervisors interviewed by my researchers generally estimated that almost all of their charges were behind in school. An Albuquerque, New Mexico, official admitted that detained children usually are three to five grade levels behind in reading skills. More than a third of delinquency referrals to Utah's juvenile courts receive D's in school or are failing; another 10 per cent are not in school at all.[72]

Yet, one detention home in five provides residents with no educational program whatsoever.[73] Certain children are excluded from educational programs that do exist in some institutions, often the youngsters whose needs for help are greatest. And 17 per

---

[69] Subcommittee on Penal and Judicial Reform to the Committee on Public Safety of the Council of the City of New York, "Prison Reform" (Report, Proposed Legislation and Recommendations, mimeographed, 1972), p. A-8.
[70] Ibid., p. A-18.
[71] Testimony of Peter V. Knolla, director, Douglas County Youth Center (Omaha, Nebraska) in "Crime in America—A Mid-America View," Hearings before the Select Committee on Crime of the House of Representatives, 90th Cong. 2d sess., 65 (1969).
[72] Utah State Law Enforcement Planning Agency, *Utah Youth Services Planning Project 1972*, p. 8.
[73] Pappenfort Census, Vol. 7, Table 44, p. 50.

cent of all children in detention facilities are not in school programs.[74]

The District of Columbia until recently provided one and one half hours of schooling per day for detained juveniles. And only after a local court ruled that detention must provide the equivalent of regular schooling did the Receiving Home begin to offer five daily hours of classes. In Indianapolis, more than half of juvenile detainees are excluded from the inadequate educational program. The superintendent of Marion County detention home admitted that "the school program is one of the sorriest things in this world." The home has too few teachers; they have no training in special education; the local school system is insensitive in its management of classes for detainees; and the home has, in fact, become a dumping ground for the least competent public school instructors.

School programs that do exist must cope with high turnover, with children who already have dropped out or failed in public school. Only dedicated and skilled teachers could cope with such a challenge, yet these children get the least effective schooling of all children.

Ironically, large numbers of children are locked away in these institutions because they have been charged with truancy. Yet the jails and detention centers often deny them an education!

In addition, half the detention homes have no remedial program, and only one in ten offers remedial schooling to all residents.[75] Ancillary services to support remedial education—such as medical tests for poor vision and other physical learning problems—usually are missing. More children receive religious instruction in detention than receive remedial schooling.[76]

Art, music, creative dance and other non-academic subjects might involve children with poor verbal skills, aid in diagnoses, permit children to express otherwise inexpressible feelings and ideas, and experience some positive achievements. Yet, the majority of confined children have no access to art, music or dance.[77] According to the district attorney of Philadelphia, Pennsylvania:

[74] Pappenfort Census, Vol. 7, Table 45, p. 51.
[75] Ibid., Tables 51 and 52, pp. 57–58.
[76] Ibid., Table 54, p. 60.
[77] Ibid., Tables 55 and 56, pp. 61–62.

The Youth Study Center has a school program, but it is geared to an estimated three-week detention period. Thus, the program simply repeats itself every three weeks with only slight changes. A child who is in custody for six months will receive the same three-week course approximately eight times.[78]

The voluntary education at the Bernalillo County Detention Home in Albuquerque, New Mexico, has only one classroom for academic subjects. Only about half the children participate on any one day. But, imaginatively, dropouts from the regular school system are allowed to come to classes with detainees. The purpose of this plan is to reach children turned off by school and motivate them to return to school, as well as servicing children in detention.

An innovative program developed more than a decade ago at the Contra Costa County Juvenile Hall in Martinez, California,[79] presented practical study subjects in concentrated units, each lasting only one to two weeks. All units were taught with a variety of techniques, emphasizing audio-visual aids and pupil participation, and included courses in such subjects as "human development," "child care," "courtship and marriage," "emotional growth," "body care and grooming," "legal rights and responsibilities of children," and "planning for your future," venereal disease or drug addiction. Traditional academic subjects, and arts and crafts instruction, were available for children who expressed interest.

Fewer than 30 per cent of detention homes also provide vocational programs and fewer than a fifth of detained children are involved in the programs which do exist.[80]

Another priority for a juvenile detention facility ought to be a recreation and physical education program; yet more than a third have *no* program of physical education either.[81]

NCCD instructs that juvenile recreation or activities programs must be more intensive in a short-term detention facility than in a longer-term facility; they must meet the varied needs of the residents while serving as a useful diagnostic tool and to aid in treatment.[82] Sherwood Norman, an expert in this field, noted that a

[78] 1970 Senate Hearings at 4710.
[79] See S. Norman, *Detention Practice: Significant Developments in the Detention of Children and Youth* (Paramus: NCCD 1960), pp. 91–92.
[80] Pappenfort Census, Vol. 7, Tables 57 and 58, pp. 63–64.
[81] Ibid., Table 59, p. 65.
[82] NCCD, *Standards and Guides for the Detention of Children and Youth,* p. 69.

recreation program is "no frill"; it is essential to fill time, teach and treat. It must allow children to express themselves, to create, to accomplish and to vent hate and energy.[83] Obvious as this proposition appears, many detention homes have no planned recreation. Some institutions supply a few uninteresting books, a set of checkers, a pack of cards, a Ping-Pong or pool table, a TV, and call it indoor recreation. Others let kids go outdoors for a while on nice days to play catch, and call it outdoor recreation.

In Albuquerque, children at the Bernalillo County Detention Home were locked in their rooms at least five times a day for a half-hour or hour at a stretch, with nothing to do but stare at the dingy walls, talk or fight. Extreme security risks were not allowed outside at all.

In the District of Columbia Receiving Home children spend hours simply milling about or watching other people playing Ping-Pong. At the home, new children are locked up by themselves in a tiny room with a bed, a toilet and sink, or they are kept in a crowded dayroom with other new arrivals. There is nothing to do but listen to a radio or play cards. In the Receiving Home Annex at Cedar Knoll, I have seen boys languishing in dark rooms, leaning against broken metal lockers or lying across tables—as dejected as dogs in a pound.

After-school hours, evenings and weekends in these centers are especially bleak periods. Children do clean-up chores, watch TV, play Ping-Pong or have "free time." But what is free time when you are not free?

In the Bucks County, Pennsylvania, detention facility, arrested juveniles go to school from 8:30 to 11:30 A.M. After lunch they help clean up; some wash dishes. If the weather permits they go outside until 4 or 4:45 P.M.; if not they have "general recreation" —or more clean-up. After a five o'clock dinner they have "free time" until 9 P.M., when they shower and go to bed. Saturday mornings, when there are no classes, they clean their rooms and the rest of the home.

At the Waxter Detention Home in Maryland, where there were serious disturbances in 1971, the evening program consists mainly of movies: gangster dramas or Westerns for the boys, and love stories for the girls, hardly useful models under the circumstances.

[83] Norman, *Detention Practice*, pp. 108–10.

Most often, the major problem is idleness. Juvenile detainees spend much of their time in "lock-up." In large and chronically overcrowded big city jails this practice is a typical grievance of adult inmates. Even the minimal programmed recreation—usually an hour a day in an outdoor courtyard—often will be denied to serve the "administrative convenience" of the guards who move the prisoners in and out. The D. C. Jail in Washington recently saw the macing and beating of protesting inmates, who simply wanted some minimal indoor recreation during a rainy weekend.

Even institutions with good programs usually separate new arrivals in a special receiving unit, for twenty-four hours, where they have nothing to do but watch TV or play cards. If a child is referred over a weekend, he may not be processed into the general population until the following Monday.

Authorities recommend that for young people the process of rehabilitation[84] should begin in the detention home. Detention facilities should be structured not as warehouses for children but to meet the programmatic goals of rehabilitation. The atmosphere should be cheerful. The physical structure must be healthy and comfortable; it should also be suitable for rehabilitative programming. Since a program involves education, recreation, counseling and medical care, the plant should include classrooms, a gym, "quiet rooms," individual counseling rooms, visiting areas, an infirmary and outdoor sports fields—as well as space for sleeping, eating and bathing.

Many jurisdictions take pride in their expensive new juvenile detention centers. But the report of an LEAA-funded juvenile justice project in Pima County, Arizona, says:

> Many communities still hire architects to build new and better detention homes and each and every one since the 1930's has taken the same basic design with narrow hallways, with security fixtures and furnishings . . .

But in Pima County, where a new center was opened in 1968, children need not spend the bulk of the time in their rooms. The building has an open plan, "designed so the administration must program for the staff to be involved with a child while he is in custody." The custody has been a notable success, according to

[84] See, generally, NCCD, *Standards and Guides for the Detention of Children and Youth,* and Norman, *Detention Practice.*

the Pima County report. With "24 hour staff supervision and 16 hour staff and child involvement," the center has had "no staff members attacked, no escapes accomplished, and vandalism held to a degree that is hardly worth mentioning . . . The only place that we have experienced vandalism is in those areas of detention that are constructed along traditional lines."[85]

Some recently built detention facilities that have classrooms, play areas and separate dining rooms end up using them not for the purposes that they were built to accommodate but merely to warehouse the overflow of youngsters referred to their care. Homes with separate sleeping quarters convert activity rooms to makeshift dormitories by stacking kids on mattresses squeezed together on the floor. Homes with classrooms designed to permit individualized attention are deluged with pupils; they must cut on special programs and even exclude some kids from school programs altogether.

In Albuquerque, New Mexico, where the girls' quarters at the Bernalillo County Detention Home are sunny, with bright bed spreads, the boys' quarters are stark cubicles, with two slablike double bunks, a metal shelf, a basin and commode. Each window is darkened by dirt and obscured by a close, heavy grating.

At the Marion County Detention Center in Indianapolis, Indiana, dreary, windowless sleeping rooms are designed to hold one child each, but the dayroom often becomes an impromptu dormitory for the ever present overflow. Nor are there windows in any of the rooms the children use in the center; when they go to court next door, they pass through an underground tunnel. No one can see them; they cannot see the light of day.

In all the facilities visited, the classrooms were much the same; there were always bars somewhere, or blank walls unbroken by windows. Few centers are really places where a child can forget, even momentarily, that he is locked up.

MEDICAL OR PSYCHOLOGICAL CARE

Many of the youngsters apprehended by the police or referred to the juvenile courts by social service agencies and schools are

[85] Pima County Juvenile Court Center, "New Model of Juvenile Justice" (June 30, 1972), pp. 24–25.

the children of poor families and are physically impaired, diseased or malnourished. Since children contract communicable diseases easily, the first service they should receive in custody is a medical checkup, with preventative care and treatment of any health problems discovered.[86] Of the more than 20,000 youthful detainees examined by the staff of New York City's Montefiore Hospital from mid-1968 to late 1971, 45 per cent were found to have medical problems.[87] The Montefiore Hospital program, which provides thorough intake examinations for all new residents at one of the city's largest detention centers, and offers follow-up treatment both during detention and after release, is, unfortunately, atypical.

Only about half of the nation's detention homes give routine physical examinations at intake, and over one quarter give no admission examinations at all;[88] 18 per cent of juvenile detention facilities can make no professional medical services available at any time, while almost half provide no dental services.[89] Few detention homes have full-time medical staff or hospital affiliations. The care which is provided usually is administered by an "on-call" doctor or nurse. Systems of medical care delivery which emphasize emergency treatment overlook detection of less obvious medical problems and subvert the diagnostic function of juvenile detention.

Only four Illinois jails give routine medical attention to all inmates; almost half conduct no medical exams at intake. The rest may afford some treatment to some prisoners, if they demand it or show obvious symptoms of illness.[90]

But even if juveniles themselves were to receive preferential treatment in medical care in jail, they would remain locked up in close proximity to other inmates with undiagnosed or untreated illness.

The need for and lack of treatment for psychological problems are also severe. Administrators claim that most children in detention have emotional or behavior problems.[91] Yet only about 4

[86] Norman, *Detention Practice.*
[87] "Montefiore Hospital and Medical Center Program at Juvenile Center" (mimeographed, December 7, 1971), p. 1.
[88] Pappenfort Census, Vol. 7, Table 21, p. 26.
[89] NCCD Correction Survey, p. 18.
[90] Mattick and Sweet, *Illinois Jails,* p. 171.
[91] Pappenfort Census, Vol. 7, Table 8, p. 12.

per cent of all detention homes give psychological tests to all the children at admission. One child in five is tested or evaluated for psychological problems on entering detention,[92] one in eight or nine received psychiatric diagnosis.[93] Treatment is even rarer; fewer than 2 per cent of center inmates receive it.[94] At most juvenile detention institutions, no children are seen regularly by any psychiatrists, psychologists, social workers or other professionals.[95] In 1965, professional social workers comprised only 3 per cent of the personnel of juvenile detention facilities.[96]

Programs are likely to be mere time-filling devices or unco-ordinated attempts at mass "therapy." There are few staff reviews of the children in custody.[97] Few facilities have any in-service training for staff.[98] And, while the majority of detention homes claim to conduct some casework or therapy with the families of their wards,[99] the inadequacy of staffing and casework within the institutions leaves the quality and intensity of these outside contacts open to question.

The NCCD sums up the objectives of detention care as provision of secure custody and physical care, constructive and satisfying programs, individual guidance through social casework and social group work, and observation and study of the child.[100] These worthy and sensible objectives are met rarely. Indeed, sometimes children are even robbed of food, the basic ingredient of care.

In many jails, especially those where the sheriff is paid so much per inmate per day, the food is horrible—this because the sheriff is able to pocket whatever he can save on meals. In one South Carolina jail youngsters were fed thin soup or beans. In another, they got only corn bread and powdered milk for their evening meals, seven days a week.

This policy also encourages locking children up, for the more inmates, the more the sheriff can make.[101]

[92] Pappenfort Census, Vol. 7, Tables 25 and 26, pp. 30–31.
[93] Ibid., Table 28.
[94] Ibid., Tables 29 and 30, pp. 34–35.
[95] Ibid., Table 35, p. 40.
[96] NCCD Correction Survey, p. 19.
[97] Pappenfort Census, Vol. 7, Table 38, p. 43.
[98] NCCD Correction Survey, p. 20.
[99] Pappenfort Census, Vol. 7, Table 37, p. 42.
[100] NCCD, *Standards and Guides for Detention of Children and Youth*, p. 36.
[101] H. James, *Children in Trouble: A National Scandal* (New York: Pocket Books, 1971), pp. 29–30.

In the face of such reports, the claim of the juvenile justice system to be a wise parent to wayward children seems a farce.

PUNISHMENT AND ABUSE BY STAFF

Much of the time, personnel and funds that could be devoted to education and care of children in detention are given over to negative programs. Institutions continue to emphasize punishment, and threats of punishment, as a mode of control. They duplicate—with untried, unconvicted children—the typical shortcomings of the whole American correctional system.

Only a minority of all children detained are dangerous to society. Many more have difficulties dealing with authority. Whatever a child's problems, the use of force reinforces those problems. Children's courts and institutions were not meant to punish, but to help. This is especially true of institutions for children who are only suspected of or charged with misconduct. But what was intended is seldom achieved.

When children in detention attempt to release pent-up energy, bred of inactivity and idleness—when they talk back to staff, speak when the rules command silence, smoke, fight or violate institutional regulations—they may be beaten, placed in solitary confinement, stripped or otherwise abused and humiliated.

The use of "solitary" or "isolation" is widespread in detention, despite its wide condemnation by theoreticians and practitioners. At almost every detention facility I have visited or seen described, there are tiny cells reserved for punishment. The rate of their use, and reasons for that use, vary from "home" to "home." At some, every rule infraction (and there always are a variety of rules, many intolerably vague) is punishable by solitary. In Albuquerque, the assistant director of the Bernalillo County Detention Home admitted that his staff was employing solitary as a "solution" to many problems that should be dealt with in other ways.

The isolation cell is used in some institutions only when the staff believes that violent behavior can be controlled in no other way. Even in these cases, the way in which the practice is conducted seems unnecessarily harsh. Boys in solitary are stripped to their underwear or allowed only pajamas; when isolation cells have mattresses they are often removed during the day. Some cells have no windows; most are too small to allow much movement. Staff visit the locked-up child in some cases; often, children are left totally alone. The time a child may be isolated can be limited to a few hours; or may extend to days or even weeks.

A Duke University survey team uncovered these inhumane practices at a longer-term juvenile institution in North Carolina:

> The harshest form of punishment involves being placed in solitary confinement, in the quiet room or, as the boys and staff call it, the jug. . . . If a child attempts to run away, is caught smoking, is acting out in class, or is involved in related offenses, he is placed in the jug. The jug itself consists of a small room in which a slab of rock serves as a bed. An offender must strip down to his underwear. He may only read a Bible, he has only two meals a day. At 5 o'clock in the evening he is given a mattress on which to sleep; at 6 o'clock the next morning the mattress is removed and the bare rock is all the boy has to rest on.
>
> The central office has issued rules for the implementation of quiet room procedure. Each boy must be checked by a doctor within a few hours of confinement. This rule is seldom followed. Another rule limits a stay in the quiet room to 7 consecutive days. To circumvent this rule a boy is briefly removed from the jug on the seventh day and returned immediately for another 7 consecutive days. Many of the boys we have talked to spent an average of 10 days for a single offense. One particular boy claimed he had spent 21 days in the jug.[102]

In October 1971, the director of Miami, Florida's, Dade County Youth Hall admitted that its population of 250 was about five times the institution's designed capacity. The young inmates, he explained, were assigned to quarters not according to their offenses or personality types, but by physical size; so that way, each would have at least a chance to defend himself against his roommates. "There's just not enough room to do it any other way," the director said. "Many of them are runaways; many have drug problems. I wouldn't doubt if a few were prostitutes. There wouldn't be any way to keep them from teaching these things to one another."

According to a complaint filed against the Wayne County Youth Home in Detroit, children who are confined there as victims of parental abuse become subject to the cruelty of the staff: they are

[102] A Report on the North Carolina Juvenile System: Courts, Correction, and Aftercare. Mimeographed, 1969, Duke Center on Law and Poverty.

punished with solitary confinement, brutal exercise routines and beatings. The behavior which called forth these punishments included speaking out of turn, inattention and looking out of windows.

Bizarre corporal punishments are common in juvenile detention facilities. According to a Harvard student who posed as a sixteen-year-old inmate of the John J. Connally Youth Center in Roslindale, Massachusetts, one common punishment was to hold boys' heads under water. For minor infractions of rules, they were beaten with fists by the other teen-agers, who participated under threats of being forced to "run the gauntlet" themselves.[103]

Even modern institutions preserve primitive practices. In the new Rome, Georgia, regional detention center, for example, an investigative journalist learned of an eleven-year-old black girl who had been punished by a whipping with a belt. He also reported finding "girls" locked in their rooms for hours because during a meal they 'looked at the boys' who eat in the same dining area."[104]

An article described the cumulative impact of prolonged detention and punishment on one young girl pseudonymed "Claudia Sutton":

> She grew up in Chicago and she was declared "neglected" at the age of 15 and put into the custody of the State of Illinois. The State didn't have any place to put her so it decided to "detain" her "temporarily," in the Audy Home on the Near Southwest Side of Chicago.
>
> The Audy Home is the first stop—and sometimes the last—for many of the children of Cook County who fall into the hands of the law. It is an overcrowded fortress with concrete walls 12 feet high, barred windows, and solitary confinement. Over the years it has served as a dumping ground for juveniles, ranging from potential rapists to children whose parents simply don't want to be bothered with them. As with most such institutions, the Home is not geared to the least guilty of them. Its whole operation is—has to be—to control the worst of them, which means that the least guilty must endure what the worst offenders deserve.
>
> While Audy calls itself a "home," and insists that its function is rehabilitative, few observers agree. As long ago as 1964 the

[103] The children's jails of Detroit, Miami and Roslindale are described in Bagdikian, "Juvenile Prison: Society's Stigma," Washington *Post*, February 3, 1972, p. A-2.
[104] James, *Children in Trouble*, p. 36.

National Conference on Crime and Juvenile Delinquency said that the "programs of the Audy Home are essentially punitive." And, more recently, the Chicago *Daily News* observed that the Audy Home "has the chilling, barren, alien look of a dayroom in a mental hospital."

Imagine what detention in such a place would mean to a highly emotional teenager like Claudia Sutton. As the months passed and she got no word as to the status of her case—and only rebuffs in answer to questions—she became increasingly frightened and emotional. After more than a year of imprisonment without cause, she resorted to the only means she had to draw attention to herself: she became "troublesome"—noisy, restless, hard-to-handle.

This, of course, disturbed her guards. Their job is not to worry about justice, but about order. Their response to Claudia was, therefore, not to try to solve her problem, but to solve *theirs*. They put her in solitary.

Solitary confinement in the Audy Home is the "Blue Stone Room," named for the blue tile on its floors. Claudia's cell was a 6' by 12' room with a single light, no washbasin, no windows (except in the door), no bed (except an air mattress on the floor), and a toilet without a seat. She was shut into this room on six or seven different occasions. The longest span was for 15 consecutive days. This did little for her emotional problems and did nothing to help get her out of jail. Meanwhile the months piled up. Finally, after 16 months in the Audy Home, the distraught girl figured out her own way to get out: she'd commit suicide. Her attempt failed but she did get out: she was transferred to a state hospital for the insane. The last time people from the outside saw her, she was bound into a straitjacket. The way that the law, and the state, had cared for the child was to take her from her home and turn her into a suicidal maniac.[105]

A young girl with an IQ of 150 was degraded and dehumanized by her experience in Illinois. A Chicago legal aid attorney told a congressional committee:

Vicki was nine years old on 13 September 1966 when her mother admitted that she had neglected the child upon the advice of social workers who had previously indicated to the mother that if she admitted neglect, the State of Illinois, through one of its agencies . . . would find a boarding school placement for her daughter. Vicki, at the time, was a brilliant girl who received excellent

[105] William B. Furlong, "When Children Go To Jail," *Good Housekeeping,* March 1972, pp. 98, 299–300.

grades in school but was beginning to "act out" and truant from school. Her mother had been separated from Vicki's father since prior to her birth. She worked, and the babysitters alleged that they could no longer control the girl.

The mother admitted neglect and Children's Division was made guardian, who placed her in an orphanage. Three months later, the orphanage stated that they did not have the facilities to maintain the child properly. Vicki was then placed in the Audy Home by her guardian state agency with the permission of the Juvenile Court of Cook County. The Audy Home is a maximum security institution for the pre-trial detention of delinquent children. At the time she was placed there in 1967, there were over 400 delinquent, neglected, mentally retarded and emotionally disturbed children in a small three-story, brick building surrounded by a 12 foot high one foot thick, concrete wall. The children were mixed together, and there are external and internal security features to the building. The superintendent of that institution has, for years, stated that neglected, mentally retarded and emotionally disturbed children should not be mixed in with the delinquent children in that building. Vicki remained at the Audy Home for eight months, and several psychiatric and psychological reports were prepared at that time. These reports indicated that she should be placed in a residential treatment center and not in a foster home. They indicated that with help, Vicki, because of her brilliance and tenacity, would be a most welcome and contributing member of society. However, her guardian ultimately decided that the girl was emotionally disturbed and placed her into the Elgin State Hospital, against the advice of a Juvenile Court psychologist . . .

[W]hile at Elgin State Hospital, she spoke to a psychiatrist on three occasions. On the first occasion, it was after she had spent a long period of time in restraints after slapping a guard, and the third time, he told her that he was going to prosecute her for assault for attacking another guard.

While at Elgin, Vicki, as other inmates, received daily shots and pills of a drug administered to keep her and others in a state of acquiescence, apparently used primarily for the benefit of the staff, who are understaffed and overworked. She was in restraints on several occasions for disobeying rules and on one occasion, she slapped a matron and was placed in restraints for 28 consecutive days. She was allowed up, attacked another matron, and was placed in restraints for 30 consecutive days. After the second period of binding, she was brought to the Kane County [a county west of Chicago in which the state mental hospital is located] Juvenile Court and prosecuted for assault . . . She was then placed with the Department of Corrections at Geneva, a security penal institution for delinquent girls euphemistically called a "training school." After being incarcerated, the girl was placed in a maximum security cottage and, over the next year, was placed in solitary confinement on nine different occasions for periods between two and six days.

Vicki has now been with the Department of Corrections for almost a year. Other girls who have committed much more serious crimes have come and gone in the meantime. However, her behavior continues to be angry and threatening; her mother is not in a position to take her back home; and her guardian, the Department of Children and Family Services, apparently, does not wish to assume the burden of attempting to place her in an institution which could aid her. Therefore, she remains in prison. . . . [S]he has been pushed from pillar to post, from a maximum security institution for pre-trial detention of delinquent youth, to a mental institution, to a prison for teenage juvenile girls only because her mother could not control her as a nine year old . . .

Nor is Vicki's case an isolated example, another 15-year-old girl was adjudicated a neglected child and spent over 13 consecutive months in the Audy Home. One reason that she spent such a long period in this maximum security institution was that her file had been lost between the Intake and Placement Departments of the Department of Children and Family Services. Thus, for six months the girl sat in the Audy Home while no one really knew what was becoming of her.

During litigation involving her, we read some confidential records of the Department of Children and Family Services and discovered that an Assistant Director of that Agency had suggested that the girl should be released from custody in the hopes that she would commit a delinquent act while outside the Audy Home for which she could be prosecuted and, hence, sent to Geneva (the institution run by the Department of Corrections). However, this was not necessary, because she attacked a male guard while at the Audy Home and was prosecuted for assault. The case never came to trial, because the girl suffered a nervous breakdown in the Audy Home and had to be transferred to a mental hospital.[106]

106 Testimony of Patrick T. Murphy in "Juvenile Confinement Institutions and Correctional Systems," Hearings before the Subcommittee to Investigate Juvenile Delinquency of the Committee on the Judiciary, U. S. Senate, 92d Cong., 1st sess., 209–10 (1971) (hereafter cited as 1971 Senate Hearings).

Morris Raley, El Paso County's chief probation officer, responded to complaints that the detention home was "pure hell," with the words: "It isn't intended as a resort hotel." Were the children's stories of cruel neglect in detention true? Raley replied:

> I'm not going to say. I'm going to say, draw your own conclusions. Many times a child is booked in for protective custody, which is not a legal charge, but is for their protection. Later, we find that the child is completely incorrigible, by their own admission and by a statement from the parents. They exhibit that incorrigible behavior here, too, believe you me.[107]

Questioned as to how children show incorrigibility, Raley displayed a ball of string, and commented: "[O]riginally it was a T-shirt which one of the boys was wearing in a room. In a few hours' time this boy removed that shirt, started unraveling and rolling the twine. That is the T-shirt in its present form." This exchange followed:

> Interviewer: Why do you think he did that, Mr. Raley?
> Raley: More to try to strike back at anyone, especially his parents.
> Interviewer: Isn't it possible that the child made that ball of twine because he was bored, because he had nothing better to do?
> Raley: Not necessarily. Many of them will take any action to, as they see it, get even with their parents or the guards.
> Interviewer: How would you account for this behavior on the part of the children?
> Raley: I would say a lot of it is due to the coddling, permissiveness of parents, permissiveness of law enforcement—of everyone concerned.
> Interviewer: Are you able to overcome this permissiveness?
> Raley: Some of it.

Some juvenile institutions, all too few, have reported notable successes with positive behavior modification programs as an alternative to punishment.[108] These institutions reward good conduct. They award points (usually represented by coupons or scrip) for desirable conduct, attitudes or accomplishments. The child who attends classes regularly, earning good grades, finishing

[107] "This Child Is Rated X," NBC, broadcast May 2, 1971.
[108] Testimony of Trip Sizemore, 1971 Senate Hearings at 217.

an art or shop project, or simply avoiding fights can spend his "earnings" to "buy" canteen items, extra recreation or gym time, admission to social events, or even a private room, weekend passes or furloughs. Positive reinforcement is combined with a practical introduction to the economics of the world outside the institution.

The quality of care in juvenile detention institutions cannot be measured in classroom time, numbers, movies shown or hours allowed for visiting. Important as these variables are, the real standards are the institution's overall atmosphere and the ways in which the children are treated. Buildings may be new and beautiful, classes may be small, gyms may be large and the staff may be large and professional. For the children in detention, however, the most important thing is how people deal with one another within the institution.

In its *Standards and Guides for the Detention of Children and Youth,* the NCCD emphasizes the need for a coherent philosophy of treatment. It explains that children who are detained often have been improperly treated by parents, teachers, police; many have lost or never learned respect for authority. Thus a detention program should help children learn to relate constructively to authority. Respect cannot be bought by permissiveness or enforced by repression. It must grow in response to an approach to the handling of the children which is consistent and firm, yet friendly.

Basic to the proper handling of children—or of persons in any situation—is respect for the individual, even though his behavior may be rejected. "We like you even though we may not like what you do and will not permit you to do it"—this attitude toward a child should be so evident that he readily feels at ease with the staff.

Supervision of treatment in detention should be less a matter of rules and regulations than of firm yet warm and understanding day-to-day relationships. They entail (a) formal and casual contacts during admission and at the time of release, (b) activities engaged in by children and staff together, (c) the program content itself, (d) the manner in which adult authority is exercised over a group, (e) the manner in which adult authority is exercised over an individual child, particularly in the presence of his peers, (f) the manner in which group and individual interviews are conducted. . . . *The staff must have a basic belief in the best characteristics of each child and in his capacity for developing them.*[109]

[109] NCCD, *Standards and Guides for the Detention of Children and Youth,* pp. 78–79.

ABUSE BY PRISONERS

The atmosphere of neglect and brutality in a jail or detention facility, like the lack of supervision, lack of engrossing and constructive activities, stimulates bullying and abuse among the inmates themselves.

Late in 1971, a fourteen-year-old at the Thomas J. S. Waxter Detention Home, Maryland's only designated juvenile detention facility, claimed that he had been raped by several other boys.[110] Designed for forty children, the institution housed 101 at the time of the alleged incident; most slept on mattresses spread on the floors. The child's charge had not been tested by a medical examination, but no one denied that tension among the center's young inmates had resulted in beatings. During a recent interview with one of my associates, the assistant supervisor would not deny that there had been homosexual rapes at the center.

In fact, none of the detention home administrators we interviewed would deny that beatings and homosexual rapes occurred in their institutions. They said in defense of their institutions that there are fewer than before, or that the problem had been "overplayed." When a child has been cornered, stripped and sodomized, and then terrorized into silence by threats of reprisal, the incident cannot be "overplayed." "Less often than before" is too often for him.

There are many lurid stories of rape and other sexual abuse of children in jail or in detention homes. Several examples will suffice to demonstrate the horror of such experiences.

Pat Barker, an official of the Oklahoma Crime Commission, who was once a bad check artist, recalled his own jail experiences in an interview:

> . . . [I]t's frightening. You're in a detention room with sleeping accommodations for 32 and 40 people. Some people have to sleep on the floor. I've seen people raped, specially young kids. You can get a kid as young as fourteen years old, and several 16. These young boys would come in, and if they were fresh and young the guys who run the tank and lived in the first cell, they would take these young guys if they wanted to. They would take the kid,

[110] Watson and Bowman, "Assaults Reported at Md. Youth Center," Washington *Post,* November 18, 1971.

forcibly hold him, and someone would rape him right in the rear.
I just flat saw it happen . . . The guards in jail make rounds periodically, but they don't have enough manpower . . . Some of [the
kids] go to pieces, just right there and then, kids who can't hack
it and are torn apart. They cry all the time, just nervous, scared of
their shadows. Others just get embittered and next time some
young kid comes in they turn around and become the raper instead of the rapee. So it depends on the individual . . . [If the kid
tells the guards] they better yank him out of there or his life isn't
worth a nickel.[111]

A story in *Kiwanis* described a Missouri experience:

When a seventeen-year-old Missouri farm boy was jailed in 1963
on suspicion of stealing tools, his older brother tried to bail the
lad out.

"Don't worry about him," a deputy sheriff told the brother at
the St. Francois County Jail; "We'll just scare him."

Two days later the boy was dead. He had been stomped to
death after being sexually assaulted by two vicious older prisoners.
The sheriff was on vacation and the jail inmates had been left
unattended at night.[112]

The district attorney of Philadelphia testified before a Senate
committee on the problem:

Our investigation led to a number of conclusions and I will summarize them in this way: First of all, that sexual assaults were
epidemic in the Philadelphia prison system. The specific offenses
which we determined to exist involved 156 sexual assaults on at
least 97 different victims.

We found, secondly, that virtually every slightly built young
man committed by the courts is sexually approached within hours
after his admission to prison.

We found, in addition, that aggressors tend to be older, larger,
and more serious offenders than are the victims. So when an individual is taken into custody, he faces a substantial risk of being
a victim of attack within the prison system itself. . . .

I would say that more than half of those who were assaulted
were youngsters. The patterns which are followed make the
younger men more desirable, more attractive to be the potential

111 Bagdikian, "A Human Wasteland in the Name of Justice," *Washington
Post,* January 30, 1972, p. A-16.
112 Murray T. Bloom, "The Local Jail: Where Crime Pays," *Kiwanis,* May–
October 1966.

victims. The younger men tend to be weaker, less worldly wise in terms of what goes on in the prison, and the younger people were the natural victims of this kind of attack. . . .[113]

Such stories are terrible to tell and to read. The experience must be terrifying. They reflect the irony of juvenile "justice" at its worst.

CASE STUDIES OF PROMISE AND HOPE

Not everything in the juvenile justice world is so depressing. An imaginative, daring and promising experiment in correctional reform—the most impressive one in the country—began in Massachusetts in 1969 under the leadership of then Youth Services Department head (now in Illinois) Jerome Miller. In a few years, this mild-mannered soft-spoken former Catholic seminarian deinstitutionalized the state's juvenile correction system. Aided by reported scandals in the existing youth facilities (hardly unique to Massachusetts) and the support of a sympathetic governor, Miller came to his job with no experience in correctional administration. He found a staff of 900, a $12 million budget (90 per cent went to staff and institutions), and an annual flow of about 1,300 youngsters between seven and seventeen years old (about 80 per cent were repeaters) who came from the state's juvenile court system for stays averaging about ten months.[114]

Acting on his theory that institutions are bad: expensive, perversely anti-correctional, classist and run for the benefit of employees who often are incompetent, political appointees antagonistic toward reform, Miller decided to shut his institutions, let staff atrophy (they could not be fired because of Civil Service regulations), and contract with various local private institutions to provide services for his young clients.

---

[113] Testimony of Arlen Specter, district attorney of Philadelphia, Pennsylvania, in "Juvenile Delinquency," Hearings before the Subcommittee to Investigate Juvenile Delinquency of the Committee on the Judiciary, U. S. Senate, 91st Cong., 1st sess., 4695 (1970) (hereafter cited as 1970 Senate Hearings).

[114] The story of this reform movement is reported in the September 16, 1972, *Saturday Review: Education,* Vachon, "Hey, Man, What Did You Learn in Reform School? Well, uh, Like How to Disconnect a Burglar Alarm," pp. 69–76.

Foster homes, halfway houses, group homes, psychiatric agencies, even the state's elite private prep schools now handle these youngsters under contracts with Miller's department. Parole and probation have increased; new volunteer and personal advocate programs have been begun. Court liaison officers were assigned to the juvenile courts to develop community remedies for the children coming before the courts. Educational and vocational training counseling have been made available; crisis intervention centers, opened by private and public agencies, provided mental health services. Outward Bound programs and narcotic centers are used. Forestry Camp programs were expanded. Shelter care facilities were created to provide residential treatment as an alternative to detention in appropriate cases. Grants-in-aid were provided to cities and towns that increased local community programs for young offenders in their area. An intensive care security unit was set up at Worcester Medical School to handle disturbed and dangerous young delinquents. Community aftercare was provided.

These are the alternatives traditionally followed by people of affluence for their own troubled children; Miller merely provided similar services for those who cannot afford these alternatives for their children. He used young people, many of whom were veterans of juvenile institutions, to run many of his department's programs.

A Detained Youth Advocate Program was developed. One hundred youth advocates are paid to provide counseling and referral services to youths during the crucial period between their arraignment and adjudication. The youngster avoids detention; the advocate may keep him in his home while talking with the family and exploring community programs which would suit the youngster's problem. The advocate develops a work or educational program with and for the youngster, eases him into it, and is available for aid in times of crisis. The aim is to get the child back home when practicable and oversee reintegration with his family. The advocate then comes to court with a plan which the court may adopt in place of an adjudication. Thereafter, follow-up services also will be provided.

The advocates are selected from universities, community action groups, Aid for Dependent Children mothers, civic or religious organizations, and then are trained. Miller estimated that as many as 5,200 youngsters benefited from this service by the end of the first year of the program, set up to operate in seven urban cities throughout the state.

Because group homes were regarded as expensive and unsuccessful, the department trained and hired professional foster parents. They work full time and have access to relevant community programs which seem suited to the problems of their charges.

A parole aide program was started to deal with the 1,400 youngsters on parole status who were receiving inadequate supervision and counseling by adult officers to whom they could not relate. The aides are youths between eighteen and twenty-two years old selected by the local community, the department and Tufts Medical Health Center, who come from similar backgrounds as their wards but who have "made it."

Miller told me he asked the legislature for a reduced budget to run his department; and at that his program's recidivism rates were better than those of the institution-based department he replaced. His beginning was auspicious.

Miller's guiding philosophy is worth considering. He assumed that children in trouble usually come from troubled and inadequate homes (90 per cent on welfare, 60 per cent with serious alcoholic or narcotics problems, with parents lacking in education and work skills, frequently with criminal records). The historic moralism of the past juvenile system, which purported to reform wicked children by incarcerating them, was, in his view, perverse and resulted in a crass, custodial system. Institutions for children intensify their criminal careers, Miller says. The century-long experiment of "saving boys and girls from lives of idleness, destitution, crime and depravity, by destroying them with misguided zeal for reform" is a failure.

The way to accomplish reform, in his view, is to dismantle and replace state institutions dealing with problem children and to replace juvenile correctional institutions with community-based facilities. Juvenile jails could be eliminated if alternatives were found and used.

In Miller's judgment, the juvenile court "is not the best agency to manage therapeutic services to youth in trouble." It is comparable to "the emergency room of the general hospital," providing limited treatment to poor people with widely varied problems.[115] The juvenile court should act rather as a referral agency to varied community resources for youth services.

[115] See Massachusetts Office of Planning, "A Strategy for Youth in Trouble" (Report, February 25, 1972).

A wide variety of community prevention, diversion and treatment programs have been used by Miller's department to replace what were the state's typical, traditional warehouses and poorhouses for children. All seek to keep these children out of the stigmatizing and corrupting, official juvenile justice system, to provide helpful, realistic services to meet the particular needs of the youngsters who become state wards, and to get them back home quickly, whenever possible. They include programs to direct youngsters from the juvenile system by "developing pre-judicial dispositions alternatives for children who have committed no crimes, pose no threat to society, and need community-based rehabilitation programs"; and alternatives to institutions for those who cannot be diverted but who need something other than crude imprisonment. Acts which would not be criminal if committed by adults would be eliminated from juvenile court jurisdiction.[116]

During the early 1970's, the state of Kentucky moved in the same direction as Massachusetts. The state legislature passed a series of new bills in 1972 and the Department of Child Welfare took significant steps to cut down on the institutionalization of children and to develop community-based alternatives to juvenile detention.

The Kentucky Department of Child Welfare acted in the belief that exposing delinquents to more sophisticated young offenders in large institutions teaches youngsters more sophisticated criminal behavior and stigmatizes them as outlaws. The new legislation and the department's recent actions were "designed to keep children out of jails immediately after apprehension" and to prohibit the institutionalization of truants, runaways and incorrigibles under eleven.[117]

The department defined its guiding philosophies as threefold: (1) "to correct problems in the family, thereby keeping families together" and preventing delinquency that results from a "child acting out in a socially unacceptable way in order to draw attention to his needs"; (2) to keep "children who have not committed

[116] Miller has left Massachusetts and is now doing a similar job in Illinois.
[117] The new juvenile justice laws are found in Kentucky Rev. Stats., §§208 060, .110, 120, 1380, and .430. Mr. Frank Coots of the Kentucky Department of Child Welfare provided information on the design and implementation of new programs.

serious offenses out of institutions"; and (3) to try to rehabilitate young offenders in homelike settings wherever possible.

The department soon was able to report that commitments to institutions decreased 46 per cent and that recommitments dropped drastically. According to its figures, it costs $6,500 annually to support a child in an institution, compared to $500 to place him on probation.

To carry out its policy, the department devised various schemes for what it calls "short-term structured treatment," enabling it to resort to institutionalization only as a last resort. One official recently wrote to me reporting that the state is "closing down two of its 12 residential facilities and converting four others to facilities incorporating community-based treatment programs such as group homes and halfway houses," as a result of these recent changes.

Along with eliminating the duration of juvenile detention and assuring constitutional rights to young offenders and the expungement of their records if they stay out of trouble for two years, the state Department of Child Welfare developed over thirty county committees of private citizens and community resources, the home-maker services which help families stay together, private day care services. It set up a diversion project, providing intensive services and employing ex-offenders. It set up foster care programs for children who are particularly difficult to place, such as those with mental health problems. It developed special foster homes, emergency shelter homes, group homes and purchased specific care from private institutions and agencies.

An innovative group home in Boulder County, Colorado, Attention Home, founded in 1967 after a church-sponsored study revealed that children were routinely held at the local jail or at the overcrowded Denver Juvenile Hall, thirty miles away, provides temporary placement for troubled children. Residents attend local schools and participate in community activities. Parents are encouraged to visit and to contribute to their children's support. Almost half the young residents eventually return to their families, many others are placed in permanent foster homes. The Attention Home is run entirely by volunteers and with community donations of money, goods and services. The total operating cost for 1967 was $7,300. The daily cost per child was only $5.67, much less than the fifteen-to-twenty-dollar-per-day cost of conventional detention care.

Unfortunately, temporary foster parents are difficult to recruit, and group homes are few and limited in capacity. The juvenile court intake staff, which must make formal "placements" of many children who come into the court's jurisdiction, has only limited discretion to explore alternatives to institutional detention for PINS cases and dependent or neglected children.

DECRIMINALIZATION AND DEINSTITUTIONALIZATION

Detention of juveniles would be drastically reduced if PINS and dependency-neglect cases were removed altogether from juvenile court jurisdiction. Decriminalization of conduct which is prohibited "for children only," would remove thousands of children from court-controlled institutions. This shift would work only if alternatives were available to respond to neglected and troubled children. One such mechanism is the system of "Youth Service Bureaus" advocated by the President's Crime Commission in 1967.[118] Youth Service Bureaus are community-based organizations providing a broad range of services to youth in trouble. They are dedicated to diverting young people from the criminal and juvenile courts.

A recent comment on juvenile law in Ohio proposed that:

> The category of children who would be referred to the Youth Service Bureau would include truants, incorrigibles, "waywards," runaways, children "found in a disreputable place," and those who associate "with vagrant . . . or immoral persons." The recently enacted Ohio Juvenile Court Act labels these children "unruly" and reserves the "delinquent" label for those children who have committed acts which, if committed by an adult, would be a crime. This classification is important in that the "unruly" child may not be committed to the legal custody of the Ohio Youth Commission unless the court finds, upon further hearing, that the child has not been amenable to the treatment or rehabilitation provided by the other dispositions available to the juvenile court. But the juvenile court is still given primary jurisdiction over the unruly child.[119]

118 President's Commission on Law Enforcement and Administration of Justice, *The Challenge of Crime in a Free Society* (Washington, D.C.: Government Printing Office, 1967).
119 Comment, "A Proposal for the More Effective Treatment of the 'Unruly' Child in Ohio: The Youth Service Bureau" 39 *U. Cincinnati L. Rev.* 275 (1970).

Acting as brokers between troubled young people and community agencies, neighborhood Youth Service Bureaus would have
no power to order institutionalization. One bureau diverted as
many as 50 per cent of the local delinquent children from the
justice system. The population of Indiana's institutions for delinquents dropped 40 per cent in the year fourteen bureaus were
established in that state.[120]

Local bureaus adapt both their organizational structure and the
range of services they offer to the needs of the communities they
serve. This emphasis on flexibility allows the bureaus to respond
to the individual needs of their young clients. Some, such as the
Washtenaw Youth Service Bureau in Ann Arbor, Michigan, work
primarily with other community agencies trying to develop new
programs for youth and new approaches for dealing with problem
children within the existing system. This emphasis on institutional
reform may be well suited to the needs of an upper-middle-class
community such as Ann Arbor.

Most Youth Service Bureaus, however, emphasize personal contact with children as a means of preventing delinquency. In
Bridgeport, Connecticut, the staff of the bureau deals directly
with youth who are referred to the bureau by other agencies or who
voluntarily seek out the help of the bureau when they feel themselves in need of help. The staff deals with many problem children
by referring them to community agencies set up to handle certain
specific problems. The staff also offers counseling and takes the
initiative in finding needed services when, as is often the case, no
appropriate services are offered in the community.[121]

Youth Service Bureaus have no power to order institutionalization. Their function is to provide means for the troubled child to
avoid the institutions which have proven unsuccessful in the past.

A parent, child, neighbor, teacher, police officer may bring a
child's conduct to the attention of a Youth Service Bureau, but
the bureau acts only with the consent of the child and the aggrieved party, if there is one. If it fails, the matter may still be the
subject of a complaint in juvenile court.

The bureau, unlike the courts, can intervene and deal directly

[120] S. Norman, *The Youth Service Bureau,* p. vi.
[121] Youth Development and Delinquency Prevention Administration, U. S.
Department of Health, Education, and Welfare, *National Study of Youth
Service Bureaus* (Casebook, 1973).

with the causes of the child's problem. To the court, a neglected child cannot be returned to his home environment, and is, therefore, a candidate for detention—although he is not accused of any wrongdoing. The bureau, on the other hand, can move to improve the child's home environment. Parents can be referred to counseling services or to vocational training programs. The child can be placed in a neighborhood day care center. Specialized welfare department caseworkers ("homemakers") can be assigned to work with the family. "Protective services" caseworkers can provide relatively intensive supervision of a potentially unhealthy home environment. In extreme cases of dependency and neglect, the bureau can arrange a foster home placement under less restrictive regulations than a court.

A habitual truant may have poor vision or dyslexia. The bureau can provide eyeglasses or special education. A pregnant teen-ager does not need institutionalization. She needs family counseling, education in prenatal care, advice on abortion or adoption procedures, and, perhaps, short-term residence in a specialized group home. Most Youth Service Bureaus, unfortunately, now receive a high percentage of their clients through the juvenile courts, and thus cannot enter a child's case until after a juvenile court hearing —too late to circumvent pre-adjudication detention.

As the Youth Service Bureau movement grows, and the range of community services on which individual bureaus can call becomes richer and more varied, the argument in favor of the legislative decriminalization of "children only" offenses becomes increasingly persuasive. Why should truancy, for example, be a legal offense? By taking such offenses out of court, and giving the Youth Service Bureaus exclusive jurisdiction, the legislatures can assure that compulsory institutionalization for minor misbehavior will not be employed. The juvenile jail or the detention facility is not a "home," the myth that it ever could be has haunted the child reform movement for almost a century.

The development of Youth Service Bureaus should no longer be a matter of local option; the states themselves, through their departments of welfare and social services, should be required to provide coverage for their entire populations of adolescents and children.

Because even symptomatic youthful misbehavior may have its victims—the neighbor with a broken window, or the youngster hurt in a schoolyard fight—decriminalization would require new mechanisms for conciliation, mediation and compensation. One such mechanism, the "neighborhood court," with an informal jurisdiction over certain conflicts, is already in operation, in the Bronx Neighborhood Youth Division Program in New York City. The program is a "judicial" component of this specialized Youth Service Bureau, known as the Forum. "Judges," each a community resident who has received special training in techniques of informal conflict resolution, sit in panels of three. A youngster who appears before the Forum is represented by an Advocate—a young community resident employed by the program.

It is an error, too commonly committed in juvenile detention practice, to assume that any child charged with a "serious" delinquent act must be subject to some form of pretrial control. An assault charge, for example, may be the result of an isolated schoolyard battle. Automobile joyriding—technically grand larceny in most jurisdictions—often is a one-time experiment. Many accused delinquents, and especially those with no prior records, can be safely and immediately released back to their families pending trial. These children need detention or supervision even less than PINS cases, who often have serious family problems which make immediate home release problematic.

It is with the children who do not need pretrial control that police and juvenile court intake workers can make their most significant contribution to reducing detention rates. Judicial intervention is important; no child should be held longer than twenty-four hours without a judicial detention hearing. To effect sweeping changes, juvenile court judges must be prepared to enforce and promulgate policies for police and intake workers to observe—policies which direct all personnel involved in the decision concerning detention to seek the least restrictive alternative in every case.

The low rates of detention already accomplished in some jurisdictions—ranging down to 5 per cent of all juveniles arrested—are testimony that effective screening is possible, but to be effective, screening must be conducted on a seven-day, twenty-four-hour basis.

Whether a right to bail does or should exist in juvenile cases is a hotly debated issue. An equivalent of the adult system's "release on own recognizance"—release into the custody of the family

—is not always possible since some youngsters accused of delinquent conduct, who would otherwise qualify for pretrial release,
have no stable family to which to return. For them, the non-
institutional alternatives should be available: temporary foster
homes and group homes.

Systems of conditional home release should also be devised, as,
for example, "pretrial juvenile probation," the assignment of an
accused delinquent to a court-affiliated caseworker early after
apprehension. If the child is released to his home, he then can be
required to report to this caseworker periodically in the interim
before hearing. The system provides supervision without detention; in some cases, it may even be the beginning of a positive
caseworker–client contact which will persist through and beyond
the juvenile court proceedings.

Jurisdictions that have the inadequate casework staff for intensive supervision may use volunteers, such as those that began
to be used in the mid-1960's in Boulder County, Colorado, and
Royal Oak, Michigan. By 1970, an estimated 10,000 unpaid local
citizens were serving as juvenile probation aides in at least 125
juvenile courts throughout the nation.[122]

An Indianapolis experiment demonstrated that a professional
probation worker can reduce the pretrial recidivism rates of juvenile clients dramatically if he is assigned a small caseload. Volunteer probation workers, specially trained and supervised by
numbers of the juvenile court staff, now teach and oversee recreation in the local juvenile detention center, and work with children
released by the court pending trial.

The "Home Detention Program" in St. Louis returns apprehended youthful offenders to their own homes, or places them in
"surrogate" group homes, when "the case is not of a notorious sort
that makes the child wholly unacceptable to the community." A
"community youth leader"—recruited from the ranks of the unemployed—takes over the case. He has no office hours and no
office and a maximum caseload of five children. The youth leaders
involve themselves intensively with the children and their families:

> In one case, for instance, one of the Youth Leaders practically
> functioned as a parent briefly, "baby sitting" with several children

122 I. Scheir and L. Goter, *Volunteers in Court: A Manual* (Youth Development and Delinquency Prevention Administration, U. S. Department of
Health, Education, and Welfare, 1972).

while the father was working and the mother was in the hospital. In another instance, the Youth Leader took a family of six in his car and drove them all to the hospital in order that the mother might give permission for medical treatment for her son. In still another case, a Youth leader, in checking on one of his boys, found him at home ill along with his brothers and sisters, in a dwelling without heat or electricity. He contacted the Welfare Agency and saw to it that the problem was properly handled.[123]

The Home Detention Program operates at a daily cost of $8.22 per child, compared to the $17.54 cost of a day's care at the St. Louis secure juvenile detention center. In the program's first six months of operation, none of the 157 boys who came under its supervision absconded; during the same six months, there were five successful escapes from the juvenile detention center. No program client committed a serious offense against a person; but five young inmates of the detention center committed serious assaults on other inmates, and another beat a staff member severely. In-home supervision can be cheaper and more effective —and more humane—than the use of secure detention.

The St. Louis program is significant in one other respect—it is a privately developed, privately operated program, conducted by a contractor to the federal Department of Health, Education, and Welfare. In developing group homes, supervision projects, diagnostic centers, and other alternatives to conventional juvenile detention, localities should be ready to rely on the expertise of private contractors for services public agencies are too sluggish or tradition-bound to provide.

There will, nevertheless, remain a residuum of "hard to place" children, who need secure detention. While sophisticated youthful offenders will have to be detained in specialized close-security facilities or even in adult jails, compulsive runaways and chronic petty offenders, often the most deprived or the most disturbed children within the juvenile court's jurisdiction, may fit none of these programs.

The model juvenile detention center envisioned by NCCD— with intensive programming, thorough diagnosis, high-quality educational services and the best possible simulation of a warm and

---

[123] Research Analysis Corporation, "Progress Report at Six Months, The Home Detention Program, St. Louis, Missouri (September 30, 1971 to March 17, 1972)" (mimeographed, 1972).

accepting atmosphere—must continue to exist for such children. But the courts must insure that such centers as remain are not allowed to degenerate into juvenile jails.

A slightly more difficult problem is presented by those youngsters who do need some form of temporary secure detention. Some communities, especially in rural areas, are unable financially to provide specialized custodial care locally for children who are accused of serious criminal offenses and are likely to flee or do real harm if not detained. Thus, they continue to rely on jails to hold unadjusted youths. One solution is the "regional detention facilities," operated by state agencies and multi-county authorities, or by individual counties which contract with others.[124] Another is the private contracting for services in the community where conditions are appropriate.

The final problem in emptying the adult jails of young people is the existence of a small percentage of prematurely sophisticated, highly dangerous criminal offenders who are "juveniles" in age only. Some of these young people would not qualify for pretrial release under even the most liberal standards now proposed for adult defendants. To confine them in specialized juvenile detention facilities, along with a heterogeneous population of less hardened youths, would subvert constructive programming by requiring a continued emphasis on high security.

They may be confined in adult jails, with the provision that the decision to detain will be subject to early, thorough, and automatic judicial review, or they may be placed in a new kind of juvenile detention facility, with severely limited capacity and intensive diagnostic services.

An end to the holding of children (excluding the small hard core referred to above) in adult jails need not await any more far-reaching reform of the juvenile justice system. Young people do not belong in jail. That goal must be accomplished now, through the strict enforcement of existing statutes, and the enactment of new prohibitory legislation where required, through centralized state administration of local jails, vigorous inspection and enforcement of jail standards and active intervention by the juvenile bench and bar.

No community should permit itself to continue jailing those

[124] For a model regional detention plan see J. Downey, "State Responsibility for Juvenile Detention Care."

children who do not need secure detention of any kind, merely because it has not devised alternatives. The children whose only real offense is need—the truant, the dependent or neglected youngster, the "incorrigible" child—will even be better off in their own inadequate home environments than behind bars in the environment of the common jail. Emptying local jails of all young prisoners accused of acts which are offenses "for children only" may actually stimulate the development of new social service approaches to their problems.

Nevertheless, faced with an influx of children into already overcrowded institutions, many detention administrators are seeking reform by more bricks and mortar. The executive director of NCCD reported that state and local governments had plans to spend more than $1 billion for new institutions by 1975. Of this amount, $177,000,000 was to go to new juvenile institutions. Yet experiences demonstrate that the more we build new buildings the more we fill them. It is easy to urge physical expansion; it is harder to develop comprehensive intake screening procedures, supervised release programs, shelter care facilities, community-based group living programs, and other non-institutional alternatives.

Lack of vision and lack of motivation complicate the future. Many detention administrators are only qualified for the jobs that now exist. Trained to run a warehouse, they now lack the background and training to supervise programs based on intensive diagnosis. If they push too hard for alternatives to institutionalization, they may eliminate their own jobs.

The NCCD has reported that by 1975, new juvenile detention facilities with a total of more than 7,000 beds will be constructed throughout the nation. Of these new beds, about 5,000 will be in separate detention homes; almost 2,000 will be in segregation wings of local jails.[125] It would be optimistic to believe that these beds will be used rarely. But optimism is not realistic. Children are the most helpless of all prisoners. Juvenile justice wears a mask of benevolence, but the practice of detaining juveniles is as resistant to permanent change as the jailing of adults.

The phenomenon, if it can be called that, which delivers poor offenders almost always, and affluent offenders almost never, to

125 NCCD Correction Survey, p. 27.

an unnecessarily expensive and unfortunately ineffective detention system is especially and glaringly destructive to young offenders. The director of a home for delinquent boys recently reported that his inmates from wealthy or middle-class families are referred there by private psychiatrists, while poor children are invariably referred by the juvenile court. The presence of both rich and poor youngsters in this home may seem to indicate that all classes of juvenile delinquents receive equal treatment; but the director's remark pointedly demonstrates the differences these youngsters encounter in their contacts with officialdom. One group was referred privately by their parents; the other group went through the stressful police, detention and juvenile court system before getting to this home. Most institutions for delinquents are awful, and poor juvenile offenders are the ones who end up in the terrible public institutions for detention which their wealthier counterparts ordinarily are able to avoid.

The 1967 President's Crime Commission reported that 90 per cent of the youth in America have done something for which they could be committed by a juvenile court. According to Sheldon and Eleanor Glueck, only 5 per cent of the children who are put in institutions for juvenile delinquency (that would be 20,000 of the 400,000 children in detention at the time of the last national crime commission survey) come from families in "comfortable circumstances."

A recent study in Contra Costa County, California, graphically illustrated this phenomenon. According to this study, 46.3 per cent of the nation's usual crop of arrested juveniles were released by the police after some informal handling and without charges being preferred. Many were simply reprimanded and released; in some cases the victim did not prefer charges, or there was insufficient evidence for a charge, or restitution was made. In California, 48.2 per cent, slightly more than the nationwide average, were released in this fashion. But an analysis of practices in the upper-middle-class suburban community of Lafayette in Contra Costa County revealed that the proportion of juveniles released after arrest was 80.8 per cent.

Correspondingly, 47.8 per cent of the juveniles arrested throughout the United States were referred to a juvenile court. In California, 46.5 per cent were referred to a juvenile court, but in

Lafayette, only 17.9 per cent. Nationwide, 6 per cent of the juveniles arrested were eventually institutionalized; in California, 5.3 per cent; in Lafayette only 1.3 per cent.

The report concludes: "These data clearly indicate that the . . . adjustment without benefit of the formal agencies of juvenile justice for middle-class suburban youth at the law enforcement level is considerably above the national and state averages." Furthermore, this process of disposing of delinquency in an informal fashion by law enforcement agencies is a phenomenon which the report said "is also found at the probation department level, and within the juvenile court structure."[126]

A recent study of 30,000 court actions in one state, substantiated by studies in other states, disclosed that juveniles who are members of racial minorities and the lower (economic) classes are especially likely to be apprehended, charged, referred, tried, adjudicated delinquents and committed. According to this report, the converse is true as well: "persons from higher socio-economic strata (but from similar sex, age, and offence categories) are more likely to receive probationary services than to be institutionalized and to receive clinical treatment services where these exist."[127]

It seems a common insight, if not a scientifically provable one, that all people transgress, but not all—in fact, very few—end up labeled and treated as criminals as a result. One study of 6,000 offenses admitted by youths in one area found that only 1.5 per cent were "brought to public attention by arrest or juvenile court hearing."

While it is arguable that poor children commit more wrongs, the discrepancy in the disposition of criminal cases may be due more particularly to the fact that upper- and middle-class families are able to deal with their children's problems privately. In fact, poor children sometimes are put in institutions for their own good regardless of the seriousness of their offense (for lack of a good home, for example), while children from prosperous backgrounds are usually released—also for their own good—even though they may have committed serious offenses.

[126] Carter, *Middle-Class Delinquency—An Experiment in Community Control* (1968) mimeographed.
[127] Vinter, "The Juvenile Court as an Institution," in President's Commission on Law Enforcement and Administration of Justice, *Task Force Report: Juvenile Delinquency and Youth Crime,* p. 87.

One writer has argued that providing alternatives that are available to people of means to poor children in trouble should be as much a matter of pragmatics as it is a clear case of equal justice.

A wholly private and unofficial system of correctional treatment has long been available to the violent scions of the socially fortunate. In every middle-class community there are psychiatrists specializing in the treatment of the errant youth of the well-heeled, frequently with the full approval of the police and judicial authorities.

Should private out-patient treatment prove inadequate, there is a nationwide network of relatively exclusive residential facilities outside the home community. Every Sunday The New York Times publishes two pages of detailed advertisements by private boarding schools catering to the needs of "exceptional youths" who are "unreachable" by means of "conventional educational methods."

It would be wrong-headed and disingenuous to cite these facts as instances of dishonest official connivance with wealth or privilege. If anything, they reflect an honest recognition that the private, unofficial treatment of offenders is vastly superior to most available public programs. Keeping children out of reformatories is a widely approved and worthy objective, irrespective of whether the children are rich or poor. The scandal lies in the fact that such alternatives are denied to the poor, through nothing more deliberate than the incidental fact of their inferior economic position. The inequity of this situation provides one of the strongest moral grounds for overcoming it. Once it is recognized that the "new" approaches advocated for the correctional treatment of all are essentially similar to those already serving the well-to-do, the ethical argument for making these services universally available becomes virtually unassailable.[128]

A recent national commission report on correction, in response to the problems of juveniles, made the following recommendations:

Each State should enact legislation by 1975 limiting the delinquency jurisdiction of the courts to those juveniles who commit acts that if committed by an adult would be crimes.

[128] Richard Korn, "Issues and Strategies of Implementation in the Use of Offenders in Resocializing Other Offenders," (Joint Commission on Correctional Manpower Resource, Washington, D.C. 1968), p. 75.

The legislation should also include provisions governing the detention of juveniles accused of delinquent conduct, as follows:

1. A prohibition against detention of juveniles in jails, lockups, or other facilities used for housing adults accused or convicted of crime.

2. Criteria for detention prior to adjudication of delinquency matters which should include the following:

a. Detention should be considered as a last resort where no other reasonable alternative is available.

b. Detention should be used only where the juvenile has no parent, guardian, custodian, or other person able to provide supervision and care for him and able to assure his presence at subsequent judicial hearings.

3. Prior to first judicial hearing, juveniles should not be detained longer than overnight.

4. Law enforcement officers should be prohibited from making the decision as to whether a juvenile should be detained. Detention decisions should be made by intake personnel and the court.

The legislation should authorize a wide variety of diversion programs as an alternative to formal adjudication. Such legislation should protect the interests of the juvenile by assuring that:

1. Diversion programs are limited to reasonable time periods.

2. The juvenile or his representative has the right to demand formal adjudication at any time as an alternative to participation in the diversion program.

3. Incriminating statements made during participation in diversion programs are not used against the juvenile if a formal adjudication follows.

Legislation, consistent with Standard 16.8 but with the following modifications, should be enacted for the disposition of juveniles:

1. The court should be able to permit the child to remain with his parents, guardian, or other custodian, subject to such conditions and limitations as the court may prescribe.

2. Detention, if imposed, should not be in a facility used for housing adults accused or convicted of crime.

3. Detention, if imposed, should be in a facility used only for housing juveniles who have committed acts that would be criminal if committed by an adult.

4. The maximum terms, which should not include extended terms, established for criminal offenses should be applicable to juveniles or youth offenders who engage in activity prohibited by

JAILS

the criminal code even though the juvenile or youth offender is
processed through separate procedures not resulting in criminal
conviction.[129]

[129] National Advisory Commission on Criminal Justice Standards and Goals,
Detention and Disposition of Juveniles, standard 16.9, p. 573 (Washington,
D.C.: LEAA).

7

REVOLUTION AND LAW REFORM IN THE JAILS

Our jails are besieged. In press reports from Boise, Idaho, to Newark, New Jersey, the same story has been dramatically told. The headlines and the copy repeat the theme. A dilapidated, antique, overcrowded jail—an incident, trivial in itself but an explosive spark under prevailing incendiary conditions, sends jail inmates on a rampage destroying property, taking hostages, making demands—a major police reaction with phalanxes of armed troopers with rifles, gas, dogs—surrender of prisoners, arrests, a public investigation, wide but short-lived press coverage, establishment promises for change—six months later, everything is back to where it all started and long-term inmate cynicism replaces short-term rage. The basic problems remain. As one commentator said after visiting New York City's jails after the riots of 1970: "Nothing has changed. It is as if the riots never happened."

Neither a planned national, political conspiracy, as some observers have charged, nor isolated peculiarities of any one locality, these episodes are part of a civil rights revolution behind bars generated by the long-time failures of jail institutions. Riots in jails can be expected to continue until fundamental reforms occur and until adequate means for redress of legitimate grievances are supplied. Jack Newfield reported the comments of one frustrated,

enraged inmate at the Manhattan Jail during the riot of 1970:
"We have no mouth and we must scream."[1]

The *Freeworld Times*[2] printed a scorecard of penal institutions,
describing some of the jail riots that occurred around the country
in the fall of 1971.

—Hundreds of inmates at the Civic Center Jail in San Jose, California, burned bedding and broke windows to complain about
overcrowding. One inmate told why: "It's the only way we can
get anybody to listen."

—Five hundred inmates at the Dallas County Jail rioted, resulting
in the death of one inmate; their purpose, to protest overcrowding,
poor food and inadequate medical care. In response, the city purchased $20,000 worth of riot control equipment.

—Ninety inmates of the Suffolk County Jail in Boston rioted to
demand that the press be admitted to the jail to observe conditions inside. The sheriff was quoted as responding: "As far as I'm
concerned they have no grievances and I have no plans to talk to
any of them. . . . We can't run our institutions if we provide a
platform for them."

—Inmates of the San Joaquin County Jail in California refused to
leave their cells for one day, demanding improved conditions,
food and recreation.

—At the Cumberland County Jail in Bridgeton, New Jersey, inmates held a peaceful sitdown demanding exercise, better mail
service and access to the public defender.

—When nineteen inmates at the Solano Jail in Fairfield, California,
broke windows and toilets and burned bedding, the sheriff refused to divulge their demands or to negotiate: "I told them we're
not going to discuss anything with them in hostility," he announced.

—At the Bexar County Jail in San Antonio, Texas, a "citizens' committee and jail inmates" complained about medical and recreational needs there and the beating to death of an inmate by another
inmate.[3] Sheriff Bill Hauck told inmates:

> "You're lucky you stopped this before I got here, or else I would
> have used some gas and let you start talking to me.
> "If you start this one more time, I'll put you on bread and water

[1] *Bread and Roses Too*, p. 335.
[2] Most of the following examples are drawn from the January 1972 issue, p. 6.
[3] San Antonio *News*, May 19, 1969; August 26, 1969; September 29, 1969.

for three days. The law says I must give you a solid meal once every 72 hours and that's exactly what I'll do.

"If you start any more trouble, and as long as you're causing trouble, you'll be eating bread and water and I'll be outside eating steak—and I believe I'll outlast you."

If they start trouble up there again, they'll sure regret it, because as long as I'm sheriff of this county, I'm going to run the jail, not the prisoners.

Later, he was quoted as saying: "No one asked those people to get in jail and that is a jail, not a hotel. They are not there for comfort and entertainment." One local official, commenting on the inmate killing, told Hauck:

I'm certainly not blaming you. You run the finest jail in the State; but you're never going to give the taxpayer full protection. I'm certainly not going to curtail services to a taxpayer to give nurse-maid service to the prisoners. They've got a better place to live there than they do at home. They fight at home and they'll fight in jail.

Ironically, often after violent public counterattacks, public officials admit the legitimacy of inmate demands.

For the second time in seven weeks, inmates of New York City's jammed-up jails mutinied last week for quicker trials, lower bail and better conditions behind bars. Rebels in four lockups—some masked with Arab-style headgear—took more than 25 hostages, smashed windows, burned bedding, hung out banners ("Help!") and rained debris into the streets. Mayor John Lindsay pleaded on TV for peace, and police counterattacked Brooklyn's jail, the most riotous, with tear gas and billies. But authorities granted that the mutineers had a case; armistice talks began—and a panel of judges convened an unheard-of bail hearing inside the walls to knock down the often exorbitant cost of freedom.[4]

When inmates at the Tombs, Manhattan's nineteenth-century jail, rioted in the summer of 1970, even the guards held hostage agreed with the legitimacy of the inmates' demands; yet reprisals were the response. Inmates at the Manhattan, Brooklyn, Long Island and Queens jails rioted to demand speedier trials and decent conditions while awaiting trial in jail. After negotiators promised no reprisals if the rioting ended, inmates released their

[4] *Newsweek,* October 12, 1970, p. 50.

hostages only to be savagely beaten. Later, many inmates were indicted for their participation in the riots.

When inmates at the D. C. Jail held guards and the city's reform-minded correction chief hostage in the fall of 1972, I participated in negotiations. All hostages were released after almost twenty-four hours of talks; but the inmates later were indicted despite promises of no reprisals. At a court hearing, inmate representatives announced their grievances. A class action lawsuit that had been brought years before this outbreak in the name of all inmates at the D. C. Jail will result in some improvements, but that case has been in court for years already. A new jail being planned is likely to repeat most of the basic deficiencies of the old one.

As arrest rates rise, as the public temper rises contemporaneously and tougher techniques and longer incarceration become more popular, as judicial backlogs postpone detained defendants' trials to intolerable levels, as the bar neglects its duties to its clients behind bars, as public monies are depleted, the dangerous temperature of our jails rises to the point of spontaneous combustion. Repressive measures add fuel to the fire.

The protesting inmates' lists of specific grievances are remarkably alike. Fundamental to them all is a desire to be treated with some measure of personal dignity. The most damaging part of imprisonment, prisoners say, is the demeaning and dehumanizing stripping away of personal identity that begins when they enter the institution's receiving room. Such treatment is especially enraging when it is applied to pretrial detainees, who compose the majority of most jail populations, and who have been convicted of nothing.

One former convict stated what has become a standard complaint:

> All inmate requests and efforts outside the standard daily prison routine are purposely made extremely difficult: adding names to the list of approved correspondents or visitors; applications for job or quarters changes; special letters to persons not on mailing lists, etc. It is often weeks or months before a simple request is answered; sometimes they are not answered at all.[5]

Correctional administrators demand broad authority free from judicial control on the basis of statutory delegations of power or

[5] Ostro, "Why U.S. Prisons Are Failing," *National Catholic Reporter,* August 27, 1969, p. 2.

the practical needs of running large custodial institutions. Statutes regulating the maintenance and care of inmates and the power of their keepers to control them are rare, and such legislative standards as do exist are for the most part vague and unenforced. Health and housing standards, for example, rarely are applied to jails.

THE "HANDS-OFF" DOCTRINE

As recently as ten years ago, courts generally denied any responsibility for supervising the treatment of jail inmates. Maintaining that separation of powers demanded this, they steadfastly refused to examine claims other than those dealing with defendants' criminal trials. Courts would look carefully at the trial; but they would forget the prisoner at the jailhouse door. Some denied that they had jurisdiction to review the management of penal institutions,[6] or that it was politically wise for them to do so in any event.

Two groups of Supreme Court cases in the 1960's contributed to a lessening of the traditional judicial reluctance to intervene in cases involving prisoners' grievances. The Court began to scrutinize various aspects of police and prosecutorial conduct that allegedly prejudiced the rights of defendants and to fashion ways to enforce these rights when law enforcement officials ignored them.[7] The Court also resurrected a nineteenth-century statute passed to enable blacks to enforce their newly granted constitutional rights against state officials. In 1961, the Court ruled that federal courts had a duty to hear claims of interference with federally protected rights by state officials brought under the federal Civil Rights Act,[8] regardless of whether the petitioners had first exhausted their state remedies.[9]

[6] E.g., *Garcia* v. *Steele,* 193 F. 2d 276, 278 (8th Cir. 1951), "The courts have no supervisory jurisdiction over the conduct of the various institutions . . ." *Dayton* v. *Hunter,* 176 F. 2d 108 (10th Cir. 1949), cert. denied, 338 U.S. 888 (1950); *Sutton* v. *Settle,* 302 F. 2d 286, 288 (8th Cir. 1962).
[7] E.g., *Miranda* v. *Arizona,* 384 U.S. 436 (1966); *Escobedo* v. *Illinois,* 378 U.S. 478 (1964); *Mapp* v. *Ohio,* 367 U.S. 643 (1961).
[8] 42 U.S.C. §1983 (1964). Federal court jurisdiction of cases based on the Civil Rights Act is based on 28 U.S.C. 1343 (1964).
[9] *Monroe* v. *Pape,* 365 U.S. 167 (1961).

The "hands-off" doctrine was used by both state and federal courts. Federal courts facing claims of state prisoners cited the need to avoid any federal–state conflict as a further rationale for declining jurisdiction. Even claims based on the violation of rights guaranteed by the federal Constitution were rejected:

> A prisoner may not approve of prison rules and regulations, but under all ordinary circumstances that is no basis for coming into a federal court seeking relief even though he may claim that the restrictions placed upon his activities are in violation of his constitutional rights.[10]

In 1964 the Court explicitly ruled that state prisoners are entitled to the protections of the Civil Rights Act,[11] but in state courts, prisoners' remedies are still quite limited,[12] despite a few notable cases involving inmates of local jails.[13]

The Warren Court, known for its liberal decisions in areas of civil rights and civil liberties generally, did little in the area of correctional reform.[14] Interestingly, Chief Justice Burger, touted as a traditionalist who would lead a more conservative court back to the old verities by strictly construing the Constitution, has spoken out about the need to attend to the correctional process and has pushed the organized bar to assume more responsibility in this area.

On the positive side, also, during the last decade the bar has begun to concern itself more responsibly with public interest law. Young lawyers, in particular, have led a movement toward reform. Foundation-funded programs, university-based organizations, OEO-sponsored groups, local public defender organizations and public interest lawyers have begun actively to pursue correctional law reform.

---

[10] "The prison system is under the administration of the Attorney General . . . and not of the district courts" (*Powell* v. *Hunter,* 172 F. 2d 330, 331 [10th Cir. 1949]).

[11] *Cooper* v. *Pate,* 378 U.S. 546 (1964) (*per curiam*).

[12] E.g., *Maryland* v. *McCray,* No. 45, Md. Court of Appeals, December 1, 1972.

[13] E.g., *Commonwealth of Pennsylvania ex rel. Bryant* v. *Hendrick,* 440 Pa. 83, 280 A. 2d 110 (1971); *Wayne County Jail Inmates* v. *Wayne County Board of Commissioners,* Civ. Action No. 173217 (Cir. Ct., Wayne County, Mich., May 18, 1971).

[14] Two exceptions are *Mempa* v. *Rhay,* 389 U.S. 128 (1967), applying due process of law requirements to the probation revocation process, and *Johnson* v. *Avery,* 393 U.S. 483 (1969), allowing inmates to use "jailhouse lawyers" when they were without adequate assistance.

The basic rights of human dignity, freedom and privacy had been presumed not to apply to prisoners. Only through years of laborious, case-by-case litigation has this presumption begun to be reversed.[15]

THE RIGHT TO BASIC NECESSITIES

Without an enforceable fundamental right to protection of his health and safety, a prisoner's other rights are meaningless. Yet even in the elemental areas of food and medical care, judges hesitate to impinge on the discretion of prison officials.[16] However, recently, a federal court of appeals ruled that a warden's withholding of all food for fifty-one hours during an apparent riot, justified a claim for deprivation of constitutional rights, and another district court invalidated the use of the traditional diet of bread and water for punishment.[17]

Recent court decisions have given prisoners an enforceable right to have their illness diagnosed and treated by a physician, and some courts have ruled that refusal by state or local authorities to provide an inmate with needed medical care is actionable under the federal Civil Rights Act.[18] Still, officials have wide discretion about what kind and how much medical treatment is required.[19]

Statutes in several states specifically authorize punishments by

[15] For an analysis of prisoners' rights cases, see Goldfarb and Singer, *After Conviction.* This chapter adapts the material in Chap. VII of *After Conviction,* which pertains to jails, adds recent developments and refers to relevant prisoners' rights cases.

[16] See *Hughes* v. *Turner,* 14 Utah 2d 128, 378 P. 2d 888 (1963); *Holt* v. *Sarver,* 300 F. Supp. 825, 832 (E.D. Ark. 1969).

[17] *Dearman* v. *Woodson,* 429 F. 2d 1288 (10th Cir. 1970); *Landman* v. *Royster,* 333 F. Supp. 621 (E.D. Va. 1971).

[18] See *Talley* v. *Stephens,* 247 F. Supp. 683 (E.D. Ark. 1965); *McCollum* v. *Mayfield,* 130 F. Supp. 112, 114–15 (N.D. Cal. 1955). But see *Gittlemacker* v. *Prasse,* 428 F. 2d 1 (3d Cir. 1970); *Owens* v. *Alldridge,* 311 F. Supp. 667 (W.D. Okla. 1970); *Willis* v. *White,* 310 F. Supp. 205 (E.D. La. 1970). *Isenberg* v. *Prasse,* 433 F. 2d 449 (3d Cir. 1970); *United States ex rel. Hyde* v. *McGinnis,* 429 F. 2d 864 (2d Cir. 1970); *Pennsylvania ex rel. Gatewood* v. *Hendrick,* 368 F. 2d 179 (3d Cir. 1966), *cert. denied,* 386 U.S. 925 (1967).

[19] A federal court has upheld a refusal by Wisconsin prison authorities to permit an inmate's use of the mails to solicit medical assistance from the Veterans Administration regarding a foot ailment that prison doctors had been unable to cure. *Goodchild* v. *Schmidt,* 279 F. Supp. 149 (E.D. Wis. 1968). See also *Willis* v. *White,* 310 F. Supp. 205 (E.D. La. 1970) (rejection of syphilitic prisoner's request for out-of-prison treatment).

prison officials, including solitary confinement, the use of chains and shackles, forfeiture of earnings, reduction in diet and the loss of statutory "good time," and corporal punishment.[20] As of 1968, administrative regulations authorized prison personnel to whip inmates in Mississippi and Arkansas. Legislation in all states but one has abolished corporal punishment as a sentence for a crime,[21] but statutes that limit the use of corporal punishment or the time an inmate can be kept in solitary confinement, can be easily circumvented. One warden of a Massachusetts jail admitted that the state's limitation of solitary confinement to ten consecutive days[22] is complied with by allowing a prisoner to leave his cellblock once before being put back for another ten-day period.

CRUEL AND UNUSUAL PUNISHMENT

Until the late 1960's, courts consistently refused to review the punishments imposed on prisoners by their keepers.

The prohibition of "cruel and unusual punishment" found in the Eighth Amendment is directly applicable to cases of prison brutality, yet the few cases in which the Supreme Court has used the Eighth Amendment to eliminate some form of criminal punishment all have been somewhat bizarre: in 1910, chaining of prisoners;[23] in 1958, penalizing a wartime deserter with the loss of his citizenship;[24] in 1962, the designation of a drug addict, who is sick, as a criminal on the ground of addiction alone.[25]

On the other hand, barbarous penalties, like sterilization, capital punishment, the civil disabilities that accompany a conviction and so on, have escaped the Court's condemnation. In one jail

[20] See *Jackson* v. *Bishop*, 404 F. 2d 571, 575 (8th Cir. 1968).
[21] See *State* v. *Cannon*, 55 Del. 587, 190 A. 2d 514 (1963), *rev'd on other grounds,* 55 Del. 597, 196 A. 2d 399 (1963).
[22] Mass. Ann. Laws ch. 127, 39–41 (1965).
[23] *Weems* v. *United States,* 217 U.S. 349 (1910).
[24] *Trop* v. *Dulles,* 356 U.S. 86 (1958). Noting the rarity of the imposition of statelessness as punishment for crime, the four concurring justices suggested that "any technique outside the bounds of these traditional penalties [fines, imprisonment and execution] is constitutionally suspect" (p. 110).
[25] *Robinson* v. *California,* 370 U.S. 660 (1962). This case marked the first time the Court ruled that the prohibitions of the Eighth Amendment apply to the states. Cf. *Powell* v. *Texas,* 392 U.S. 514 (1968).

case I tried, the district court heard about the macing and hosing of inmates of the D. C. Jail, an outrageous overreaction by guards to a jail disturbance, but refused to take any action. Courts have looked at the severity of sentences, but not the severity of their administration.

In two cases in which the Supreme Court was asked to apply the Eighth Amendment to the treatment of prisoners rather than to the statutory sentence for a crime, escaped prisoners had urged that serious prison brutality in Georgia and Alabama prisons, would make extradition a cruel and unusual punishment. The Court ordered their return on the ground that they had failed to exhaust state remedies.[26] Justice Douglas, in dissent, protested:

> [I]f the allegations of the petition are true, this Negro must suf-
> fer torture and mutilation, or risk death itself to get relief in Ala-
> bama . . . I rebel at the thought that any human being, Negro
> or white, should be forced to run a gamut of blood and terror
> in order to get his constitutional rights . . . The enlightened view
> is indeed the other way.[27]

The Court has said, however, in words that offered promise for the future: "[t]he Eighth Amendment expresses the revulsion of civilized man against barbarous acts—the 'cry of horror' against man's inhumanity to his fellow man."[28] The amendment's basic concept "is nothing less than the dignity of man. . . . [It] must draw its meaning from the evolving standards of decency that mark the progress of a maturing society."[29]

For years, lower federal courts also ruled that the Eighth Amendment does not prohibit the most brutal conditions of solitary confinement.[30] But then in 1966, in *Jordan* v. *Fitzharris*,[31]

---

[26] *Sweeny* v. *Woodall*, 344 U.S. 86 (1952); *Dye* v. *Johnson*, 338 U.S. 864 (1949) (*per curiam*). See also *Stewart* v. *State*, 475 P. 2d 600 (Ore. 1971).
[27] 344 U.S. at 92–93 (dissenting opinion).
[28] *Robinson* v. *California*, 370 U.S. 660, 676 (1962) (Douglas, J. concurring).
[29] *Trop* v. *Dulles*, 356 U.S. 86, 100–01 (1958) (separate opinion). See also *Weems* v. *United States*, 217 U.S. 349, 372–73 (1910).
[30] E.g., *Ford* v. *Board of Managers*, 407 F. 2d 937 (3d Cir. 1969); *United States ex rel. Knight* v. *Ragen*, 337 F. 2d 425 (7th Cir. 1964), *cert. denied*, 380 U.S. 985 (1965); *Williams* v. *Wilkins*, 315 F. 2d 396 (2d Cir.), *cert. denied*, 375 U.S. 852 (1963); *Roberts* v. *Pepersack*, 256 F. Supp. 415 (D. Md. 1966), *cert. denied*, 389 U.S. 877 (1967); *Roberts* v. *Barbosa*, 227 F. Supp. 20 (S.D. Cal. 1964); *Ruark* v. *Schooley*, 211 F. Supp. 921 (D. Colo. 1962); *Blythe* v. *Ellis*, 194 F. Supp. 139 (S.D. Tex. 1961). But see *Fulwood* v. *Clemmer*, 206 F. Supp. 370, 377 (D.D.C. 1962) (two years' solitary con-

a federal district judge held a full hearing at the Soledad Correctional Training Facility in California to determine the truth of a prisoner's charges that he had spent twelve days in solitary confinement in a filthy "strip" cell as punishment for a disciplinary infraction, without adequate heat, light or ventilation, without bedding, clothing, adequate medical care or any means of keeping himself clean. The court was convinced that intervention was required in this case

> [to] restore the primal rules of a civilized community in accord with the mandate of the Constitution of the United States. . . .
>
> In the opinion of the court, the type of confinement depicted in the foregoing summary of the inmates' testimony results in a slow-burning fire of resentment on the part of the inmates until it finally explodes in open revolt, coupled with their violent and bizarre conduct. Requiring man or beast to live, eat and sleep under the degrading conditions pointed out in the testimony creates a condition that inevitably does violence to elemental concepts of decency.

The court issued a permanent injunction against the imposition of cruel and unusual punishment as part of solitary confinement. Under its order, "use [of a strip cell] must be accompanied by supplying the basic requirements which are essential to life, and . . . as may be necessary to maintain a degree of cleanliness compatible with elemental decency in accord with the standards of a civilized community."[32]

A year later, the United States Court of Appeals for the Second Circuit held that if an inmate could prove he had been subjected to "debasing conditions" he would have established that his Eighth Amendment rights had been violated. An inmate said he had been kept in a strip cell for consecutive periods of thirty-three

---

finement not "reasonably related" to disturbance of prison peace); accord *Wright* v. *McMann,* 321 F. Supp. 127, 145 (N.D.N.Y. 1970) (seventeen months' segregation unconstitutionally disproportionate to offense of refusing to sign safety sheet).

[31] 257 F. Supp. 674 (N.D. Cal. 1966).

[32] The Court advised the defendants that adoption of the disciplinary practices recommended by the American Correctional Association would satisfy constitutional requirements. American Correctional Association, *Manual of Correctional Standards* (3d ed. 1966), pp. 414–15. The standards limit punitive segregation on a restrictive diet to a maximum of fifteen days and suggest that the cells be evenly heated, adequately lighted and ventilated and contain toilets, washbowls and bathing facilities.

and twenty-one days, under conditions similar to those in *Jordan v. Fitzharris;* the district court had ruled that the complaint did not sufficiently show a denial of inmate's constitutional rights and that his remedy, if any, was in the state courts. The appellate court ruled that

> civilized standards of human decency simply do not permit a man for a substantial period of time to be denuded and exposed to the bitter cold of winter in northern New York State and to be deprived of the basic elements of hygiene such as soap and toilet paper . . . [Such] subhuman conditions . . . could only serve to destroy completely the spirit and undermine the sanity of the prisoner. The Eighth Amendment forbids treatment so foul, so inhuman and so violative of basic concepts of decency.[33]

Although the Supreme Court has never considered a challenge to methods of prison discipline based on the Eighth Amendment, its unanimous action on the validity of a confession by a prisoner who had spent fourteen days in the punishment cell of a Florida prison after a prison riot may indicate the action it would take in such a case. The Court ruled that the confinement voided the confession:

> For two weeks this man's home was a barren cage fitted only with a hole in the corner into which he and his cell mates could defecate. For two weeks he subsisted on a daily fare of 12 ounces of thin soup and eight ounces of water. For two full weeks he saw not one friendly face from outside the prison, but was completely under the control and domination of his jailers. These stark facts belie any contention that the confession extracted from him within minutes after he was brought from the cell was not tainted by the 14 days he spent in such an oppressive hole . . . The record in this case documents a shocking display of barbarism which should not escape the remedial action of this Court. . . .[34]

Nevertheless, solitary confinement is an accepted method of discipline, and courts have consistently refused to rule that it

[33] The Court cited *Weems* v. *United States*, 217 U.S. 349, 378 (1910). See also *Sostre* v. *Rockefeller*, 312 F. Supp. 863 (S.D.N.Y. 1970), *aff'd in part, modified in part, rev'd in part sub nom. Sostre* v. *McGinnis*, 442 F. 2d 178 (2d Cir. 1971) (*en banc*); *Hancock* v. *Avery*, 301 F. Supp. 786 (M.D. Tenn. 1969).

[34] *Brooks* v. *Florida*, 389 U.S. 413, 414–15 (1967) (*per curiam*).

constitutes cruel and unusual punishment *per se*,[35] or, with few exceptions, that its duration must be limited to a specified period.[36] Yet solitary confinement deprives a prisoner of exercise, companionship and mental stimulation; it can be extremely severe.[37] Cruelty need not involve the infliction of bodily pain,[38] for even "enforced idleness can be cruel punishment, particularly when it is only to protect [the prisoner] from bodily harm [by his fellow prisoners]."[39]

In *Sostre* v. *Rockefeller*,[40] a New York prisoner spent thirteen months in solitary confinement. He was not permitted to use the prison library, read newspapers, see movies or attend classes. The federal district court that enjoined continuation of this form of punishment said, "the crux of the matter is human isolation—the loss of 'group privileges.'" Going beyond existing definitions of cruel and unusual punishment, which heretofore had required extreme physical conditions accompanying solitary confinement, the court found that

[35] "Solitary confinement in and of itself does not violate Eighth Amendment prohibitions, and the temporary inconveniences and discomforts incident thereto cannot be regarded as a basis for judicial relief" *Ford* v. *Board of Managers*, 407 F. 2d 937, 940 (3d Cir. 1969); Accord, *Burns* v. *Swenson*, 430 F. 2d 771, 777–78 (8th Cir. 1970). *Courtney* v. *Bishop*, 49 F. 2d 1185 (8th Cir.), *cert. denied*, 396 U.S. 915 (1969); *Abernathy* v. *Cunningham*, 393 F. 2d 775, 777 (4th Cir. 1968); *Graham* v. *Willingham*, 384 F. 2d 367 (10th Cir. 1967); *Holt* v. *Sarver*, 300 F. Supp. 825, 827 (E.D. Ark. 1969); see *Stroud* v. *Johnston*, 139 F. 2d 171 (9th Cir. 1943) (confinement of the "Bird Man of Alcatraz" in an isolation cell for life accepted as within the range of administrative discretion); cf. *Ray* v. *Neil*, Civ. No. 5590 (M.D. Tenn., order entered, December 29, 1969) (warden ordered to permit James Earl Ray some time out of his isolation cell for recreation, work and exercise).
[36] *Sostre* v. *McGinnis*, 442 F. 2d 178 (2d Cir. 1971) (*en banc*); *Beishir* v. *Swenson*, 331 F. Supp. 1227 (W.D. No. 1971).
[37] In the most recent edition of its *Manual of Correctional Standards* (1966), p. 413, the American Correctional Association stated:
> Perhaps we have been too dependent on isolation or solitary confinement as the principal method of handling the violators of institutional rules. Isolation may bring short-term conformity for some, but brings increased disturbances and deeper grained hostility to more.
[38] *Weems* v. *United States*, 217 U.S. 349, 372–73 (1910).
[39] *Ray* v. *Neil*, Civ. No. 5590 (M.D. Tenn., order entered, December 29, 1969). See also *Davis* v. *Lindsay*, 321 F. Supp. 1134 (S.D.N.Y. 1970) (segregation of detainee because of her notoriety violates her right to equal protection despite availability of same facilities given rest of the jail population).
[40] 312 F. Supp. 863 (S.D.N.Y. 1970).

punitive segregation . . . is physically harsh, destructive of
morale, dehumanizing in the sense that it is needlessly degrading,
and dangerous to the maintenance of sanity when continued for
more than a short period of time which should certainly not exceed fifteen days. . . .

Subjecting a prisoner to the demonstrated risk of the loss of his
sanity as punishment for any offense in prison is plainly cruel and
unusual punishment as judged by present standards of decency.

The court of appeals reversed.[41] It said that prolonged segregation might be "counterproductive as a correctional measure and
personally abhorrent," but the conditions in this case, which included rudimentary implements of personal hygiene, a reasonable
diet and the opportunity for daily outdoor exercise and communication with other prisoners, were "several notches above those
truly barbarous and inhumane conditions" previously found cruel
and unusual. The court noted the absence of any testimony that
the confinement threatened the prisoner's physical or mental health
and pointed out that a physician visited him daily. It refused to
place an upper limit on the duration of the punishment; the continued confinement in this case could have been ended by the
prisoner's agreement to abide by institutional rules.

This decision has been relied on in subsequent cases, as authority for declining to interfere with segregation imposed as punishment on pretrial detainees in local jails.[42] The even greater
claim of the unconvicted defendant to be free from such severe
punishment has been all but ignored.

At the opposite extreme from isolation is the punishment inherent in the inhuman overcrowding that plagues so many local
jails.

The court in *Holt* v. *Sarver* was the first to go beyond standards
set by correctional administrators and enforce the policies underlying the prohibition against cruel and unusual punishment in ruling that overcrowded prison conditions ran afoul of the Constitution:

Without undertaking to state with specificity the exact point at
which one of the isolation cells becomes "overcrowded" rather
than simply "crowded" . . . the Court finds that the cells have
been chronically overcrowded . . .

[41] *Sostre* v. *McGinnis*, 442 F. 2d 178 (2d Cir. 1971) (*en banc*).
[42] E.g., *Clements* v. *Hamilton*, No. 7001 (W.D. Ky., May 3, 1972).

[T]here are limits to the rigor and discomfort of close confinement which a State may not constitutionally exceed. . . . [T]he prolonged confinement of numbers of men in the same cell under the conditions that have been described is mentally and emotionally traumatic as well as physically uncomfortable. It is hazardous to health. It is degrading and debasing; it offends modern sensibilities, and, in the Court's estimation, amounts to cruel and unusual punishment.[43]

In several recent cases, indignant courts have ordered an end to overcrowded and unsanitary conditions in jails and detention centers. One federal district court ordered the immediate release of the inmates who had served the longest terms in order to reduce the number of confined prisoners.[44] Other federal courts have ordered relief, based on the Eighth Amendment, from overcrowding, lack of light, sanitation, ventilation, exercise or adequate supervision, in jails in New Orleans,[45] Little Rock,[46] Detroit[47] and two California counties.[48] One of the district judges, who actually visited the jail in question, said he had come

to the inescapable conclusion that Greystone should be razed to the ground. Confinement in cells at Greystone, under the almost unbelievable conditions which prevail there, offends elemental concepts of decency and is of such shocking and debasing character as to constitute cruel and unusual punishment for man or beast.[49]

A state court ordered two pretrial detainees transferred out of the Holmesburg Prison in Philadelphia, where conditions were termed "an affront to the dignity of man" and outside "the limits of civilized standards." Authorities had thirty days to correct the most flagrant abuses; after that, the court presumably would act on similar petitions.[50]

[43] 300 F. Supp. 825, 833 (E.D. Ark. 1969).
[44] *Curley* v. *Gonzales,* Civ. No. 8372 (D.N.M., February 13, 1970).
[45] *Hamilton* v. *Schiro,* 338 F. Supp. 1016 (E.D. La. 1970).
[46] *Hamilton* v. *Love,* 328 F. Supp. 1182 (E.D. Ark. 1971).
[47] *Wayne County Jail Inmates* v. *Wayne County Board of Commissioners,* Civ. Action No. 173217 (Cir. Ct., Wayne County, Mich., May 18, 1971).
[48] *Brenneman* v. *Madigan,* 343 F. Supp. 128 (N.D. Cal. 1971); *Dean* v. *Young,* No. 123849 (N.D. Cal., March 17, 1971).
[49] *Brenneman* v. *Madigan* at 4. See also *Anderson* v. *Nosser,* 438 F. 2d 183 (5th Cir. 1971) (conditions of pretrial detention of racial protest demonstrators at the Parchman State Prison in Mississippi).
[50] *Commonwealth of Pennsylvania ex rel. Bryant* v. *Hendrick,* No. 1567

Recent scientific studies have shown that marked, demonstrable physiological and psychological damage is done to animals isolated for prolonged periods or overcrowded beyond permissible territorial imperatives. Studies in "sensory deprivation," where men were placed in dark, soundproofed, but comfortable rooms, have demonstrated that confinement resulted in definite biochemical and neurological changes of an indefinite duration. It is likely that forced and uncomfortable solitary confinement or overcrowding may have similar drastic effects. In the D. C. Jail case,[51] this line of evidence was developed through expert witnesses. When untried detainees are involved, any conditions beyond those necessary to ensure presence at trial are subject to challenge as punishment without due process of law, forbidden by the Fifth and Fourteenth Amendments, as well as under the more stringent Eighth Amendment standard. In *Jones* v. *Wittenberg,* the court stated: "[Detainees] are not to be subject to any hardship except those absolutely requisite for the purpose of confinement only, and they retain all the rights of an ordinary citizen except the right to go and come as they please."[52]

In *Lollis* v. *New York State Department of Social Services,*[53] a court faced with a challenge to the solitary confinement of a fourteen-year-old girl in an unfurnished "strip room" at a New York training school relied heavily on the opinions of several experts in adolescent psychology concerning the harmful effects of such confinement. One witness warned of the danger in prolonged exposure to sensory deprivation—"a state of affairs which will cause a normal adult to begin experiencing psychoticlike symptoms, and will push a troubled person in the direction of serious emotional illness. . . . [I]solation is a condition of extraordinarily severe psychic stress; the resultant impact on the mental health of the individual exposed to such stress will always be serious, and

---

(Court of Common Pleas for Philadelphia County, August 11, 1970), *aff'd* 440 Pa. 83, 280 A. 2d 110 (1971). See also *Jackson* v. *Hendrick,* 11 *Criminal Law Reporter* 2088 (Philadelphia Court of Common Pleas, April 7, 1972) (Philadelphia's entire penal system violates Eighth, Fourteenth, First and Sixth Amendments).

[51] *Campbell* v. *Rogers,* Civ. Action No. 1462–71 (U. S. District Court for the District of Columbia).

[52] 323 F. Supp. 93 (N.D. Ohio 1971). See also *Tyler* v. *Ciccone,* 299 F. Supp. 684 (W.D. Mo. 1969); *Anderson* v. *Nosser, Hamilton* v. *Love, Brenneman* v. *Madigan, Commonwealth of Pennsylvania ex rel. Bryant* v. *Hendrick, supra.*

[53] 322 F. Supp. 473 (S.D.N.Y. 1970).

can occasionally be disastrous." The court ruled that the confinement violated the Eighth Amendment's ban on cruel and unusual punishment.

Corporal Punishment. Disciplining prisoners by the use of any corporal punishment—beating, torturing and so on—is prohibited by statute, administrative regulation or court decision[54] in the federal and in practically every state penal system. Yet corporal punishment is common in the nation's prisons and jails.

After the September 1971 uprising and taking of hostages at New York's Attica prison, prisoners sought a federal court injunction against further physical reprisals by guards. Prisoners and one National Guardsman testified that

> . . . beginning immediately after the State's recapture of Attica on the morning of September 16, guards, state troopers and correctional personnel had engaged in cruel and inhuman abuse of numerous inmates. Injured prisoners, some on stretchers, were struck, prodded or beaten with sticks, belts, bats or other weapons. Others were forced to strip and run naked through gauntlets of guards armed with clubs which they used to strike the bodies of the inmates as they passed. Some were dragged on the ground, some marked with an "X" on their backs, some spat upon or burned with matches, and others poked in the genitals or arms with sticks.[55]

Despite its acceptance of the testimony for the purposes of its decision, the district court denied the injunction because of the assurances of prison authorities that the reprisals would not continue.

The court of appeals reversed, holding that "even if some corporal punishment may be permitted under the Constitution, the mistreatment of the inmates in this case amounted to cruel and unusual punishment in violation of their Eighth Amendment rights." In the circumstances, the appellate court was not satisfied with the officials' assurances, in the absence of further proof:

> If the abusive conduct of the prison guards had represented a single or short-lived incident, unlikely to recur, or if other correc-

---

[54] See *Talley* v. *Stephens,* 247 F. Supp. 683 (E.D. Ark. 1965); *Jackson* v. *Bishop,* 404 F. 2d 571 (8th Cir. 1968).
[55] *Inmates of Attica Correctional Facility* v. *Rockefeller,* 453 F. 2d 12 (2 Cir. 1971).

tive measures had been taken to guarantee against repetition, injunctive relief might be denied, despite the heinous character of the conduct. . . .

Here, however, the conduct of some of the prison guards, state police and correctional personnel, as testified to, was not only brutal but it extended over a period of at least several days, with one serious incident occurring much later.[56]

After the New York City jail riots of the summer of 1971, inmates charged that they had been promised no reprisals if they would stop their rioting and surrender; but they were beaten by guards as they emerged from the riot scene. In negotiating the release of hostages and an end to a disturbance at the D. C. Jail, the first concern of the inmates involved was a promise of no reprisal. The commissioner of corrections and a federal district court judge both ordered that there be no reprisals and the public defender service monitored the jail in the aftermath of the negotiated peace.

Prisoners who are beaten by guards or subjected to other sadistic forms of punishment should be permitted to bring legal action under statutes forbidding corporal punishment. However, statutes providing criminal sanctions may preclude civil suits by injured prisoners,[57] and prosecutors are likely to be reluctant to prosecute fellow officials. A civil action for damages or for an injunction, predicated on the standards dictated by the Eighth Amendment, may provide the only realistic and effective remedy.[58]

Every prisoner has a right to be free from violence, including sexual threats or assaults. Brutalities from officials or inmates, nevertheless, continue free from interference. Particularly in institutions where inmates stay for short periods of time and there is frequent turnover in population, inmates are subject to almost constant threat of physical or sexual attack by other inmates.[59] This is a fact of life in all jails.

In one unusual case, however, a federal court refused to ex-

[56] *Gonzales* v. *Rockefeller,* 10 *Criminal Law Reporter* 2227 (2d Cir., December 1, 1971).
[57] Cf. *Ridgway* v. *Superior Court,* 74 Ariz. 117, 122, 245 P. 2d 268, 272 (1952).
[58] See *Jackson* v. *Bishop,* 404 F. 2d 571 (8th Cir. 1968).
[59] See, e.g., *Holt* v. *Sarver,* 309 F. Supp. 362, 377 (E.D. Ark. 1970), *aff'd* 442 F. 2d 304 (8th Cir. 1971).

tradite an escaped prisoner to Georgia[60] because it was shown to be ". . . the custom of the Georgia authorities to treat chain-gang prisoners with persistent and deliberate brutality [and] that Negro prisoners were treated with a greater degree of brutality than white prisoners."

Unfortunately, legal remedies in this area are rare. Jailers have been held liable for failure to take reasonable steps to protect in-mates from beatings or sexual attacks by other prisoners.[61] How-ever, such remedies rarely compensate the victim or protect him from further attack; indeed, any action he takes against other stronger or more sophisticated prisoners is likely to bring retalia-tion. Inmates who request maximum security confinement for their own protection, must suffer the same loss of privileges as prisoners in maximum security as punishment. A federal court of appeals recently ruled that such "voluntary" deprivations are not forbidden by the Constitution, despite a strong dissent questioning why a prisoner "must choose between a reasonably safe life more miserable than that of other well-behaved prisoners and the risk of serious physical injury and death?"[62]

In a few cases, prison and jail officials have been held liable in damages for negligently failing to protect prisoners from injuries by other prisoners.[63] But the right to bring a future damage suit does not protect a prisoner. Some attorneys petitioned for the release of prisoners whom officials have been unable to keep safe from attack, and in a few reported instances, judges have ordered untried prisoners released from jail[64]—or transferred to another

[60] *Johnson* v. *Dye,* 175 F. 2d (3rd Cir.), *rev'd per curiam on other grounds,* 338 U.S. 864 (1949).
[61] *Ratliff* v. *Stanley,* 224 Ky. 819, 7 S.W. 2d 230 (1928); *Hixon* v. *Cupp,* 5 Okla., 545, 49 P. 927 (1897); *Riggs* v. *German,* 81 Wash. 128, 142 P. 479 (1914); see also *United States* v. *Muniz,* 374 U.S. 150 (1963); *Whitree* v. *State,* 56 Misc. 2d 693, 290 N.Y.S. 2d 486 (Ct. Cl. 1968); but see *Adams* v. *Pate,* 445 F. 2d 105 (7th Cir. 1971).
[62] *Braden* v. *Jackson,* No. 71–1400, 4th Cir., March 21, 1972 (Craven, J., dis-senting).
[63] In *Roberts* v. *Williams,* 302 F. Supp. 972 (N.D. Miss. 1969), *aff'd 9 Crim-inal Law Reporter* 2052 (5th Cir., April 1, 1971), a claim by a prisoner against the prison official who permitted an inmate trusty to handle a shotgun which discharged and injured the plaintiff was ruled actionable under the federal Civil Rights Act. According to the court, callous indifference on the part of officials toward the safety of prisoners may constitute cruel and un-usual punishment even where there is no specific intent to inflict harm.
[64] New York *Times,* September 28, 1968, p. 65.

jail[65] for their own safety. A young defendant who was detained in the Philadelphia jail prior to his trial was ordered released by Court of Common Pleas judge Alexander F. Barbieri, in an unpublished order dated September 26, 1968, when the judge found that prison authorities had been unable to protect him from ten homosexual attacks. The district attorney agreed that keeping the defendant in jail under these circumstances would constitute cruel and unusual punishment.

In *Holt* v. *Sarver*,[66] a federal district judge agreed to permit a suit on behalf of all the inmates of the Cummins Farm Unit of the Arkansas State Penitentiary. Prisoners complained that most were housed in open barracks, patrolled only by inmate "floorwalkers," who were ineffective in preventing nighttime assault. The court recognized a constitutional right of prisoners to a reasonable degree of protection by the state while they are incarcerated:

> It is plain . . . that the State must refrain from imposing cruel and unusual punishments on its convicts. . . .
> [T]he State owes to those whom it has deprived of their liberty an even more fundamental constitutional duty to use ordinary care to protect their lives and safety while in prison . . .

The court noted the inadequate resources that the state had allocated to its prison farms; yet it ordered the commissioner of corrections generally to allocate the department's limited resources in such a way that there would be a substantial start toward alleviating the unsafe conditions.

Few prisons or jails provide even minimum precautions necessary for the safety of the inmates without judicial intervention. Nor have legislatures traditionally shown readiness to provide the authority or the funds for basic institutional changes. Many courts have deferred taking even modest progressive steps towards requiring protection of inmates' safety, usually on separation-of-powers grounds. Simple changes, giving each prisoner an individual room or cell, or hiring more guards, have been denied because they would cost more money than legislators have ap-

[65] *Commonwealth of Pennsylvania, ex rel. Bryant* v. *Hendrick, aff'd* 440 Pa. 83. 280 A. 2d 110 (1971). The court noted that the petitioners' lives were in danger at Holmesburg. See also *State of West Virginia ex rel. Pingley* v. *Coiner*, H.C. No. 70–181 (Cir. Ct. of Randolph County, May 6, 1971), *rev'd* 186 S.E. 2d 220 (1972).
[66] 300 F. Supp. 825 (E.D. Ark. 1969).

propriated for correction or detention.[67] Remedial steps might "disrupt the Penitentiary or leave [prison authorities] helpless to deal with dangerous and unruly convicts."[68]

In a suit by inmates of the New Orleans Parish Prison, a federal district court ordered New Orleans city officials to correct unsafe conditions at the city jail despite its finding that the sheriff responsible for the jail was "doing the best he can with the facilities and means available to him."[69] A federal judge presented with the results of inspections of a county jail in Georgia by the state fire marshal and the county Board of Health pronounced the jail "unfit for human habitation" and ordered that no prisoners be housed there starting eight months after the order. In the interim, the jail population was severely curtailed and its upper floor condemned.[70]

If prisoners are to realize the potential scope of Eighth Amendment protections, other common prison and jail practices should be challenged as cruel and unusual punishment. Chief among these are the denial of heterosexual relations, the requirement that pretrial detainees may not work and that the prisoners work for little or no pay, and the warehousing of prisoners with no attempt at rehabilitation.

Long, enforced sexual abstinence, especially among young people, is a cruel and unnecessary form of punishment, and the refusal to allow married prisoners sexual relations with their wives must increase their alienation and the disruptive effect of imprisonment on family life. To date, no court has ruled that a prisoner has a right to sexual relations while he is in prison, and somewhat surprisingly, apparently no prisoner has attempted to obtain such a ruling.[71] While there is some question about whether convicted prisoners may lawfully be deprived of these rights, there should be no question where unconvicted detainees are concerned. Pretrial

---

[67] Cf. *Upchurch* v. *State,* 51 Hawaii 150, 152; 454 P. 2d 112, 114 (1969). While recognizing that the state legislature might be at fault for failing to appropriate the funds needed for a modern prison, the court refused to find the state liable on that theory.

[68] *Holt* v. *Sarver,* 300 F. Supp. 825, 833 (E.D. Ark. 1969).

[69] *Hamilton* v. *Schiro,* C.A. No. 69–2443 (E.D. La., June 25, 1970).

[70] *Hodge* v. *Dodd,* No. 16171 (N.D. Ga., May 2, 1972).

[71] In one case a wife tried unsuccessfully to obtain a court order allowing her conjugal visits with her incarcerated husband. *Payne* v. *District of Columbia,* 253 F. 2d 867 (D.C. Cir. 1958) (*per curiam*).

defendants theoretically are not in jail to be punished; therefore, there is no rationale for denying them normal social contacts.

LABOR

Prisoners from Georgia and Arkansas penitentiaries recently claimed that forced labor, performed for the economic benefit of the state, violates the Thirteenth Amendment's ban on slavery and involuntary servitude. However, since the Thirteenth Amendment specifically exempts work done as "punishment for crime" it appears to offer little hope to prison inmates.

Requiring prisoners to work without due compensation may, however, be argued as constituting cruel and unusual punishment prohibited by the Eighth Amendment. Enlightened prison administrators feel that prisoners should be paid at least the minimum wage and then be required to pay for their room, board and any extra food and personal items they care to purchase in prison, and to contribute to the support of their dependents. Under this system, the families of prison inmates could be taken off public welfare. More important, the self-supporting inmates would have more self-respect and a sense of responsibility.

The convicted inmate may be in a jail on a work or school release program while he serves out his sentence; he stays in the jail at night to sleep and eat, or he may be employed at the jail in housekeeping. But jail inmates awaiting trial may not work, according to the prevailing rationale, because they have not been convicted. They are forced to be idle, perhaps a worse fate than forced labor.

Warehousing: Right to Rehabilitation. Two recent prisoners' rights cases have raised a novel and potentially explosive legal question: Can a state incarcerate a convicted criminal without making any effort to rehabilitate him? Arkansas prisoners sought, with some success, an injunction prohibiting prison officials from incarcerating them "without providing meaningful rehabilitative opportunities" and requiring the authorities "to formulate and implement a plan of rehabilitation including adequate vocational, educational, medical and other programs for all inmates of the

institutions operated by defendants."[72] In Georgia, prisoners unsuccessfully sought a judicial declaration that sentencing convicts
to county work camps, where no effort was made to rehabilitate
them, constituted cruel and unusual punishment.[73]

The notion of a right to rehabilitation seems to have arisen as
a concomitant of the developing "right to treatment"[74] in the area
of civil commitment.[75]

There are substantial problems in applying the "right to treatment" rationale to prison inmates. Unlike foreign criminal codes,
which frequently specify rehabilitation as a central purpose of imprisonment, American criminal statutes give little guidance as to
the overall policy reasons for incarcerating criminals. According
to the American Correctional Association, whose statement of
the purposes of the prison system is widely accepted (on paper),
the purpose of rehabilitation is basic to our entire correctional
system. However, the only judge to have considered the question
refused to adopt the primacy of rehabilitation:

> In years past many people have felt, and many still feel, that a
> criminal is sent to the penitentiary to be punished for his crimes
> and to protect the public from his further depredations. Under
> that view, while there is no objection to rehabilitation, it is not
> given any priority. . . .
>
> Given an otherwise unexceptional penal institution, the Court
> is not willing to hold that confinement in it is unconstitutional
> simply because the institution does not operate a school, or pro-

[72] *Holt* v. *Sarver*, 309 F. Supp. 362, 364 (E.D. Ark. 1970), *aff'd* 442 F. 2d
304 (8th Cir. 1971).
[73] *Wilson* v. *Kelley*, 294 F. Supp. 1005, 1012 (N.D. Ga. 1968), *aff'd per
curiam*, 393 U.S. 266 (1969): "[A] work camp per se does not constitute such
'inhuman, barbarous or torturous punishment' as to violate the Eighth Amendment."
[74] The phrase "right to treatment" first was used by Birnbaum, "The Right to
Treatment," 46 *A.B.A.J.* 499 (1960). See also editorial, "A New Right," 46
A.B.A.J. 516 (1960).
[75] See *Rouse* v. *Cameron*, 373 F. 2d 451, 453, 455 (D.C. Cir. 1966). The
court intimated that even if there had been no applicable statute, it might
have found a constitutional right to treatment. *Nason* v. *Superintendent of
Bridgewater State Hospital*, 353 Mass. 604, 233 N.E. 2d 908 (1968). The
patient had sought a transfer to a different institution, where treatment would
be available. *Whitree* v. *New York*, 56 Misc. 2d 693, 290 N.Y.S. 2d 486 (Ct.
Cl. 1968). *People ex rel. Ceschini* v. *Warden*, 30 App. Div. 2d 649, 291
N.Y.S. 2d 200 (1968) (*per curiam*).

vide vocational training, or other rehabilitative facilities and services which many institutions now offer.[76]

There is no agreement even among experts on what constitutes correctional "treatment." Is it a series of "group therapy" sessions run without professional participation or supervision? Is it vocational training on outdated machinery? A totally therapeutic community? Or can any effort to impel prisoners to engage in some useful activity, even if only to perform janitorial services, be termed "treatment"?

Experts also have questioned the value of treatment programs in correctional institutions:

> [T]reatment may *not* be humanitarian . . . treatment may be an invasion of civil rights . . . treatment may be harmful . . . [B]efore one decides on treating a person, even a convicted criminal, one must consider whether leaving him alone may not be better, better for him and better for society . . .
>
> I agree [that a right to treatment] is an important right, and it must become a protection for individuals. But it must *not* become a cover for depriving people of their liberty . . .
>
> [W]e freely commit people and call it treatment.[77]

It could be argued that prisoners should be accorded a constitutional right to treatment. At a minimum, this should include for each prisoner the development of a rehabilitative plan designed to develop his talents and meet his particular needs. Plans might encompass schooling, professional or vocational training, medical or psychiatric attention and provision for earning money to support dependents. The treatment rhetoric should not be used to deny prisoners their liberty unnecessarily or paradoxically to deprive them of their constitutional rights.

[76] *Holt* v. *Sarver*, 309 F. Supp. 362, 379 (E.D. Ark. 1970), *aff'd* 442 F. 2d 304 (8th Cir. 1971).

[77] "The Illusion of Treatment in Sentences and Civil Commitments," address by Sol Rubin at the University of South Carolina, March 29, 1968, printed with changes at 16 *Crime and Delinquency* 79 (1970). See also President's Commission on Law Enforcement and Administration of Justice, *Task Force Report: Correction*, pp. 58–59:

> There is a decided danger that the existence of special facilities will imply a comparable existence of special expertise encouraging society to shuffle off on correctional institutions problems that should be dealt with elsewhere. There are many indications that this has been the result, for example, of schools for defective delinquents and programs for sexual psychopaths.

The right to treatment would not apply to pretrial detainees in jails except implicitly in underscoring their rights not to be subjected to anti-rehabilitative or grossly punitive incarceration. However, for the sentenced jail inmate, who often is young, a minor offender, an alcoholic or addict, arguments are strongest that there should be a positive program available for their period of detention.

Cumulative Effect of Unconstitutional Conditions. In 1970 a federal district judge in Arkansas, rather than limiting his decision to a consideration of specific abuses practiced on particular prisoners, ruled that conditions in the Arkansas system, including a delegation of authority over prisoners to armed trusty inmates, the physical danger to prisoners from trusties and other inmates in the open barracks and the complete absence of efforts to rehabilitate the inmates confined there, made it cruel and unusual punishment to sentence anyone to an Arkansas prison:

> After long and careful consideration the Court has come to the conclusion that the Fourteenth Amendment prohibits confinement under the conditions that have been described and that the Arkansas Penitentiary System as it exists today, particularly at Cummins, is unconstitutional. . . .
>
> It is one thing for the State to send a man to the Penitentiary as a punishment for crime. It is another thing for the State to delegate the governance of him to other convicts, and to do nothing meaningful for his safety, well being, and possible rehabilitation. It is one thing for the State not to pay a convict for his labor; it is something else to subject him to a situation in which he has to sell his blood to obtain money to pay for his own safety, or for adequate food, or for access to needed medical attention.[78]

This far-reaching decision establishes the precedent that, while specific and sometimes trivial conditions may not in themselves be outlawed on constitutional grounds, together they may be sufficient to convince a court that an entire correctional system is constitutionally deficient. It has had a far-reaching effect on decisions condemning jails, and is the most frequently cited precedent for

[78] *Holt* v. *Sarver*, 309 F. Supp. 362, 381 (E.D. Ark. 1970), *aff'd* 442 F. 2d 304 (8th Cir. 1971).

the all-encompassing orders by federal judges concerning both the physical facilities and the procedures used in local jails.

CIVIL RIGHTS IN JAIL

A number of judicial decisions have concluded that constitutionally protected civil liberties also apply—at least to some extent —to people in jail. They have responded to inmate claims to the right to practice a religion, to be free from racial discrimination, to communicate freely, to vote, to enjoy privacy and to have the parallel rights with others when they are accused of crimes. In large institutions with special problems of discipline, special constraints on liberty apply; still, the courts in dealing with such cases have relied heavily on precedents in cases brought by free men.

Religion. The courts were first impelled to abandon their "hands-off" attitude in the area of religious freedom, "one of the fundamental 'preferred' freedoms guaranteed by the Constitution,"[79] and one regarded as serving "the rehabilitative function by providing an area within which the inmate may reclaim his dignity and reassert his individuality."[80] Government provides prisoners with chapels, ministers, free sacred texts; nevertheless a danger exists that "prison personnel will demand from inmates the same obeisance in the religious sphere that more rightfully they may require in other aspects of prison life."

Courts distinguish between a prisoner's absolute right to religious beliefs[81] and his qualified right to engage in religious practices.[82] Much of the litigation involving religion in jail has

---

[79] *Pierce* v. *LaValle,* 293 F. 2d 233, 235 (2d Cir. 1961).

[80] *Barnett* v. *Rodgers,* 410 F. 2d 995, 1002 (D.C. Cir. 1969). See also *Brown* v. *Peyton,* 437 F. 2d 1228, 1230 (4th Cir. 1971): "One of the principal purposes of incarceration is rehabilitation and rehabilitation is a moral and intellectual process. Criminals and prison communities may be benefitted by the free exercise of religion."

[81] E.g., *Pierce* v. *LaValle,* 293 F. 2d 233, 235 (2d Cir. 1961); *Sewell* v. *Pegelow,* 291 F. 2d 196 (4th Cir. 1961).

[82] "Within the prison society as well as without, the practice of religious beliefs is subject to reasonable regulations, necessary for the protection and welfare of the community involved" (*Long* v. *Parker,* 390 F. 2d 816, 820 [3d Cir. 1968]).

revolved about the question of what restrictions on religious practices are reasonable in the institutional setting. Some courts have
deferred to the opinions of prison authorities[83] on the reasonable-
ness of restrictions on religious practices. Others demand "reasons
imperatively justifying the particular retraction of rights."[84]

Although some courts have disagreed, prisoners generally have
been permitted to receive religious literature unless the authorities
can prove to the satisfaction of the court that the literature creates
a "clear and present danger" to discipline.[85]

The equal protection principle has been applied to small or less
conventional groups,[86] with many states providing chaplains,
chapel facilities and even religious medals. State statutes or administrative regulations prohibiting racial or religious discrimination or granting inmates the right to hold religious services in
prison chapels must be applied to all religious groups, some courts
have held.[87] Since it may not always be practical for officials to
treat members of all religious groups with strict equality, exceptions have been allowed, but only when reasonable. For example,
a state need not provide a full-time chaplain for every denomina-

[83] *Abernathy* v. *Cunningham*, 393 F. 2d 775, 779 (4th Cir. 1968) (prison
officials may prohibit the receipt of Black Muslim publications).
[84] *Barnett* v. *Rodgers*, 410 F. 2d 995, 1001 (D.C. Cir. 1969) (jail officials must
make an effort to accommodate dietary restrictions of Black Muslim prisoners).
[85] *Long* v. *Parker*, 390 F. 2d 816, 822 (3d Cir. 1968); cf. *Knuckles* v. *Prasse*,
435 F. 2d 1255 (3d Cir. 1970) (Black Muslim literature could constitute
clear and present danger to institution); *Walker* v. *Blackwell*, 411 F. 2d 23,
29 (5th Cir. 1969); *Brown* v. *Peyton*, 437 F. 2d 1228 (4th Cir. 1971); but
see *Abernathy* v. *Cunningham*, 393 F. 2d 775 (4th Cir. 1968).
[86] But see *Jones* v. *Willingham*, 248 F. Supp. 791, 794 (D. Kan. 1965), where
the court ruled that a warden's actions in refusing to allow Muslims the same
privileges given members of other religious faiths was not arbitrary, capricious
or unlawful. In fact, the warden "not only was fully justified in imposing on
the plaintiff and others professing Muslim beliefs the restrictions of which
the plaintiff now complains, but it was his duty to so act."
[87] *Sewell* v. *Pegelow*, 291 F. 2d 196 (4th Cir. 1961), *appeal dismissed per
stipulation*, 304 F. 2d 670 (4th Cir. 1962); *Fulwood* v. *Clemmer*, 206 F. Supp.
370 (D.D.C. 1962); *Shaw* v. *McGinnis*, 14 N.Y. 2d 864, 200 N.E. 2d 636
(1964); *Brown* v. *McGinnis*, 10 N.Y. 2d 531, 180 N.E. 2d 791, 225 N.Y.S. 2d
497 (1962).
Others have reached similar conclusions on the constitutional grounds of
freedom of religion and equal protection of the laws.
E.g., *Cooper* v. *Pate*, 378 U.S. 546 (1964); *Long* v. *Parker*, 390 F. 2d 816
(3d Cir. 1968); *Northern* v. *Nelson*, 315 F. Supp. 687 (N.D. Cal. 1970);
Delaware ex rel. Tate v. *Cubbage*, 210 A. 2d 555 (Del. 1965); but see *Gittlemacker* v. *Prasse*, 428 F. 2d 1 (3d Cir. 1970).

tion,[88] but a group may not be denied the right to hold its own religious services because it is not recognized."[89]

In the past decade, many religious-freedom claims have concerned Black Muslims. Religious beliefs, like political doctrines of black racial supremacy, were not originally deemed protected by the First Amendment.[90]

One federal court of appeals dismissed complaints that Muslim prisoners were subjected to a diet that offended their religious practices.[91] The Muslim religion forbids all consumption of pork and requires special foods and mealtimes during the month of December (Ramadan). Yet when Muslims in the District of Columbia Jail complained that two thirds of their meals contained pork, the Court of Appeals for the District of Columbia said:[92]

> There is no finding as to whether any particular "considerations underlying our penal system" warrant the tax on conscience that the jail's food service policies require appellants to endure. Nor is there a finding as to whether that program could not be administered in such a way as to lighten or eliminate its burden on free religious exercise. . . .
>
> Certainly if this concession is feasible from the standpoint of prison management, it represents the bare minimum that jail authorities, with or without specific request, are constitutionally required to do, not only for Muslims but indeed for any group of inmates with religious restrictions on diet.[93]

[88] *Gittlemacker* v. *Prasse,* 428 F. 2d 1 (3d Cir. 1970); see *Rockey* v. *Krueger,* 306 N.Y.S. 2d 359 (Sup. Ct. 1969) (W.D. Mo. 1968); cf. *Sharp* v. *Sigler,* 408 F. 2d 966 (8th Cir. 1969).
[89] *Theriault* v. *Carlson,* 339 F. Supp. 375 (N.D. Ga. 1972) order, 353 F. Supp. 1061 (N.D. Ga. 1973).
[90] *In re Ferguson,* 55 Cal. 2d 663, 361 P. 2d 417, 12 *California Reporter* 753, cert. denied, 368 U.S. 864 (1961); cf. *In re Jones,* 57 Cal. 2d 860, 372 P. 2d 310, 22 *California Reporter* 478 (1962); but see *Fulwood* v. *Clemmer,* 206 F. Supp. 370 (D.D.C. 1962); *Delaware ex rel. Tate* v. *Cubbage,* 210 A. 2d 555 (Del. 1965); *Brown* v. *McGinnis,* 10 N.Y. 2d 531, 180 N.E. 2d 791, 225 N.Y.S. 2d 497 (1962).
Some officials, however, continue their refusal to recognize the Muslim religion. The supervisor of the Nassau County Jail testified in a New York court that Islam is not accepted as a religion at the jail. New York *Times,* December 12, 1969, p. 57.
[91] *Walker* v. *Blackwell,* 411 F. 2d 23, 25–26 (5th Cir. 1969). The point seems to have been confused with the Muslims' special requests concerning Ramadan discussed below.
[92] *Barnett* v. *Rodgers,* 410 F. 2d 995 (D.C. Cir. 1969).
[93] Courts have not required authorities to make special arrangements for

The constitutional prohibition against the establishment of religions covers not only official interference with religion but official encouragement of religion, as well. Atheists and agnostics have complained that prisoners are released to attend religious services while alternative activities by non-religious groups are banned.

Free Expression. The law regarding free expression in correctional institutions was the last aspect of correctional life to change and is still in constant flux.[94] Prison officials remain essentially unchecked by the speech and assembly provisions of the First Amendment. They have been left free to censor communications[95] and to screen out "reasonably objectionable,"[96] "inflammatory"[97] or "subversive"[98] articles or publications.[99]

In a far-reaching decision dealing with an institution for pretrial detainees in Rhode Island, a federal court forbade officials to screen out all but "hard core pornography," basing its ruling on the freedom of publishers to circulate printed materials to prisoners.[100]

A federal district court recently broke new ground by ruling

Ramadan on the basis "that considerations of security and administrative expense outweigh whatever constitutional deprivation petitioners may claim" (*Walker* v. *Blackwell*, 411 F. 2d 23, 26 [5th Cir. 1969]).

[94] Judicial rulings that have resulted in increased freedom to speak, write or assemble formerly were based on some other protection, such as access to court or equal protection of racial or religious groups.

See, e.g., *Edwards* v. *Duncan*, 355 F. 2d 993 (4th Cir. 1966); *Lee* v. *Tahash*, 352 F. 2d 970 (8th Cir. 1965). See also *Rockey* v. *Krueger*, 306 N.Y.S. 2d 359 (Sup. Ct. 1969) (right to wear a beard if religion so requires); *Long* v. *Parker*, 390 F. 2d 816 (3d Cir. 1968) (right to receive religious or racially oriented publications); cf. *In re Hayell*, 2 Cal. 3d 675, 420 P. 2d 640, 87 *California Reporter* 504 (1970) (pursuant to Cal. Penal Code 2600, prisoners may receive all printed matter except those in prohibited categories).

[95] *Brabson* v. *Wilkins*, 19 N.Y. 2d 433, 227 N.E. 2d 383, 280 N.Y.S. 2d 561 (1967); *Wilson* v. *Kelley*, 294 F. Supp. 1005 (N.D. Ga. 1968), *aff'd per curiam*, 393 U.S. 266 (1969).

[96] *Jackson* v. *Godwin*, 400 F. 2d 529, 540 (5th Cir. 1968).

[97] *Walker* v. *Blackwell*, 411 F. 2d 23, 29 (5th Cir. 1969).

[98] *Rivers* v. *Royster*, 360 F. 2d 593 (4th Cir. 1966); cf. *Shakur* v. *McGrath*, 69 Civ. 4493, at 8–9 (S.D.N.Y., mem. December 31, 1969).

[99] In *Sostre* v. *McGinnis*, 442 F. 2d 178 (2d Cir. 1971) (*en banc*), the court ruled that a prisoner cannot be punished for possession of "inflammatory" or "racist" literature that might "subvert prison discipline," leaving open the question of the constitutional standards necessary to justify the confiscation. The district court's order requiring officials to submit regulations governing the receipt, distribution, discussion and writing of political literature was reversed.

[100] *Palmigiano* v. *Travisono*, 317 F. Supp. 776 (D.R.I. 1970).

that, although "certain literature may pose such a clear and present danger to the security of a prison or to the rehabilitation of prisoners that it should be censored," protection of prisoners' limited First Amendment rights require several procedural safeguards when reading materials are withheld. Specifically, the court ordered that literature cannot be screened by prison officials without: notice to a prisoner that literature addressed to him has been censored or withheld; an opportunity to present arguments, either oral or written, in favor of a finding that the literature is acceptable; and a decision by a body that can be expected to act fairly.[101]

It is common for jails to have strict rules about reading materials, justifying them on the ground that they are necessary for administrative reasons: to cut contraband and for paternalistic, moralistic reasons. The D.C. jail authorities allowed inmates at the city jail to read only books and magazines sent directly from publishers. As a result of a class action suit in the federal district court, the city agreed to the following stipulated regulation:

> Every resident is entitled to receive publications from any source, and is not limited to receiving publications directly from the publisher. Every resident is entitled to receive publications through the mail or brought to the jail for his use. The resident may keep his publications in whatever room or cell he may occupy.

Rights of speech and advocacy are less protected in the jails. Severe disciplinary sanctions were brought against one prisoner for urging a sit-down demonstration to protest mistreatment,[102] another was segregated and transferred for "agitating" by posting on the prison bulletin board and circulating a letter to the governor suggesting prison reform. In both these cases the court ruled against the prison.

Unfortunately, prison inmates rarely obtain access to sympathetic outsiders to voice their grievances; they are not usually permitted to publish books or articles in magazines of general circulation or even to give sermons to those on the outside.

The chief barrier to communication with the outside world is the complete control by officials of an inmate's visitors, his correspondents, the number of letters he may write and the subject

---

[101] *Sostre* v. *Otis,* 330 F. Supp. 941 (S.D.N.Y. 1971). The court found that the recent establishment of a broadly based review panel of prison officials from different disciplines satisfied the third criterion.
[102] *Roberts* v. *Pepersack,* 256 F. Supp. 415, 429–30 (D. Md. 1966), *cert. denied,* 389 U.S. 877 (1967).

matter and language of his letters. Jail regulations generally limit the volume as well as the contents of outgoing mail.

The courts generally have endorsed such restrictions on the use of the mails. Judges have sustained not only the prohibition of unacceptable correspondents but also of "unacceptable sentiments and points of view."[103]

Many of the rationales used to justify interference with prisoners' mail have no application to jails, where most inmates are in pretrial status. Yet even those cases that have overturned some of the restrictions on jail inmates' mail generally do not make this distinction, continuing to give great weight to the security needs of the institution.[104]

Despite the allowance of virtually unlimited discretion to correctional officials to control mailing and visiting rights, courts have made an inroad into this area in cases involving complaints to judges and other government officials. A prisoner's letter to a state senator describing conditions of the Virginia State Penitentiary was intercepted by an official who did not believe "it is the prisoner's place to be describing to the State Senator his description of how we operate the penitentiary." In ruling that prison authorities may not suppress complaints to executive officials, the court stated:

> If the operation of the prisons and the treatment of the inmates is lodged solely in the Executive, generally without any possibility of judicial restraint, there ought to be open avenues of complaint by prisoners to those in general charge of their immediate jailers. Executive capacity to prevent abuses and excesses on the part of subordinate officials would be greatly impaired if the most fruitful sources of information are dammed up or diverted.[105]

Likewise, a federal district court prohibited District of Columbia prison officials from punishing a prisoner for making "false accusations" against the officials in a complaint to the District commissioners.[106] The complaint had been made in accordance with procedures approved by the commissioners, and the ensuing punishment therefore interfered with the prisoner's right to seek

---

[103] *McClosky* v. *Maryland,* 337 F. 2d 72 (4th Cir. 1964) (censorship of anti-Semitic statements termed an "essential adjunct of prison administration").
[104] See, e.g., *Lamar* v. *Kern,* 349 F. Supp. 222 (S.D. Tex. 1972).
[105] *Landman* v. *Royster,* 333 F. Supp. 621 at 657 (E.D. Va. 1971).
[106] *Roberts* v. *Pegelow,* 313 F. 2d 548, 551 (4th Cir. 1963).

redress of his grievances.[107] These kinds of restrictions will be outlawed some day,[108] but as yet they still stand.

In one of the few decisions to give explicit recognition to the special rights of pretrial detainees, a federal district court prescribed these standards for inmates awaiting trial in Toledo jails:

1. There shall be no censorship of outgoing mail.
2. There shall be no limitation on the persons to whom outgoing mail may be directed.
3. There shall be no censorship of incoming letters from the prisoner's attorney, or from any judge or elected public official.
4. Incoming parcels or letters may be inspected for contraband, but letters may not be read.
5. Proper arrangements shall be made to insure that prisoners may freely obtain writing materials and postage.
6. Indigent prisoners shall be furnished at public expense writing materials and ordinary postage for their personal use in dispatching a maximum of five (5) letters per week.[109]

The court recognized the special protection due pretrial detainees, relying heavily on a unique opinion dealing with a Rhode Island prison housing pretrial inmates. There the court had ruled that:

[O]fficials at the Adult Correctional Institution have used such controls to suppress any criticism of the institution or institutional officials. I fail to appreciate such an attitude which smothers information to the public about prisoners and prison life—it serves

[107] See also *Brabson* v. *Wilkins*, 19 N.Y. 2d 433, 227 N.E. 2d 383, 280 N.Y.S. 2d 561 (1967); *Sostre* v. *Rockefeller*, 312 F. Supp. 863 (S.D.N.Y. 1970); *Sostre* v. *McGinnis*, 442 F. 2d 178 (2d Cir. 1971) (*en banc*); Accord *LeVier* v. *Woodson*, 443 F. 2d 360 (10th Cir. 1971); *Shaffer* v. *Jennings*, 314 F. Supp. 588 (E.D. Pa. 1970); cf. *Meola* v. *Fitzpatrick*, 322 F. Supp. 878 (D. Mass. 1971) (censorship of correspondence with the courts violates the Fifth Amendment).
[108] See *Sostre* v. *Rockefeller*, 312 F. Supp. 863, 876 (S.D.N.Y. 1970), *aff'd in part, modified in part, and rev'd in part sub nom. Sostre* v. *McGinnis*, 442 F. 2d 178 (2d Cir. 1971) (*en banc*), holding that officials may not punish an inmate for writing militant letters, possessing political literature or refusing to answer questions about a political organization, where his activities caused no reasonable apprehension of a disturbance or security risk. "It is not a function of our prison system to make prisoners conform in their political thought and belief to ideas acceptable to their jailers." See also *Carothers* v. *Follette*, 314 F. Supp. 1014 (S.D.N.Y. 1970).
[109] *Jones* v. *Wittenberg*, 330 F. Supp. 707, 719 (N.D. Ohio 1971); see also *Brenneman* v. *Madigan*, 343 F. Supp. 128 (N.D. Cal. 1971); but see *Henry* v. *Ciccone*, 315 F. Supp. 889, 892 (W.D. Mo. 1970).

no rational social purpose supportive of prison objectives. It merely serves to destroy one of the few vehicles prisoners have of informing the public which should know so that it can exercise its responsibility in a meaningful way. Furthermore, it is my view that censorship for such reason is an unconstitutional infringement of the First Amendment rights of the plaintiffs, including the right to petition for redress of grievances.

Officials of the Adult Correctional Institution have also taken it upon themselves to read and screen outgoing mail to protect the public, including the courts, from insulting, vulgar letters. This is not their function—they are not the protectors of the sensibilities of the public which can protect itself.[110]

The court forbade prison officials to open, read or inspect any outgoing mail without a search warrant and to read (as opposed to inspecting for contraband) letters to prisoners from correspondents on their approved mailing lists.[111]

A federal court told officials of a Michigan county jail that they could not censor mail to or from courts, attorneys or public officials.

Unlike the cases [dealing with convicted prisoners], we are here confronted with a county jail whose inmate population includes a large percentage of pre-trial detainees. To such prisoners the right to confidential correspondence with one's attorney is especially important.[112]

Progress has begun in the vital areas of insuring the access of the press and private citizens to prisons and jails. A federal court of appeals has ruled that prisoners may write uncensored letters to the news media to complain of general prison conditions or personal grievances.[113] Another court recently ordered the federal Bureau of Prisons to permit individual interviews of inmates by the press, subject to administrative or disciplinary intervention in specific cases. In language as apt to jails as to prisons, the court recognized:

Prisons are public institutions. The conduct of these institutions is a matter of public concern. Whenever people are incarcerated,

[110] *Palmigiano* v. *Travisono*, 317 F. Supp. 776 (D.R.I. 1970).
[111] See also *Morales* v. *Turman*, 326 F. Supp. 677 (E.D. Tex. 1971); *Carothers* v. *Follette*, 314 F. Supp. 1014, 1021, 1025 (S.D.N.Y. 1970).
[112] *Jansson* v. *Grysen*, No. G–130–71 C.A. (W.D. Mich., June 5, 1972).
[113] *Nolan* v. *Fitzpatrick*, 451 F. 2d 545 (1st Cir. 1971).

whether it be in a prison, an insane asylum, or an institution such as those for the senile and retarded, opportunity for human indignities and administrative insensitivity exists. Those thus deprived of freedom live out of the public's view. It is largely only through the media that a failure in a particular institution to adhere to minimum standards of human dignity can be exposed.[114]

One court has enjoined Rhode Island officials from preventing private citizens from attending inside meetings of the National Prisoners' Reform Association.[115]

Racial Discrimination and Segregation. Discrimination against minorities in the treatment of inmates and the hiring and promotion of guards and other employees is most obvious in the South, where black inmates perform most of the menial tasks and black employees are virtually non-existent, but the problem exists in virtually all jails.[116]

Regulations that deny black inmates the right to receive "non-subversive" newspapers and magazines that are oriented toward blacks, while allowing white inmates to receive publications of general circulation, have been deemed a denial of equal protection.[117]

The first federal court to be presented with a claim rejected the argument that racial segregation of prisoners (including a walled-off compartment for blacks in the dining hall) was unconstitutional: "by no parity of reasoning can the rationale of *Brown* v. *Board of Education* . . . be extended to State penal institutions."[118] Since then, other courts have upheld such challenges under the equal protection clause of the Fourteenth Amendment, without requiring specific proof of discrimination or unequal facilities. The first case involved institutions for juveniles, where

[114] *Washington Post Co.* v. *Kleindienst,* Civ. Action No. 467–72 (D.D.C., April 5, 1972), p. 4; see also *Burnham* v. *Oswald,* Civ. No. 1971–132 (N.D.N.Y., May 16, 1972).
[115] *National Prisoners' Reform Association* v. *Sharkey,* Civ. Action No. 4884, 347 F. Supp. 1234 (D.R.I. 1972).
[116] See, e.g., *Wilson* v. *Kelley,* 294 F. Supp. 1005 (N.D. Ga. 1968), aff'd per curiam, 393 U.S. 266 (1969).
[117] *Jackson* v. *Godwin,* 400 F. 2d 529 (5th Cir. 1968); *Rivers* v. *Royster,* 360 F. 2d 593 (4th Cir. 1966). See also *Ownes* v. *Brierley,* 452 F. 2d 640 (3d Cir. 1971).
[118] *Nichols* v. *McGee,* 169 F. Supp. 721, 724 (N.D. Calif.), *appeal dismissed,* 361 U.S. 6 (1959).

the analogy to public education was the most obvious.[119] More recently, state prisons and local jails in Alabama, Georgia, Arkansas and Virginia have been ordered to desegregate.[120] The federal judicial policy generally has been that "the danger to security, discipline, and good order must presently exist and be apparent to justify any segregation. This prohibits any standard policy or program of segregated custody at state, county, or local level."[121] Arkansas officials were excused temporarily from immediate desegregation of the barracks on the grounds that it "would create disciplinary problems that Respondents are not able to solve at the moment and would tend to make the already bad situation at the Penitentiary substantially worse than it is."[122] Nebraska officials, on the other hand, were not permitted to house separately those white prisoners who objected to living with blacks on the basis of possible disruptions that could be caused by integration.[123]

While integration is now the generally enforced public policy, seething close to the surface and often boiling over is the problem of constant exploitations of minorities by majorities. The situations sometimes are reversed in correctional institutions where

[119] See *State Board of Public Works* v. *Myers,* 224 Md. 246, 167 A. 2d 765, 769 (1961). See also *Board of Managers* v. *George,* 377 F. 2d 228, 232 (8th Cir. 1967); *Singleton* v. *Board of Commissioners,* 356 F. 2d 771 (5th Cir. 1966); *Crum* v. *State Training School for Girls,* 413 F. 2d 1348 (5th Cir. 1969); *Montgomery* v. *Oakley Training School,* 426 F. 2d 269 (5th Cir. 1970). But see *Edwards* v. *Sard,* 250 F. Supp. 977 (D.D.C. 1966).

[120] *Holt* v. *Sarver,* 309 F. Supp. 362, 382 (E.D. Ark. 1970), *aff'd* 442 F. 2d 304 (8th Cir. 1971); *Mason* v. *Peyton,* Civ. No. 5611-R (E.D. Va., ordered entered, October 16, 1969); *Wilson* v. *Kelley,* 294 F. Supp. 1005 (N.D. Ga. 1968), *aff'd per curiam,* 390 U.S. 333 (1968). See also *Bolden* v. *Pegelow,* 329 F. 2d 95 (4th Cir. 1964) (injunction against segregated barbershops in District of Columbia prison).

[121] *Wilson* v. *Kelley,* 294 F. Supp. 1005, 1009 n. 5 (N.D. Ga. 1968), *aff'd per curiam,* 393 U.S. 266 (1969). An exception occurred once in a District of Columbia case, where a district judge ruled that in a prison with a ratio of approximately ten black inmates for every white, the policy of having six integrated and sixteen all-black dormitories could not be considered discriminatory. *Edwards* v. *Sard,* 250 F. Supp. 977 (D.D.C. 1966); cf. *Dixon* v. *Duncan,* 218 F. Supp. 157 (E.D. Va. 1963) (District of Columbia prison officials may not force white prisoners to live in integrated dormitories while giving black prisoners a choice between integrated and all-black dormitories).

[122] *Holt* v. *Sarver,* 309 F. Supp. 362, 381–82 (E.D. Ark. 1970), *aff'd* 442 F. 2d 304 (8th Cir. 1971): "It must be remembered that we are not dealing here with school children. We are not dealing with free world housing; we are not dealing with theatres, restaurants, or hotels. We are dealing with criminals, many of whom are violent, and we are dealing with a situation in which the civilian personnel at the Penitentiary are not in control of the institution."

[123] *McClelland* v. *Sigler,* No. 71–1310, 8th Cir., March 22, 1972.

outside minority groups often outnumber incarcerated whites due
to the disproportionate number of minority races in jail. It is beginning to appear that segregation in jails may be less a technique
for prejudicing minority groups than a way to protect them.

Privacy. Within the jail, inmates have been given no right to
claim constitutional immunity from searches of their persons or
their personal property. "It is obvious that a jail shares none of the
attributes of privacy of a home, an automobile, an office, or a hotel
room. . . . [O]fficial surveillance has traditionally been the order
of the day."[124]

Denial of privacy has gone further to deny consensual sexual
relations, heterosexual or homosexual. Prisoners usually are forbidden to contract marriages (without cohabitation) unless they
have official permission. No court has yet ruled that this complete
control over every aspect of a prisoner's existence is impermissible,
no matter how it relates to his criminal career or his security in
custody and regardless of the propriety of the criteria imposed.
When untried inmates are jailed only because of their poverty,
the inappropriateness of this lack of privacy is especially compelling.

Voting. The common practice of permanently disenfranchising
prisoners seldom has been challenged by ex-convicts.[125] Inmates
who were qualified to vote have been denied the right to cast
ballots in prison or jail; their legal challenges have, so far, been
unsuccessful.[126]

124 *Lanza* v. *New York,* 370 U.S. 139, 143 (1962). But see *Palmigiano* v.
Travisono, 317 F. Supp. 776 (D.R.I. 1970):
> Though this court has focused mainly on the issue before it as it relates
> to the First Amendment, it is of the opinion that the conduct of the . . .
> officials of indiscriminately opening and reading all prisoner mail in-
> cluding that of unconvicted awaiting trial inmates, whether the same
> be from the inmates or members of the free society, is a violation of
> the Fourth Amendment.

125 See *Green* v. *Board of Elections of New York,* 380 F. 2d 445 (2d Cir.
1967); *cert. denied,* 389 U.S. 1048 (1968) (refusal to convene three-judge
district court upheld); *Beacham* v. *Braterman,* 300 F. Supp. 182 (S.D. Fla.
1969), *aff'd without opinion,* 396 U.S. 12 (1969) (three-judge court convened but disqualification upheld); *Stephens* v. *Yeomans,* Civ. No. 1005–70
(D.N.J., October 30, 1970) (three-judge court ordered to consider felon's
right to vote).

126 *Ray* v. *Commonwealth,* 263 F. Supp. 630 (W.D. Pa. 1967); cf. *Coffin* v.
Reichard, 143 F. 2d 443, 445 (6th Cir. 1944), *cert. denied,* 325 U.S. 887
(1945). The right of ex-offenders to vote has been recognized, though, in

As one federal court in Pennsylvania saw it, the right to vote just is not that important:

> It is only where fundamental, humane and necessary rights are breached that the constitutional protections become involved.
>
> These do not include the right to vote, nor can they include any rights which interfere with the Warden's duty and function of seeing to the enforcement of the incarceration and the fulfillment of sentence after conviction.[127]

The Supreme Court, interpreting an Illinois election law as not affording unconvicted prisoners awaiting trial the right to absentee ballots, declined to rule that the law denied prisoners the equal protection of the laws:[128] "there [was] nothing to show that a judicially incapacitated pre-trial detainee [was] absolutely prohibited from [voting];" thus it was not unreasonable for the legislature to refuse them absentee ballots while granting ballots to persons who could show an "absolute inability to appear at the polls."

This tortuous line of reasoning may be changing. In its most recent decision dealing with the subject, the Supreme Court ordered a lower three-judge court to hear the claims of inmates confined awaiting trial in Philadelphia who challenged a state statute that barred them from obtaining absentee ballots. It said, unanimously, that its earlier decision did not involve an absolute prohibition against voting and thus did not "foreclose the subject."[129]

Recently, voting officials have provided absentee ballots to unconvicted inmates of several local jails, and a recent federal court of appeals decision requiring the convening of a three-judge court to consider whether deprivation of the right to vote on conviction of a felony violates the equal-protection clause of the Constitution,[130] may augur the end of the restriction even as it applies to convicted felons.

---

recent cases: for example, *Ramirez* v. *Brown,* Calif. Sup. Ct. March 30, 1973, reported in 2 *Prison Law Reporter* 189 (1973).

[127] *Goosby* v. *Osser,* 452 F. 2d 39 (3 Circ. 1971).

[128] *McDonald* v. *Board of Election Commissioners,* 394 U.S. 802 (1969). Ill. Rev. Stat., ch. 46, 19-1 and 19-3 (1967).

[129] *Goosby* v. *Osser,* 12 *Criminal Law Reporter* 3075 (January 17, 1973).

[130] *Dillenburg* v. *Kramer,* No. 7102647 (9th Cir., November 16, 1972).

Charges of Criminal Conduct in Jail. A prisoner suspected of committing a crime while in jail is "entitled to the rights of any suspect who is walking the streets."[131] The only exceptions appear to relate to Fourth Amendment search and seizure protections. A difficult problem of double jeopardy[132] occurs, however, when an inmate faces a criminal charge in addition to disciplinary action by jail authorities. One prisoner convicted of participating in a prison riot was sentenced to a term of nine years and eight months, to run consecutively with the term he was then serving; but prison officials also ordered him confined to a punishment cell for thirty-five days.[133] Another prisoner, who stood trial for killing a guard and was acquitted of murder on a plea of self-defense, was "padlocked" in a solitary cell; more than a year after the acquittal, a federal district court, in deference to the discretionary authority of the superintendent over disciplinary matters, denied his request for release from solitary.[134]

After the uprising at the Attica prison in September 1971, the state provided forms on which inmates could request or waive counsel; prisoners claimed that refusal to co-operate with the in-

[131] Barkin, "Prison Policy," p. 19; see, e.g., *Mathis* v. *United States,* 391 U.S. 1 (1968) (warning of rights); *Brooks* v. *Florida,* 389 U.S. 413 (1967) (*per curiam*) (voluntariness of confession); *Blyden* v. *Hogan,* 320 F. Supp. 513 (S.D.N.Y. 1970) (warning of rights before inmates signed consent-to-interview forms following riots); Bureau of Prisons, "Policy Statement 2001.1" (February 19, 1968) (warning of rights, counsel, self-incrimination).

[132] See *Benton* v. *Maryland,* 395 U.S. 784 (1969).

[133] *Brooks* v. *Florida,* 389 U.S. 413 (1967) (*per curiam*). The lower-court decision was reversed on other grounds, the contention of double jeopardy apparently not having been raised.

[134] *Jones* v. *Peyton,* 294 F. Supp. 173 (E.D. Va. 1968).

In the first case to recognize this dilemma, the double-jeopardy argument was not made. However, the court examined a further problem created by subjecting the same conduct to criminal prosecution and administrative discipline. Although a criminal suspect has the right to remain silent in the face of police questioning since *Miranda* v. *Arizona,* a prisoner choosing to do so may have to sacrifice the right to explain his conduct to the prison disciplinary committee before being punished. Because of the difficulty involved in making this choice, the court ruled that any prisoner charged with a prison rule violation that may be punishable by state authorities must be provided with counsel. Another federal decision vacated the administrative penalties imposed in such circumstances, leaving open the question of whether it would grant procedural safeguards in future hearings or grant immunity from the use of an inmate's statements in future criminal proceedings.

See *Clutchette* v. *Procunier,* 328 F. Supp. 767 (N.D. Cal. 1971); *Miranda* v. *Arizona,* 384 U.S. 436 (1966); *Carter* v. *McGinnis,* 351 F. Supp. 787 (W.D.N.Y., November 1972).

vestigation, regardless of the possibilities of self-incrimination, could lead to administrative reprisals, and requested an injunction against any interrogations except in the presence of counsel.

A federal court of appeals upheld the denial of injunctive relief, citing the dearth of evidence of improper questioning of prisoners, and the existence of the adequate legal remedy of excluding any illegally obtained evidence from future trials. According to the court, "Plaintiffs' incarceration as the result of prior convictions for unrelated offenses, while it does not strip them of Sixth Amendment rights . . . does not confer upon them greater rights to counsel than those of citizens outside of the prison walls." A dissenting opinion, emphasizing the subtle pressures that could be applied to deter prisoners from requesting counsel and the resulting dilemma of choosing between possible prosecution and administrative reprisal, concluded that a prisoner's need for counsel may exceed that of a suspect in the usual criminal investigation.[135]

ACCESS TO COURT

Although jail officials consistently have been accorded wide powers to limit and censor inmates' communications with the outside world, administrative restrictions on correspondence may not operate to deny prisoners the right of reasonable access to the courts.[136]

The Supreme Court affirmed the right of access to court in 1941.[137] Although the aim of regulation of prisoners' rights might be laudable, it had the effect of abridging their rights to apply to federal courts for legal relief.[138] Other cases have held that both the due process and the equal protection clauses of the Fourteenth Amendment (and, presumably, the due process clause of the Fifth Amendment) prohibit the application of even reasonable regulations to keep a prisoner from filing a timely appeal from his conviction.[139]

[135] *Gonzalez* v. *Rockefeller,* 10 *Criminal Law Reporter* 2227 (2d Cir., December 1, 1971).
[136] *Lee* v. *Tahash,* 352 F. 2d 970 (8th Cir. 1965).
[137] *Ex parte Hull,* 312 U.S. 546 (1941).
[138] See also *White* v. *Ragen,* 324 U.S. 760, 762 n. 1 (1945) (right of access by state prisoners to state courts).
[139] E.g., *Dowd* v. *United States ex rel. Cook,* 340 U.S. 206 (1951); *Cochran*

Courts have also recognized that for inmates who can secure their rights only through judicial decrees, protection of their access to the courts is basic to the enforcement of all other rights.[140] The access principle has been reaffirmed where prisoners claimed mistreatment in prison, and sought release.[141]

There is less concern about the effect of officials refusing to permit inmates to file civil suits, but several courts have held that due process of law requires that prisoners be given prompt hearings on all their claims, civil or criminal.[142]

Access to the courts may be blocked notwithstanding judicial efforts to the contrary.[143] For example, censorship of the mail alerts jail officials to complaints even before they reach the courts (there is a trend in recent cases to prohibit the practice of screening outgoing mail); and although prisoners may not be disciplined for bringing suit against prison officials, reprisals do occur.[144]

---

v. *Kansas*, 316 U.S. 255 (1942); *Hymes* v. *Dickson*, 232 F. Supp. 796 (N.D. Cal. 1964); *People* v. *Howard*, 166 Cal. App. 2d 638, 334 P. 2d 105 (Dist. Ct. App. 1958); *Warfield* v. *Raymond*, 195 Md. 711, 71 A. 2d 870 (1950).

[140] *Coleman* v. *Peyton*, 362 F. 2d 905, 907 (4th Cir.), *cert. denied*, 385 U.S. 905 (1966) (dictum); *Stiltner* v. *Rhay*, 322 F. 2d 314, 316 (9th Cir. 1963), *cert. denied*, 376 U.S. 920 (1964).

[141] E.g., *Talley* v. *Stephens*, 247 F. Supp. 683 (E.D. Ark. 1965); *Fulwood* v. *Clemmer*, 206 F. Supp. 370 (D.D.C. 1962); *In re Riddle*, 57 Cal. 2d 848, 372 P. 2d 304, 22 *California Reporter* 472 (1962); *In re Ferguson*, 55 Cal. 2d 663, 361 P. 2d 417, 12 *California Reporter* 753, *cert. denied*, 368 U.S. 864 (1961); *Kahn* v. *LaValle*, 12 App. Div. 2d 832, 209 N.Y.S. 2d 591 (Sup. Ct. 1961) (dictum).

[142] *Tabor* v. *Hardwick*, 224 F. 2d 526 (5th Cir. 1955); *Seybold* v. *Milwaukee County Sheriff*, 276 F. Supp. 484 (E.D. Wis. 1967); *Diaz* v. *Chatterton*, 229 F. Supp. 19 (S.D. Calif. 1964) (federal funds not available to transport prisoners from state prison to appear at trial or pretrial hearings in ordinary civil action); *Kirby* v. *Thomas*, 336 F. 2d 462, 464 (6th Cir. 1964). *Peterson* v. *Nadler*, 452 F. 2d 754 (8th Cir. 1971); *Thomas* v. *Gordon*, No. 71–C–168 (W.D. Wis., January 27, 1972).

[143] E.g., *Spires* v. *Bottorff*, 317 F. 2d 273 (7th Cir. 1963) *cert. denied*, 379 U.S. 938 (1964), where the court held that a prisoner might have a cause of action under the Civil Rights Act against a state judge who claimed he was "agitated with" the prisoner's demands for copies of the charges that had led to his conviction, and induced the warden to prevent him from corresponding with him or the clerk of his court; *Fulwood* v. *Clemmer*, 206 F. Supp. 370 (D.D.C. 1962); *In re Riddle*, 57 Cal. 2d 848, 372 P. 2d 304, 22 *California Reporter* 472 (1962).

[144] See, e.g., *Carothers* v. *Follette*, 314 F. Supp. 1014, 1020 (S.D.N.Y. 1970) (copies made of any letters to a judge in which a prisoner complains of his treatment). *Andrade* v. *Hauck*, 452 F. 2d 1071 (5th Cir., 1971); *United States ex rel. Cleggett* v. *Pate*, 229 F. Supp. 818, 821–22 (N.D. Ill. 1964). *Sostre* v. *Rockefeller*, 312 F. Supp. 863, 869 (S.D.N.Y. 1970), *aff'd in part*,

In most jails, neither a reason nor a hearing need be given before a prisoner is administratively punished. Indeed, it may be impossible to show that disciplinary measures resulted from an attempted exercise of constitutional rights. When prisoners are able to inform the courts that such punishments stemmed from legitimate efforts to air grievances in court, judges have no problem in condemning the reprisals and enjoining their repetition.[145]

Counsel. One of the most common and most serious problems of jail inmates is the absence of effective counsel. Few people in jail can afford lawyers; those who can afford them often get poor service.

Several years ago, the California Supreme Court,[146] recognizing the crucial relationship between the ability to afford and secure an attorney and a prisoner's ability to exercise his legal right of access to court, ruled that prison authorities could not use their power to censor prisoners' mail to screen out letters to attorneys even when the mail criticizes the prison regime. Yet prisoners continue to complain that their letters documenting jail abuses to attorneys lead to reprisals by the authorities. Several federal courts have insisted that there is no legitimate purpose for which mail to or from attorneys should be read by officials. In one case, although an agreement permitting the opening of mail from attorneys in order to inspect for contraband was approved by the court, officials could open it only in the presence of the inmate. Other courts have permitted officials to read mail to attorneys to assure themselves that they concern only the legality of an inmate's detention or the treatment he is receiving in jail.[147] The

---

modified in part, rev'd in part sub nom. Sostre v. *McGinnis,* 442 F. 2d 178 (2d Cir. 1971) (*en banc*); *Meola* v. *Fitzpatrick,* 322 F. Supp. 878 (D. Mass. 1971).

[145] E.g., *Meola* v. *Fitzpatrick,* 322 F. Supp. 878 (D. Mass. 1971). In *Smartt* v. *Avery,* 370 F. 2d 788 (6th Cir. 1967), a federal court invalidated a parole board regulation that postponed for one year the parole eligibility of any inmate who filed a habeas corpus petition in court. The court ruled that the parole board could not penalize prisoners for exercising their constitutional and statutory right of access to court by withholding a privilege (consideration for early release) that would otherwise have been granted.

[146] *In re Ferguson,* 55 Cal. 2d 663, 361 P. 2d 417, 12 *California Reporter* 753, *cert. denied,* 368 U.S. 864 (1961). Cf. *McCloskey* v. *Maryland,* 337 F. 2d 72 (4th Cir. 1964) (prisoner has no constitutional right to seek legal assistance in spreading anti-Semitic propaganda).

[147] *Brabson* v. *Wilkins,* 19 N.Y. 2d 433, 227 N.E. 2d 383, 280 N.Y.S. 2d 561

particular importance to pretrial detainees of unfettered correspondence with their attorneys has been recognized by a few
courts which forbid jail officials to read or interfere with attorney
or judicial mail.[148]

Inmates have the right to consult privately with their attorneys
in the institution at reasonable times.[149] Although visual surveillance of a prisoner's interview with his attorney is permitted,[150] electronic eavesdropping is not; obviously a criminal
defendant cannot be properly represented by counsel unless he
can be assured confidentiality.[151]

The case law concerning the access of convicted prisoners to
counsel and the recent prohibition of unreasonable restrictions on
the activities of "jailhouse lawyers"[152] has not been applied to
unconvicted inmates of local jails. Nor have jail officials been required to provide access to law libraries,[153] since all unconvicted
defendants presumably have appointed or retained counsel.[154]

The mechanical problems of assuring convenient access to law
libraries for men and women in jail is minor, however, when compared to the very practical and far-reaching problems caused by
the absence of effective counsel. The time in jail pretrial is particularly important to a defendant. That so few people in jail have
legal help, despite public defender and other public interest law
organizations, is a fundamental, institutional problem which must

---

(1967); *Lee* v. *Tahash*, 352 F. 2d 970, 974 (8th Cir. 1965). Cf. *McDonough*
v. *Director of Patuxent*, 429 F. 2d 1189 (4th Cir. 1970) (obtaining of psychiatric, financial and legal assistance for court hearing to redetermine finding of
defective delinquency); *Sostre* v. *McGinnis*, 442 F. 2d 178 (2d Cir. 1971)
(*en banc*); see also *Wright* v. *McMann*, 321 F. Supp. 127, 142 (N.D.N.Y.
1970); *Freeley* v. *McGrath*, 314 F. Supp. 679 (S.D.N.Y. 1970).

[148] *Jansson* v. *Grysen*, No. G–130–71 C.A. (W.D. Mich., June 5, 1972);
Palmigiano v. *Travisono*, 317 F. Supp. 776 (D.R.I. 1970); see also *Jones* v.
Wittenberg, 330 F. Supp. 707 (N.D. Ohio 1971); *Brenneman* v. *Madigan*,
343 F. Supp. 128 (N.D. Calif. 1971).

[149] *Rhem* v. *McGrath*, 326 F. Supp. 681 (S.D.N.Y. 1971). *In re Allison*, 425
P. 2d 193, 57 *California Reporter* 593 (Sup. Ct.), *cert. denied*, 389 U.S. 876
(1967).

[150] *Konigsberg* v. *Ciccone*, 285 F. Supp. 585, 596097 (W.D. Mo. 1968).

[151] The defendant need not show that the information actually was trans-
mitted to the prosecutor. *State* v. *Cory*, 62 Wash. 2d 371, 382 P. 2d 1019
(1963). Cf. *Lanza* v. *New York*, 370 U.S. 139 (1962). See Annot., 5 A.L.R.
3d 1360, 1375–79 (1966).

[152] *Johnson* v. *Avery*, 393 U.S. 483 (1971).

[153] Cf. *Younger* v. *Gilmore*, 404 U.S. 15 (1971).

[154] *Wayne County Jail Inmates* v. *Wayne County Board of Commissioners*,
Civ. Action No. 173217 (Cir. Ct., Wayne County, Mich., May 18, 1971).

be answered adequately if true reform and justice is ever to come to America's jails.

DISCIPLINE AND CLASSIFICATION
PUNISHMENT OF INMATES FOR INFRACTIONS
OF INSTITUTIONAL RULES

Although some jails publish inmates' handbooks listing the regulations that prisoners are expected to obey, most do not, and an inmate may have no idea of the in-house rule he has violated until he is punished.[155] Even where written rules exist, they may be so vague as to be meaningless. One pervasive regulation outlaws any manifestation of "disrespect" toward correctional officers. Courts have attempted to prevent punishment of prisoners for exercising their constitutional or statutory rights,[156] but when jail officials impose punishment for violation of some unwritten regulation no real protection applies.[157] Scant progress has been made in establishing in prison or jail the usual standard of criminal law—namely, that conduct may be punished only when forbidden by a written regulation drawn with enough specificity to inform potential violators what conduct is forbidden.[158]

Reliable methods even for determining whether an infraction in fact has occurred exist in few jails. In most states, there are no hearings before inmates are put in solitary confinement; guards' reports alone can keep prisoners in solitary for many months. Officials uniformly have the power to segregate troublesome inmates in emergencies. In a recent case, a court refused to invalidate the use of this power to keep a prisoner in segregation for seven months before he was given any type of hearing.[159]

[155] See *Howard* v. *Smyth*, 365 F. 2d 428 (4th Cir. 1966) ("for the good of the institution").

[156] E.g., *Johnson* v. *Avery*, 393 U.S. 483 (1969); *Smartt* v. *Avery*, 370 F. 2d 788 (6th Cir. 1967); *Howard* v. *Smyth*, 365 F. 2d 428 (4th Cir. 1966).

[157] See *Landman* v. *Peyton*, 370 F. 2d 135, 139 (4th Cir. 1966).

[158] But see *Jones* v. *Wittenberg*, 323 F. Supp. 93 (judgment), 330 F. Supp. 707, 720 (order) (N.D. Ohio 1971):

Discipline imposed shall have a direct relationship to the institutional rule violated . . . This obviously requires that the rules of the jail, and the penalties for violation, must be established in advance, and made clearly known to all inmates.

[159] *Burns* v. *Swenson*, 430 F. 2d 771 (8th Cir. 1970); cf. *Williams* v. *Robin-*

The 1970's have seen a growing number of challenges to the power of correctional officials to discipline prisoners without due process protections. In the case of *Sostre* v. *Rockefeller*,[160] a federal district court ruled that a prisoner retains his right to procedural due process in the institution. A prisoner who "was, in effect, 'sentenced' to more than a year in punitive segregation without the minimal procedural safeguards required" was entitled to collect damages.[161] That court at least "would not lightly condone the absence of such basic safeguards against arbitrariness as adequate notice, an opportunity for the prisoner to reply to charges lodged against him and a reasonable investigation into the relevant facts—at least in cases of substantial discipline."[162]

In *Morris* v. *Travisono*,[163] a federal district judge mediated negotiations between lawyers representing Rhode Island prisoners and those representing prison officials. The officials agreed to the adoption of provisional regulations to govern disciplinary procedures, including, among other steps, a written charge by the reporting officer or employee; a hearing before a disciplinary board; and automatic review of the record by the warden of the institution. In the D. C. Jail suit also, the federal district court ruled that no prisoner could be reclassified to a worse status without a hearing and a lawyer, and ordered around-the-clock available phones to the public defender's office.

Some federal courts presented with broad challenges to various disciplinary practices have begun to adopt the position that the degree of procedural protection afforded depends on the severity of the punishments that can be meted out.[164]

---

son, 432 F. 2d 637 (D.C. Cir. 1970); cf. *Carter* v. *McGinnis*, 320 F. Supp. 1092 (M.D.N.Y. 1970); *Smoake* v. *Walker*, 320 F. Supp. 609 (S.D.N.Y. 1970).

[160] 312 F. Supp. 863 (S.D.N.Y. 1970). This protection "applies to charges for which he may receive punitive segregation or any other punishment for which earned good-time credit may be revoked or the opportunity to earn good-time credit is denied."

[161] See also *Wright* v. *McMann*, 321 F. Supp. 127, 141–42 (N.D.N.Y. 1970).

[162] On appeal, a majority ruled that "[a]ll of the elements of due process recited by the district court are not necessary to the constitutionality of every disciplinary action taken against a prisoner." The court stated that it did not consider the present case an appropriate vehicle for spelling out the due-process requirements to apply to New York prisons. *Sostre* v. *McGinnis*, 442 F. 2d 178 (2d Cir. 1971) (*en banc*).

[163] 310 F. Supp. 857 (D.R.I. 1970).

[164] See also *Nolan* v. *Scafati*, 430 F. 2d 548 (1st Cir., 1970). Cf. *Meola* v. *Fitzpatrick*, 322 F. Supp. 878 (D. Mass. 1971), with *Brown* v. *Brierley*, 316 F. Supp. 236 (W.D. Pa. 1970).

Two district courts have gone the farthest in prescribing procedural protections for prison discipline. Prisoners at San Quentin brought a class action challenging all disciplinary procedures at the prison, and the court ordered that the requirements of "rudimentary due process" be satisfied—notice of the charge, the right to call and cross-examine witnesses, counsel or a counsel substitute, decision by an unbiased fact-finder and equal access to any right to appeal.[165]

A federal district court in Virginia concluded that the same procedural requirements prescribed in the San Quentin case should prevail whenever any time in solitary confinement, transfer to maximum security or loss of good time is imposed or a prisoner is padlocked in his own cell for more than ten days. When lesser penalties are imposed, verbal notice, the opportunity for a hearing before an impartial decision maker with cross-examination of the complaining officer and the presentation of testimony in defense may not be omitted.

Most cases involving pretrial inmates ironically have offered fewer protections in disciplinary hearings than those involving state prisons.[166] A federal judge, in a Jefferson County, Kentucky, jail case, said that unlike convicted prisoners, jail inmates did not require due process protections on the specious ground that their sentences could not be prolonged or increased by administrative action.[167] This rationale overlooks the awful realities of life in jail, the effect of pretrial jail records on a sentencing judge, as well as the special claim to fair procedure of the innocent inmate jailed only because of his inability to raise cash bail.

An inmate's future chances for parole[168] or, in the case of a pretrial detainee, the severity of his sentence if he is convicted, can be affected by a record of disciplinary infractions determined without the required administrative safeguards.

[165] *Clutchette* v. *Procunier,* 328 F. Supp. 767 (N.D. Cal. 1971). The court mentioned that all these safeguards might not be necessary in every case and suggested guidelines, such as the length of time in isolation (ten days) or the possibility of increasing a prisoner's sentence.

[166] An interim consent order entered in the D. C. Jail case involving pretrial detainees specified a right to retained counsel in all jail disciplinary hearings, *Campbell* v. *Rogers,* Civ. Action No. 1462–71 (U. S. District Court for the District of Columbia).

[167] *Clements* v. *Hamilton,* No. 7001 (W.D. Ky., May 3, 1972).

[168] *West* v. *Cunningham,* No. 71–1392 (4th Cir., February 23, 1972).

The far-reaching state court decision concerning the Detroit jail held that:

> All disciplinary hearings must include four elements of due process: (1) notice (including specific advice of the charge), (2) an opportunity to be heard, (3) a fair hearing, and (4) an impartial decision-making body (drawn from noncustodial staff of the sheriff). However, the jail need not provide counsel since the issues are simple and no technical rules of evidence or procedure apply. It need not allow inmates to call witnesses on their behalf because such would prolong the hearings and open up the possibility of inmate coercion, intimidation, extortion, and reprisal. It need not allow inmates to know the identity of cross-examine witnesses against them because such would in too many cases "throw the accuser to the wolves."[169]

CLASSIFICATION OF INMATES

Recently, prisoners have begun to question the traditional assumption that they are completely subject to administrative discretion in assignment to facilities and programs. Under what circumstances are some prisoners assigned to work for the profit of the state while others receive schooling and vocational training?[170] Can defendants who are being detained prior to their trial be subjected to more onerous conditions than other convicted inmates of a jail because officials consider them special security risks?[171] Can a convicted murderer be required to spend all his

[169] *Wayne County Jail Inmates* v. *Wayne County Board of Commissioners*, Civ. Action No. 173217 (Cir. Ct., Wayne County, Mich., May 18, 1971).
[170] See *Wilson* v. *Kelley*, 294 F. Supp. 1005 (N.D. Ga. 1968), *aff'd per curiam*, 393 U.S. 266 (1969).
[171] Complaint at 11, *Shakur* v. *McGrath*, 69 Civ. 4493 (S.D.N.Y., filed October 1969). The complainants, thirteen of the "Panther 21" defendants, argued that
> [S]ince plaintiffs have not been charged with infraction of any detention center rules or regulations, and since there has been no explicit or implicit reason given for their treatment, such treatment . . . constitutes cruel and unusual punishment, for where there has been no crime, *any* form of punishment must be looked upon as being cruel and unusual.
They claimed that other inmates subjected to such onerous conditions allegedly have committed some serious infraction of institutional regulations after entering the jail. Ibid., pp. 11–12. In an interview, Commissioner of Correction George F. McGrath stated that the special treatment was justified because the defendants' high bail indicated that they were security risks and

time locked up in a maximum security cell in order to protect him from other prisoners?[172]

Rhode Island prisoners confined to a "Behavioral Control Unit" challenged the procedures that put them there on the grounds that they could not adjust to the general prison population or that they were a serious threat to the security of the institution.[173] New regulations adopted through negotiations between the prisoners and administrators provided for periodic review of inmates' classifications by a board, written notice to inmates, hearings with an opportunity for defense, announcement of decisions and an opportunity for review. The judge said that he would review the reclassifications of the complaining prisoners. No similar cases have yet been decided.[174]

REMEDIES

The most obvious judicial power over the administration of the correctional system—the sentencing power of judges—rarely has been used to stimulate reform.[175] Judges could refuse to sentence defendants to jails that did not meet constitutional standards. Some courts have backed up their general orders to release pretrial defendants with specific requirements to change constitutionally unacceptable practices causing these problems (overcrowding, for example) in jails.[176] But generally judges have not acted to use their sentence power for reformative purposes. In one case

because their presence in the jail population might cause a riot. New York *Times,* February 28, 1970, p. 36, col. 3.

[172] See *Ray* v. *Neil,* Civ. Action No. 5590 (M.D. Tenn., order entered, December 29, 1969). In handing down his temporary order that Ray be given some recreation, work and exercise, Judge William E. Miller said: "[E]nforced idleness can be cruel punishment, particularly when it is only to protect him from bodily harm" (Washington *Post,* December 30, 1969, p. A-7).

[173] *Morris* v. *Travisono,* 310 F. Supp. 857 (D.R.I. 1970). Cf. *Walker* v. *Mancusi,* No. 72-1081 (2d Cir., September 20, 1972).

[174] Recently, a few courts have begun to look beyond the obfuscating labels, such as "administrative" versus "punitive" segregation, used by correctional officials, to the real privileges and deprivations involved in different types of custody. If the deprivations are significant, some procedural protections will be required. *Urbans* v. *McCorkle,* 334 F. Supp. 161 (D.N.J. 1971); *Guajardo* v. *McAdams,* C.A. No. 70-4-570 (S.D. Tex., September 25, 1972).

[175] But see *United States* v. *Alsbrook,* 336 F. Supp. 973 (D.D.C. 1971).

[176] See, e.g., *Jones* v. *Wittenberg,* 323 F. Supp. 93 (N.D. Ohio, 1971).

where a defendant tried to assert a claim of denial of rights in jail in his appeal, the court ruled that his mistreatment in jail before trial was irrelevant to his conviction.[177]

Prisoners have been able to use other means of remedy: civil suits for damages against correctional officials or against the state or federal government; damage suits or injunctions against state officials under the federal Civil Rights Act; *mandamus* against correctional officials; habeas corpus; criminal prosecutions against officials who act illegally; contempt for failure to obey court orders to keep prisoners safe; and class actions. Most such strategies have been used by convicted prisoners, but jail inmates can use them also. The class action approach brought under the federal Civil Rights Act also has been employed successfully in this context.

CIVIL SUITS AGAINST OFFICIALS

In tort suits for damages due to negligence, prisoners have protested lack of adequate food, clothing, shelter, medical care or protection from physical assault. The courts, responding, usually applied the ordinary standard of civil liability for negligence, requiring jail officials to exercise due care to ensure the safety of inmates in their custody.

> A sheriff owes to a prisoner placed in his custody a duty to keep the prisoner safe and free from harm, to render him medical aid when necessary, and to treat him humanely and to refrain from oppressing him.[178]

A New York court found the failure of a warden and a prison physician to provide an injured prisoner with medical care was

---

[177] *State* v. *Williams*, 157 Conn. 114, 249 A. 2d 245 (1968).

[178] *Thomas* v. *Williams*, 105 Ga. App. 321, 326, 124 S.E. 2d 409, 413 (1962); *Kendrick* v. *Adamson*, 51 Ga. App. 402, 403, 180 S.E. 647, 648 (1935). See also *Ex parte Jenkins*, 25 Ind. App. 532, 58 N.E. 560 (1906); *Farmer* v. *State ex rel. Russell*, 224 Miss. 96, 79 So. 2d 528 (1955); *State ex rel. Morris* v. *National Surety Co.*, 162 Tenn. 547, 39 S.W. 2d 581 (1931); *Kusah* v. *McCorkle*, 100 Wash. 318, 170 p. 1023 (1918). In an Oklahoma case a jury found a sheriff negligent for failing to isolate an inmate's smallpox-ridden cellmate, as a consequence of which the sick prisoner's roommate contracted the disease and died. The court allowed the inmate's wife to recover from the sheriff in a wrongful-death action. *Hunt* v. *Rowton*, 143 Okla. 181, 288 p. 342 (1930).

"the neglect of a duty imposed by law."[179] The death of a prisoner in West Virginia who received no medical care was held in violation of a statute providing that "when any prisoner is sick the jailer shall see that he has adequate medical attention and nursing."[180] A Kentucky court said that a statute requiring jailers to "treat prisoners with humanity, and furnish them with proper food and lodging during their confinement," applied when a jailer knew of an inmate "kangaroo court" and failed to protect a prisoner from it.[181] But in three other states, courts have refused to find jail officials liable. In Maryland and Massachusetts the "hands-off" attitude of the courts precluded prisoners' tort suits against negligent officials without a showing of malice or an intent to cause the prisoner bodily harm.[182]

> It is inconsistent with the purpose for which prisons are established, and with the discipline which must be maintained over prisoners, that the officials should be responsible to the prisoners, in private actions, for mere negligence in the performance of their duties.[183]

An Illinois court held that any duty imposed to provide necessary medical care was owed to the public and not to individual prisoners; thus a violation could lead to a statutory penalty, but not civil liability.

The majority of states allow damage actions against negligent jail employees: still, it often is extremely difficult to prove an inmate's case to the satisfaction of a jury. Inmates cannot bring civil suits as long as they remain in jail in some places and suits, therefore, can only be brought years after an injury occurred.

Few lower-level custodial employees can pay significant money judgments rendered against them. A private employer would be compelled to assume liability for injuries inflicted by his em-

[179] *McCrossen* v. *State,* 277 App. Div. 1160, 101 N.Y. 2d 591, 592 (Sup. Ct.), *appeal denied,* 302 N.Y. 950, 98 N.E. 2d 117 (1950). The court noted a statutory duty to "protect and preserve the health of inmates." New York Correctional Law, 46 (McKinney 1968).
[180] *Smith* v. *Slack,* 125 W. Va. 812, 26 S.E. 2d 387 (1943).
[181] *Ratliff* v. *Stanley,* 224 Ky. 819, 7 S.W. 2d 230 (1928).
[182] *O'Hare* v. *Jones,* 161 Mass. 391, 37 N.E. 371 (1894); *Carder* v. *Steiner,* 225 Md. 271, 170 A. 2d 220 (1961). See also *State ex rel. Clark* v. *Ferling,* 220 Md. 109, 151 A. 2d 137 (1959); *Williams* v. *Adams,* 85 Mass. (3 Allen) 171 (1861).
[183] *O'Hare* v. *Jones,* 161 Mass. 391, 392–93, 37 N.E. 371, 372 (1894).

ployees, but the government—in this case a local jail—has no such responsibility—the doctrine of sovereign immunity dictates that a sovereign can do no wrong and generally may not be sued without its consent.

In the past few years the federal government,[184] the District of Columbia[185] and more than one third of the states[186] have eliminated this immunity by law or judicial decision.[187] The Supreme Court ruled in 1963 that the Federal Tort Claims Act applies to prisoners,[188] but the exemptions are many. "Any claim arising out of assault, battery, false imprisonment, false arrest, malicious prosecution, abuse of process, libel, slander, misrepresentation, deceit, or interference with contract right."[189]

Actions by officials based on a statute or an administrative regulation or that involve an official's exercise of discretion are almost always excluded.[190]

In a case I tried, involving the District of Columbia Jail, an epileptic said she was denied her medicine while in a punishment cell. The District of Columbia denied responsibility, claiming that the complaint referred to discretionary acts protected by the

---

[184] Federal Tort Claims Act, 28 U.S.C. §1346 (b) (1964).

[185] See *Spencer* v. *General Hospital,* 425 F. 2d 479 (D.C. Cir. 1969) (*rehearing en banc*); *Baker* v. *Washington,* 448 F. 2d 1200 (D.C. Cir. 1971).

[186] See, e.g., *Stone* v. *Arizona Highway Commission,* 93 Ariz. 384, 381 P. 2d 107 (1963); *Muskopf* v. *Corning Hospital District,* 55 Calif. 2d 211, 359 P. 2d 457, 11 *California Reporter* 89 (1961); *Hargrove* v. *Cocoa Beach,* 96 So. 2d 130 (Fla. 1957); *Molitor* v. *Kaneland Community Unit District No. 302,* 18 Ill. 2d 11, 163 N.E. 2d 89 (1959); *Haney* v. *City of Lexington,* 386 S.W. 2d 783 (Ky. 1964); *Williams* v. *City of Detroit,* 364 Mich. 231, 111 N.W. 2d 1 (1961); *Spanel* v. *Mounds View School District No. 621,* 264 Minn. 279, 118 N.W. 2d 795 (1962); *Rice* v. *Clark County,* 79 Nev. 253, 382 P. 2d 605 (1963); *McAndrew* v. *Mularchuk,* 33 N.J. 172, 162 A. 2d 820 (1960); *Kelso* v. *City of Tacoma,* 63 Wash. 2d 913, 390 P. 2d 2 (1964) (abrogation partly based on statute); *Holytz* v. *City of Milwaukee,* 17 Wis. 2d 26, 115 N.W. 2d 618 (1962).

[187] See Arvo Van Alstyne, "Government Tort Liability: A Decade of Change," 1966 *University of Illinois Law Forum* 919.

[188] *United States* v. *Muniz,* 374 U.S. 150 (1963).

[189] E.g., Federal Tort Claims Act, 28 U.S.C. §2680(h) (1964) (exemptions to liability).

[190] E.g., Federal Tort Claims Act, 28 U.S.C. §2680(a) (1964):
Any claim based upon an act or omission of an employee of the Government, exercising due care, in the execution of a statute or regulation, whether or not such statute or regulation be valid, or based upon the exercise or performance or the failure to exercise or perform a discretionary function or duty on the part of a federal agency or an employee of the Government, whether or not the discretion involved be abused.

sovereign immunity doctrine. The case was dismissed by the district court but remanded for trial by the court of appeals.[191] The plaintiff eventually was awarded substantial damages.

FEDERAL CIVIL RIGHTS ACT

The federal Civil Rights Act of 1871 originally passed to protect freed Negroes recently has been used to protect citizens generally from institutional deprivations. It provides a basis for redressing grievances against state or local officials including jail personnel.[192]

For many years, the Civil Rights Act was not an effective remedy for prisoners. In 1961, however, the Supreme Court revitalized the act. In many federal courts, the *Monroe* v. *Pape*[193] decision reversed the "hands-off" attitude toward state prisoners. Anyone clothed with authority by a state or local correctional system —a prisoner who is made a trusty and given power over other prisoners, for example, or even private persons acting in concert with state correctional officers—could be held liable under the act. Federal court action became for many the most direct route for resolution of local jail inmates' grievances if they could claim that the state deprived them of a federal statutory right or a constitutional right guaranteed by the Fourteenth Amendment.[194]

Federal courts have been reluctant to award compensatory damages to prisoners in cases brought under the act. In addition, the doctrine of sovereign immunity survives as a bar to the

[191] *Anthony* v. *District of Columbia*, No. 32,010 (D.C. Cir., December 2, 1969) (remanded for reconsideration in light of *Spencer* v. *General Hospital*, 425 F. 2d 479 (D.C. Cir. 1969).
[192]

> Every person who, under color of any statute, ordinance, regulation, custom, or usage, of any State or Territory, subjects, or causes to be subjected, any citizen of the United States or other person within the jurisdiction thereof to the deprivation of any rights, privileges, or immunities secured by the Constitution or laws, shall be liable to the party injured in an action at law, suit in equity, or other proper proceeding for redress.

42 U.S.C. §1983 (1964). See generally, *Carter* v. *Carlson*, 447 F. 2d 358 (D.C. Cir. 1971).
[193] 365 U.S. 167 (1961).
[194] See generally, *Benton* v. *Maryland*, 395 U.S. 784 (1969); *Palko* v. *Connecticut*, 302 U.S. 319 (1937).

liability of many states and municipalities under the Civil Rights Act and thus prevents the statute from serving as an adequate means to compensate prisoners for the effects of illegal actions by jail personnel.

Even when damage suits against government officials can be brought by jail inmates, courts can only hear individual cases on a piecemeal, after-the-fact basis. When an inmate is beaten or starved, transferred to a mental institution, forbidden to practice his religion or held incommunicado, it is of secondary importance that some distant day he may be able to collect damages, or his jailer may be held criminally liable. The inmate needs to be able to win his rights quickly and to force prison administrators to respect these rights. The most effective means is the injunction.[195] Another is the declaratory judgment which defines rights and obligations; correctional officials determine what appropriate action is required,[196] but the court can oversee.[197] For ex-

---

[195] In *Monroe* v. *Pape*, 365 U.S. 167 (1961). See *Eisen* v. *Eastman*, 421 F. 2d 560, 569 (2d Cir. 1969); *Sostre* v. *Rockefeller*, 312 F. Supp. 863, 881–83 (S.D.N.Y. 1970), *aff'd in part, modified in part, rev'd in part sub nom. Sostre* v. *McGinnis*, 442 F. 2d 178 (2d Cir. 1971) (*en banc*). *McNeese* v. *Board of Education*, 373 U.S. 668 (1963); *Houghton* v. *Shafer*, 392 U.S. 639 (1968) (*per curiam*). E.g., *Houghton* v. *Shafer*, 392 U.S. 639 (1968) (*per curiam*). The Supreme Court explicitly held that an exhaustion of state remedies was not a prerequisite to bring a suit under the Civil Rights Act. Lower courts also have said that state and local prisoners need not test every state administrative or judicial remedy before seeking relief in the federal courts. Yet these opinions show confusion over whether the Civil Rights Act excuses exhaustion of state and administrative remedies in every case, or only where application for relief through state channels clearly would be futile. The Supreme Court has added to this confusion by reiterating that exhaustion is unnecessary, while taking care to examine available state remedies and demonstrate their inadequacy for dealing with the claims raised.

[196] Declaratory Judgment Act, 28 U.S.C. §2201 (1964): "In a case of actual controversy within its jurisdiction . . . any court of the United States, upon the filing of an appropriate pleading, may declare the rights and other legal relations of any interested party seeking such declaration, whether or not further relief is or could be sought."

"Further necessary or proper relief based on a declaratory judgment or decree may be granted, after reasonable notice and hearing, against any adverse party whose rights have been determined by such judgment" (Ibid., §2202).

[197] Declaratory judgments are useful where judicial actions may be warranted but the court is reluctant to enter an area of supposed administrative expertise or where its decision would necessitate an appropriation of additional funds by a state legislature. Cf. *Upchurch* v. *State*, 51 Hawaii 150, 153; 454 P. 2d 112, 114 (1969).

ample, in New York, a writ "in the nature of mandamus"[198] was
granted to compel the commissioner of correction to permit a
Black Muslim prisoner the free exercise of his religion.[199] But
in another state, *mandamus* requires proof that the official has
shown "not merely error of judgment, but perversity of will, pas-
sion, prejudice, partiality, or moral delinquency."[200]

Most statutes dealing with the rights of prison inmates are extremely broad and ambiguous. In one federal case,[201] prisoners
who claimed that freedom to practice their religion had been
denied were not permitted a writ because there was no statute to
implement the constitutional right to free exercise of religion. The
court stated that *mandamus* cannot be issued unless the duty of
the administrative officer to act is clearly established and defined
and the obligation to act is peremptory.[202]

The nature of *mandamus* conflicts with the natural hesitancy
of judges to meddle in areas where they know little and where the
political risks are great. Until specific correctional standards are
promulgated to define prisoners' rights and the responsibilities of
correctional officials, this remedy will be of limited use in correctional reform efforts.

---

[198] Prison officials may be forced to take affirmative action respecting prisoners' rights where prisoners are successful in obtaining a writ of *mandamus*.
Although *mandamus* could provide an efficient means for courts to oversee
administrative action, legislatures and courts have imbedded within the remedy so many intricacies that it is seldom used in prisoners' cases.

Mandamus is the appropriate procedure for controlling the ministerial
(non-discretionary) acts of executive officials, for requiring officials to exercise their discretion and for preventing the abuse of administrative discretion. *Mandamus* may not be used, however, to control the manner in
which discretion is exercised. The difficulty lies in applying this theory to
specific instances. As with sovereign immunity, lines must be drawn dis-
tinguishing ministerial from discretionary acts.

[199] *Brown* v. *McGinnis,* 10 N.Y. 2d 531, 180 N.E. 2d 791, 225 N.Y.S. 2d
497 (1962).

[200] *State ex rel. Shafer* v. *Ohio Turnpike Commission,* 159 Ohio St. 581, 591,
113 N.E. 2d 14, 19 (1953).

[201] *White* v. *Clemmer,* 295 F. 2d 132 (D.C. Cir. 1961).

[202] In addition, administrative remedies must be exhausted before this type
of judicial relief is sought. The court did not inquire, however, whether any
administrative remedies existed in fact.

HABEAS CORPUS

Habeas corpus has been the chief method for prisoners to challenge the legal authority for their confinement. Before the Civil War this classic writ, considered by state courts to have been authorized by common law tradition, as well as by statute, was used more by state than federal courts. In 1867 Congress authorized the federal courts to grant habeas corpus "in all cases where any person may be restrained of his or her liberty in violation of the constitution, or of any treaty or law of the United States . . ." Both state and federal prisoners then began using the federal courts to challenge their detention on constitutional grounds.

For the better part of a century, only prisoners who challenged the legality of their conviction could get habeas corpus petitions; but in 1944, a federal court of appeals[203] said that prison inmates who claim that the conditions of their imprisonment violate constitutional guarantees, could seek habeas corpus protection. The Sixth Circuit Court of Appeals ruled that

> A prisoner is entitled to the writ of habeas corpus when, though lawfully in custody, he is deprived of some right to which he is lawfully entitled even in his confinement, the deprivation of which serves to make his imprisonment more burdensome than the law allows or curtails his liberty to a greater extent than the law permits.

Two years later, Judge Learned Hand said that habeas corpus is available "whenever else resort to it is necessary to prevent a complete miscarriage of justice."[204] In 1963 the Supreme Court expressed its approval of this expanded use of the writ.[205]

An Idaho court,[206] ordered a hearing on a petition for habeas corpus in which a prisoner said he had been beaten, denied medical care, forced to live under extremely unsanitary condi-

[203] *Coffin* v. *Reichard,* 143 F. 2d 443 (6th Cir. 1944).
[204] *United States ex rel. Kulick* v. *Kennedy,* 157 F. 2d 811, 813 (2d Cir. 1946) *rev'd on other grounds,* 332 U.S. 174 (1947) (habeas corpus cannot be used where direct appeal is permitted).
[205] *Jones* v. *Cunningham,* 371 U.S. 236 (1963); *Carafas* v. *LaValle,* 391 U.S. 234 (1968).
[206] *Mahaffey* v. *State,* 87 Idaho 228, 392 P. 2d 279 (1964).

tions and unjustly held in solitary confinement for prolonged periods of time. A West Virginia court granted a habeas corpus petition and ended the prison term of a defendant it had sentenced for robbery because of testimony about unsafe and anti-rehabilitative conditions in the penitentiary, a bold action that was reversed on appeal.[207] A Pennsylvania court used habeas corpus to transfer two pretrial detainees from the Holmesburg Prison to another jail because of conditions at Holmesburg which it said constituted cruel and unusual punishment.[208]

Even where available, federal court review through habeas corpus can take a long time. Prisoners must still exhaust all alternate remedies first,[209] though the extent to which the exhaustion requirement applies to habeas corpus attacks on prison conditions is not clear.

When an inmate awaiting state trial in the Manhattan House of Detention for Men claimed that he was being denied legal materials necessary for him to prepare for his trial,[210] his petition for a writ of habeas corpus was dismissed for failure to exhaust

[207] *State of West Virginia ex rel. Pingley* v. *Coiner,* H.C. No. 70–181 (Cir. Ct. of Randolph County, May 6, 1971) *rev'd* 186 S.E. 2d 220 (1972).

[208] *Commonwealth of Pennsylvania ex rel. Bryant* v. *Hendrick,* 7 *Criminal Law Reporter* 2463 (Court of Common Pleas for Philadelphia County, August 11, 1970), *aff'd* 444 Pa. 83, 280 A. 2d 110 (1971). Recognizing the possibility of a large number of habeas corpus petitions from other untried prisoners, the court announced that it would decline to hear them for a thirty-day period in order to give officials the opportunity to eliminate the most flagrant abuses. Surprisingly, no further petitions were filed.

The expansive view of habeas corpus in this case is not unanimous, however, particularly among state courts. Recently, a Florida prisoner, whose request for prison officials to forward a written complaint to the United States Attorney General by certified mail was refused, filed a petition for a writ of habeas corpus in the state court. The court ruled that even if the prisoner's constitutional rights had been violated by the officials' inaction, a writ of habeas corpus cannot be issued to a prisoner not entitled to immediate release from confinement. The Supreme Court denied *certiorari,* and the decision was later cited with approval by a court in another state. See *Wilwording* v. *Swenson,* 439 F. 2d 1331 (8th Cir. 1971), *rev'd per curiam on other grounds,* 404 U.S. 249 (1971). *Granville* v. *Hunt,* 411 F. 2d 9 (5th Cir. 1969); *McNeal* v. *Taylor,* 313 F. Supp. 200 (W.D. Okla. 1970); *Schack* v. *State,* 194 So. 2d 53 (Fla. Dist. Ct. Appeals), *cert. denied,* 386 U.S. 1027 (1967); *Brown* v. *Justice's Court,* 83 Nev. 272, 428 P. 2d 376 (1967).

[209] 28 U.S.C. §2254 (1964); *Johnson* v. *Dye,* 338 U.S. 864 (1949) (*per curiam*); 28 U.S.C. §2254(b)-(c) (1964).

[210] See section on Access to Court, supra. The petitioner was unrepresented by counsel. Cf. *Gideon* v. *Wainwright,* 372 U.S. 335 (1963).

state remedies.[211] When he tried to appeal the denial, a law clerk told him that the New York Code of Criminal Procedure "does not authorize an appeal from the orders of the General Sessions Court denying your application to be furnished with law books. Under the circumstances, there is no further action to be taken by this Court in the matter." The federal petition was then filed, yet an assistant New York County district attorney informed the court the prisoner still might apply for relief from the Supreme Court of the State of New York, and the federal petition was dismissed. Whether this man's request ever received consideration by a federal court before his criminal trial is not known. But the enormous deterrent these procedural requirements impose upon the unsophisticated inmate in jail may render the remedy ineffective.

At present, few correction departments have established procedures for hearings or other methods of resolving prisoners' grievances. If some administrative complaint procedures should be developed in the future, courts could be expected to require prisoners to use these administrative channels before taking their grievances to court.[212]

Prisoners' attorneys have begun to file an increasing proportion of suits under the federal Civil Rights Act rather than attempting habeas corpus relief. In *Rodriguez* v. *McGinnis*,[213] a prisoner sued officials under both the Civil Rights Act and federal habeas corpus, claiming that he had been improperly deprived of good time which, if credited to his sentence, entitled him to immediate release. The district court ruled that the case was predominantly a Civil Rights Act claim, with a habeas corpus petition included as an adjunct to ensure full relief if the prisoner should prevail. The appellate court reversed. Since the complaint sought relief from custody, it said, it was in fact an application for habeas corpus and required the exhaustion of state remedies. The Supreme

[211] *Barone* v. *Warden,* 209 F. Supp. 309 (S.D.N.Y. 1962).
[212] Exhaustion of federal administrative remedies was required in *Paden* v. *United States,* 430 F. 2d 882 (5th Cir. 1970); *O'Brien* v. *Blackwell,* 421 F. 2d 884 (5th Cir. 1970); *Hess* v. *Blackwell,* 409 F. 2d 362 (5th Cir. 1969); *Smoake* v. *Willingham,* 359 F. 2d 386 (10th Cir. 1966).
[213] 307 F. Supp. 627 (N.D.N.Y. 1969), *rev'd,* 451 F. 2d 730 (2d Cir. 1971); cf. *Jones* v. *Decker,* 436 F. 2d 954 (5th Cir. 1970); *Denney* v. *State of Kansas,* 436 F. 2d 587 (10th Cir. 1971); *Sinclair* v. *Henderson,* 435 F. 2d 125 (5th Cir. 1970); *United States ex rel. Hill* v. *Johnston,* 321 F. Supp. 818 (S.D.N.Y. 1971); *Edwards* v. *Schmidt,* 321 F. Supp. 68 (W.D. Wisc. 1971).

Court has ruled that where the remedy sought concerns the fact or duration of confinement, habeas corpus is the appropriate procedure, and where a case concerns conditions of confinement, the Civil Rights Act is the appropriate statute.[214]

Most recently, the Supreme Court, over the lone dissent of Chief Justice Burger, summarily reversed the dismissal of a federal habeas corpus petition against conditions of maximum security confinement in a state penitentiary, for failure to exhaust all conceivable state judicial remedies. The Court ruled that the complaint might be read as pleading a cause of action under the Civil Rights Act, and hence not subject to the requirement of exhaustion.[215]

CRIMINAL ACTIONS AGAINST OFFICIALS

In theory, officials who abuse or assault or murder inmates in their custody can be criminally prosecuted.[216] In practice, prosecutors have been reluctant to invoke local criminal statutes against fellow officials. When sensational publicity and investigations by state and federal authorities resulted in the prosecution of several Arkansas prison employees under a state statute making it a felony to exceed punishments prescribed by the State Penitentiary Board,[217] the Arkansas Supreme Court upheld the dismissal of all charges, holding the statute void as an unconstitutional delegation of legislative power.[218]

[214] *Preiser* v. *Rodriguez,* 41 *U. S. Law Week* 4555 (May 7, 1973).

[215] *Wilwording* v. *Swenson,* 439 F. 2d 1331 (8th Cir. 1971), 404 U.S. 249 (1971) (*per curiam*), *rev'd.* Following the decision in *Wilwording,* the Court of Appeals for the Second Circuit reconsidered its decision in *Rodriguez* v. *McGinnis* and this time voted to affirm the decision of the district court. However, the existence of seven separate concurring and one dissenting opinion offers graphic evidence of the continued confusion. *Rodriguez* v. *McGinnis,* 10 *Criminal Law Reporter* 2365 (2d Cir., January 25, 1972) (*en banc*).

[216] E.g., *Bush* v. *Babb,* 23 Ill. App. 2d 285, 162 N.E. 2d 594 (1959) (statutory duty to provide medical care owed to public but not to individual prisoners; only state can sue for violation); *Ridgway* v. *Superior Court,* 74 Ariz. 117, 245 P. 2d 268, 272 (1952) (criminal statutes concerning offenses against children cited as the proper remedy for floggings and other punishments of boys in institutions for juveniles).

[217] Ark. Stat. Ann. 46–158 (1964).

[218] *State* v. *Bruton,* 246 Ark. 288, 437 S.W. 2d 795 (1969).

In a few extreme cases, almost all involving southern prisons, the United States Department of Justice has reacted to the failure of states to prosecute by obtaining federal indictments of local officials under the criminal provisions of the federal Civil Rights Act.

Deputy sheriffs in Alameda County, California, were indicted for violating the civil rights of persons arrested in connection with the "People's Park" incidents in Berkeley.[219] Two of the deputies were accused of "forcing a prisoner to place his head against a metal pole at the jail and then clubbing the opposite side of the pole," three others of "holding, beating, choking and striking" a prisoner while booking him. According to the county sheriff, the United States attorney responsible for the indictments had "taken these deputies and thrown them to the wolves," setting a "terrible example of law enforcement."[220]

Only the extraordinary, shocking misconduct of jailers is likely ever to result in their indictments. And, in any event, the indictment and conviction of a jail guard can at most have a potentially deterrent effect against similar misconduct and a deserved punitive effect on the guard himself. For the aggrieved inmate it is a last resort, but a less than adequate remedy.

CONTEMPT

The contempt power is the traditional legal weapon by which courts have enforced their orders. By definition, one is held to be in contempt upon disobedience to an existing order. It rarely has been used to support prisoners who are seeking enforcement of court orders.

In 1889 a federal district judge in Georgia sentenced a defendant to a local jail.[221] Later he read in a newspaper of the prisoner's disorderly conduct and the consequent disciplinary

---

[219] In three cases decided in the 1950's, federal appeals courts ruled that summary or corporal punishment of convicts could violate the federal Civil Rights Act, regardless of whether the punishments were authorized by state law. *United States* v. *Jackson,* 235 F. 2d 925 (8th Cir. 1956); *United States* v. *Walker,* 216 F. 2d 683 (5th Cir. 1954); *United States* v. *Jones,* 207 F. 2d 785 (5th Cir. 1953).

[220] Washington *Post,* February 4, 1970, p. A-3.

[221] *In re Birdsong,* 39 F. 559 (S.D. 1889).

measures imposed by the jailer: "He was chained by the neck to the grating of the cell, and by the time he stands up until this morning, and lives a day or two on bread and water, he will probably be willing to be disciplined." Outraged, the judge ordered an investigation and directed the jailer to show cause why he should not be held in contempt of court. The jailer was fined fifty dollars plus court costs—the fine to be suspended as long as the offense was not repeated. This is the first reported case of a sentencing judge's use of the broad, inherent contempt power to discipline a jailer for violating his implicit responsibility for the safekeeping of prisoners committed to his custody by the court. The judge reasoned that the abuse of power was so extreme and so dangerous that some judicial remedy simply had to be established. Unfortunately, this precedent has been disregarded: the first reported case was virtually the last.

In 1906, the Supreme Court punished a county sheriff and others for permitting a prisoner to be lynched. A federal court had ordered that the Negro be detained in jail safely pending appeal of a rape conviction.[222] Justice Oliver Wendell Holmes, Jr., characterized the alleged offense as a conspiracy "to break into the jail for the purpose of lynching and murdering [the prisoner] with intent to show contempt for the order of this court . . ."

In the D. C. Jail case, attorneys for all the inmates at the jail brought a contempt action against jail officials when protesting inmates and innocent observers were brutally hosed and maced by guards. The court scolded the supervising jail officials but denied contempt on the technical ground that there was no proof that the offenders had "wilfully" disregarded the court order. A federal judge in Virginia, however, recently held state correctional officials in contempt of its orders for failing to implement its prior order concerning disciplinary proceedings,[223] and another federal judge in Georgia held the director of the federal Bureau of Prisons and his chief chaplain in contempt for disobeying his court's order to notify all wardens of the court's order to provide certain recognition and to allow certain practices of an exotic religious cult in prison.[224]

[222] *United States* v. *Shipp,* 203 U.S. 563 (1906).
[223] *Landman* v. *Royster,* 354 F. Supp. 1292 (Fed. Dist. Ct. E.D. Va., January 29, 1973) ($25,000 fine suspd.).
[224] *Theriault* v. *Carlson* 339 F. Supp. 375 (N.D. Ga. 1972), order, 353 F. Supp. 1061 (N.D. Ga. 1973).

The contempt power could be expanded to provide another appropriate recourse for prisoners' claims of maltreatment, but it probably will not be used often because of the political nature of the remedy and the practical problems of proof.

The use of contempt could be expanded as an effective technique for controlling jail officials; but it is limited to after-the-fact situations. It is of no use when the abuse does not arise out of a case not already before the court.

CLASS ACTIONS

Class actions brought for or against representatives of a group were developed by courts of equity as an answer to the practical problems of multi-party litigation. They are made to order for litigation by transient jail inmates aimed at general jail conditions.

Where jail inmates are uneducated, unaware of their rights or of the means for implementing them, or unrepresented by counsel, a class suit can provide the only practical means for presenting their grievances to a court. Class suits frequently are more efficient and economical than individual actions and save time for the courts, defending prison officials, and attorneys.

With few exceptions,[225] however, class suits against jail officials have not been allowed by the state courts, although in recent years, several notorious and successful cases have made increased recourse to class actions more likely in the future.

Most of the growing number of challenges to conditions of local jails have been brought as class actions. Courts have permitted class actions on behalf of inmates of the Cook County Jail,[226] the New Orleans Parish Prison,[227] the county jail in Little Rock, Arkansas,[228] the D. C. Jail,[229] and two county jails in California,[230] among other places.

On the other hand, a federal district judge refused to permit

[225] *Wayne County Jail Inmates* v. *Wayne County Board of Commissioners,* Civ. Action No. 173217 (Cir. Ct., Wayne County, Mich., May 18, 1971).
[226] *Inmates of the Cook County Jail* v. *Tierney,* No. 68 C 504 (N.D. Ill. 1968).
[227] *Hamilton* v. *Schiro,* 338 F. Supp. 1016 (E.D. La. 1970).
[228] *Hamilton* v. *Love,* 328 F. Supp. 1182 (E.D. Ark. 1971).
[229] *Campbell* v. *Rogers,* Civ. Action No. 1462–71 (U. S. District Court for the District of Columbia, 1971).
[230] *Brenneman* v. *Madigan,* 343 F. Supp. 128 (N.D. Cal. 1971); *Dean* v. *Young,* No. 123849 (N.D. Cal., March 17, 1971).

inmates of the Milwaukee County Jail to bring such a lawsuit because of his doubts that adequate notice could be given to the members of the class, many of whom were transients and held in jail for only a short time.[231]

A unique approach to litigation has emerged in these jail cases in a number of large cities during the last few years, and it has been successful in every instance to date. In several cities—Philadelphia, Detroit, Little Rock, Baltimore, New Orleans, San Francisco and Alameda counties, California, and Washington, D.C., notably—class action lawsuits have been brought in the names of all inmates in the city or county jails, contesting the aggregate of the prevailing practices and conditions at those jails. The legal thrust of these cases has been two-pronged. First, it has been alleged that the sum of the conditions at the jail constitute cruel and unusual punishment in violation of the Eighth Amendment of the United States Constitution. Second, it has been argued that since most jail inhabitants are in pretrial status, their being deprived of certain of their rights, often more than convicted inmates in prison, violates the presumption of innocence and the equal protection and due process clauses of the Constitution.

The first position, one which has been accepted by a number of courts already, that inhuman jail conditions generally constitute cruel and unusual punishment, would seem to apply to most jails, especially the large overcrowded urban jails where conditions generally are egregious, where the facilities are awful and the general practices and treatment are excessive. The versatility of this legal approach is that while bad ventilation, inadequate recreational facilities, unacceptable medical care, crowded cells, physical abuses and unfair disciplinary proceedings or any of the other typical aggravated jail conditions and practices in and of themselves might not be deemed deprivations of constitutional proportions, the aggregate of all of these conditions in one place clearly adds up to a classic example of what our contemporary civilized notions are of cruel and unusual punishment.

This argument is made all the more forceful when a second

---

[231] *Shank* v. *Peterson,* 8 *Criminal Law Reporter* 2397 (E.D. Wisc., January 12, 1971). Since any judgment in the case would have little effect on these "transients," it is not clear why this obstacle was considered insurmountable.

ingredient is considered. The overwhelming majority of the people who are subjected to these onerous jail conditions are in pretrial status, have not yet been convicted of a crime, are entitled to a presumption of innocence and have not been incarcerated to be punished, but simply to be detained until their trial. As one court has said: "Punitive measures in such a context are out of harmony with the presumption of innocence."[232] Most of the class action cases considered this point and stressed that not only should pretrial detainees not suffer cruel and unusual punishment but suggested that any punishment suffered beyond the simple fact of detention itself (which is the only purpose of denial of bail), is if not cruel and unusual punishment certainly a violation of fundamental Fifth and Fourteenth Amendment rights.

In most of the decisions to date in these cases, while courts have singled out particular inadequacies of the local jails in question which were most shocking, they ended up deciding the case on the broader ground that the aggregate of all of the conditions elevated the case to one of constitutional proportions. In the San Francisco case, for example, *Smith* v. *Hongisto,* the trial judge seemed most concerned about the inadequate medical facilities, but he also noted the poor quality of jail food, unsanitary conditions, overcrowding, poor procedures involving visitation, mail, recreation, staff and the terrible isolation cells. At one point, the court stated that these specific complaints ". . . each taken alone would be insufficient to amount to such total deprivation of medical care or even such gross inadequacies as would constitute violation of 8th Amendment rights." But he said when all of the individual items considered were taken as a whole, a clear Eighth Amendment problem was present. That court noted that the problems he detailed with great specificity ". . . are universally applied to detainees without regard to the threat any individual might constitute," and indeed apply especially to the many people in pretrial detention status.

In these class action cases, the courts have gone into great detail about the specific conditions of the jails involved and, shocked by the revelations, reached the broad constitutional questions

[232] *Anderson* v. *Nosser,* 438 F. 2d 183, 190 (5th Cir. 1971). The Alameda County case, *Brenneman* v. *Madigan,* 343 F. Supp. 128 (N.D. Cal. 1972), contains a good discussion of this point.

raised in the complaints. Furthermore, they did not hesitate to issue strong specific orders for improvement with time limitations.

In a case involving the Jefferson Parish Jail in Louisiana, the court was concerned about specific situations at the jail, particularly the many mentally disturbed people who are housed there and the physical conditions of the place which the court called "a combination medieval dungeon and zoo," used simply to "stow" people. The court ordered better exercise, reduced population, improved medical treatment, classification procedures, compliance with state sanitary and health laws and more vocational rehabilitation programs. It also stated that, in dealing with people in jail on pretrial status, "obviously, under our constitution, society may not punish at all those who are merely charged with a crime, for they are presumed innocent until proved guilty beyond a reasonable doubt."

In both the Detroit and New Orleans jail cases, the courts required that a plan be submitted which would deal with the specific existing conditions and which would, within a set time period, assure the improvements required by their interpretations of the Constitution's cruel and unusual punishment provisions. In both of these cases, the conditions involved were typical ones which exist in almost all jails: unsanitary conditions, overcrowding, lack of supervision and recreation and medical care, inadequate protection of inmates from each other and from precipitous punitive and administrative practices of jail personnel.

These cases are proliferating around the country; they have been successful; they have led to the beginnings of local improvements, although in all cases reforms have come frustratingly slowly. In a similar class action, in which I have acted as co-counsel with the city's public defender service, questioning the constitutionality of the general conditions at the D. C. Jail, the case has been pending for over three years, during which time there have been two riots, a contempt proceeding against jail officials, numerous pretrial hearings, but no final adjudication. We have managed to extract from city administrators and correctional officials a series of consent orders granting numerous of our requested changes and refining the issues of the case. However, we have yet to have our trial.

While the approaches of all of these cases have been similar, in our case in the District of Columbia, I have made one further argument which has not been raised elsewhere and which really gets to the fundamental question about jails. I have argued that not only do all of the excessive conditions and unusual procedures in the jail constitute an unconstitutional form of cruel and unusual punishment but, in addition to these extraordinary conditions, the normal operations and conditions of the jail in and of themselves constitute a form of cruel and unusual punishment.

My argument on this point proceeds along the following lines. It is generally agreed that physically hurting or beating a prisoner as a form of punishment—for example, pounding a prisoner with a blackjack—would be a form of cruel and unusual punishment that would not be tolerated. Indeed, most states have outlawed corporal punishment of any kind. Yet in jails, where theoretically men are not sent for punishment of any kind but rather to await trial, we regularly are subjecting inmates to subtle but equally damaging forms of punishment which also should be considered constitutionally impermissible.

In the past few decades, scientists have demonstrated that conditions of extreme isolation and overcrowding result in scientifically demonstrable forms of physical and psychological stress and damage. If that is so, and if the Constitution's cruel and unusual punishment provisions are to be read in the light of evolving and contemporary views about what is cruel and unusual, then in every jail like the one in my city, where men are either caged in minuscule, awful cells, or crowded into large dormitories—again, most of them in pretrial status—the normal everyday operation of the jail can cause physical and psychological damage and thus may be viewed as a form of cruel and unusual punishment which by its very nature, should be prohibited by the Eighth Amendment. This question has not yet been decided.

These cases are fascinating examples of social engineering by lawyers and courts. The complaints and documentation that have initiated the cases were extensive, well researched, imaginative. Many of the judges personally visited the institutions and held protracted hearings which went into great detail about the operations and conditions of the institutions. The judges reacted with shock at what they found and took firm reformative positions, irrespective of their reputations as liberals or conservatives, hardliners or soft touches. Judge Christenberry wrote, in the New Orleans Parish case:

> Prison life inevitably involves some deprivation of rights, but the conditions of plaintiffs' confinement in Orleans Parish Prison so shock the conscience as a matter of elemental decency and are so much more cruel than is necessary to achieve a legitimate penal aim that such confinement constitutes cruel and unusual punishment in violation of the Eighth and Fourteenth Amendments of the United States Constitution.

The court's opinions have been factually exhaustive (the opinion in the case involving the Philadelphia Jail, for example, ran 264 pages) and legally imaginative. The courts in their opinions went into elaborate detail describing the physical conditions, the programs (or, more aptly, the lack of programs), the overcrowding, the absence of facilities and services, the procedures at disciplinary proceedings and the forms of punishment exacted in reaching often ringing constitutional positions.

While the courts were solicitous about the problems officials had in bringing about changes in jails, and realistic about the political facts of life, they also were adamant in their insistence upon requiring conformance with constitutional standards.

In a number of cities, the judges asked for special reports, outside consultants and set up timetables for changes. The costs and the political problems surrounding jail reform were not allowed as excuses. As one court put it in its decision:

> The Court is aware of the difficulties of the situation. No one supposes that if our prisons improve, we shall be free of crime; if they become models for the world, this will not occur; but at least by dealing with our prisoners justly we shall have made a start.[233]

In sum, some courts have moved remarkably in jail reform, from the "hands-off" policies of the past, and jumped in, if the judicial metaphor may be continued, with both their hands and feet.[234]

[233] *Jackson* v. *Hendrick*, 11 Crim. L. Reptr. 2088 (Penn. Ct. Comm. Pls., April 7, 1972).
[234] I have maintained contact with the courts and attorneys around the country who I know are dealing with class action jail cases in the last several years. In my files are numerous complaints and decisions, interim orders and court reports regarding these cases. Due to the evolving nature of this area of litigation, and the scarcity of reported decisions, to date no list can claim

NON-JUDICIAL ALTERNATIVES FOR RESOLVING GRIEVANCES

Courts are hesitant to extend their review of prisoners' grievances for fear of being inundated with claims. Even with minimal research facilities, prisoners have the time and ingenuity to generate an enormous amount of litigation. In 1964, federal and state prisoners filed 6,240 petitions in federal district courts alone. By 1971 this figure had nearly tripled—to 16,266.[235]

If legal advice were regularly available, the many groundless complaints could be screened out. Legal assistance also would save the courts time by producing petitions that are better drafted and contain less irrelevant material than those written by unaided inmates. Administrators might be more likely to relieve unnecessary deprivations of jail life if the community pointed out their irrationality and, if necessary, put pressure on the officials to eliminate them. But prisons and jails present low-visibility social problems.

In certain other countries, private citizens have organized for prison reform. KRUM in Sweden has counterparts in Denmark (KRIM), Norway (KROM) and Finland (the November Movement). The organization, composed of present and former convicts, students, professors, businessmen, politicians and others,

completeness. However, the following cases should be considered by anyone interested in the field:

Jackson v. *Hendrick,* Philadelphia, Pennsylvania Court of Common Pleas, No. 71-2437, filed April 7, 1972; *Hamilton* v. *Schiro,* United States District Court, Eastern District of Louisiana, New Orleans, C.A. No. 69-2443; *Holland* v. *Donnelon,* United States District Court, Eastern District of Louisiana, New Orleans, 71-1442; *Smith* v. *Hongisto,* United States District Court, Northern District of California, filed March 15, 1973, C-70-1244RHS; *Wayne County Jail Inmates, et al.* v. *Wayne County Board of Commissioners,* Wayne County, Circuit Court, Michigan C.A. No. 173217; *Hamilton* v. *Love,* United States District Court, Eastern District of Arkansas, Eastern Division, filed June 2, 1971, No. LR-70-C-201; *Brenneman* v. *Madigan,* United States District Court, Northern District California No. C-70-1911AJZ; *Garnes, et al.* v. *Taylor, et al.,* complaint pending, United States District Court, District of Columbia; *Stinnie* v. *Gregory,* United States District Court, Eastern District of Virginia, complaint filed Civil Action No. 554-70-R; *Smith and Fluker* v. *Carberry, et al.,* United States District Court, Northern District of California, Civil No. C-70-1244.

235 Administrative Office of the United States Courts, "Annual Reports of the Director" (1964 and 1971).

serves as a watchdog to ensure decent treatment of prisoners and to promote alternatives to prison cells.

Organizations such as these could exist in this country. Private groups such as the District of Columbia's Visitor Service Center, which handles the personal, social welfare problems of jail inmates through volunteers or refers them to appropriate agencies is a rare phenomenon in this country, however.

In Denmark confidential complaints from prisoners may be sent to an ombudsman, who seeks to resolve problems with prison officials on the scene. But if that does not work they may deal directly with administrators and the director of prisons. In Italy a surveillance judge (*giùdice di sorveglianza*) makes decisions on the transfer and release of prisoners and ensures that prisons are administered according to law. Although the visiting judge has no power to order officials to change their procedures, he can report irregularities to his superior, the Minister of Justice. A similar institution, *juge de l'application des peines,* has been created in France.[236]

In the Netherlands a three-member team from the Ministry of Justice, trained in law, psychology and counseling, visits all institutions where people are confined. Their responsibility is to inquire into the bases for confinement, listen to the prisoners' grievances and report to the Minister of Justice on cases that appear to call for a remedy. Chief Justice Burger described these teams, and the desirability of an American grievance procedure:

> In a sense these trained teams are like bank examiners, or health inspectors. Their method provides a regular avenue of communication designed to flush out the rare case of miscarriage of justice and the larger number of cases in which the prisoner has some valid complaint or deserves reexamination of his sentence. The mere existence of such an avenue of communication exercises a very beneficial influence which is in many respects far superior to our habeas corpus process. With us, the prisoner hopes that some distant proceeding before a remote judge will enable him to have his cries heard; with them, the prisoner meets face to face with trained counselors who give him a sympathetic hearing, ask questions, make a record of his complaints, and bring his valid grievances to the attention of higher authority.

[236] Seewald, "The Italian Surveillance Judge," 45 *Nebraska L. Rev.* 96, 97–98 (1966).

The National Council on Crime and Delinquency recently recommended that every state correctional department establish a
grievance procedure under which all grievances communicated by
prisoners to the head of the department would be investigated by
a person or agency outside the department and a written report of
the findings would be submitted to the department and the
prisoner.[237]

The Maryland legislature has created an Inmate Grievance Commission to which any state prisoner may complain. Unless his
complaint is found "on its face wholly lacking in merit," the inmate will be given a hearing. He may call and question witnesses
and, if he can afford it, employ an attorney. If the decision is in
his favor, it is reviewed by the secretary of public safety and
correctional services.[238]

A bill passed by the California legislature but vetoed by the
governor[239] would have created a correctional ombudsman responsible to the legislature to receive complaints from prisoners
and to recommend changes to the administrators involved or to
suggest new legislation. A recent proclamation by the governor of
Minnesota established the first state correctional ombudsman,
responsible to the governor, with the authority to investigate complaints from prison and jail inmates, their families, probationers,
parolees and correctional staff. The ombudsman's office has
been funded on a pilot basis by a federal grant. The federal Bureau
of Prisons has an Office of Review, staffed by lawyers, to investigate institutional complaints. In Oregon, the superintendent of the
penitentiary has appointed a former prison guard to act as prison
ombudsman. Both inmates and staff members report that the
ombudsman has done much to relieve tensions by calling individual injustices or oversights to the attention of the superintendent.

The greatest potential for non-judicial remedies to effect
broader, systemic change appears to lie in the work of private
groups. The Pennsylvania Prison Society had been permitted to
put an ombudsman into the Philadelphia prison system, but after
the ombudsman, an ex-offender approved by prison officials, had
worked for a month, the officials asked that he be removed and

[237] A Model Act for the Protection of Rights of Prisoners (1972), p. 5.
[238] Md., Art 41 Ann. Code §204F (1971).
[239] Assembly Bill No. 1181, introduced March 25, 1971.

replaced with someone else. A year later, they decided that jail conditions no longer warranted independent review.

The Center for Correctional Justice, a private, non-profit OEO-funded organization in the District of Columbia, during its first few months provided local offenders with access to legal counseling and representation in both civil and criminal matters through contracts with community legal services agencies. The center assumes the role of an ombudsman within the institutions, attempting to resolve grievances through negotiation with administrators. It has developed formal grievance procedures, culminating in arbitration, currently being implemented in Massachusetts and California, and has begun to experiment with collective bargaining. In Cleveland, a mediator from the National Center for Dispute Settlement has been involved in protracted negotiations and some arbitration at the Cuyahoga County Jail.

Originally developed by labor and management groups as an alternative to strikes and other methods of economic disruption, the flexibility of collective bargaining techniques has been demonstrated in the fields of public employment, student–university relations and community conflicts. It is particularly appropriate where prisoners have begun to organize into unions, generally led by ex-prisoners, to bargain for higher rates of pay and better working conditions.

Several incentives operate—one, the avoidance of frequent litigation: another, the possibility of reducing tensions among prisoners. Prisoners' unions present new challenges. Should officials be required to reorganize unions? Do prisoners have legal status to operate and impose sanctions? Two unions in California and unions in New York (the latter with the backing of a recognized outside union), Michigan, Rhode Island, Massachusetts, Maine, Maryland and Delaware, have sought to bargain collectively with officials concerning standard union demands for higher wages and better working conditions. One of the California unions also addressed itself to inadequate medical care, indeterminate sentencing laws and parole practice.

To date, none of the officials involved has agreed to recognize a prisoners' union. Legal battles are under way simply to establish the unions' right to send their newsletters into the prisons.[240] The fight for recognition undoubtedly will reach the courts, where

[240] *Goodwin* v. *Oswald*, 462 F. 2d 1237 (2d Cir. 1972).

lawyers for the fledgling unions can be expected to raise both the First Amendment issues of freedom of association and right to assemble and petition for redress of grievances, and the more specific right of unions to achieve recognition under the federal and state labor laws.

Administrative problems in the criminal justice system would be relieved if there were some direct and expeditious means to filter and handle prisoners' complaints. For example, a complaint to an ombudsman might be required before grievances could be aired in court. In the long run, such a procedure would save considerable time and expense, and might defuse many incendiary but minor problems.

Jails will remain lawless so long as the law permits. The cycle of lawlessness is a vicious one; it is as much a product of our own creation as it is of those marked law violators inside. The presumption must be reversed that upon entry into jail, people lose their rights. Except those few rights which are absolutely required to maintain their civilized detention, men in jail should be treated with decency, humanity and according to constitutional dictates.

Grand juries and other governmental and quasi-governmental bodies have the job of screening jails in most places, but rarely carry it out. In response to complaints, the Nassau County, New York, district attorney used fifteen undercover agents to investigate conditions at the Nassau County Jail, and in 1972 issued a public report about conditions there.[241] One of this prosecutor's conclusions was:

> When an inmate had a complaint or a grievance, he felt that he had no recourse within the prison system. If he wrote a complaint to a high ranking officer or the warden, it had to be submitted, unsealed, to the guard on duty—who often was the very individual against whom the complaint was made. Most inmates believed that their complaints never reached the staff members to whom they were addressed and that a written complaint was an exercise in futility. Many of them did not submit complaints because they feared they would be further harassed or even suffer loss of "good time" [the time deducted from their original sentence for good behavior].
>
> Some method of assuring inmates that complaints and griev-

[241] S. Cahn, "Report on the Nassau County Jail," *Crime and Delinquency* (1973), adapts the report's findings. The full report was issued on April 11, 1972.

ances will be forwarded to someone in authority must be developed. Whatever method is chosen, the inmates should be able to believe that their complaints and grievances are being properly reviewed by someone who is not automatically prejudiced against them. Operatives indicate that this would go a long way to reduce the pettiness and frustration that exist within the institution.

The prosecutor announced that undercover monitors would be placed in the jail regularly to assure against lapses.

Here in Nassau County, this report is not a conclusion but merely a beginning. Once the presence of our agents became known, the attitudes and performance of certain staff members improved markedly. . . .

We announce this publicly, emphasizing that we will hold accountable all who violate the law, including correctional staff members. If our system of justice is to be at all effective, we must be as strict with those whose task it is to administer punishment as we are with those who we judge must be punished.

In New Orleans, Louisiana, the federal district court found that shocking conditions at the city's jail amounted to unconstitutional punishment of the inmates, and commissioned a master to report and to supervise the decision for the court. The master conducted a thorough survey, and the court adopted his findings. This technique is a useful one since courts have neither the time, expertise nor inclination to do this kind of supervisory work despite their responsibility.

Whether it is a master for a court, an undercover agent of the district attorney, an ombudsman who is independent of the correction department or some other outside agency, it is crucial that some monitoring agent be assigned to assure that jails do not disintegrate into outlawry.

Chief Justice Burger recently stated in a speech before the National Conference of Christians and Jews that, with a properly functioning grievance system:

[T]he hour-to-hour and day-to-day frictions and tensions . . . can be carried up through channels so that the valid grievances can be remedied and either guided to a proper solution or dissipated by exposure.

This, in essence, is what every penal institution must have—the means of having complaints reach decision-making sources through established channels so that the valid grievances can be remedied and spurious grievances exposed.

If we are really going to have any chance of making prison inmates useful members of society, the institution is the place to teach the fundamental lesson that life's problems are solved by working within the system—not by riots and destruction of property.

As courts become more involved with the jails, and as the bar begins to meet its responsibility to provide full representation to jail inmates, both prompted by a growingly restless and demanding jail clientele, conditions will improve. But without community involvement in providing alternate and augmentative services, and without public attention and continuous pressure to insist on jail reform, those efforts will be inadequate and ephemeral.

The press, too, must live up to its self-heralded responsibility to watchdog jails. The press often has been delinquent, interested in jails only when riots are exploding or when some bizarre incident occurs. If jails are to improve, the press must keep "the pitiless light of public glare" on the typically shadowed, ignored life behind jail walls.

8

TOWARD A NEW
CONCEPT OF JAILS

In 1972, I was asked to testify as an expert witness in a case which contested conditions at the Jefferson Parish Prison—a medium-sized jail outside the city of New Orleans. After the complainant's lawyer, a young law professor from Tulane, questioned me about the faults I had seen in the jail and about my suggestions for preferable alternatives, an interesting line of cross-examination began.

During the direct examination I had tried to make the point that under our present system the only legal and proper purpose for pretrial detention was containment: to assure that a defendant would show up for trial and to protect the community during the interim from dangerous defendants. After that, there was no further need, nor was it legally proper, to exact all the other common deprivations of the typical jail. I referred to the ugly prison garb, the senseless censorship of mail and reading material, the arbitrary curbs on visitation, the absence of adequate recreation and work opportunities, the disgusting prison fare, the onerous regulations and practices which prevailed at that jail and in jails all over the country.

Jails, like all other total institutions, are operated, I argued, for the convenience of the administrators. The consumers, the clients of the institution, have rights, too, I suggested; especially when they have been institutionalized involuntarily and have not been convicted of any crime. The punitive conditions in jails raise serious legal and moral questions. These practices and procedures in the extreme amount to cruel and unusual punishment and more generally can be questioned as unconstitutional denials of equal protection of the law when they apply to pretrial detainees in jails. A man who makes bail or is released in some other fashion before trial, need not undergo these deprivations. Two conclusions were clear: first, only for extraordinary reasons should detention be required before trial; and, second, any detention should be less punitive than is customary. For convicted defendants, the jail rarely if ever is the right place.[1]

The defense counsel asked me a long line of questions, inquiring whether I would allow jail inmates to mingle, to partake in unlimited recreation, to have unlimited visits, to work, to cohabit sexually. To each question I responded that I felt jail inmates should be permitted to do all these things and more since their partaking in such activities need not detract from the ability of jail administrators to assure their presence at trial and to maintain the segregation of dangerous defendants from the free community. Once contained, they should be punished no more.

After having led me down this path, the defense counsel, obviously pleased with his ability to push me into what he thought was an obviously untenable position, announced his surprise that an outsider to the local scene, a supposed expert, would make such outlandish, bizarre suggestions recommending practices which he felt would be considered exotic in his community. I was proposing, he said, no more than a kind of hotel for criminals.

Perhaps this critic caught a crucial point which needs to be made. Hotel is a loaded word, connoting coddling and imprudence; but jails are not supposed to be prisons. Jails do have some proper custodial functions, but they can be carried out in a totally different institution. This notion is not as radical as it might seem. A recent report by a presidential commission faulted the treatment of inmates in jails and made the following recommendations:

> 1. Persons detained awaiting trial should be entitled to the same rights as those persons admitted to bail or other form of pretrial release except where the nature of confinement requires modification.
>
> 2. Where modification of the rights of persons detained await-

[1] For fuller discussion of this point, see infra.

ing trial is required by the fact of confinement, such modification should be as limited as possible.

3. The duty of showing that custody requires modification of such rights should be upon the detention agency.

4. Persons detained awaiting trial should be accorded the same rights recommended for persons convicted of crime as set forth in Chapter 2 of this report. In addition, the following rules should govern detention of persons not yet convicted of a criminal offense:

a. Treatment, the conditions of confinement, and the rules of conduct authorized for persons awaiting trial should be reasonably and necessarily related to the interest of the state in assuring the person's presence at trial. Any action or omission of governmental officers deriving from the rationales of punishment, retribution, deterrence, or rehabilitation should be prohibited.

b. The conditions of confinement should be the least restrictive alternative that will give reasonable assurance that the person will be present for his trial.

c. Persons awaiting trial should be kept separate and apart from convicted and sentenced offenders.

d. Isolation should be prohibited except where there is clear and convincing evidence of a danger to the staff of the facility, to the detainee, or to other detained persons.

5. Administrative cost or convenience should not be considered a justification for failure to comply with any of the above enumerated rights of persons detained awaiting trial.

6. Persons detained awaiting trial should be authorized to bring class actions to challenge the nature of their detention and alleged violations of their rights.[2]

We must decide whether the jail is an institution that needs to be improved or one that needs to be replaced. The answer is, it seems to me, that the American jail operates as an archaic, unacceptable social institution; it needs to be changed fundamentally.

To achieve fundamental reform is not to make what the inmates call "sweet joints," to "paint the bars," to provide no more than a cleanup of existing institutions. A new institution (physical and programmatic) is required to deal with persons who require some form of pretrial institutionalization. Other persons awaiting trial do not belong in any institution. As one recent report stated:

[2] National Advisory Commission on Criminal Justice Standards and Goals, *Report on Corrections* (1973), p. 133, standard 4.8.

In considering whether administrative cost and inconvenience should justify alterations or limitations on the rights of persons awaiting trial, the presumption of innocence dictates that different rules be applicable. Conviction for an offense against society may place some limits on the expenditures an offender can reasonably require. Society authorizes detention of presumably innocent persons solely to assure presence at trial. If the cost in authorizing such detention fully respective of the rights of pretrial detainees is prohibitive, then society should develop some alternative means of providing that assurance.[3]

Those who need such a new institution include: (1) the pretrial detainee who may not otherwise show up for trial, or who is too dangerous to be released; (2) the offender whose problem is one of health or welfare, not punishment; who needs to be held in order to be examined and channeled to an appropriate specialized institution; and (3) the convicted offender who requires some local correctional institution to house him during that period when he is being reintegrated into the community. A new concept for an institution to replace our present jails should make certain presumptions.

Ideally, jails as we have known them should be eliminated. They should be replaced by a network of newly designed, differently conceived metropolitan (in the big cities) and regional (in rural areas) detention centers. No convict would serve a sentence in the proposed metropolitan and regional detention centers which would replace jails. Instead, correctional authorities would have to service convicted defendants[4] in prisons or in community correctional programs.

Removing convicted defendants from the jails would leave two problems. What would be done to replace convicted defendants serving long sentences who perform housekeeping functions in jail? And what would be done with the mass of convicted misdemeanants now in jails who are serving short sentences?

Those long-term convicts who are used as the maintenance men in the local jails neither provide nor receive crucial services. Their housekeeping functions could be assumed by others. Those con-

[3] National Advisory Commission on Criminal Justice Standards and Goals, *Report on Corrections*, p. 134.
[4] For a detailed analysis of how and in what way correctional institutions should operate, see Goldfarb and Singer, *After Conviction* (Simon & Schuster, 1973).

victs who are dangerous or who have committed such serious crimes that the community would not tolerate either their release or their participation in a community correctional program should complete their sentence in a traditional prison. Alternative prison institutions or community programs should do more for them than the present prisons, and certainly more than jails do.

The short-term convicted misdemeanant presents a more difficult problem. The national survey of correction completed in 1967 stated that the overwhelming percentage of prisoners in the correctional system are misdemeanant offenders,[5] convicted of such offenses as vice, drunkenness and vagrancy; others are "casual offenders in marginal cases" for whom jails perform "miscellaneous social tasks for which they are ill-suited and which they generally do not perform as well as programs specifically aimed at doing such tasks."

These defendants are kept in jails at wasteful public costs, although the services made available to them are minimal. Probation is used infrequently, if at all; and when it is employed, it is "sparse and spotty." Rehabilitative programs are unusual. Jails with programs designed for misdemeanants are rare.[6] Parole is "extremely limited." (Part of the problem here is that most institutional stays are very brief, usually for about two months.) Jail programs for misdemeanants are rare.

The characteristic social problems endured by many inner-city defendants rarely are best handled in maximum security facilities. This class of misdemeanant has minimal penal problems and major social needs.

If jails were abolished, the correctional establishment would be forced to detain and institutionalize only dangerous misdemeanants and those who need special correctional assistance. The others would be diverted into appropriate community correctional programs.

The detention centers of the future would house those defendants in pretrial status who present clear and demonstrable threats of flight before trial or whose personal dangerousness warrants limited pretrial detention. They also would serve as reception, diagnostic, classification and referral institutions for those

[5] The President's Commission on Law Enforcement and the Administration of Justice, *Task Force Report: Corrections,* Chap. 7, pp. 72–81.
[6] Ibid., pp. 77–78.

who have been arrested but could be serviced better in other institutions, particularly youngsters, alcoholics, addicts, physically and mentally sick people. Thirdly, these centers could be used as dormitories to house convicted convicts who are placed in community programs without residential facilities—halfway in and halfway out defendants; defendants on work release and furlough status and defendants who participate in restitution programs. These individuals would not be detained for correction: they simply would be provided a dormitory service.

These future detention centers should be administered not by the police but by the local Human Resources Department or its counterpart agency. With several distinct functions and roles, they would have to be divided into three separate wings. One wing would be for detention only. A second wing would be to provide diagnosis to inmates and refer them to appropriate outside programs or institutions, only housing defendants short-term in the course of their treatment or diagnosis. The third wing would be a dormitory only, providing only augmenting social services to assist transition back to a completely free status.

A deputy would supervise each of the three component parts of the center: a court or police official would run the pretrial facility; a medical official would supervise the diagnostic and referral wing; a social welfare or correctional department official would direct the third wing, for people in the community housed under correctional supervision. Each state Human Resources Department should have the statutory obligation to set strict standards for these detention centers and inspect them regularly to assure the standards are met.

WING I. THE PRETRIAL DETENTION OF DEFENDANTS TO PREVENT FLIGHT OR CRIME

The first wing—for detention—would house dangerous adult and juvenile defendants for limited times before trial under special conditions and under court orders. While far too many people end up in jail because they cannot afford bail, too many people who present clear and present dangers of hurting others are able to avoid detention because of the vagaries of the money bail system.

To a great degree, we have ended up with a paradox of injustice: many of the wrong people are in jail while many of the wrong people are on the street. Freedom that is against the public interest should not be bought, nor should imprisonment result simply from one's disadvantaged economic status.

The only way to perfect the pretrial system is to abolish money bail completely and to devise an open and careful scheme for determining pretrial release and detention. A new pretrial system should be developed. It should include a clear judicial procedure which would strike a reasonable balance between proper demands for detaining the few defendants who are dangerous and assuring the freedom of the many defendants who are not. Some defendants may require some supervision short of jail. Some people should be detained to protect others. Detention should not result from the fact that a defendant cannot afford a bail bond; it should arise only when defendants are demonstrably dangerous.

In my earlier book, *Ransom,* I suggested that the American bail bond system be scrapped, that a fair pretrial detention system be developed, and that these goals be carried out in a new pretrial proceeding which I detailed there and which I will summarize and expand upon here.[7]

This new pretrial procedure would govern the status of all criminal defendants from the time of arrest until trial. The pretrial procedure would take place in two steps: the first, a judicially sanctioned release procedure, would cover the great majority of cases; the second, a pretrial detention hearing, would affect—I should guess—about 10 per cent of the criminal cases.

Step 1 would include two classes of situations: one, the majority of cases when the judicial process is called into play and supervised release is ordered; the other, when a summons would suffice, and the judicial pretrial process could be avoided or significantly limited. There would never be more than the briefest and most perfunctory incarceration prior to trial under a Step 1 proceeding; there could be pretrial imprisonment only after a Step 2 proceeding, which would deal only with this issue, instituted only in prescribed situations, and carried out in carefully prescribed situations, in a procedurally circumscribed manner and administered in a special facility. When appropriate officials decide

[7] For a fuller treatment, see Goldfarb, *Ransom,* Chap. 7.

to initiate the criminal process against a person whom they believe or suspect committed a crime, they would proceed under Step 1 in one of two ways.

If the crime is not a serious one (a petty offense, some misdemeanors), the first approach would be followed. Instead of arrest or at the time of arrest (but without taking a person physically into custody), or a very few hours thereafter (if there had been an arrest, booking, perhaps some brief incarceration demanded by the particular exigencies of the case), the defendant would be summoned by a delegated police official to appear in court at a later date for trial. If refused the summons in one of these situations, a defendant could demand to be brought before a court which, except for some extraordinary reason, would release him and order him to appear for arraignment or trial.

This phase of Step 1 would include both the true police summons (instead of an arrest) and police ROR (that is, summons soon after arrest and a limited background investigation). The defendant would have to agree to appear in court as a condition of his release. Administrative officials of the court in charge of overseeing the pretrial release system would be responsible (in conjunction with the police) for record keeping, trial notification and general control of this group of defendants during the time they are free in pretrial status.

If the crime is a serious one (aggravated misdemeanors or felonies), the accused would immediately be brought under the control of the courts (under similar time requirements, usually within forty-eight hours, as now exist in general practice regarding mandatory appearance before a judicial officer for arraignment). Depending on the nature of the crime, the background of the defendant, and any other meaningful circumstances of the case, the court then would either order the defendant to appear for later arraignment or trial, and release him or place him under the control of a designated official for investigation and then release him under the supervision of that court officer, whichever seemed appropriate.

Under either phase of Step 1, both unnecessary imprisonment and improper release based on the absence or presence of money bail would be eliminated, and with it would disappear the role of the bondsman in the administration of justice. His function would not be allowed and it would not be needed.

Where a summons is issued, there is no imprisonment. In other cases, at the first meeting with a defendant, the judge would order appropriate controls short of imprisonment to assure the defendant's presence at trial. This might be a simple order by the court to be there; or it might be an order when to appear with an assignment to and the assumption by some third party of the responsibility to insure his presence. If appropriate (and it would be in most cases) the court would make an assignment to some administrative court official to investigate the defendant's background and supervise the defendant and assure his appearance at trial. This function could be assigned to any court official, even one who dealt solely with this task. That responsible official could fulfill his duty to assure the defendant's presence at trial by any program short of imprisonment.

The supervisory officer for the court could draw on the techniques of any sensible program to administer defendants' releases. He might require a defendant to report to him periodically; or to turn over his driver's license or passport; or to deposit a bank book, even a sum of money if it were an appropriate control and as long as release was not dependent solely on the ability to make a financial deposit and detention did not result from inability to afford the sum. Only a letter or a phone call to keep in contact would be necessary in some cases. In others, third party parole could be used. Under this concept, the assistance of an organization, employer, counsel, a relative, or a member of the clergy is enlisted to supervise the defendant prior to trial.

The point is that the court official, with the opportunity to satisfy himself that the defendant is not dangerous and can be released, as would be the case most of the time, should not be limited in the variety of methods by which he could administer this Step 1 release proceeding.

Flight would present a problem for the court and police, but experienced law enforcement officials have pointed out that fugitives from justice are relatively rare.[8] There is no reason to believe that the bail bond system would have prevented or terminated even these escapes. To this low figure of fugitives must be added the impressive record of the FBI in hunting down and capturing even this small percentage of people. The police investigative

[8] Goldfarb, op. cit., p. 243.

agencies are quite adept at this function; of the few defendants who become fugitives, even fewer get away. Natural deterrents like lack of money to hide indefinitely, the inevitable personal ties to one's home, people and community and the omnipresent paper world of records we are all tied to combine to minimize the problem of flight.

Where there is a real and obvious danger of flight, detention under Step 2 could be considered.

The courts have both punitive and administrative powers to deal with the inevitable but unusual cases when a defendant does not appear for trial. They also have the contempt power to punish swiftly any violation of their orders to appear for trial. Fleeing from a trial could be made a crime in those places where it is not already. Proof of flight may be offered at trial as evidence of a defendant's consciousness of guilt. If a defendant is not dangerous and he escapes, it is not a serious problem anyway.

Charging fees for bonds or imprisoning the non-risk defendants, as is now done, is an unsatisfactory way to deal with these relatively few cases. The present system imprisons the mass of defendants to protect against the potential few who might flee or do harm. The proposed system would free the mass of defendants who deserve freedom and provide a special machinery to deal differently with the exceptions.

All defendants then would be released prior to trial:

a. In petty offenses and minor misdemeanor cases after only a summons to appear, or a brief arrest and then a summons by a police official who would administer the bookkeeping needed to record and administer the event, or

b. in more serious cases, after being brought swiftly before a court and either

   (1) simply ordered by the court to appear, or
   (2) ordered to appear and after some investigation placed under third party control or official supervision.

My estimate is that Step 1 would probably cover 80–90 per cent of all criminal cases; it would assure the release of most defendants under a rational scheme. It would take no more time or administrative effort than present procedures, possibly less.

Step 2 would cope with the relatively small, special and very important class of cases for which compelling reasons exist to warrant special detention until trial. This procedure would attempt

JAILS

to balance the safety of society with the rights of accused individuals, to secure a proper relationship between public control and personal freedom.

Such a procedure must take into account the need to prevent unnecessary and predictable crimes, especially crimes of violence, whenever possible; and the importance of maintaining the working philosophy about crime that no man should lose his liberty without due process of law, that accusation is not conviction, that until conviction a man is presumed innocent and the burden is on the government to prove otherwise.

The Step 2 proceeding would occur soon after arrest, at the time of arraignment. It would be allowed only in special prescribed cases. If the prosecutor feels that there are strong reasons why it is in the public interest for a defendant to be detained prior to trial, he could seek the court's sanction for commitment. The court also could initiate this proceeding, but, it could be invoked only in the prescribed situations.

A statute should list the cases where the Step 2 proceeding would be permitted. This law should include crimes of extreme violence, pathological crimes; subversion cases where violence, sabotage or treason were involved; and cases where recidivism or obstruction of justice is anticipated. Defendants who would not co-operate with the court official in charge of release also could be included here. In no other case would a Step 2 pretrial detention be permitted.

To warrant this invocation of commitment, the government should be required to make a very strong showing of the existence of these special conditions. In the Step 2 proceeding, the defendant must have the fullest and fastest opportunity, with counsel, to oppose the government by presenting arguments in his defense. Careful and sensitive procedures would have to be developed to satisfy the touchy constitutional questions about self-incrimination and the right to counsel which arise here.

Only if the court should decide after a speedy, full and fair hearing to order special commitment would the defendant be incarcerated. Even in this case, every step should be taken to make this a special kind of detention. No imprisonment is pleasant, and calling it something else does not make it any better. Even the renowned legal scholar Blackstone, who argued that preventive detention not only was necessary but was eminently fair, recognized the prejudicial penal aspect of private detention:

> But this imprisonment, as has been said, is only for safe custody, and not for punishment; therefore, in this dubious interval between the commitment and trial, a prisoner ought to be used with the utmost humanity, and neither be loaded with needless fetters nor subjected to other hardships than such as are absolutely requisite for the purpose of confinement only; though what are so requisite must too often be left to the discretion of the gaolers, who are frequently a merciless race of men, and, by being conversant in scenes of misery, steeled against any tender sensation.[9]

Admittedly, there is a chance that this procedure would be declared unconstitutional because, no matter how circumscribed and how restrained, it does sanction imprisonment without the traditional trial and all its concomitant protections. In the context of today's punitive jails, this argument is persuasive; a new kind of detention institution probably would be required to save even the most carefully designed pretrial detention procedures from constitutional challenge.

A pragmatic argument must be accepted to support this admittedly precipitous procedure: it is that since we frequently practice preventive detention under the present bail system and since *it* has never been considered unconstitutional, Step 2, which provides a much more clear and more direct procedure surrounded with more careful safeguards perhaps would not be considered unconstitutional either.

Some means for preventive detention exists in all other systems of law. There is no official procedure for this practice in the United States, however, though serious problems prove the need for one. In an ad hoc unofficial way we now either release dangerous defendants and react after the damage is done or lock them up through unofficial routes by misusing bail procedures as a makeshift substitute. The proposed procedure is an attempt to accommodate vital if competing interests clearly, directly and with fairness.

How carefully Step 2 was implemented would be an important factor in assaying whether it was a reasonable and fair procedure. The courts and legislatures would have to build a body of law

[9] Blackstone (Jones), Vol. 2, p. 2523, s. 337.

around such general guiding propositions as: How much proof would be necessary to invoke Step 2 successfully? Precisely what crimes would fall within the general categories of eligibility that are suggested? How could the time factors be controlled to allow defendants realistic and fair opportunities to oppose or appeal from these proceedings?

The trenchant question has been asked me: Once condoning preventive detention under these restrictive circumstances, how can one stop there? Would this lead to arrests for investigation? Once accepting the idea behind preventive detention, why wait for a formal indictment or criminal charge to detain? Why not detain all the evil people and prevent their future crimes? Why not have preventive detention even after acquittals or dropped charges, to protect society?

The answer is that lines must be drawn. Concepts need not be taken to their logical extremes to test their validity in limited cases. But the question does raise an important caveat about any scheme of pretrial detention. If used, it must be done carefully. The basic point, it seems to me, is that the proposed Step 2 proceeding would result in far less improper official conduct and less pretrial incarceration than under the present bail system, and that the procedure would better protect both society and defendants.

Under Step 2 the power to set money bail could not be perverted to deal circuitously with problem cases. For judges to misuse their judicial powers as they do now in denying bail for speculative, preventive purposes or for idiosyncratic reasons is wrong and degrades the judicial process. In those cases where detention is proper, there would be a specified mechanism to deal with the particular exigencies of each particular case. The individual against whom this procedure is invoked could insist that the charges against him be specified, and proved. He would have an opportunity to refute them.

There would be less chance for judges to abuse their powers —their reasons and the basis for them would appear on an appealable record. Detention would be less punitive than it is under existing procedures. The individual's trial would be expedited. His period of incarceration would be made as tolerable as possible. He could receive medical and other special services if they were warranted.

If this two-step procedure was adopted, the jails would be emptied of the many poor defendants who are neither dangerous nor likely to flee, and yet are the majority of most jail populations. The money saved by eliminating them from the jail system could be used to administer the judicial system to supervise this part of the pretrial process. Those who would be detained under the pretrial procedure would be relatively few. Their incarceration would be limited by the calendar preferences they could demand. Their numbers would be limited enough to allow the pretrial facilities to remain relatively small. Their unique status would require that these facilities could not become ersatz prisons.

A great deal must be done to make this incarceration less personally destructive than is the case during pretrial detention. A special facility or wing of the future pretrial detention facility (separate from any convicted prisoners) should be used. It should be made as physically pleasant as possible. No cells or cages or crude, crammed dormitories would be permitted.

A prisoner's family should be allowed to visit at any reasonable time. The defendant should be able to work at controlled employment to earn some reasonable income during this time before trial. He should be assisted to find re-employment if he is acquitted. All social and medical services that would be helpful to him or his family ought to be provided. Where the crime charged or the background of the defendant indicates some special problem, voluntary treatment could begin immediately. Particularly in the cases of the uncontrollable recidivist criminal, or the pathological or insane criminal, this proceeding could convert into a more permanent medical supervision if that were found to be appropriate.[10]

This pretrial incarceration should not be counted as an arrest record if the defendant is acquitted. Trial dates should be expedited by giving calendar preferences to these cases. The time of pretrial detention should be reduced from any subsequent sentence after the trial. The defendant should be released at the time of trial, and the fact of his incarceration should not be brought to the jury's attention.

I fully realize that this suggested proceeding raises serious constitutional problems which cannot be dismissed lightly. To de-

[10] Such a person might well be transferred to Wing II of the detention facility for medical diagnosis and referral; see p. 430 infra et seq.

prive any accused defendant of his liberty without a trial by jury, for committing no consummated wrong or no proscribed action, is fundamentally in conflict with the basic American way of doing things. This is so no matter how the incarceration is specialized. However, there is some precedent for this kind of a proceeding in existing civil commitment practices where individuals may be incarcerated without the ordinary trial process because it is deemed necessary to society and to the individual himself to take such a step.

If these changes in effect make the facility a sort of short-term hotel for the containment of involuntarily registered and closely supervised clients, then that reality can be faced. A jail is not a prison and there is no good reason why it should look or operate like one. Even though it would have an incidental, similar function—detention—the similarities must end there. The pretrial detention facility and the correctional facility used after conviction are fundamentally different institutions with different basic purposes. This wing of the detention center of the future would reflect those differences in every way: architecturally, administratively and programmatically.

WING II.   THE INTAKE, CLASSIFICATION AND REFERRAL AGENCY FOR SPECIAL CASES

The second wing of the jail of the future would be completely segregated from the others; with a medical staff and orientation, it would serve a diagnostic and referral function for sick defendants and those with special problems.

The two-step pretrial arraignment procedure advocated for adults would also apply to children. Only the patently dangerous young offender—never the non-criminal, uniquely juvenile offender—would be detained in the juvenile section of Wing I described earlier. The juvenile court and the administrators of early entry parts of that system would determine and supervise appropriate community controls of youngsters involved in the system. Detention could result only in the special circumstances described earlier regarding dangerous defendants, and then under careful, special procedures.

a. *Young Offenders and Juveniles in Trouble*

In the juvenile system, however, the release practices are more difficult to design than those for the adult system. Unlike the case of most adult detention, some form of pretrial residential care for juveniles often is necessary. In many instances, a youngster first comes to the attention of the juvenile court because of problems in his normal home environment; depending on the nature of the trouble at home, such a crisis may prompt the child to commit a peculiarly juvenile offense, or it may stimulate a parent or guardian to file a "PINS" petition against the child. Under these circumstances, it would be unrealistic to release children in trouble to await court action at home. While generally the artificially maintained duality which now exists between the adult "criminal justice system" and the counterpart "juvenile justice system" is a false and pernicious one, in the case of pretrial services, the needs of adults and young people differ significantly in this one regard.

A variety of pretrial, non-detention alternatives to America's atrocious "child jails" exist. These alternatives, outlined above in Chapter 5, are not, in the traditional sense, forms of juvenile detention. But proposed systems for group homes, foster homes and even so-called "home detention" do involve significant restrictions on a youngster's freedom. Because they require that new temporary residential arrangements be made for children, or that existing arrangements be modified significantly, these alternatives to pretrial custody are very sensitive and peculiarly demanding.

With children, unlike adults, it cannot be assumed that the pretrial placement which most closely approximates an individual's pre-arrest status is the most desirable placement. Before a realistic pretrial placement is made for any child in trouble, some inquiry into the child's background and family situation is required. In addition to providing the basis for such a temporary placement, an early investigation into a child's background may provide valuable clues to the causes of his or her predicament—the scars of parental child abuse, the signs of a crippling but correctable learning problem, or the symptoms of a lingering physical illness.

As it is presently constituted, the juvenile justice system is particularly ill suited to making necessary inquiries concerning children in trouble. The juvenile court intake officer has time and skill enough to make only an uninformed and largely intuitive choice between detention and release. From this point forward, all discretion lies with the juvenile detention system's own staff. Unfortunately, thorough testing and competent evaluation of children in trouble is a rarity.

The diagnostic wing of the detention center of the future, through its "one-stop" referral center for troubled adult arrestees, could have a key role to play in a rationalized, humanized system of juvenile detention. In the past, social reformers have insisted on a clear separation between the adult and juvenile justice systems. All too often, the result has been that children in trouble inhabited "the worst of both worlds." Conventional thinking in the area of juvenile detention takes the desirability of complete segregation of adult and juvenile detainees as an absolute tenet. All too often, the result is that young people inhabit institutions even viler than those reserved for adults, and receive services which are unresponsive to their needs.

As the detention center of the future replaces the present network of overcrowded, undersupervised, overly secure jails with new facilities planned to realize new objectives, many of the traditional arguments against jointly housing adult detainees and children in trouble might disappear. Considerations of efficiency suggest that when a jurisdiction invests in a centralized diagnostic wing of a detention center for adults, and staffs that center with professional medical personnel, social workers and counselors, the same center also should provide threshold diagnostic services for children. Anticipating this function for the diagnostic wing of the new detention center, its designers should provide from the outset for a specialized children's section—with separate living, dining and recreation areas, but with access to common medical facilities and to the offices of professional staff members whose skills can benefit adults and children alike.

A large group of children in trouble would not become residents of the diagnostic wing or the detention wing. This group would include the youngsters whose "crimes" are minor, and whose family ties strong; they would be released to their parents by a police officer immediately after arrest. Rather than taking such children into custody, the arresting officer would merely leave a notice of violation, returnable at a set hearing date, with the parents. This group of children would include those with responsible families who could not be located immediately by an arresting officer, but could later be traced by the juvenile intake staff of the detention center. For them, the diagnostic wing would provide merely a neutral place to wait until a family member appeared to take custody.

For many other children, however, an immediate and unconditional release could do more harm than good. The existing juvenile detention system, which gives little or no attention to threshold evaluation, does these children a disservice. Some youngsters are released back to the very conditions which precipitated the crisis leading to their arrest. Others are confined under equally unsatisfactory conditions for long periods. A few are referred to alternative non-custodial residential facilities or specially supervised programs; but such referrals are unusual, the result of good fortune.

By instituting procedures under which children who could not be released immediately and unconditionally, would be held in diagnostic custody for a period not to exceed forty-eight hours, the juvenile justice system could rationalize its detention decisions. During this brief stay in the children's diagnostic section, each child could be evaluated individually and adequately. Public and private pretrial service agencies, which would maintain liaison offices at the diagnostic wing, could be consulted, as could referral agencies specializing in service brokering between the child and the community. Urgent medical needs could be treated and less urgent ones identified.

The minority of troubled children who require secure detention could be isolated in the detention wing and referred to the juvenile court for an immediate hearing—analogous to the Step 2 hearing in the adult pretrial procedure outlined above. At the end of forty-eight hours, every arrested child should have been brought before the court or released into the care or under supervision of a designated pretrial service program after receiving a notice of the next scheduled hearing date in his case.

The use of the diagnostic wing of the new detention center as a screening center for children in trouble could not itself solve the problems of juvenile detention. Each community also would have to provide an adequate range of alternative pretrial housing and supervision programs for young people. The savings which would accrue from an end to wholesale juvenile detention could be expected to contribute toward financing this alternative care network. The Youth Service Bureau model, which has met with notable success in the few jurisdictions where it has been tested, suggests that an umbrella organization operating outside the juvenile justice system could assist children.

The child's brief stay in the diagnostic wing of the new detention center might fill another need as well. All experts agree that the implementation of diversion is the key to reform in juvenile justice: the best way to protect children from abuse in juvenile courts, reform schools or training homes is to see that as few children as possible ever come into contact with these institutions. At the diagnostic wing an important diversion program could be administered. During the forty-eight-hour evaluation period, the child and the state could agree to a diversion "contract"; in appropriate cases, if the child then met its terms—whether by attending school, by participating in a specified program, making restitution, or merely by staying out of further trouble—charges might be dismissed.

Today, as many as 50 per cent of all charges lodged against children are "adjusted," but the very informality of this haphazard diversion procedure casts doubt on its effectiveness. Ad hoc adjustments relieve pressure on the system, but they may do little or no good for the child. By formalizing early exit procedures within the juvenile justice system, and by providing the diagnostic wing of the new detention center as a meeting ground for all persons concerned in the decision to divert, the architects of criminal justice reform could extend the benefits of true diversion to young people.

b. *Sick Defendants*

The physically or mentally sick defendant (discussed in Chapter 3) poses a perfect example of the kind of person who should be serviced by this second wing of the detention center.

Providing every prisoner who is detained with high-quality diagnostic services, and with any required preventive or corrective medical care should be a major priority of any detention system. The general scrutiny of all arrestees to discern public health problems and suggest candidates for related, non-penal institutions and programs should be the other major function of this medical wing.

To provide such services and care, this wing of the detention center must have new equipment and larger medical budgets, nurses or medical paraprofessionals, meaningful amounts of physicians' time and the space and materials medical employees need to work.

Furthermore, new strategies of co-operation with other public and private institutions must be devised. At best, a large urban detention center cannot provide all the services its mixed population of sick inmates may require; a jail infirmary cannot become a complete substitute for a hospital; and specialist doctors will not be available to serve as full-time jail staff members. Before the health of the inmate population can be improved substantially, walls of isolation between the jail and the community must come down.

Affiliation agreements between local detention administrators and nearby public health facilities (particularly teaching hospitals) would be one direct and efficient means of improving the delivery of health care to detained inmates. Under such an agreement, medical teams would be available for duty inside and hospital beds would be available for inmates outside the detention center. The gulf between the limited care to which inmates now have access and the complete care to which all free patients can at least aspire would narrow or close. Such reform would be expensive; and it would require that both the jailing system and the health care establishment abandon their traditional habits of insularity.

In preceding chapters, I have suggested some ways in which existing jails, with their mixed assortment of sick and healthy inmates, could intervene usefully in the lives of their wards. A properly staffed, well equipped and fully affiliated jail medical unit could offer several services to the inmate population. It can provide a wide range of low-intensity services to a large number of detained people. It can assure that no inmate's medical problem goes unrecognized and undiagnosed. It can provide post-release referrals to community treatment services. In many instances, it can initiate the delivery of simple, urgent health care services during detention.

The detention center of the future should be treating the limited inmate population in its diagnostic wing at the same time as it checks and diagnoses all other arrestees who are not required to be detained. Many miscellaneous prisoners for whose health today's jail is responsible would not be detained in the first instance under fair and rational pretrial release procedures along the lines of those recommended earlier. Other "problem prisoners" in today's jail, including the drunkenness offender, the addict and the police "mental health pickup," could be taken to specialized hospital-like facilities immediately; incarcerating them need not be a function of the detention center of the future. Instead, many defendants could be examined and released while the medical staff and resources of the center concentrated on delivering high-intensity services to the relatively small and coherent population in detention.

Under the pretrial release procedures proposed, a defendant's dangerousness or risk of flight would be the only justifications for his pretrial detention. The defendants detained under such procedures would have their share of medical problems. As is the case with most jail inmates today, many prisoners received at such a detention facility would be men or women who have had little or no prior professional medical attention. Diagnostic and treatment resources could be concentrated on giving these prisoners the aid they need and want.

This medical wing then would provide a short battery of tests and a basic physical examination of all arrested defendants during the brief time between their arrest and arraignment. The only exceptions would be those defendants whose crimes were so minimal, dangerousness so unlikely and condition apparently normal that an early decision to release has been made by the police or juvenile authorities. Perhaps, this group, too, should be required to submit at some date before their trial or other disposition of their case to this brief public health examination. Clearly they should be given the option of submitting to this examination and any course of treatment which is recommended. The recommendation of the staff of this wing would be available to assist the court in determining release conditions under the proposed Step 1 proceeding.

Secondly, for all those defendants who are detained under Step 2, submission to diagnosis and recommended referral to appropriate outside programs should be required, at least where there is a relation between the offense charged and the condition diagnosed. This would lead to alternate treatment programs and diversion in many cases if the court adopted the medical wing's recommendations. If there is no relation between the offense and the condition diagnosed, I would recommend that any subsequent referrals be only on a voluntary basis.

In some cases this useful social service could be strictly a public health function, tangential to the criminal justice system. In other cases, it could lead to major alternative correctional programs such as with the cases of alcoholics and addicts.

The currently fashionable term "diversion" embraces a variety of programs. Some of these programs supply complete alternatives to criminal prosecution, others provide participants with an opportunity to defer and possibly avoid prosecution, still others merely provide special services outside the criminal justice system for defendants awaiting trial.

All diversion programs have one thing in common: before any accused offender can be removed from the criminal justice system and introduced to useful social and medical services, his personal problems first must be recognized and analyzed. No present functionary or institution of the criminal justice system is required or prepared to fulfill this professional diagnostic responsibility—least of all the present jail and its staff. Routine jail intake procedures now overlook even the grossest physical, psychological and social handicaps; they are completely inadequate to discover the subtler, often equally crippling, personal problems of people in trouble.

The diagnostic wings of the detention centers of the future should concentrate any professional skills which exist in the present criminal justice system, and would add and co-ordinate new professional capabilities the pretrial system badly needs. As a "one-stop" center for social service and medical examination and referral, it would replace the haphazard aggregation of part-time physicians, probation officers, court social workers and volunteers who now share inadequately this responsibility.

The medical wing of the proposed new multipurpose detention facility would provide for hospital wards, secure individual rooms and dormitories, interview areas, physicians' offices, medical laboratories as well as office space for representatives of community programs which accept referrals.

The diagnostic wing would not dispense long-term treatment. Only when an inmate was in need of immediate help would its personnel provide short-term, crisis intervention medical services. No inmate would be held there beyond the brief period (usually days and rarely more than weeks) required to assess his problems and to complete a referral. Not every person diverted through the diagnostic wing would be a complete volunteer, but its diversion procedures would be designed to encourage the client's participation in the referral process.

The class of people who would be served by this diagnostic wing would be the people who are most seriously mis-served by present-day jails: the men, women and children whose offenses are identical with, or directly caused by their afflictions.

The diversion of alcoholics and addicts concerns a large and special class of arrestees worth individual attention. The gradual reform of law enforcement regarding alcoholics, outlined in Chapter 5, could provide the eventual decriminalization of the offense of public intoxication. Even where the offense remains on the statute books, there is an increasing interest in non-criminal alternatives for handling the public drunk.

Decriminalization will not, however, end the problem drinker's involvement with the criminal justice system. Intoxicated men and women will continue to be arrested for a variety of alcohol-related criminal offenses, ranging from simple disorderly conduct to manslaughter in the course of drunken driving. Police will continue to bear primary responsibility for removing helpless and vulnerable drunks from the streets.

Of all the emerging alternatives for dealing with alcoholic petty offenders and simple drunks, the medical detoxification unit or "sobering-up station" is the most promising. Short-term care for acute intoxication and alcoholic withdrawal is simple, inexpensive and effective. For some problem drinkers, detoxification proves to be the first step on the long, difficult road to abstinence, sobriety and future avoidance of the criminal justice system.

Experiments in a number of American cities have demonstrated that the usefulness of specialized detoxification units has two significant, practical limitations. The first of these limitations is the police officer's common reluctance to bring even seriously intoxicated men and women to the local "Detox." Often this reluctance is the result of the unit's inconvenient location, the time-consuming paperwork involved in admitting a drunk to the unit or the officer's dislike for non-law enforcement duties.

The second limitation is the detoxification unit's typical separation from medical and social aftercare systems which could provide continuing support for its short-term patients. By definition, a detoxification unit is a limited-purpose facility, set up to deliver a few days of high-quality sobering-up service at low cost. Referral help, where it is provided at all, generally amounts to an administrative afterthought.

Both these limitations could be offset or eliminated by making the detoxification unit a part of the new detention center's diagnostic and referral section. As a centrally located, professionally administered and law enforcement-oriented facility, the new center could offer an alcoholic detoxification program which tradition-minded police officers could accept.

The "alcohol ward" of the detention center of the future—a humane and scientific version of the notorious "drunk tanks" of today's jails—would receive a variety of patients. In addition to simple, public drunks (picked up for their own protection, at their own request or after violation of a minor public intoxication ordinance), the ward also could house severely intoxicated drunken drivers, disorderly persons and even arrestees charged with serious alcohol-related offenses. Unlike the chronically overcrowded specialized detoxification units, which often must limit the care they provide to two or three days of medication and bed rest, the new center could be programmed and staffed to provide the five to seven days of care which experts agree is required for thorough detoxification.

With its complete medical-social diagnostic staffing, the new center could provide drunks with services beyond the capability of any specialized detoxification unit. During the sobering-up period, the patient would have the opportunity to undergo a full physical examination, and a battery of psychological tests. For the Skid Row drunk, this sort of evaluation can be especially useful: often his intoxication masks serious physical and psychological handicaps which have never been diagnosed or treated. Evaluation and diagnosis would enable the professional staff of the new diagnostic center to design individualized aftercare plans for alcoholic detoxification programs, making use of all available community resources. Medium-term residential alcoholic treatment centers, AA groups, halfway houses, sheltered workshops, out-patient mental health facilities, even family units from which the drunk presently is estranged, all could be resources to which the center might refer appropriate cases.

On completing detoxification, most patients from the new center's alcohol ward could be discharged outright. In jurisdictions where public drunkenness is fully decriminalized, there would never be any criminal charges against them; their stay in the alcohol ward would have been voluntary from the outset. In other jurisdictions, successful detoxification could be made a condition for the later automatic quashing of a summons or notice of violation issued at the time of a drunkenness arrest.

Where the condition of a simple drunk indicated it was necessary and apt (and where local statutes permitted), physicians could initiate proceedings leading to short- or medium-term civil commitment to a public alcoholic treatment center or mental hospital. Those patients who were charged with minor alcohol-related offenses (other than simple drunkenness itself) would be eligible for immediate pretrial release under the Step 1 release procedure already described. Only a tiny minority (repeaters or those charged with manslaughter, perhaps) might be subject to a later Step 2 pretrial detention hearing and possible detention.

Before leaving the alcohol ward, each detoxified patient would have the opportunity to discuss and plan his future program with a specialist counselor, to question or modify the planned program and ultimately to accept or reject it. In some cases, this conference would be the first step in a true scheme of diversion; acceptance of participation in aftercare referrals might be wholly voluntary, flowing from the confidence created by a positive detoxification experience. On whatever terms the aftercare referral is made, however, the personnel of the new center would assume responsibility for completing the connection with the facility or agency to which the patient is referred. Counselors would be available to accompany each patient from the alcohol ward to the next way station, and to help him avoid relapse.

Building alcoholic detoxification services into the detention centers of the future would assure the institutionalization of the tentative measures which some communities have taken to assist indigent problem drinkers. Incorporation of an alcohol ward into the diagnostic wing of the new detention center would amount to the necessary recognition that alcohol is America's favorite intoxicant, and problem drinking is an inevitable and major problem. If the excesses of America's underprivileged problem drinkers must remain a law enforcement or police problem, at least the poor drinkers will be provided the humane and scientific treatment which their affliction deserves and their wealthier counterparts usually get.

Alcohol, the public drunk and the alcohol-related offense will be widespread social problems in any foreseeable American society. The same is not necessarily true of narcotics, narcotics addiction and drug-related crime. The heroin epidemic, urgent as it is today, may be on its way toward being checked, reversed and controlled by a combination of law enforcement and public health strategies. For the moment, however, narcotic drug use is a unique public problem: an easily contracted social disease which has criminal activity as one of its most prominent symptoms. Any modern detention facility must be designed, staffed and programmed to identify and assist arrested narcotics addicts.

Even if the heroin problem should be controlled, the procedures and techniques developed for use with heroin addicts during their initial confinement may be adaptable for use with men and women suffering from new or as yet unidentified crime-producing diseases.

For trained professional or paraprofessional staff, the diagnosis of narcotics addiction presents no substantial problems. A routine of physical examinations, coupled with interviews and urinalysis testing, will miss few active narcotics users. Every new jail should be designed to perform this identification function quickly and accurately in a non-penal, medical setting. When properly performed, addict-identification of arrestees can be completed within only a few hours.

Under the pretrial release procedure of Step 1 outlined above, many accused offenders (those not apparent addicts) would be released immediately after arrest, without any formal preliminaries other than the issuance of a police summons. These accused offenders would not be subject to screening for drug use, and the addicts among them would go undetected and untreated—at least temporarily. To this extent, the jail of the future would not perform the complete task of identifying every addict who comes into contact with the criminal justice system unless all arrestees were required to submit to testing, even if released prior to their trials.

The diagnostic personnel of the medical wing of the detention center could identify addicts charged with serious offenses, addicts whose condition had aroused the concern of police officials or judicial officers supervising pre-release proceedings, and addicts who—regardless of the nature of their alleged offenses—requested medical help at the time of arrest. As the criminal justice system operates today, the number of addicts in the last category would be minimal; the risks of identifying oneself as a narcotics user to an arresting officer are serious despite the possible personal benefits from self-identification. In a system where diagnostic centers earn a reputation for providing high-quality care on a non-stigmatic, non-punitive basis, however, the crisis of an arrest might stimulate addicts to seek long-term care through the jails themselves.

In devising operating diagnostic procedures for the jail of the future, a number of difficult legal and policy questions remain to be resolved. Could a police release supervisor or a judicial officer properly deny a summons or a Step 1 conditional release to a defendant whom he merely suspected of addiction, until the individual had submitted to medical tests? Would it be proper for an arrestee who is diagnosed as a heroin addict to be offered a choice between release with a treatment condition and pretrial detention leading to an early trial, when non-addicted defendants from similar backgrounds and charged with similar crimes are routinely released on their own recognizance without special conditions? Could a system with a built-in bias against all forms of pretrial institutionalization formulate an acceptable set of exceptions which applied solely to narcotics addicts? None of these questions can be answered authoritatively. But they must be considered before the new center's real potential for intervention in addiction can be assessed.

Assuming, however, that relatively large numbers of narcotics addicts can be persuaded or compelled to make their condition known to the professional diagnostic staff of the new jail, a number of valuable treatment services can then be provided for them at the pretrial stage. In the diagnostic wing, housing could be provided for those identified narcotics addicts who were ordered into preventive pretrial detention after a Step 2 release hearing. Here, methadone for detoxification could be dispensed on individualized schedules, rather than on the standardized schedules now employed. For detainees who chose to undergo narcotic withdrawal without tapering dosages of methadone, other forms of assistance could be provided—ranging from the dispensation of tranquilizing drugs to counseling by staff members. Another housing area might be set aside for voluntary detoxification patients—men and women who are eligible for pretrial release, but who first wish to end their immediate drug dependency under specialized medical supervision.

Most of the addicts identified in the diagnostic wing of the new jail, however, would not be "detoxed" there. Instead, they immediately would be placed in a public or private community drug treatment program. For some, acquiring and honoring a treatment affiliation would be an administratively imposed condition of their pretrial release, which they would be able to challenge at a special judicial release hearing. For others, treatment would be a voluntary option, proposed by members of the detention center's medical or counseling staff, and accepted by these arrestees because of its likely social and medical benefits, and not for collateral reasons.

Most of the addicts referred from the diagnostic wing to longer-term addiction treatment will not be true volunteers. Instead, they will have been diverted with a promise that entry into treatment will earn them an initial deferred trial as a concession from the prosecution, and that success in treatment could earn them the additional concession of a dismissal of charges. Working out a treatment placement for these addicts will not be a simple process: it will involve co-operation between the center's diagnostic and counseling staff, the administrators of treatment programs receiving referrals, the prosecutor's office, the arrestee's attorney and the defendant himself.

One of the most significant practical limitations of many existing addict diversion programs is that the crucial individuals who must make the decision to divert a defendant lack regular contacts and a routine meeting ground. The diagnostic wing, which would be designed to provide office space for treatment program staff and prosecutors, would serve this function. The diagnostic staff would have an opportunity to recommend placement; gradually, they would acquire practical experience by which to test their theories of placement. The addict and the program each would have an opportunity to inspect the other critically before making a commitment. The rate of "first-time" diversion successes could be expected to increase as the decision making bearing on diversion improved.

The success of a full-scale diagnostic detention facility could resolve the present debate over treatment alternatives for criminal addicts. The choice of program placements offered through the diversion on referral mechanisms of the facility would be as wide as the range of medical and non-medical treatment services available in the community: outpatient detoxification and supervision, the therapeutic community residence, methadone maintenance and narcotic antagonist treatment all could be made available as alternatives to prosecution. The final power of choice or refusal would be with the addict himself.

The diagnostic wing could serve another important function. Some studies have indicated that addiction chemotherapy programs benefit when the patient can be stabilized on his new maintenance or blocking drug in a hospital setting. But few operating programs can call upon enough hospital beds in the community to allow for routine inpatient stabilization. For addicts about to be diverted into chemotherapy, the facilities of a diagnostic jail itself could fill this need.

For diverted addicts entering treatment programs which do not involve chemotherapy, and for those who do not require or desire inpatient stabilization, the diagnostic staff could perform one additional service: its members could take responsibility for referring these addicts from the detention center to the office, clinic or residence where their treatment is to begin. Within a few days of entering the diagnostic wing for addiction screening, identified addicts could be on their way under professional supervision to a treatment program which they have selected for themselves with professional guidance.

The jail critic can do more than criticize present institutions and allude to empty moralisms about the need for "a better way" or "the need to divert defendants from the criminal justice system." Ample public and private programs exist to which defendants are being diverted from the criminal justice system and which have proved their worth on economic, administrative, public safety as well as humanitarian grounds. We need only use, co-ordinate, expand and perfect those better, available techniques to meet the problems of most jail inmates.

When the prototypical jail population is diverted and located elsewhere in large enough numbers, the institution itself loses some of its problems (overcrowding, for example) and the treatment of remaining populations can be evaluated at different and more professional levels. The overused criminal justice apparatus, for which the jails are the dumping grounds, will be improved, as will the chances of those unfortunate jail citizens who could be diverted under such a reform program.

WING III.   DORMITORIES FOR COMMUNITY CORRECTIONAL PROGRAMS

The third wing of the detention center should be a dormitory for convicts working under correctional programs in the community. These programs could be expanded if they had the residential base that this wing would provide. Use of services in Wing II would also be available where appropriate to residents of this third wing of the detention center.

While the present system of jails does nothing for convicts, and while I feel that convicted defendants should be kept either in real correctional institutions or in the community (whichever is best suited to each case), the future detention institution could service the correctional establishment without available community homes by providing dormitory services for certain individuals under their supervision. They would not be imprisoned in this new facility; those who would live in the wing would be convicts in partial release programs who do not have homes in the community.

The lack of available facilities and community hostility to correctional homes in its midst has limited the swing toward community correctional programs. This new public institution then could fill a void. It would allow more recourse to middle ground treatment of offenders, between outright release and complete imprisonment. Now, men cannot go on parole status unless they can prove they have a job and home to go to. If a man is ready to return to the community but does not have either a job or home, this facility would provide a vital service. Furthermore, it could provide halfway-in alternatives for individuals who need some supervision short of prison. Youngsters and minor offenders could be sentenced to serve short or part-time sentences on work release; their programs could be administered and housed in this part of the new detention facility.

Work Release. Work release, sometimes referred to as work

furlough or day parole, is a widespread but underused practice, which enables prisoners to be released during the working day to private employment, requiring that they return behind bars after work.[11] The technique also has been used to allow part-time release to participate in academic or vocational training programs or for voluntary service in the community.[12]

The notion behind work release is a most sensible one and the practice has historic roots. Prisoners frequently have been released to work under lease arrangements and women prisoners have been allowed to work as indentured domestics. These early schemes, however, were no more than painful forms of bondage.

The first major work release program, the one which is considered to be the beginning of the progressive movement toward community correction, was the Huber Law, passed in 1913 in Wisconsin. It authorized sentenced misdemeanants to retain a job while they served their sentences in local jails. While no state followed Wisconsin's lead for forty years, in the last few decades, work release programs have proliferated in numerous jurisdictions, notably North Carolina, Maryland, the District of Columbia and in the federal system. By the beginning of the 1970's, thirty-five states had some such program.

The values of the work release concept are obvious. Inmates are allowed to do a decent day's work in the free world to which they eventually must return. Inmates are relieved of the dreary, droning existence of correctional institutions for most of the day. They are able to earn a wage at prevailing civilian rates, adding to their feeling of self-esteem: they can support their families (and pay taxes) and pay their own way through their correctional experience saving needless public costs. These programs involve the community in the resocialization of convicted offenders, a goal commonly espoused by the experts. While some correctional administrators dislike the administrative chores that work release programs require, most jailers speak favorably of their experiences with such programs.

Yet, despite these benefits, few people have been given the chance to participate in such a program. The small minority of individuals who are too dangerous to be allowed in the free com-

---

[11] For a fuller discussion of this subject, see Goldfarb and Singer, *After Conviction*, pp. 527–52.

[12] E.g., see Florida Rev. Stats. 945.09[1]b.

munity without jeopardizing the safety of the public should not be allowed into programs like this.

In various places the correction system uses the work release concept in different ways. A judge may sentence a minor offender to a work release program instead of prison. Work release may be used as a pretrial condition of bail. In several places, work release is used as a pre-release technique to begin easing a person who has served most of his sentence in prison back into the community.

A unique experiment undertaken jointly by the District of Columbia Department of Correction and the city's public housing agency is employing work release prisoners to renovate vacant or vandalized public housing units. The prisoners, many of them skilled laborers, live in the housing projects they are renovating, receive full union wages for their work and in some cases receive job training from the private contractors supervising the project. One official reported: "We are rehabilitating people and houses at the same time."

Halfway Houses. On the rise in this country is the use of the halfway house as an alternative between the free community and total prison. Typically, halfway houses are used for men who have served most of their sentences and are able to be released from prison early to ease their transition back into the community. Typically, such men will be in a halfway house for several months while they get a job, visit their families increasingly, get assistance from staff in their transition to freedom.

Some judges have used a halfway-in as well as a halfway-out technique. That is, they sentence certain inmates to a halfway house, taking them out of the unsupervised environment they came from but at the same time not thrusting them into a totally closed prison system. This technique provides judges with a sentencing alternative for the many men for whom neither release nor imprisonment is appropriate.

Again, for the class of convict who would qualify for such programs, the metropolitan detention center could be the barracks. Supervision and control would be provided while an inmate worked his way back to freedom.

Furloughs. Inmates in prisons may be released to the community temporarily on furloughs. Sometimes this is done for extraordinary reasons like the death of a member of the family; at other times, a furlough may be used as a reward or an inmate will be released to spend a holiday with his family or to attend a special event.

The furlough concept should be expanded and used in non-emergency situations. It is an important technique to ease the ultimate transition of all prison inmates back to the community. The metropolitan detention center could be used to house men temporarily on furloughs under planned, short-term correctional programs (seeking a job to qualify for parole, for example) aimed at graduating the move from total incarceration to complete freedom.

Restitution Houses. An innovative nuance on the basic scheme of correction in the community would be to require men to work and use part of their earnings to make restitution to the victims of their crimes. While this idea has not been used in work release programs to date, I view it as a promising technique for expanding the uses of work release.

Minnesota recently began a program employing this scheme, which could be adapted more broadly. There, selected convicted inmates serving sentences in prison for property offenses are given the option of serving their sentence in a community halfway house which is run by the correction department but administered by a joint correction department-citizen board of directors. To qualify, the convict must work out a contract with the victim of his offense to pay him an agreeable restitution for his wrongdoing. Correction officials supervise the house and assist in training the convict and getting him a job. Once he pays off his victim pursuant to their contract, he may be released. The inmate also pays his own living expenses (and taxes and family support) while living at the community house.

The fundamental idea behind this program is that in the large majority of crimes (especially property offenses), restitution and reconciliation between an offender and his victim should be the key goals of correction. Once assuring that this process is completed, society has intervened appropriately and the inmate has been punished sufficiently, has proved his correction and warrants release. This idea is a sound one and could be expanded widely to great advantage.

Part-time Prisoners. Other variations on the work release theme might be suggested, and they all make sense. In Sweden I visited

one correctional institution near Uppsala which released its inmates during the day to attend classes at a nearby university. Indeed, the prison at Lorton, Virginia, allows some of its prisoners
to attend the Federal City College in Washington. The notion
behind these programs is that not everybody in prison is a natural
laborer; some have intellectual promise. Such people should qualify for release to educational programs just as laborers can profita-
bly be released to go to their jobs.

In Denmark, I visited one institution which held offenders only
on weekends. Certain offenders were allowed to work at their jobs
and remain at home with their families all week, but were required
to serve their sentences at the prison piecemeal and in a way which
least destroyed their normal lives.

In England, juvenile offenders are allowed to work off their
minor sentences, and indeed to avoid prosecution completely in
some cases, by reporting to the police for work assignments after
school and on weekends.

All these community-based correctional schemes make sense.
If the trend continues and more programs develop, there will be
an even greater need for dormitories in the community to house
convicts working in community programs. The metropolitan detention center of tomorrow could be a dormitory and administrative center for community-based correctional programs like
these.

The recent National Advisory Commission on Criminal Justice
Standards and Goals referred to these needs in its 1973 Report
on Corrections:

Jail Release Programs

Every jurisdiction operating locally based correctional facilities
and programs for convicted adults immediately should develop
release programs drawing community leadership, social agencies,
and business interest into action with the criminal justice system.

1. Since release programs rely heavily on the participant's self-
discipline and personal responsibility, the offender should be involved as a member of the program planning team.

2. Release programs have special potential for utilizing specialized community services to meet offenders' special needs. This
capability avoids the necessity of service duplication within corrections.

3. Weekend visits and home furloughs should be planned regu-

larly, so that eligible individuals can maintain ties with family and friends.

4. Work release should be made available to persons in all offense categories who do not present a serious threat to others.

5. The offender in a work-release program should be paid at prevailing wages. The individual and the work-release agency may agree to allocation of earnings to cover subsistence, transportation cost, compensation to victims, family support payments and spending money. The work-release agency should maintain strict accounting procedures open to inspection by the client and others.

6. Program location should give high priority to the proximity of job opportunities. Various modes of transportation may need to be utilized.

7. Work release may be operated initially from an existing jail facility, but this is not a long-term solution. Rented and converted buildings (such as YMCA's, YWCA's, motels, hotels) should be considered to separate the transitional program from the image of incarceration that accompanies the traditional jail.

8. When the release program is combined with a local correctional facility, there should be separate access to the work-release residence and activity areas.

9. Educational or study release should be available to all inmates (pretrial and convicted) who do not present a serious threat to others. Arrangements with the local school district and nearby colleges should allow participation at any level required (literacy training, adult basic education, high school or general educational development equivalency, and college level).

10. Arrangements should be made to encourage offender participation in local civic and social groups. Particular emphasis should be given to involving the offender in public education and the community in corrections efforts.[13]

Changing the function and architecture and administration of jails from awful correctional institutions to useful, helpful social service agencies makes sense. There is ample evidence that the new detention centers would be cheaper, safer and sounder than the present haphazard, onerous, counter-productive network of jails.

Unless outside agencies—particularly the bar, and the press, to be sure—are constantly involved in watchdogging the administration of this system of detention facilities, there is reason to fear

[13] Standard 9.9, p. 306.

that it too might degenerate into a perverse and totalitarian institution.

In the past, public scrutiny of its jails has been minimal, episodic, usually attending extraordinary and sensational events—a death, a riot, an exposé. The day-to-day operations of so crucial an institution carrying out such vital public chores must be carefully and regularly monitored. The press does not live up to its avowed public responsibilities when it neglects this job; and in the past it has done an incomplete job at best.

The bar, too, must do more of what the public legal services programs and private-based public interest lawyers have begun to do in the last decade. That is, the bar must fully represent the poor, under-represented if not misrepresented class of people who traditionally find themselves institutionalized.

If the press and bar must act on the line, the courts must resist old fears of intruding on the correctional process and oversee that the system operates in a constitutional manner. However dependent, incapacitated and punished, citizens always retain their fundamental rights as human beings. The most beneficent and supervisory government must act within constitutional constraints. The common notion that institutionalized people are total pawns of government must be changed. Historical and fundamental American notions of justice can no longer be denied to helpless and poor people. The public institutions of our country must incorporate the standards and motives of the private sector which are based on goals of social service and human decency.

A suitable standard and goal of these new detention centers would be the assurance of liberty and justice for all: even for those people who inhabit the ultimate ghetto.

INDEX